The Tuning of Place

The Tuning of Place

Sociable Spaces and Pervasive Digital Media

Richard Coyne

The MIT Press
Cambridge, Massachusetts
London, England

For information about special quantity discounts, please e-mail special_sales @mitpress.mit.edu

This book was set in Stone Sans and Stone Serif by Toppan Best-set Premedia Limited. Printed and bound in the United States of America.

Library of Congress Cataloging-in-Publication Data

Coyne, Richard.
The tuning of place : sociable spaces and pervasive digital media / Richard Coyne.
p. cm.
Includes bibliographical references and index.
ISBN 978-0-262-01391-8 (hardcover : alk. paper)
1. Ubiquitous computing. 2. Mobile computing. 3. Online social networks.
I. Title.

QA76.5915.C695 2010
006.7'54—dc22

2009033440

10 9 8 7 6 5 4 3 2 1

To Kathleen

Contents

Preface

How do pervasive digital devices influence the way people use spaces? This book examines the concept of tuning as a way of understanding how people adjust their interactions with one other and with the places they occupy. I propose that mobile phones, smartphones, personal stereos, handhelds, wearables, other pervasive digital devices, and the networks that support them become the means of making incremental adjustments within spaces—of tuning place.

The book develops an understanding of how pervasive media help to formulate a sense of place through their capacity to introduce small changes, in the same way that tuning a musical instrument invokes the subtle process of recalibration. Murray Schafer coined the term *the tuning of the world*. I adopt his emphasis on the importance of sound in the creation of environments, the implied contrast between sound and vision, and the small-scale, incremental change. There is a strong social aspect to place making. Ubiquitous devices are obviously tools for social interaction. The tuning of place is also the tuning of social relations.

Pervasive digital media integrate information processing and computation into the world of everyday objects and environments, as computer components become smaller, more powerful, better connected, and less costly. Cell phones, smartphones, portable audiovisual devices, and the convergences among them herald the development of new and inventive ways of secreting computational capability into household goods, equipment, clothing, vehicles, and new kinds of commodities barely conceived. Such devices depend on omnipresent networks, infrastructures, and methods of content distribution. There is also a pervasive aspect to the development of these systems, the democratization of innovation whereby it is claimed that any small developer, producer, publisher, artist, or user can establish a niche in content provision, programming, and customization, abetted in no small part by interfacing with and reporting via the participative media of the World Wide Web and its progeny.

Rather than catalog achievements and predictions this book presents a framework for discussing how pervasive digital media can inform developers, designers, and users as they contemplate interventions into the environment. Processes of tuning can be expanded to a consideration of intervention, calibration, wedges, habits, rhythm, tags, taps, tactics, thresholds, aggregation, noise, and interference—themes highly relevant to pervasive computing and that structure the content of this book. I expect this orientation toward the art, design, and culture of digital media to be instructive to anyone interested in understanding the world of technology and how the smartphone generation tunes its relationships with place.

This book builds on my critique of the digital economy and its narratives about the gift society, *Cornucopia Limited*,[1] in which I examined Marxist, neo-Marxist and other critical positions in relation to global markets, capital, and cultures of digital consumption. A previous work, *Technoromanticism*,[2] examined the romantic legacy in information technology design and proposed alternatives to celebratory cyberspace narratives. An even earlier book, *Designing Information Technology in the Postmodern Age*,[3] critiqued the technorationalist imperative and promoted the theme of metaphor in place of a belief in blind, impersonal calculation and the imminence of artificial intelligence. This fourth book in the series emerged from my long-standing commitment not only to architecture, cultural theory, and computers, but also to issues of sound, behind which lurks the master metaphor of architecture as "frozen music."[4] I am fortunate to have been able to work closely with several experts in music and sound, from whom I have learned a great deal about priorities outside of the visual confines of architecture. In particular I would like to acknowledge the contributions of Pedro Rebelo, Peter Nelson, and Martin Parker.

This book is also the culmination of work carried out with the generous support of the UK Engineering and Physical Sciences Research Council (EPSRC) and the Arts and Humanities Research Council (AHRC). The first of three funded projects was supported by the AHRC's Designing for the 21st Century initiative and was titled Orienting the Future: Design Strategies for Non-place (EP/C513878/1), with a follow-on project, Branded Meeting Places: Ubiquitous Technologies and the Design of Places for

Meaningful Human Encounter (AH/E507654/1). Along the way I was supported by the AHRC on a speculative study, Inflecting Space: Correlating the Attributes of Voice with the Character of Urban Spaces (AHRC 112333). Collaborators in these projects included Peter Nelson, Martin Parker, Stephen Cairns, Robin Williams, Jane Jacobs, Ewan Klein, Elizabeth Davenport, Susan Turner, Jennifer Willies, and Ray Lucas. Alan Dix, Peter Excell, Ann Light, William Mackaness, Vlad Tanasescu, and Chris Speed provided further insights. Mobile Acuity Ltd, directed by Anthony Ashbrook, stimulated several of the practical insights explored in this book. It is also the product of extended discussions with the project research team of Henrik Ekeus, Mark Wright, James Stewart, Penny Travlou, and John Lee. In particular I would like to acknowledge the enormously imaginative experimentation and development of Henrik Ekeus and Mark Wright. The book is also the fruit of much experimental design work by students too numerous to mention in our Master of Science in Design and Digital Media and Master of Science in Sound Design programs at the University of Edinburgh, and key PhD projects by Aghlab Al-Attili, David Fortin, Anastasia Karandinou, Leonidas Koutsoumpos, and Dermott McMeel.

Introduction

In *Technics and Civilization,* published in 1934, Lewis Mumford observed that the routines of medieval monasteries and the subsequent technologies of timetables and clocks promoted the diurnal rhythms that "helped to give human enterprise the regular collective beat and rhythm of the machine; for the clock is not merely a means of keeping track of the hours, but of synchronizing the actions of men."[1] Clocks and timetables help people coordinate their activities. Presumably pervasive digital media and communications devices continue this trajectory of coordinating and synchronizing people's activities to one another, a phenomenon described in the context of mobile phone usage by Castells et al. as "micro-coordination."[2] Thinking of digital devices in this way, as mechanisms people use to synchronize their relationships and interactions, provides a way to discuss how digital devices impact on people's lives and on the places they inhabit.

Pervasive devices also foreground synchronization as a technical operation that ensures that the state of the diary on your handheld device corresponds to the state of the diary on your computer. Pervasive, interconnected media require that you are dealing with the same information whether on cell phone, personal digital assistant (PDA), laptop, web browser, or other device. You may think of networks and connections both as enabling file transfer and as facilitating the synchronization of data, for which there are certain evolving practices—such as connecting your PDA to your laptop via a docking device at the end of the day and sometimes waiting a few seconds or minutes for changes to be registered on both devices. Wireless connectivity between devices, to servers, and to data "clouds"[3] inevitably involves awareness of a process that needs to be monitored and managed. Synchronization can therefore present itself as a weakness in the flow. The users of ubiquitous devices feel their data is vulnerable when the synchronization process gets interrupted, or does not function, and data loses integrity.

Synchronization also involves alignment against a standard, the regular subdivisions and inexorable ticks of clock time—the "actions of men" coordinated by reference to an external, machinic, predictable, and unconditional progression of time. Focusing on synchronization draws theorists of culture and technology to the role of clocks, schedules, and other mechanisms as mediators of social interaction. Such processes are interesting, for the way people invent, interact with, and resist synchronization is instructive of social conditions. But for my purposes synchronization already presumes too much, as if information provides the key to understanding the relationship between place and pervasive media.[4] Hence my focus is on processes of tuning. The concept of tuning helps theorists, developers, and users to think integratively of synchronization as a practice, or a series of practices, rather than only a technical operation outside the control or concern of human agency.

Tuning has direct relevance to the human organism's relationship to its surroundings. Biologists (chronobiologists) Russell Foster and Leon Kreitzman resort to the tuning metaphor in examining the way organisms adjust themselves to the cycles of the days and seasons. They link this fine-tuning to an animal's ability to anticipate, or to "create future."[5] The philosopher Martin Heidegger invites similar attention to attunement as a basic human condition. The German word understood as attunement is *Stimmung*, which Heidegger's translators relate to the tuning of a musical instrument, but also connecting to a mood or atmosphere.[6] Behind the concept of a "state-of-mind," popular among psychologists, lies the primordial condition of "being-attuned." For Heidegger, attunement is a condition that may pervade a whole group. It is invisible in any social situation and often goes unremarked. Paraphrasing Heidegger, attunement is primarily social rather than a characteristic of the individual, and without it individuals cannot really lay claim to personal moods or feelings. To what are people attuned? In Heidegger's philosophy the phenomenon under discussion is generally a condition that precedes anything that might be explained through causes. Therefore people are not attuned to some external standard, and certainly not to clock time. It is fair to say social beings simply are attuned, a state occasionally manifested as a public mood: mourning, outrage, joy, restlessness, expectancy, excitement, or resistance. In the terminology of this book it is helpful to think of the agency of attunement as widely distributed, engaging sociability, conversation, the mass media, digital communications, and other means of cultural creation, preservation, and transmission. For Heidegger, attunement also comes before any sense of time or space.

The philosopher and sociologist Alfred Schutz develops the tuning theme further, drawing attention to the "mutual tuning-in relationship" that becomes manifested as a sense of sociability or a "We."[7] This tuning-in relates less to the matter of synchronizing according to regularized clock time and more to the duration,[8] or the "inner time," of lived experience. Schutz uses music to explain this attunement. Ensembles of musicians are engaged in a complex play of anticipation. Any musician reading a score "has not only to interpret his own part which as such remains necessarily fragmentary, but he has also to anticipate the other player's interpretation of his—the Other's—part and, even more, the Other's anticipations of his own execution."[9] Tuning-in is an interpretive and relational process concerned with contingent human interactions and participation in human solidarity. My use of *tuning* in this book is intended to embrace tuning-in and attunement, opening up an examination of the micropractices by which designers and users engage with the materiality of pervasive digital media and devices, including the inexorable accumulation of small changes, divisions, and ticks of such devices.

So tuning provides a richer metaphor for the interconnected digital age than Mumford's trope of synchronization. Musicians tune musical instruments, mechanics tune internal combustion engines, and managers "fine-tune" their budgets, but people also use instruments, machines, and spreadsheets to tune their interactions with one another. By this reading, musicians might think of musical instruments as devices for tuning the interactions among ensemble players and with an audience. The social grouping and its spatial presence are the first consideration, with the instruments serving as vehicles for facilitating human interactions.

If tuning addresses the coordination of time increments, then what does it say about spatial increments? It is common to contrast the mathematical and mechanical orderings of space against the more engaged, experiential, contingent notion of place.[10] According to Edward Relph, "places are territories of meanings, meanings that arise from the experiences of living, working or visiting somewhere, appreciating its architecture, being familiar with its routines, knowing its people and having responsibilities towards it."[11] In other words, places are inhabited spaces, particularly as populated by people, their concerns, memories, stories, conversations, encounters, and artifacts.[12] The tuning of place is a set of practices by which people use devices, willfully or unwittingly, to influence their interactions with one another in places. It is sound theorist Murray Schafer who brought the relationship between tuning and place into sharp relief. In *The Tuning of the World* Schafer suggested that we should think of the occupants of space as composers and performers, responsible for giving form and beauty to their environment through sound.[13] Whether or not people aspire to compose or perform, they may at least assume the role of instrument tuners, as if performing, or preparing to perform, in ensembles of players located in places.

If place is about the way people inhabit, interact, socialize, and remember, then tuning connects to the lived experience of temporal and spatial adjustment. By this reading time and space are the derivative, abstracted, and disengaged manifestations of what inhabitants ordinarily experience unreflectively simply as being in a place, positioning themselves, adjusting, and tuning. This accords with geographer Doreen Massey's constructional characterization of space: "because space . . . is a product of relations-between, relations which are necessarily embedded in material practices which have to be carried out, it is always in the process of being made."[14] While synchronization suggests a mechanical process arbitrated by the standard of time as a regular pulse, tuning suggests human contingency that pertains exclusively neither to time nor to space. Whereas synchronization pertains to time, tuning applies both to time and space.

Commentators who focus on synchronicity tend to look to a condition in which everything happens at once, a language of instants: instant travel, immediate access to information.[15] Tuning brings to the fore the processes by which people seek or arrive at the aligned condition, recovering when things drift, retuning and detuning.

In this book I wish to access the phenomenon of tuning by attending to the mechanistic as well as the social, which I think fold into one another, not least as meditation on the materiality of the mechanical provokes renewed thought of the everyday.[16] I will problematize the human's relationship with technologies and place by amplifying otherwise underdeployed metaphors derived from sound and the materiality of digital devices.

The tuning metaphor has not escaped those who theorize pervasive media.[17] Tuning pervades the human animal's relationship with its environment. I adjust, tweak, and tune my environment. I flick the light switch, turn down the electric radiator, and turn up the stereo. With such microadjustments I shape spaces to suit my immediate requirements and those of fellow occupants, and through operations far less costly and requiring less foresight and planning than relocating a window, moving the fireplace, or raising the roof. It is helpful to think of tuning as a form of constrained microdesign, oriented to immediate circumstances. The concept of tuning draws attention to what some have termed *subarchitecture*.[18] This is the condition by which "one takes one's place" in a public place to optimize one's position to hear, be heard, or enjoy quiet. It is a stratum of design activity that does not require the costly and expert positioning of structural elements. Anyone can tune, or attempt to tune, their place without recourse to expert knowledge.

The materiality of space and that of sound often converge through meteorological metaphors. The Situationists of the 1960s attempted to turn architecture into the pursuit of "atmospherics," in the meteorological as well as the phenomenal sense.[19] The boundaries of atmospheric zones rarely follow the boundaries of buildings, and require subtle means of control and adjustment.

Atmospheric adjustment inevitably is social. In polite circumstances a person will consult other occupants of a room before opening a window or turning on the radio. Comfort and discomfort are shared phenomena. There is a richly social aspect to this spatial tuning. As suggested by Schafer's democratization of environmental modification, occupants' interventions are more in the manner of a collaborative and spontaneous performance than a concerted plan instituted by a single designer or a class of experts. Tuning reflects back on design. As sociologist Bruno Latour asserts, "all designs are 'collaborative' designs,"[20] and in this sense design is tuning on a grand scale, or a collection of many tuning operations. Thinking of design as a collaborative micropractice also helps design theorists and developers understand further how ubiquitous digital media are complicit in the tuning of place.

Many ubiquitous media and devices, such as cell phones, smartphones, digital cameras, and streamed media players are conspicuously social media, dedicated to communication. Mobile phone functions are arguably more social than clocks. Urban dwellers saturated in pervasive media use ubiquitous devices to tune their interactions with one another: to organize meetings, coordinate travel, tell each other what they are doing and where they will be. Not all pervasive devices facilitate the transmission of messages, but even clocks, global positioning systems (GPS), personal organizers, game consoles, and other ubiquitous devices bring synchronization and communication into the arena as basic social functions,[21] not least as the consumers of such services identify meeting places, share online diaries, and play multiuser computer games. In his book titled *Mobilities*, John Urry highlights some of the subtle practices introduced by mobile connectivity. The office worker can phone ahead if she is running late, change venues, and be more selective in offering invitations to meetings: "clock-time is increasingly supplemented by a negotiated 'network' or fluid time of mobile communications."[22] A judicious text message or phone call can act as a reminder, or a hint, and can nudge someone to do something or move into a different mode of practice: for example, to start preparing paperwork for signing, to fulfill family obligations, to reciprocate a dinner invitation. But the tuning of place suggests that the influences people exert on one another go beyond those between two agents seeking to affect each other's behavior.

Pervasive digital devices have obvious spatial aspects: phones connect across distances, GPS locates people in space, computer games and streamed media synthesize spatial environments, personal stereos apparently confine the listener to a sensory container—all of these devices are distributed across space. Short text messages, or tweets, are propagated through the Internet and phone networks to signal the change in position of a friend ("I am in the park") or the state of arbitrary objects, as when the transport enthusiast receives an automated text message that London's Tower Bridge is raised. As instruments of social tuning, ubiquitous devices also abet the formation of place, as the context in which people interact, in synchronic face-to-face encounters or indirectly through artifacts, devices, and the stories people tell, implicating concepts of identity, memory, history, and meaning.

What activities are tuned through pervasive digital media? If pervasive devices abet the tuning of place, then researchers and designers need to expand their understanding of the role of such technologies from synchronization or coordinating schedules to aligning human practices. Humans are social creatures, mimicking, copying, and learning from one another.[23] As well as conveying messages, the communicative functions with which pervasive media are concerned facilitate sharing practices. According to a tradition of social theorizing, from Thorstein Veblen and Erving Goffman to Michel Foucault, human society sets in train certain institutions, practices, and artifacts by which it regulates itself.[24] To the extent that people order their lives by timetables, agree to military drills, keep their elbows off the dinner table, and practice musical scales, they instill and perpetuate social norms and promote habits and customs that help identify with one group or another, decide who is in and who is out, and transmit power relations.[25] It seems that such cultural transmission is essential for getting things done. The proliferation of pervasive digital media as one of the means by which humans refine social relationships—the tuning of place—is consistent with this understanding of the crucial role of human practices, and their preservation and transmission.

How can cultural critics, commentators, designers of human-computer interactions, urbanists, and architects respond to a call for the tuning of place? Certain factors conspire against a clear articulation of the nature of place in light of pervasive digital devices. My own studies into digital media[26] corroborate findings in psychological studies that not everyone is equally adept at conceptualizing, representing, and reasoning about space or place.[27] Many users of spaces and of pervasive devices are less articulate in reflecting on and giving expression to their spatial experience than they are at disclosing insights into interpersonal relationships.[28] For one thing, the communication of spatial experience often requires aptitude in drawing, sketching, mapping, measurement, descriptive prose, and other specialized forms of representation. Digital devices are pervasive, but spatial understanding and the means to express it are not.[29] Nor is the base of evidence on which the researcher might draw incontrovertible or entirely transparent. My topic, the tuning of place, calls for a speculative resourcefulness, an orientation that draws on metaphor and imagination.

Concepts of virtual reality (VR) provide a further complication to the pursuit of place and pervasive digital media. In their article on pervasive media in 1997, Ishii and Ullmer took it for granted that people potentially "live between two realms: our physical environment and cyberspace."[30]

The apparent challenge of tangible digital media—that is, pervasive media with a particularly tactile quality—is to connect the two spaces. The concepts of cyberspace and virtual reality continue to thrive, bolstered by the power of dynamic 3D modeling and the automation of rapid perspective rendering, and their combination with networked communications. The ethereal otherness of putative virtual spatial experience occasionally dominates people's reflections on digital media and spatiality, accented by immersive, multiuser, user-created 3D environments such as Second Life, and other massively multiplayer online role-playing games (MMORPGs) and environments.[31]

The discourse of cyberspace is potent and alluring. But there is growing resistance to the concepts of virtuality and cyberspace. Many critics think the theme of virtual reality distracts from a consideration of everyday spatiality.[32] Many of those who now study pervasive media from a social perspective oppose the imaginative but nonverifiable assertions of cyberspace enthusiasts, a protest that is gaining ground among researchers into pervasive computing.[33] Concepts of space are, after all, subservient to concepts of society; space as place is socially as well as materially constructed,[34] not the product of three-dimensional representations presented to the eye. Tuning relates more strongly to concepts of augmentation, interaction, and sociability than the alignment of parallel worlds.

A further factor that renders the consideration of place and pervasive media so challenging is that many of the technologies under discussion are nascent, or at least they are not available in sufficient volume in the marketplace for their effects to be observed and studied. Whereas the consequences of pervasive mobile phones, smartphones, and personal media players are available for study, other ubiquitous devices and networks are by their nature inconspicuous or invisible. They are also undergoing transformation. As web critic Geert Lovink says of related Web 2.0 developments: "How can you do research when your object is in a state of hyper-growth and permanent transformation?"[35]

I have alluded so far only to the obvious and current mass commodities of phones, handheld devices, games, cameras, and personal stereos, but the range of ubiquity is vast, including the inconspicuous deployment of radio frequency identification (RFID) tags, smart badges, networked "specks," smart sensors, actuators and environmental controls in buildings, dynamic signage, surveillance devices, microprocessors in cars, refrigerators, toasters, and washing machines, office equipment, wearable computing, life-support, prosthetics, and assistive technology, still under development, not all tested on the market, and with spatial applications and consequences that are still coming to light. Researchers and developers characterize these under various headings: ubiquitous computing, pervasive digital media, augmented reality, tangible interfaces, wearable computers, cooperative buildings, and context-aware computing.[36]

In fact, to even list devices and technologies suggests that the sum of components captures the whole of this complex milieu. Some might regard such tallies as short changing the phenomenon of pervasive computing, which builds notions of interconnection, invisibility, and context awareness, an all-pervasive shared field of sensing, processing, communicating, and actuating, the individual components of which only reveal themselves when needed.[37] Such configurations also attest to the availability of an "Internet of things."[38] For some, the concept of pervasive digital media extends well beyond the Internet as currently understood. According to computer scientists Rolf Pfeifer and Josh Bongard, although it is likely that the world will see increased integration of ubiquitous devices with the Internet, "ubiquitous computing networks are conceptually and practically much more than another kind of Internet." They are "embodied."[39] Researchers of ubiquity often suggest that their subject area covers all computing, or at least the imminent computing of the future. Computation is well on the way to permeating the human being's entire experiential field.

In characterizing this ubiquity I have already indicated a preference for the metaphor of the computer as medium as opposed to machine or device.[40] A medium can be understood as a carrier; such as air or water that transmit sound waves. In classical information theory the medium is incidental to the message being carried, other than as a source of noise or disturbance to the message signal.[41] Under ideal conditions the medium is transparent and invisible. Harold Innes and Marshall McLuhan as leaders in the field of media theory promoted a major revision to how cultural theorists and computer hardware and software designers think of media.[42] The medium not only influences the message, but also "the medium *is* the message."[43] David Bolter and Diane Gromala articulate clearly the formative character of computer media in their book on the myth of media transparency.[44] Media are not incidental to the messages they transmit, nor are they interchangeable. Cinema did not replace live theater. Though they are complicit in the transformation of the mass media, websites do not necessarily replace newspapers. Note the emergence of free, easy-read newspapers for consumption on pubic transport, and the symbiotic relationship between web content and mainstream news. Media do not immediately replace one another, or become obsolete, as if the world is on the way to a convergent, invisible, all-encompassing cyberspace matrix or pervasive media blur. Media such as books, paintings, televisions, films, computers, portable DVD players and cell phones interact and influence one another through a process Bolter describes as "re-mediation."[45] As further evidence of the crucial role of media, consider how consumers reveal their concern about the physicality of media devices, as recognized in the market value attached to products independently of any apparent notion of function or utility. Think of designer watches, stylish handhelds, and branded laptops. People care about the medium through which this functionality is delivered, and the design of the medium is as potent as its putative content.

Ubiquity relates to processes of innovation and dissemination within mass markets. Studying commercial processes provides a further way of analyzing ubiquitous technologies[46] abetted by evidence gathered from surveys and interviews. The methods of social science prefer to analyze phenomena that are already present, but identifying and describing the mediated and ambient character of contemporary ubiquitous computing also requires insights gained from disconnected experiments along with imaginative conjecture. Were pervasive computing imminent or at hand then it might be difficult to scrutinize anyway. An understanding of ubiquitous technologies requires invention and speculation, which takes me to the matter of design.

My own discipline, architecture, has obvious concerns with place. Interaction designers sometimes draw on some of the lessons of architecture, particularly on the themes of place and space, thanks to the work of several architectural practitioners, educators, and theorists, who have pioneered aspects of computing since the 1960s,[47] and the work of contemporary commentators such as William Mitchell and Malcolm McCullough who have made explicit the connections between pervasive computing and architecture,[48] a theme about which more needs to be said.

My investigation in this book of necessity sits at the intersection of several disciplines. The sociology of technology advances understanding of how devices are being used in practice, and how they are complicit in formal and informal social organization. Interaction design develops and explores innovative technologies and applications, and positions ubiquitous technologies in contexts of embodied, situated agency and spatiality. Studies in the cultures of the senses draw attention to the problematic of human perception. Contemporary urbanism and architecture work through issues of place, space, and non-place. These disparate disciplines do not necessarily rest on common ground. Nor does the sum of their contributions lead inevitably to a consistent or inclusive picture. Their differences can reveal as much as their similarities and sympathies.

How can the researcher and social commentator structure a study of ubiquitous technologies of place? Interaction design might consider affordance, augmentation, seamlessness, usability, and integration.[49] By invoking a more provocative terminology, contemporary architectural urbanism might conscript the typology of gaps, seams, the uncanny, the sublime, dark space, warped space, and non-place in its typology.[50] In this book I structure the themes of ubiquity and the senses along the vectors set by the conspicuous character of digital media devices: their need for adjustments, the repetitive nature of their operations, their role in storing and indexing data, their locational functions, and the problematic issue of noise. As for the experiences and practices of those who use these devices, I translate these themes in terms of intervention, calibration, wedges, habits, rhythm, tags, taps, tactics, thresholds, aggregation, noise, and interference. I group these phenomena under section headings pertaining to temperament, the everyday, and the commonplace. Alternatively, they deal in tuning, time, and space. Temperament introduces the tuning metaphor in detail; the everyday pertains to the experience of temporal cycles, and the commonplace to location and issues of environment. I argue that a consideration of these prosaic and practical aspects of pervasive devices reveals socially and spatially interesting characteristics of pervasive digital media and devices, particularly pertaining to their design and to the environments they occupy and create.

In chapter 1 ("Intervention") I present the design process as an intervention into the everyday. Design is ubiquitous, conflictual, agonistic, potentially provocative, and at its core a tactical and incremental operation that works with small differences.

Chapter 2 ("Calibration") makes the case for encouraging designers and users to take into account the adjustment of digital devices in assessing their operations. Calibration practices are those instrumental processes by which models are brought into alignment, notably in the calibration of a scientific instrument against a standard, the adjustment of a building form to its ideal archetype, and of course the tuning of musical instruments. Precise manufacture and automated procedures sometimes conceal the processes of calibration, but calibration persists in the subtle and mutual adjustments required in the tuning of machines. The chapter canvases issues of recalibration, the role of registration and control points in graphic representations, the interference between representations, how the idealist tradition deals in discrepancy, and the operations of scales and musical temperament. Calibration presents as a covert operation that permeates the world as experienced, as well as the world as studied, analyzed, and engineered.

In chapter 3 ("Wedge") I start with the simple idea of the archetypal device that accomplishes the hedge or fudge to bring constructional elements, environments, and digital components into alignment. I build on this metaphor of the wedge to develop the idea of calibration as a human-oriented, contingent, and contextual process of tuning: the physical and metaphorical role of the wedge as a tool of adjustment, tunings between social actors, the tuning of metaphors, and design as tuning. I examine digital media devices as generators of, and solutions for, deviation and calibration, an insight that applies to early machines (Vitruvius's war engines), architectural artifacts, scales in music, iPods, smartphones, and other pervasive digital media.

In chapter 4 ("Habit") I examine how pervasive digital devices constitute everyday objects, which in turn implicate cycles and patterns that are also crucial in the devices' operation and reception. Habit implies routine and ritual integrated into everyday life. In this respect pervasive digital media are designed to blend into the everyday world of mundane objects. Habitat is the place where habits are born and cultivated. Pervasive digital devices are complicit in the creation and maintenance of the everyday habitat, of the schedules of broadcast media, and the everyday and ritualized practices surrounding the use of phones, media players, and digital cameras. I counterpoint the homely idea of habitat with the more aggressive, assertive operations by which people create territory.

Chapter 5 ("Rhythm") draws attention to repetition. Repetition helps define space through the regular ordering of colonnades, grids, and other architectural devices, including beacons, church bells, and alarms. Sounds offer a more covert means of ordering and claiming space than physical structures, especially when repeated, as in the case of bird calls, the criers in the marketplace, voices on the sports field, and half conversations conducted on cell phones. Digital technologies repeat and promote repetition. They also contribute to the human obsession with a world picture, through endless visual scans in ever-greater detail. It is against the sameness of repetition that differences stand in relief. A small difference can nudge an organization or set of practices into a different mode of repetition.

Among those small apparently inconsequential differences resides the world of the tag, the subject of chapter 6 ("Tags"). Tags are small indices pointing to something greater and more complex. Tags proliferate through RFID and other pervasive indexing technologies. Tags make sense in the company of other tags and contexts. As such they form languages of small changes brought into relief by ideas of collective tagging, or *folksonomies*, promoted through social network sites. Tags mark moments in time, as transient indicators of a change in state. The tag is emblematic of participative moves to adjust the environment by means of small-scale local interventions: putting your own label on a thing.

Chapter 7 ("Taps") looses the tag from its dependence on the host and further demonstrates the importance of the incremental move in understanding pervasive digital media and devices. Tags are closely related to touch, the way a tap on the door or a tap on the shoulder signifies an important moment. Tags as taps are prone to the possibilities of misunderstanding, mislabeling, persuasion, and transience. The chapter therefore promotes the sensual potential of the tag.

In chapter 8 ("Tactics") I address technologies that locate travelers and mobile workers in space. Pervasive devices increasingly deploy technologies that position people and devices. Here I demonstrate how the way locational technologies operate, and the ways people interact with them, can further an understanding of the incremental move in the design and use of pervasive digital devices. The chapter compares GPS with the tactics of simply walking about, and the extent to which each mirrors the other in its attention to detail and the small change. The chapter amplifies the extent to which the tuning of places and nonplaces are tactical throughout.

Chapter 9 ("Threshold") examines how pervasive digital devices render familiar places and activities strange. Spatial navigation involves negotiating so many thresholds and small transitions. One way people tune their relationship to place and each other is to adjust their position across, on the edge of, and in response to thresholds, processes now abetted in no small part by pervasive digital devices.

Chapter 10 ("Aggregation") outlines the trajectory of pervasive media design development. To reinforce the idea that design works as a provocation to further as yet undefined interventions, I present and analyze a working project involving smartphones. The chapter amplifies the character of design as a collaborative, participative, opportunistic, incremental, and experimental process. Design also functions as a mode of research, which is to say a way of revealing new understandings of pervasive digital media and the societies and spaces in which they operate.

Communication is impeded by noise, a type of signal distortion that is the subject of chapter 11 ("Noise"). I show how noise has two interesting characteristics that can inform an understanding of pervasive digital media. First, noise can render communication incoherent, but it does so by purveying ambiguity. A noisy channel might confuse because it conveys too many messages. Second, noise enters from the outside, from another channel, from beyond the frame. From these two characteristics, ambiguity and externality, flow an understanding of pervasive media in terms of silences and a kind of sociability that assumes someone else is listening in, an absent other. The chapter explores various means by which digital devices invoke the absent other, leading to a consideration of the role of the human voice in pervasive media.

Chapter 12 ("Interference") develops further the theme of the putative externality of noise. In any case, cultural theories of sound invoke contrasting ideas of both continuity and the cut. The externality of noise is also suggestive of impurity, anomaly, and incongruity—acceptable grist for any designer's mill. The chapter concludes with a consideration of detuning to complete this acknowledgment and verification of the role of pervasive digital media in the tuning of place.

By way of summary, my investigation is driven by five key propositions. First, design offers a preeminent mode of understanding, for which metaphors provide a potent resource.[51] Designers value associations and profusion, even an excess, of connections. In keeping with the practices relating to much cultural theory, creative designers like to draw on a wide range of varied sources.[52] The metaphor of tuning invites associations among fields such as music, sound, design, architecture, urbanism, psychology, engineering, technics, and ethnography, a cornucopia supported in no small part by the associative matrix of the World Wide Web, and the ready availability of online journals, sound files, and images, particularly through institutional subscription accessible from the work desk and while on the move. Therefore my focus on design provides license to traverse a field of rich associations.

Second, this work attends to the idea of small increments, nudges, and cues ahead of grand plans and systems. Influences among workers, politicians, and citizens are purveyed most effectively as nudges and subtle shifts in practices that are carried over into technologies, such as pervasive and mobile digital devices. In this book I seek to push to its limits the energy of the small change. I take it for granted that human relations and practices are complex and ready to be tipped into a new state, mode, or key by the judicious application of the appropriate small change, a subtle tuning to context and environment.

Third, I advance the cause for the judicious application of the small change as tactic. Deliberate interventions, responsibility, and agency are better described in terms of tactics than plans. The ways people adapt to and adopt various technologies are highly tactical, and so is design.

Fourth, the small increment, the minor shift can serve as an irritant, a foreign body, a catalyst, a transforming agent that renders what consumers of public and private space normally identify as somehow alien or strange. This is a function of much design and art in any case, to challenge accepted norms, to transform environments by offering a different take on the world. But the design process and all acts of creation are subject to such processes. In this sense any innovation has the potential to present as an opportunity for discovery. Ethnographically attuned observation releases cultural commentary from the necessity to criticize everything technological as buying into capitalist hegemony. So in response to media theorist

Geert Lovink's identification of the net user as "data dandy," "wrapped in the finest facts and the most senseless gadgets,"[53] I would add that even superfluous items of consumption have the capacity to inform users, designers, and theorists about the human condition. In order to innovate, designers, creative writers, artists, and entrepreneurs keep seeing new possibilities in the ordinary by rendering the familiar strange. What could be stranger than the ways that digital media and devices now pervade every aspect of the environment, and tune the places people inhabit?

My fifth point of course relates to sound. What follows will be permeated by a plethora of unavoidable ocular metaphors, but moderated by an acute sense of the acoustical, which provides a further means of defamiliarizing sociable spaces increasingly permeated by digital media and devices.

Temperament

1 Intervention

Whereas a sociologist or ethnographer might examine how people use ubiquitous technologies and how they relate to one another as they do so, a designer actively invents, creates, deploys, and otherwise intervenes with a technology not only to create something useful but also to advance understanding. The outcome hopefully will be better design, technique, or even better products, but also improved understanding, irrespective of the quality, functionality, or marketability of the design product. There is a place for standing back and observing ubiquitous technologies, as if from a distance, but there is also scope for engaging with the technologies under study: making, building, and tuning in order to learn. Design deploys tactics for both making and understanding the environment.

There is an argument to be made that space is "created" by such interventions in any case. From an architectural perspective it is common to think of the character of a space as determined by the elements that contain it (walls, ceilings, floor surfaces) and the elements it contains (columns, pipes, furniture). According to the philosopher Gottfried Leibniz (1646–1716), space would not exist were it not for the relationships between things.[1] Space is relational in this tradition. Space is revealed by the placement of objects, events, and people; such interventions constitute space. So a design, whether or not it contributes to comfort, safety, communication, or sociability is an intervention that not only has spatial consequences but also contributes to the making of a space. This space-making function can occur by way of setting up contrasts as well as by making the occupants comfortable. To place a forklift truck in a coffee shop would reveal something about the size, sociability, and robustness of the space. It could disclose the space to the occupants in a new way. In subtler ways, the introduction of cell phones into coffee shops and railroad compartments contributes to the definition of those spaces, and for the theoretically reflective may reveal something about the public-private characteristics of leisure and transportation spaces in general. By this reading, devices are disclosive, which can lead to particular understandings, which in turn suggest further interventions.[2]

Technologies do not conform politely to predetermined or intended functions. Philosopher of technology Don Ihde notes how a hammer may be designed to drive nails into floorboards, or remove them, but this functionality does not prevent a hammer being used as an art object, a murder weapon, or a paperweight.[3] Designers and product developers cannot anticipate easily such incidental uses, especially when dealing with innovations in dynamic contexts of use. Strategies of rapid prototyping, in concert with "agile" and "extreme" computer programming or product development, recognize that it is only when a product is placed into a context of use that many of its functions come to light.

So a carefully designed product, improvised design or combination of resources and streams from various digital sources (a mashup) is not the end of the development process, assessable only in terms of success or failure. A design can be part of an extended process that leads further. Hence my conviction that designed devices already contribute to place, space, spatiality, and spatial understanding, irrespective of their suitability for purpose. This is not to advocate populating the world with clumsy, inappropriate, and unusable products, but to recognize that devices are already constitutive of space. To enter a room is to encounter a field of complex and varying relationships that distort and inflect people's experiences in ways that many observers describe as spatial. To introduce a new intervention further tweaks, ruptures, or tunes the spatial field.

In this book I draw on intervention as a means of understanding. I endorse not only well-designed products, but also those myriad experiments, both naïve and profound, the descriptions of which populate conferences, teaching programs, blogs, and reports, both in and out of company time. They are the ordered or improvised, successful and failed products and by-products of institutional, corporate, amateur, and everyday technical practices, the configurations of hardware, software, web pages, media mixes, user innovations, and experiments in ad hoc practices that celebrate the insights that emerge simply from trying things out.[4] The concept of hacking captures aspects of this milieu as a variant of tuning practices.[5]

Hardware hacking,[6] modding, and circuit bending are practices that adapt or recycle ubiquitous electronic and mechanical components and scrap, in and out of warranty, to some experimental end, an activity that captures the opportunism of much design. As hacker, the digital *bricoleur* uses a game joystick as a musical instrument interface, deploys pressure pads from a disco mat as a movement sensor, overclocks (speeds up the central processing unit of) a computer, and turns a computer case into an aquarium. To hack is to use what is to hand when the purpose-made component is unavailable or unaffordable. As I will explore in the next chapter, tuning suggests bringing things into alignment, as if closer to an ideal state, but can also be characterized as a hack, the fine adjustment of parameters, a compensation for a condition where an ideal can never be met.

Accountable Design

Some design follows the trajectory of the improvised hack, but is there not also well-ordered design that methodically and systematically ascertains what needs to be done, counts the cost, charts and plans, integrates with other team members, delivers on time according to a program, and is accountable? After all, most hardware and software configurations alluded to in this book constitute extremely sophisticated, well-planned and well-marketed designs. My argument, pushed to its extreme, is that all design has the character of a hack, or a provisional microdesign. In so far as it can be said to exist at all, the whole, the big picture, resides with the complexities of human practices in contexts. Human practices are not planned, organized, controlled, or designed, but emerge in intricate and ad hoc ways, as so many interactive alignments and realignments. Architects and the users of spaces commonly suppose that plans, blueprints, drawings, and texts constitute expressions of some idea, and in turn represent instructions for others to follow. But another way to look at such objects is as interventions into a series of processes that are already in play, and that have to be in place before those plans have any effect.

Design as intervention can be illustrated with the idea of a master plan for a big city, such as Georges-Eugène Haussmann's plan for the boulevards of Paris, designed in 1852.[7] This was certainly a grand plan, but it was also a set of drawings, conversations with Napoleon III and the city fathers, specifications, contracts, letters, and other documents. These documents had to be interpreted, and were drawn up to be interpreted in certain ways. Haussmann was already working in a context of mutual understanding and shared practices, not least in the practices of road builders, gardeners, masons, financiers, and the imperial court.[8] Without this body of practice, many of the legacies of which are shared by twenty-first century cities, the plans would be incomplete.

Cities seem to grow incrementally and opportunistically, and plans are often overridden by changes in political circumstances.[9] But where plans exist, they also undergo similar processes. I argue here against "ideas,"[10] those supposedly transcendent visions that constitute the essence of a project, and exceed their mere implementation. I maintain that designs are objects, artifacts of incremental processes, featuring in ad hoc human practices, open to multiple interpretations, and often contested, modified, paid lip service to, and used to political ends. Designs are drawings, conversations, texts, specifications, contracts, and instructions. As such designs intervene in myriad human practices. This is not to diminish their importance, but to acknowledge the character of designs in the cultural currency of materially situated documents and practices. Similarly, the design of sophisticated digital devices and services involves sketches, drawings, CAD (computer-aided design) models, specifications, and contracts subject to the vicissitudes of human practices, supply, manufacturing, production, distribution, regulation, codes, and markets.

A design philosophy of the increment does not exclude and in fact affirms the possibility of designing for a "total user experience," encouraging designers to think creatively and expansively about how products, services, brands, websites, user support, regulations, and the whole "user experience" fit, or don't fit, together. As indicated in the UK Designing for the Twenty-first Century initiative,[11] many fields benefit from an expansion of the design orientation—for example, in thinking of health care as a design issue, and formulating strategies to promote "wellness," preparing and presenting food in ways that enhance the conviviality of the meal; ideas related to hospitality, tourism, and travel as gratifying experiences.

The design of a pay-as-you-go curbside car-sharing service illustrates the operations of such an expansive orientation to design. Investors and developers might be encouraged to think of the design of the vehicles, the profile of the fleet, the website, payment processes, forms, branding, interface with local authorities, road markings, customer support, backup, user feedback, user experience, and interfacing with other services, as well as management, business, and investment planning, all processes permeated by design and subject to contingencies. To advocate design as an incremental process is to introduce into the mix a consideration of the processes by which such a scheme might be rolled out and how designers, developers, and managers learn from mistakes before overinvesting in decisions from which it is difficult to withdraw. Advocates of the "total design" view would probably, rightly point to the need to conduct the necessary background research before embarking on serious investment. I would simply add the necessity to design in the capacity to change and adapt the design and development process, as well as the design of the products and services, taking into account their complex interrelationships.

Of course incremental development features in the discourses of biology. Charles Darwin maintained that the maxim "the law is not concerned with trifles" does not apply to science.[12] The trifles under consideration include not only the momentous consequences of the actions of the lowly earthworm in activating the earth's nutrients, but also the small and subtle incremental shifts in environments and behavior patterns that bring some species into being and extinguishes others. Small increments can have large effects. A small shift can move a big object beyond its tipping point and over a cliff.

Historian Jonathan Sterne provides a telling history of audio devices that illustrates the contingencies of product design and the nature of incremental and opportunistic development, starting with Alexander Graham Bell and Clarence Blake's "ear phonautograph" and the litany of weird, failed, and partially successful devices for the transmission of sounds to the masses.[13] It seems that, as for the urban environment, incremental and contingent processes are at work in the design of sensory apparatus.

It is a simple matter to identify the role of the increment in the long-term evolution of products. One of the justifications for the development of rigorous design methods in the 1960s was that there is now insufficient time to let designs evolve incrementally over successive generations.[14] Tools and technologies may improve the efficiency of design, but there is no escaping the increment.

Design Increments

Ubiquitous devices operate as machines for tuning the environment. Drawings, specifications, computer models, spreadsheets, lists of milestones, PowerPoint presentations, and emails likewise are tuning devices, as are the documents that purport to bring them all together. In architecture, operations with such devices constitute microdesign practices that intervene into existing practices of manufacturing and building. So too in the case of software design, or the design of computer interfaces (interaction design)—charts, tables, timelines, and specifications do not so much dictate how the project will progress but intervene into the existing practices of the programmer, designer, and project manager. Seen in this light, even supposed grand designs or policies are interventions into the environment at the microscale.

To stress the role of the incremental I therefore emphasize equipment and devices rather than systems. In their day-to-day dealings people interact with devices not systems. On a day-to-day basis people look at the subway map to find their way around, not the subway system. When travelers do refer to the system it is often to draw attention to some hegemonic condition, that of a thinly specified sense of unease, a symptom of some socially shared "attunement" to a condition of dissatisfaction with "the system." In avoiding talk of systems I prefer to think of diagrams, plans, tables, networks, and other structures deployed to give an account in some professional context or other—very often an account of failure when no particular device can be identified. In any case, sociologists of technology have expanded the concept of technical systems as socially situated, asserting that in so far as they conceive of systems at all then all technical systems are sociotechnical.[15] The representation of what constitutes the system in any particular case is already an artifact contingently embedded in human practices.

These themes approving the value of the incremental have found their way into the popular business literature,[16] according to which there is always something going on socially and culturally that can be tipped into another condition by the passing of a law, the presentation of a blueprint, a key meeting between individuals, a clip on YouTube, a well-timed or judicious wink. This tipping point is elusive, and may involve a lot of events working in tandem. A plan is a document, sequence of spoken words, or a diagram that is produced to tip one mode of practice into another, or to suppress one practice (smoking in bars) and elevate another (socializing on the street). The plan or policy assumes authority by virtue of the practices that already exist, and brings certain of those practices into sharp relief. It also tunes practices, sometimes unpredictably. The tuning of place suggests that the hard graft occurs within extant complex, pervasive, and tacit human practices. Like the rudder on a ship, a slight movement exploits the momentum of other motions to steer the vessel in a new direction.

The Agony of the Senses

Architectural and product design are commonly associated with the workshop and the studio as the loci of invention. Designers and makers of physical artifacts commonly associate workshops and studios with materials undergoing transformation: wood being cut, paint splashed about, casts molded, kilns fired up, glass blown, drum kits tested, dance moves exercised, and scenery arranged. They are richly material and therefore sensual environments, hands-on, tactile, embodied, and risky. In addition, as confirmed by the experiments of the Surrealists and the Situationists, the workshop spills into the street, the home and the office, the everyday realms of sensation.[17] Attention to such design environments promotes the role of the senses.

Ubiquitous technologies have obvious contact with the senses that are not so apparent in the world of desktop and fixed communication systems. "Handheld," "wearable," "touch sensitive," "personal," "context aware," "ambient," and "sonic" are the adjectives of contemporary interaction design, and ubiquitous devices are out there in the world of the senses. Many devices have built-in sensors, picking up vibrations of various kinds, electromagnetic signals, sounds, movement, light, heat, touch, and scent. Ubiquitous technologies and the creative environments in which they are conceived, developed, and tested constitute sensory studios, wired workshops, and living labs.[18]

So places and the devices in them implicate the senses, with the sense of hearing as a major instrument. Think of the early Sony Walkman, the cell phone, and the MP3 player or iPod, as underlined by the research of sociologist Michael Bull.[19] Ubiquitous portable electronic media found their foothold through a capacity to deliver sounds. Sound theorist Murray Schafer's identification of the occupants of space as composers and performers suggests that sound provides a potent means of understanding pervasive digital media and place. Sound implicates atmosphere, ambience,[20] and ambient computing. Concepts of tuning obviously draw from a consideration of the auditory sense.

Attention to sound, sense, body, place, and increment might imply a return to a more sympathetic and organic order of being, where creatures adapt to their environments and each other, there is harmony between part and whole, and integration between human and machine, apparently important in a world otherwise dominated by impersonal machines, ceaseless communications, and digital surveillance. To follow this line of inquiry would be to tread the well-worn path of romantic organicism.[21] Along with several theorists of the senses I conjecture an opposite trajectory, and affirm the *agony of the senses*.[22] After all, according to Aristotle sound is produced by one object striking another.[23] Cultural theorist Steven Connor makes the case well: "This notion of adversity—the *agon* of the blow or smiting—has predominated in definitions of sound."[24] The workshop is a place of noise, dust, fumes, and blisters as much as immersion in the sensuality of materials. Streets as studios harbor dirt, uneasy transitions and profane interactions. So my investigation into pervasive devices inevitably draws attention to how all the senses and the conflicts between them can enliven spatial design in architecture, digital interaction, and ubiquitous computing, as an alternative to smooth neo-organicism. Contrary to cyborg naturalism, humans need not expect to be one with their machines,[25] nor can they. For Matthew Chalmers and other proponents of a "seamful" computing, interaction designers need to be reminded of "the finite and physical nature" of digital media.[26]

In what ways are the senses agonistic? According to theorists of the senses, for much of the time the human animal is simply immersed in a sensory field.[27] Certain events momentarily bring a single sense into awareness: the unpleasant sound of a power saw working its way through stone paving, the shift in visual awareness as someone turns on the light, the aroma as one lifts the lid on a jar of coffee. The identification of any particular sense is contingent and of the moment. The individual's senses are also brought into relief in the event of conflicts or breakdowns[28] within perceptual experience. Even the identification and numbering of the senses is shown to be the site of conflict.[29] The art of *agon*, adopted by Roger Caillois as a category of game play, simply means *competition*, but as an interplay that is not always hostile or destructive.[30]

In terms of the history of media and culture, the main protagonists in this play are the senses of sight and hearing. Architectural historians remind us that design for space, as developed within the classical tradition, privileges the visual,[31] and the first theorist of space known to architecture was Marcus Vitruvius Pollio (ca. 80 BC–ca. 15 BC) who coupled design closely with vision.[32] Design suggests control, overseeing, and fixing things in place, reaching a high point with the application of perspective geometry to painting in the sixteenth century.[33]

Where sound and the other senses are mentioned in the classical architectural treatise it is frequently related to music, which translates to a concern with harmony and proportion,[34] and the potent conjunction suggested by architecture as "frozen music."[35] The classical tradition, which still pervades much thinking about technologies, promotes this harmony and unity, and decries the fragmentation perpetrated by the apparent primacy accorded to instrumental scientific knowledge, factory production, and raw calculation. The classical legacy elevates order, the harmony of the spheres, and unity, and draws architecture and music within the same orbit. But there is ample evidence of scarcely hidden conflicts between the cultures of vision and sound, between the visual arts and music, the priority given to seeing as opposed to hearing. The ancient myth of Echo and Narcissus indicates such a tension: a story of a nymph constrained to repeat only what is heard and unable to demonstrate her affections to a youth who wastes away under the thrall of his own visual reflection. Media and literary theorists Marshall McLuhan, E. A. Havelock, and Walter Ong in different ways give contemporary expression to the conflicts between the cultures of sound and vision: the former pertaining to aural culture, the latter to the visual authority of the written word.[36] The conflict implicates rival authorities, technologies, and cultures.

Vision and sound are in conflict, but sound can be construed as agonistic in any case. Sound is often emblematic of conflict. In their experience of the everyday, people often think of sound as a source of noise and annoyance. They seek visual confirmation of sounds as if to settle the matter of their source, as though sound is never enough, or complete in itself, and sounds suggest disconnection.[37] Sounds emanate from bodies that otherwise appear intact, and yet the bodies' sounds are separate from them, as are other emanations, such as vapors and scents. The agonistics of sound are obvious in the case of electronic transmission. As further evidence of the tensions within sonic experience, Murray Schafer coined the term *schizophonia*, suggestive of a pathology to describe the "split between an original sound and its electro acoustical transmission or reproduction."[38]

The agonistics of sounds are brought into relief in contemporary society when, for example, passengers encounter the disruptive effects of someone in a neighboring seat on the bus talking on a cell phone. For some this intrusion points to the need to calm things down, to put sound in its place. On the one hand sound can be invoked to placate restive spirits, for example, by chants, waves drumming the shore, humming, soft music. But sound also provides the most potent means of protesting against quietude. If you want to disrupt then you instinctively make a noise if you can.

As confirmed by the everyday experience of sound, music or ambient interventions can have opposite effects to those presumed, depending on circumstance, highlighting the problems with a formulaic approach to sound's placatory potential. In certain circumstances, sad songs can invoke happy memories; romantic ballads can switch off the desire for intimacy; and jaunty melodies can be deployed by composers and producers to heighten terror, drawing from the classical canon of gentle musical taste to invoke menace (as in *A Clockwork Orange* or *Reservoir Dogs*). Of all the arts, music lays the strongest claim to favorably influencing the emotions,[39] but neighbors will as readily voice complaint over Sibelius as Spineshank, and soothing ballads rapidly turn into grating sentiment in certain circumstances. Sound, noise, and even music are imbued with an unsettling, restive character that denies the traditional prominence accorded to concepts of harmonious unity.

Sound Gaps

Certain contemporary spatial theorists seek to break with traditions of tranquility and politeness, readily equated with vision, and characterize places as more restive. In so doing they adopt a vocabulary of gaps, fragments, and dislocated "junk spaces." Such terms are also enlisted within contemporary architecture and urbanisms as describing symptoms of spatial fragmentation.[40] As well as bringing people together, cell phones are complicit in a desire to be disconnected. Phone users may seek out social contact, but also disconnection from sociability.[41] Just as the telephone can put people in touch with one another, it is also a means to break away from the sociability of one's present company.

Sound provides an obvious foil to the dominance of the visual, and arguably encourages a more active vocabulary. The mobile phone ringtone lures its owner and its insistence repels bystanders. Sound pervades the ambient field, but it also requires attention, it modulates and distorts space as an inflection in a sentence alters meaning. Sound can assume the role of an irritant or a point source of pain. As if to abrogate any claim to completeness and unity, Schafer suggests that sound "samples details."[42] Sonic repetition and inflection provide further metaphors for the agony of the senses, and accentuate the small change, the increment, the catalytic moment, tuning and detuning. The staccato intervention of a rogue sound bite (e.g., the slamming of a car door in the middle of the night, a plate smashed in the kitchen, a glitch in the sound track) provides a metaphor for aspects of spatiality that are local, transient, contingent, and transforming, concepts that resonate with the disruptive characteristics of pervasive media.

Sounds and even smells can tip the sensually aware into a new mode of action. In their book *Nudge*, Thaller and Sunstein note that the smell of cleaning fluids in a cafeteria nudges (some) people to keep the place tidy, and warm drinks increase the incidence of a sense of bonhomie.[43] Rather than think of human behavior as conditioned by sense experiences (stimulus–response), it seems designers might think of smells, tastes, and sounds as offering the potential to amplify the tendency to exercise complex predispositions. Sudden sense impressions can tip people into a new mode of practice, a new state of awareness.

Insofar as they implicate the senses, ubiquitous digital devices may provide a local effect, but their influence extends to the scale of the domestic, the urban, and the contemporary places of transportation interchanges and transitional zones.[44] The personal stereo, digital camera, and smartphone of the urban nomad aggravate the flow, and configure space in the process, with subtlety, and incrementally.

Organisms that Think

This agonistic approach to devices and senses intersects with certain theories about thought. Theories of "situated cognition" advance instrumental explanations of how space is involved in thought processes.[45] The theories draw on concepts of timing and subtle inflection. A fish flicks against rocks and exploits the eddies in the water, some generated by its own movements, to swim faster than it could by brute strength. By this reading thought has a similar character, as opportunistic, making the most of the environment in which it takes place. Such theories deprecate the agency of the brain as master controller and instead develop notions of embodied, situated, and distributed agency in which neurons act as "tunable and modulable filters."[46] Spatiality embeds the capacity for quick cognitive responses. Such models have greater resonances with ideas about disruption, breaks, glitches, and opportunistic hacks than do well-ordered plans, the pursuit of a seamless melding of tools and bodies, or the assertion that differences between organism and machine are somehow dissolved by digital technologies.

My emphasis on tuning and the incremental hack is a variation on the theme of cooperation prevalent in studies into complexity,[47] where large numbers of independent agents each responding to their immediate environment are presumed to constitute a meta-organism that demonstrates complex and even intelligent behavior. The obvious example is a colony of termites where each creature responds to local stimuli and the colony is thereby able to build complex structures, an emergent outcome for which there is no apparent representation, plan, or program.[48] This grass-roots, unmanaged self-organization suggests a unity and harmony in small responses leading to something greater than the sum of the parts, an insight that spills into concepts of "smart mobs," interconnected mobile phone users who end up meeting in a certain place through apparently spontaneous and effortlessly negotiated agreement, and without any individual taking charge.[49] The idea of such cooperating agents also informs the ambitions for the next generation of web development, the so-called semantic web, where it is thought that computers will communicate with each other and cooperate to provide the information people need.[50]

Irrespective of the utility of complexity theory to computational and machine operations, the realms of human culture and society seem also to give prominence to concepts of the aberrant shift, the gap in the matrix, and the rogue agent. In so far as there is complex interaction within human agency I prefer to think of complicity as much as cooperation, as a series of opportunistic confederations that seeks to break its own and other webs of connection.[51] Gaps, boundaries, ruses, resistances, and inflections provide metaphors for understanding the cues, hedges, and instantaneous gambits by which people construct, move, and think their way through their social interactions and social places, using whatever media they have at their disposal. Sociologist Bruno Latour elaborates this understanding through the theatrical metaphors of actor-network theory (ANT), in which: "the very word *actor* directs our attention to a complete dislocation of the action, warning us that it is not a coherent, controlled, well-rounded, and clean-edged affair. By definition, action is *dislocated*."[52]

Agon ex Machina

Machine operations that draw on the vicissitudes of the small change and agonistics suggest indeterminacy and play. But my strategy resists tendencies toward organicism and a trend within interaction design research toward a rhetoric of fun and *friendliness*, as exemplified by Donald Norman's influential book titled *Emotional Design*.[53]

Computing has long been a hostile medium for some, and digital devices have been difficult to use. Little thought was given to the human context of their use. Convivial design rightly presents a trend in the opposite direction, toward emotion, play, creativity, and sociability.[54] But pleasure is a complex construct, and is not always usefully equated with having fun. Pleasure can rely on exertion, pain, challenge, competition, a break in tedium, reward after tedious repetitive practice, and being left alone. My strategy is to look past the supposed potential for comfort, pleasure, friendliness, and fun in interaction design. As with cheerful music, pleasure for some can be a misery for others—mobility-impaired individuals can trip over familiar things, pretty objects can invoke sad memories, and many adults are averse to cute playthings. So-called *kawaii*—or cute culture—of Japan, Korea, and China[55] apparently gives pleasure, but stylized doe-eyed depictions of smiling animals, children, and vegetables are repugnant to many. The psychologist Freud indicated the seriousness of the "pleasure principle."[56] Furthermore, serious research into fun is subject to the agonistics of commercial competition and academic tenure. Exhortations to have fun pall in political contexts of potential or actual inequality. Not least, invisible ubiquitous devices that purport to automate user pleasure, by anticipating mood, are in the company of animated dolls, puppets, ventriloquial mannequins, and pleasure devices (the "orgasmatron" in *Barbarella*). It is only too easy to see such gadgets running out of control, and as invocations of the uncanny and of darkness.[57]

Art and architecture generally resist the language of fun, which transports the Taj Mahal and the Palace of Versailles to Las Vegas, making the sublime appear ridiculous, a process that cultural theorists treat seriously.[58] Architecture abandoned the swing toward fun and emotion purveyed in some quarters in the 1960s by the provocative and ironical proposals of the Archigram movement,[59] and the dark pleasures of the erotic city of Sogo in *Barbarella*. The influential apologist of modernism Sigfried Giedion decried an architecture that is "treated as playboys treated life, jumping from one sensation to another and quickly bored with everything."[60] Where architecture and the arts generally purvey enjoyment it is in the realm of meta-pleasure, as in irony, the wry smile that comes from seeing ourselves taken in by overstatement and subterfuge. Irony cuts through the grand plan, the master design, and totalizing ideologies, and it acknowledges its own contradictions in doing so.[61] A problem with interaction design driven by conviviality is that it eschews politics, or at least politics is not easily integrated into its discourse. Ironic design leaves space for the questions "friendly for whom?" and "comfortable for whom?" My investigation into pervasive media attempts therefore to work through the spaces between populist and commercial aesthetic categories.

As I have explored elsewhere, irony is closely associated with the function of the cynic, the character who apparently eschews the grand plan and unsettles pretensions. This is also a function of the trickster, the uncomfortable entity that may be funny, but is mostly an irritant.[62] The tuning of place is an invitation to occupy the interstitial condition of the ironist, the detuner, the occupier and worrier of the gap.

In this brief survey of the role of design in understanding pervasive media, I explored designed devices as interventions that both create spaces and reveal something about the places they occupy. Design is less about abstract ideas and plans than adjustments and tunings to the environment, social relations, blueprints, models, and schedules. Effective design is also a richly sensual activity involving vision and sound, which are in many respects in conflict with one another. The senses are agonistic. Design is well understood through concepts of the hack, the opportunistic adjustment, the negotiation of rifts and gaps—themes explored in chapter 2 on calibration.

2 Calibration

Nothing brings a device into conspicuous awareness so much as its complete breakdown[1]—except perhaps the need to calibrate it, to fiddle with its functioning as preparation for its adoption into regular and habitual use. In their account of experiments in creating an electronic meeting space (which they called an "iRoom") that integrates large displays, wireless devices, and "seamless" mobile appliances, Brad Johanson and colleagues reported: "One of the big headaches in building the second version of iRoom was dealing with projector alignment and color calibration."[2] Calibration interrupts the otherwise seamless operations of digitally augmented spaces and pervasive digital media.[3]

In this chapter I will examine calibration as a major entry point for understanding the design of pervasive devices and media, a consideration that, in a bold move, I expand to the calibration and recalibration of social interactions. Pervasive digital media and ubiquitous devices are involved in the regularization and deregularization of human interactions. Tuning is a kind of calibration, the investigation of which opens the study of pervasive digital media to the possibility of a theory of discrepant phenomena.

The need to calibrate and recalibrate mechanical and electronic devices draws attention to the seams rather than to the supposed smooth integration of technologies into everyday life. Instead of glossing over such tunings as aberrant and undesirable, there is much to be gained in acknowledging and working with them. Designers, consumers, and theorists of digital media benefit from exposing calibration to scrutiny, as a feature of devices and practices of use and design. Ubiquitous digital devices need to be calibrated in order to function, but calibration also provides interesting metaphors for ubiquity and mobility. Users take possession of devices and adapt (calibrate) them to their own circumstances, needs, uses, and local context. To focus on calibration is also to recognize the need for sensitivity to place.

In keeping with the various practices by which consumers and users of digital devices orient themselves to new situations, calibration appears in rituals of inauguration: the device is procured, transported, removed from its packaging, and batteries inserted if needed; it is switched on, variously adjusted, and memory is formatted and data transferred if necessary; the device as product is inventoried, trialed, shown off, used, and shared. The process of inauguration may be repeated completely or in part at a later date. Smart design and retailing recognize the ceremony and occasion associated with the inauguration of a product, its adoption from the shelf to the personalized environment of the individual consumer.[4] The launch of Apple's iPhone augured several videos on YouTube of new owners enjoying the ritual of unpacking and inspecting this new fetish object. The ritual process continues, of course, through the product's documentation, use, repair, return, exchange, storage, decommissioning, and disposal, as well as through the services of which these elements might form a part. Calibration is the technical necessity to ensure that the device initially is fit for context. It is at the core of the inauguration ritual, relates to the functioning of the device, and constitutes a major component in designing for usability and for the user experience.

Standards

Before addressing calibration as a way of dealing with discrepant phenomena, I need to draw attention to the converse of discrepancy—that is, conforming to a standard. Calibration correlates a device to a standard. Considerations of conformity and compliance to a standard may further frustrate inconspicuous operation. But standardization is one of the hallmarks of the contemporary, interoperable communications on which pervasive digital media depend. Much as enthusiasts applaud the free-form, democratic, grassroots, open-source, incremental interventions and smart mobility of digital communications and ubiquitous media, this capability is built on complex configurations of devices that communicate with one another through standard programming languages, data formats, and protocols. The communications language of web pages and mobile devices, HTML (hypertext markup language) and XML (extensible markup language), are such standards. Further advances were made in the uses of the Internet as a medium for international communications and file exchange when web browsers adopted and implemented the Unicode character-encoding standard. Unicode standard radically expands the old ASCII character set (which is limited to 256 characters) to include the symbols, diacritical marks, punctuation, and other graphemes of hundreds of different languages. The Unicode standard essentially assigns a unique number to every character found in most written languages. Similarly, the MIME (multipurpose Internet mail extensions) standard regularizes email formats and enables visual data, sounds, and movies to be transported through interconnected media, including mobile devices and smartphones. Other standards are emerging. Though they also restrict practices and procedures, standards are complicit in extending interoperability and the dissemination of development and use (so-called Web 2.0 developments), and support anticipations of the "semantic web" deploying an RDF (resource description framework) language to supplement XML by enabling web developers to code information about relationships between objects.[5]

Lack of standardization is often identified as a major impediment to the growth of ubiquitous devices and networks.[6] For example, standards for the representation of three-dimensional building data have so far proved elusive.[7] There have been standards such as STEP (STandard for the Exchange of Product model data), aecXML (architecture, engineering, and construction XML), and other COLs (common object libraries) intended for CAD (computer-aided design), CNC (computer numerically controlled) manufacturing machines and other devices and programs that might interoperate with them. For good reasons such standards are not yet widely adopted. This lack of a suitable standard arguably impedes innovations, such as those that might derive from the direct transmission of building information to construction sites via mobile phone, and the operations of ubiquitous sensing and control devices in buildings. Of course, the difficulty in establishing CAD and CNC standards is not just that people have trouble reaching agreement, but also indicates something of the complexity of buildings and their management, and the construction process overall. Buildings are produced by teams, in which architects, engineers, surveyors, regulators, contractors, and building managers each have different requirements in how they represent buildings and building components. Different users have varying "frames of reference."[8] Standards do not necessarily meet the needs of all.

Adventurous thinkers often associate standardization with restriction and unnecessarily arcane bureaucratization, as symptomatic of the "iron cage of bureaucracy,"[9] but standardization clearly is a major enabler of the design and development of shared and distributed devices and networks. Standardization allows interoperability among devices, products, and data of different manufacturers, publishers, and suppliers. Standards can certainly restrict innovation, but they emerge as provisional components within complex sociotechnical practices. Standards sometimes are in competition with one another, developed in political and economic contexts, and agreed on, contested, and revised. Standards often only come after substantial development effort, rather than before it, and when the task of reaching agreement is seen to be worth the effort in coordination. In instrumental, economic terms, the effort of developing and upholding standards is a matter of balance and risk management.

Standards are adopted across the whole technical milieu, including in the use of procedures, codes of practice, and delivery of products, commodities, services, weights, measures, and communications. The idea of deviation could be said to start with the recognition of a standard. Habitual rule breakers often have an overly acute sense of what is allowed and what is not. Standards are interesting objects of study, especially if designers and theorists think of them in terms of human practices.[10]

Deviation often is defined as variation from a standard, but it is worth noting that those standards are dependent on discrepancy in the first place. Many standards emerge as a consequence of an event or disaster that major stakeholders do not want to see repeated: a bridge collapse, breach in network security, loss of data, inability of devices to communicate with one another. Standardization fits within strategies for the management of risk. In this light, a standard is already the product of a breakdown, glitch, or discrepancy. Programmers, interaction designers, and digital analysts do not need to presume a concept of standardization or normality in order to understand the importance of breakdown. In terms outlined in chapter 1, human beings are already attuned to each other and their environment. They participate in a mood, an attunement, out of which objects and events emerge and awake in the human animal some new realization, a breaking away from the norm, or a breakdown.[11]

Standardization involves deciding what the standards are and what they apply to, using them to inform and evaluate a design, policy, or procedure, sometimes within legislative frameworks. The application of a standard is rarely a mechanical process, and is subject to processes of human interpretation. Standards seldom cover every eventuality, and interesting design often emerges where standards conflict, or in the breach of standards.

To belabor the conventional role of standards: when designing a database application program, a programmer might need to attend to standards of data representation, as when designing a program for processing and presenting a catalog of library books, and to how that catalog of information is intended to interoperate with other catalog programs. The DCMES (simple Dublin Core Metadata Element Set) library data standard is easy to grasp in this respect, and is concerned with a much simpler domain than standards for building construction. DCMES provides an agreed series of headings for holding metadata about items kept in libraries and online. The DCMES consists of so-called metadata elements for storing textual information about an item or work (book, article, map, photograph), such as Title, Creator, Subject, and Publisher. Therefore if a programmer is designing a new database that is to be compatible with other programs, then she may be required to use these categories. If data is already stored in a different format, using different headings, and needs to be recognized by another program that only recognizes the DCMES standard, then the information has to be translated, by a human operator, or through a translation (computer) program. Translation programs provide mappings between different representations, and between rival or alternative standards.

Rather than further explain and advance the cause of standards in this chapter, I wish to focus on what their study has to say about discrepant phenomena in the tuning of place. The concept of translating from one representation to another introduces the idea of a mapping. Standardization involves mappings between formats, and is achieved by computer programs, procedures, formulas, tables, and indexes, but also by dials, lines, symbols, and lights on paper, glass, metal, and plastic.

Calibration

Portable, mobile, and ubiquitous devices need calibrating. Simple technologies pertaining to weights and measures and their portability highlight what is at stake in the adoption of standards. An engineer takes a strip of metal, lines it up against a standard-scale ruler, and creates new markings on the metal strip that correspond to the standard. The new ruler is thereby calibrated against a standard. As for standardization, calibration involves a mapping between two models. One model has general applicability and some group or other has agreed to adopt that model as the standard. There is a secondary model of marks or measurements for application in particular contexts, for example, the ruler a carpenter uses to measure the length of a cupboard. To calibrate is to implement a mapping between the two models (the standard and the blank metal strip). In the case of the scale ruler this involves a simple procedure of alignment and copying marks. Within an acceptable margin of error or variation, scale rulers are mass produced to conform to the standard. Scale rulers of course are portable items, mobile and pervasive, low-tech forms of ubiquitous media.

The translation between the discrete values in the Unicode character set involves a set of indexical relations as discrete values. The calibration of an index usually means setting up a table of mappings or pointers. But calibration is particularly applicable to standardization across continuous variables. So the length of a scale ruler or the position of marks on it can be adjusted along a continuum. Calibration involves the adjustment of increments along a variable scale.

The term *standard* has military connotations and so connects with issues of mobility. The *Oxford English Dictionary* definition of *standard* suggests a relationship with the headquarters of an army. The task of calibration implies a home base, a fixed standard, from which are dispatched so many peripatetic, mobile clones (metal scale rulers). Standardization therefore has spatial connotations, implicating concepts of stability and mobility. Calibration is also important in design in so far as design involves measurement. Design also deals with small changes, shifts, and adjustments that have important consequences. Calibration also draws attention to discrepancies between models, the gap, threshold, and sites where design often has a great deal to contribute. Furthermore, concepts of calibration are endemic to the idea of what an instrument is, and to its design, particularly in so far as instruments are concerned with measurement and precision. In these respects I regard the design of pervasive media and the places populated by them as best developed by attending to issues of calibration rather than standards. Calibration is conspicuously a dynamic and provisional practice.

Recalibration

Calibration implies a one-off procedure, but mobility demands adaptability to different contexts, and therefore the capacity for recalibration. Scale rulers are mass produced to conform to the standard with a certain tolerance, but other instruments, such as scales for weighing ingredients in the kitchen, allow for recalibration. Sometimes the cook wants to put the items to be measured in different containers, which entails placing the empty container on the scales and setting the scales to zero so that only the contents are weighed. For example, there is a control knob to set the initial reading to zero before weighing the flour. This is a limited adjustment, but in more sophisticated weighing instruments it is possible to adjust the scale to ensure that 100 grams on the scale corresponds to the standard 100-gram measure. One can procure standard weights for this purpose, which are further calibrated against a succession of derived standards that have led traditionally to the standard kilogram, a block of platinum-iridium kept in the vaults of the International Bureau of Weights and Measures (Bureau international des poids et mesures) near Paris.[12]

Instruments are also manufactured to operate in a certain range and within a known degree of accuracy. Some instruments have to be recalibrated to ensure their accuracy in that particular context of operation. They may also need recalibrating after a disturbance to their operation, or when components drift out of alignment due to wear and tear.

As for pervasive devices, calibration and recalibration are crucial in the deployment of scientific instruments.[13] The word *calibration* derives from the noun *caliber*, which refers to the diameter or bore of a cylinder, and calibration is a basic operation in the manufacture and deployment of artillery and various cylindrically shaped measuring instruments. The basic thermometer is one such tubular device that brings the issue of calibration into focus. As a prototypical measuring instrument, the thermometer consists of a thin glass cylinder joined to a hollow bulb at one end containing mercury.[14] The warmer the mercury gets the more it expands, and the higher it moves up the tube. Marks or graduations on or adjacent to the tube indicate how warm it is in the room or other medium. As everyone knows, the scale is called a "temperature scale," and the thermometer indicates the temperature.

The scale on this prototypic thermometer is decided by a simple procedure. The bulb end of the thermometer is placed in ice water for a few seconds. The level of the mercury in the tube is marked at zero degrees centigrade. The bulb is then placed in the vapor issuing from a kettle of boiling water. The mercury rises. The level at which it stops is marked off as 100 degrees centigrade. The length of the tube running between zero and 100 is marked off evenly into 100 units, yielding the basic temperature scale. Of course, the precise freezing and vapor (boiling) points of water vary with water purity, air pressure, and hence elevation above sea level. Therefore the process has to be conducted within standard conditions. Thermometers can be mass produced from the prototype created by this process, within certain degrees of accuracy and with appropriate markings, though the manufacture of glass tubes is subject to variation. Where very accurate temperature measurements are required, the markings on the thermometer tube may have to be recalibrated to account for variations in manufacture and different conditions of use.

Like clocks and mobile phones, thermometers are moved from place to place. Their context of use changes. It is tempting to think of the calibration of the thermometer as a mapping between a representation device (the glass thermometer) and some actual ("real") world condition. The instrument is perhaps a representational device for reproducing some aspect of reality. Philosophers of science often discuss the role of instruments in science in terms of this problematic. What is the reality that the reading on the thermometer represents? In fact, the use of ice water and boiling water already is a technological mediation, and the history of such scientific instruments is replete with other reference datums, such as the temperature of the human body, the temperature of a deep cellar, and even the melting point of butter.[15] So it is perhaps convenient to sidestep the issue of empirical realism, of what constitutes the reality,[16] and see calibration simply as the mapping between two technological models. This view accords somewhat with the philosopher Mary Hesse's notions about models and analogies in science.[17] It is, after all, models that are being compared against one another rather than theories being compared against pure observations. The invention, definition, and deployment of such models constitute complex sociotechnical practices.[18]

The thermometer amplifies four basic components of the problem of calibration. The first component is a standard, primary, or reference model that involves ice, water, kettle, and vapor. The second component is a model involving a bulb, tube, and mercury (the secondary model). The third component is a translation or mapping language. This is a variable means of establishing a correspondence between the two models, such as a convention of marking the side of the tube, and a procedure, such as inscribing marks at regular intervals between the freezing and boiling points. A fourth component is a context of use. The operation has to fit within an environment where it matters that the primary and secondary models are aligned in some way. The context of use of the thermometer models is wide ranging, including knowing whether or not to put on a coat before stepping outside, estimating someone's state of health, or testing the results of a chemical reaction in the laboratory.[19] Thus ice-cold and boiling water are components within a standard model, involving various technologies and procedures, against which the glass and mercury model is calibrated.

The communication of meteorological data via pervasive devices involves further levels of calibration. My smartphone and laptop provide the approximate temperature at my current location, but this information is derived from a table stored on a central server. The software on the phone pays no heed to local atmospheric conditions, but updates periodically with data pertaining to my current location and that of several other locations indicated in a menu. The information is dependent on a series of interrelated calibrations across several modalities, not least involving tuning into radio frequencies and via communication protocols. The smartphone's display with figures and icons depicting temperature at my current location draws only obliquely and circuitously on models of steaming kettles.

Calibration has applicability beyond a consideration of externally regulated and legislated standards, and any two technical models might need to be calibrated. Lest the contemporary mobile device user thinks such adjustment is a new phenomenon, the diaries of mathematician and astronomer Galileo Galilei (1564–1642) reveal an application of the importance of calibration as a local operation. Galileo mapped the movement of dark patches across the surface of the sun (sunspots) as evidence that the earth rotates and orbits around a rotating sun. He recorded these observations by hand, drawing over the image formed by the light from a telescope projected onto a sheet of paper. In order to record these observations he had to position the telescope relative to the sun but also to the sheet of paper by aligning the circumference of the sun to a circle drawn on the paper.

> In order to picture them accurately, I first described on the paper a circle of the size that best suits me, and then by moving the paper towards or away from the tube I find the exact place where the image of the sun is enlarged to the measure of the circle I have drawn. This also serves as a norm and rule for getting the plane of the paper right, so that it will not be tilted to the luminous cone of sunlight that emerges from the telescope. For if the paper is oblique, the section will be oval and not circular, and therefore will not perfectly fit the circumference drawn on the paper. By tilting the paper the proper position is easily found, and then with a pen one may mark out spots in their right sizes, shapes and positions. But one must work dexterously, following the movement of the sun and frequently moving the telescope, which must be kept directly on the sun.[20]

One model involved lenses and sunlight, the other involved paper and pen. The two models were calibrated to one another by the adjustment of distance and angle of a sheet of paper. The mapping language entailed geometrical alignment, and the context of use was a concern with planetary and solar motion.

Digital Calibration

Through processes far more sophisticated, augmented reality equipment has to deal similarly with calibration issues, particularly those that mediate the view of the environment via superimposition of a digital image in real time. The user wears a head-mounted display apparatus that projects a three-dimensional image of a streetscape, with annotations, onto a screen, through which the viewer can also see the street. Sophisticated movement tracking detects the precise location of the viewer's head so that it can generate a corresponding view in the digital model. Calibration is required to ensure that the initial conditions are set accurately, and instant calibration and recalibration is required to keep the images aligned. It is tempting to think of the necessity to calibrate the digital image with reality, but again there are two models in play: a projective model based on the way light falls onto a flat plane of glass and the computer model that has to be aligned to it.

As a simpler example, in the case of the calibration of a touch screen on a handheld device (a process now largely obsolete), the two models in play include the visual display model and the sensing model. The display is made up of a grid of pixels that are addressed and activated by the computer's central processing unit. The detection of touch on the screen is determined by variations across an electrical field that are activated when an implement (perhaps a plastic pointer or finger) touches the screen. Due to variations in manufacturing, the visual display and the sensor field are not always aligned to one another, and the screen is a composite of layers of materials the distance between which is not necessarily known with great precision. Variations in the touch pen and the way it is held also introduce discrepancies. On instruction, the user recalibrates the two layers by tapping on visible reference points on the touch screen. This sets the parameters of a function applicable across the screen surface. Technically, the calibration sets the parameters of a transformation function, as if stretching a piece of rubber with a pattern on it so that it corresponds to the pattern on a plane underneath. The transformation function is applied automatically to every subsequent touch of the screen, whichever part of the screen is contacted. The calibration is meaningful in the context of the entire instrument (display screen, touch sensors, pen) and the instrument would not be fit for purpose as a means of interaction on a handheld device without such alignment and its calibration.[21]

The central role of calibration is obvious to an audience observing a group of sound artists preparing for a performance. One performance I observed involved our sound design students improvising around everyday objects. Various sensing devices and actuators (electrical contact switches, microphones, speakers) were attached to the components of a tea party (cups, pots, plates). These in turn were connected to laptop computers and sound mixers. Such ad hoc configurations of hardware inevitably require adjustment so that signals can be received and processed to deliver the required sounds. The ensemble was to be played as a collection of instruments. Calibrating and recalibrating played a significant role in the performance, and contributed as much to the audience's appreciation as the final performance, which was unpredictable anyway, especially when audience participation was invited. Such works provide a potent reminder of the role of calibration when subjecting everyday objects to some specific purpose.

Needless to say, the processes of calibration are often occluded in the rhetoric of seamless environments and interactions, or the melding of organism and machine. For example, cybernetician Kevin Warwick has conducted a series of experiments in which he attempts computer control of the movement of his own hand: an automated clenching of the hand outside of his own will. In the experiments, electrical signals are transmitted into Warwick's arm from a computer via a series of electrodes. Such experiments are presented as if at the vanguard of machine-body hybridity.[22] Yet such operations involve elaborate and prolonged tuning, tweaking, calibrating, and recalibrating. The human nervous system apparently adapts to the external signal and the context of the signal in complex ways.[23] Digital interventions into the human frame require calibration on the part of both the machinery and the body. Philosopher of the mind Andy Clark describes how mobility-impaired individuals with digital implants lodged into the motor cortex can be trained to move a cursor on a computer screen "by thought." The patient first tries to will the movement of certain body parts: "When such efforts yield a signal, which the computer hears, a buzzer sounds so the patient knows to concentrate on that particular kind of thought," thereby controlling a screen cursor.[24] Of course the rhetoric of human-machine hybridity aims to render such calibration processes automatic.[25] But designers, commentators, and consumers might benefit from exposing the issue of calibration to scrutiny, as endemic to the device, in order to better inform their implementation and use of such technologies.

Calibration processes not only are required for pervasive digital media to operate, but also present interesting metaphors for ubiquity and mobility. The mobile device emerges from a housebound, regulated environment, and the user takes possession and adapts—calibrates—it to her own circumstances, needs, and uses. Pervasive digital media require this sensitivity to local context.

Registration and Control Points

Morphing between two images involves a similar process to that employed in the calibration of a touch screen. The familiar digital effect by which one human face appears to transform into another involves morphing: Dr Jekyll becomes Mr Hyde. In morphing, a digital artist usually indicates which points on each image are to map to the other: the tip of the nose, the corners of the eyes, the mouth, and so on. These control points form the basis of an invisible network of lines and points across images, and a mapping procedure. Viewers see the features distort as one image transforms into the other under the control of a computer program. Halfway through the morph observers see a composite image where Dr Jekyll and Mr Hyde are fused into one, or at least they see some kind of average combining the two characters.

In some cases the identification of calibration points can be automated, as in the case of stitching together two images that have an area of overlap. In this case the two images are scanned for clusters of pixels that have similar characteristics. These constitute the control points. A computer program rotates and aligns the images so that these points overlap one another as nearly as possible. The overlapping areas between the two images will already be very similar, but they are morphed to the halfway or average point to produce an apparently seamless composite image. The technique becomes very powerful when there are large numbers of miscellaneous images, only some of which overlap. There exist automated procedures for taking collections of images and organizing them in terms of overlaps to produce any number of composites, some of which may form panoramic views, as in Google StreetView, with continuous images covering very wide angles of view.[26]

Such techniques of automated image calibration, adjustment, and combination have found new application as a way of processing vast quantities of visual data from ubiquitous digital devices. The rituals of amateur photography involve capturing images of people and places, managing archives and collections, and sharing images with others. The display of photographs has expanded to the use of websites, sometimes attached to temporal and locational map information, and organized according to social groups and networks. Vast numbers of images are available from Flickr and related social networks (Facebook, MySpace, Orkut) for all to see and process.[27] Enterprising developers have created techniques for searching and stitching images from these sources, notably Microsoft's Photosynth and Seadragon for generating large composite images and panoramas from stored pictures, and even extracting three-dimensional information about a place.[28]

Mobile devices require calibration, but they also generate extensive quantities of data requiring microcoordination and calibration. In the examples here the data usually is visual and coordinated by a third party on managed and centralized servers. Increasingly, such processes occur dynamically, in real time, to some instrumental end and between devices, hinting at advanced interoperability between pervasive digital media devices.

Optical Interference

Devices may interoperate, but they may also interfere with one another's operations in some way, as when the radio waves of a mobile phone are thought to interfere with an aircraft's internal communications. There are many ways that two signals can interfere, often unpredictably, and sometimes productively, as in the case of the interference between two digital images.

Two digital images can be overlaid without the sophisticated calibration suggested by stitching panoramas. If the top image is treated as transparent then there are many ways that the two images can be combined. Commonly used image-processing software can average the color values of pixels that are aligned, or only display the maximum in one color dimension of the overlapping pixel values.[29] In the manner of a bricolage, image overlays can reveal interesting relationships between images, and generate new and startling relationships, as evident in early analog photography: for example, Man Ray's 1923 image of a feather superimposed over a pestle and a sheet of glass. Image overlays can also reveal subtle interferences between images.

Interference is most interesting where two slightly discrepant representations or models come into contact with one other. There is the well-known moiré effect in vision, where a wire mesh is superimposed on top of another wire mesh, and there is displacement in terms of their alignment relative to the eye.[30] Some cells in the top grid will be occupied by a view of the wire in the mesh behind, and some will be empty where the wires line up precisely, with a range of conditions in between. The result is an interference effect appearing as a series of light and dark curved bandings or fringes. The effect is evident in the case of various regular patterns, including those involving curved lines. Such patterns are very common, even where grids are identical, and the moiré effect was first regarded as a quality in fabrics, such as silk. As the distance and orientation of two surfaces changes, so too the interference patterns may change, like ripples appearing on a water surface. The observation of fringe banding has been related to hallucinogenic states, and op (optical) artists such as Victor Vasarely and Bridget Riley have exploited moiré effects in their work.

Optical geometry dictates that the visual alignment of two flat planes varies across the visual field. Such interference patterns are also evident when the grids are on the same plane, as when a coarse-grained photograph from a newspaper is scanned and displayed on a computer screen. The dot array of the image sometimes interferes with the grid array of the computer screen to produce banding of colors and brightness values. Rescaling an image can have a similar effect.

The moiré effect amplifies small changes. It is sometimes used in the detection of subtle deformations in materials. A grid of lines is printed onto the material to be deformed, and it is viewed through the same grid, which serves as a reference. Subtle movements in the deformed grid relative to the reference grid register as moiré fringe bands.[31] As the moiré effect exaggerates small differences, the banding provides a cue to the registration of two models and their calibration with each other. One grid is stretched or adjusted by degrees until the banding disappears.

Sonic Interference

The superimposition of sound patterns can also produce regular and detectable intensities, notably in the case of rhythm. Composers such as Xenakis and La Monte Young explored overlays of sonic textures and rhythms. Interference is also detectable in situations involving subtle differences in regular periodicities at the level of the vibrations that make up sound waves, noticeable in the case of musical tuning.

Early Pythagorean scholars theorized about the relationships between musical notes.[32] Take a harp string of a fixed length, tie one end to a nail positioned on a table, and tie a weight to the other end. Hang the weight over the end of the table so that the string is clear of the table surface, taut and of known length between its supports. Next to it place an identical string with the same tension and of the same length. When plucked, the two strings will sound in unison. They vibrate at the same frequency. If one string is shortened slightly, by adjusting one of its fixings at an end, then it will have a slightly higher pitch than the string next to it. When plucked together, they will vibrate at slightly different frequencies.

The two strings produce an aural interference effect. Momentarily, in a fraction of a second of being plucked, the two notes reinforce one another, as if in unison, and then a fraction of a second later their slightly variant oscillations produce a slight cancellation effect. This rapid succession of reinforcement and cancellation due to the slight discrepancy in their vibration can be heard as a series of beats that is at a lower frequency than either of the main frequencies. These beats are analogous to the bands of the moiré effect. If one string is vibrating at 100 Hz, and the second at 110 Hz, then the beats will occur at 10 Hz, manifested as a kind of buzzing sound. Other factors such as the resonance of the environment, the materials of the string and fixing, and whether other notes are being played at the same time influence the prominence of the effect, and how listeners might respond aesthetically to the sound. Adjusting musical instruments to control these discordant beats becomes a major tool in their calibration. A piano tuner will adjust a string by successive tightening and slackening, and listening to the varying periodicity of the discordant beats as she does so.[33] In fact, each note on the piano has several strings, tuned slightly differently to induce such beats and thereby enrich the sound, or timbre.

Tuning extends to other vibrating mechanisms. Shock absorbers in cars are tuned to provide the right degree of comfort for passengers and to maintain the vehicle's stability in handling the road. Buildings and other structures may integrate tuned vibration absorbers (TVA), "tuned so as to cancel the vibration at a particular forcing frequency," according to a technical paper on the subject.[34] Machines that have components oscillating at different rates may require tuning. Jet engines on an aircraft with slightly different rotation speeds produce a secondary vibration that may register as a throbbing sound to passengers, or as an undesirable vibration.[35] Where the two vibrating mechanisms are connected further interference ensues. Two discrepant machines, physically connected, each tugging at the other to conform to its own rhythms, can produce a set of shockwaves. The knocking or pinging of a car engine is such an effect, where the timing of the spark tends toward a different cycle from that of the fuel entering the combustion chamber. Tuning an internal combustion engine on a car or motorcycle involves adjusting valves that control the air and petrol mix to the combustion chambers for optimal performance, a process described as a refined craft in Pirsig's book *Zen and the Art of Motorcycle Maintenance.*[36] Skilled mechanics will listen to the sound of the engine, which involves the complex interrelations between oscillating components.

The tuning of a radio receiver is also a form of calibration. The listener turns a dial to adjust the sensitivity of the radio to the frequencies of transmission stations. In contemporary digital devices the process is sometimes automated, but has to be repeated when the device is moved to a new location with different reception properties. Technically, electronic tuning is known as demodulation, which hardware hacker Nicolas Collins describes as "multiple stages of amplification, filtering, and frequency shifting."[37]

Tuning in involves tuning out—filtering out unwanted frequencies, and signals that would interfere with the device's operations, distort the final output (the sounds), or produce other "interference effects." To the extent that pervasive devices rely on electromagnetic and audible signals they require selective tuning, a recalibration that involves filtering out unwanted frequencies. But interference also serves as a metaphor for the interaction between devices. In the same way that two notes not quite in unison produce a third beat, or two overlaid images produce moiré patterns, interoperating pervasive devices produce effects other than the sum of their parts. Interference banding serves as a metaphor for the rich potential, and shortcomings, within interoperating models. It also points to the potential for the generation of unintended social effects and hybrid artifacts. Images and sounds can be combined to produce not just averages, but also new entities.

Discrepancy

Fringe banding is an example of minor discrepancy in alignment, a kind of error that produces a larger effect not always undesirable. It seems that there is no escaping the productive influence of discrepancy. In his review of the legacy of second-order cybernetics, the science of control, and the human-machine relationship,[38] Ranulph Glanville underlines the observation that "error is, in itself, neither bad nor good, but endemic—it cannot be eliminated. . . . it is error that drives the system!"[39] It seems that discrepancy not only is a matter of scarcely noticed error in small things, but also is inscribed in the generative capability of the universe writ large. It is also evident in language. For Saussure, it is the tiny differences in sound patterns, "the phonetic contrasts which allow us to distinguish that word from any other," which in turn "carries the meaning."[40] Discrepancy, error, difference, and small increments are closely inscribed in the way things work as well as fail.

In this section I want to pursue the proposition that human beings inhabit a universe of small increments, in further support of an argument I have developed elsewhere against the tendency toward idealism in the study of digital media[41] and that has ample support from various traditions in philosophy, notably Pragmatism, as discussed in the context of interaction design by McCarthy and Wright.[42] Why does this matter? In his seminal work on tangible computing, Paul Dourish proposes "smoother and more natural forms of interaction and expression" that "unify computational experience and physical experience," and that "unify the physical and electronic worlds to create a blend which is more closely matched to our daily experience and abilities."[43] In so far as the design of ubiquitous technologies appeals to concepts of all-encompassing unities, schemas and typologies, and seamless interaction, they are heirs to a kind of idealism. The tendency toward an all-encompassing norm or standard is implied in McCullough's account of tuning, which has the character of bringing a network of equipment into a state "based on a qualitative, top level interpretation of the performance, and in best cases, the 'feel' of the aggregate."[44] McCullough's identification of architectural types (places for shelter, work, trade, learning, gathering) as a means to understanding the role of ubiquitous technologies is a variant on the classical and idealist traditions, where the alternative to the recognition of types is thought to lead to "chaos."[45] After all, if the universe cries out for unity, then it is the goal of technological design to abet this progression. Unity is incontrovertibly a virtue, and pervasive devices that blend and adapt are superior to devices that fragment or aggravate human experience. But the experience and observation of the heavens has always revealed discrepant phenomena. Such attention supports the imperative to attend to the gaps and the instruments that work them.

The primacy of the small increment, of subtle change, is evident in all the senses, but is arguably brought into sharpest relief through the sense of hearing. In his book *Microsounds*, Curtis Roads discusses the ubiquity of transient events that reveal an instantaneous sonic presence: "We experience the interactions of microsounds in the sound of a spray of water droplets on a rocky shore, the gurgling of a brook, . . . the crunching of gravel being walked upon, the snapping of burning embers, the humming of a swarm of bees, the hissing of rice grains poured into a bowl, and the crackling of ice melting."[46] It seems that musicians, acousticians, sound engineers, and sound designers must attend in their trade to the small temporal interval. Specialists in sonic media seem to exhibit control over increments with greater facility than a visual media artist might attend to flashes of light, momentary glances, pixels or moiré fringe banding. In working with both sound designers and visual designers, in the case of the former I frequently see computer screens showing timelines overlaid with wave forms, divided into temporal units of fractions of a second. Focusing on a single dimension, time, the analysis of sound leads inevitably to the key actions of dividing and subdividing, a compositional strategy examined by composer Iannis Xenakis: "Natural events such as the collision of hail or rain with hard surfaces, or the song of cicadas in a summer field. These sonic events are made out of thousands of isolated sounds."[47]

Small intervals, increments, and discrepancies are closely related. The detection of discrepancies between transmissions provides obvious technical utility. The time gap between the transmission and return of a signal, as in the case of sonar, provides information about distance and location. Similar processes are at work in charting the position of satellites, and depend on temporal discrepancies. Satellites feature prominently in global communications networks and enable the interoperability of much pervasive digital media. The time standard is currently set as ATI (international atomic time), the average of the time kept by several atomic clocks in laboratories across the globe, relative to a reference time and date (January 1, 1977). Atomic clocks usually are set to the radiation frequency of the chemical element cesium, which is a relatively easy chemical to monitor, and has highly stable radiation emissions.[48] It ticks at a decidedly regular rate. The positions of orbiting satellites need to be known at any instant so that a GPS receiver on earth can calculate its position relative to the satellites. Satellite positions are calculated by the miniscule time differences in the transmission and reception of radio signals relative to synchronized atomic clocks on the satellites. Time discrepancies are used to calculate the positions of satellites and enable interoperability between precise scientific, engineering, and navigational instruments.

Tools for timing are important in the context of pervasive media. Clocks and watches were among the first pervasive and portable mechanical devices to be created. Mobile devices invariably rely on timing components. Recall Lewis Mumford's observations about social synchronization through clocks. There are of course less precise technosocial models that involve the positions of celestial bodies and their discrepant cyclical rhythms. Think of the movements of the sun and the moon. It is a commonplace to note that the sun and the moon are on slightly different courses across the sky, have different periodicities, and have different effects on light, shadow, tides, and weather. From the point of view of this discussion of calibration, it is helpful to think of the solar and lunar models as two technosocial models, isolated for particular ends, that involve looking at the sky, light, shade, sticks, shadows, sundials, tides. By various means the cycles of the sun and moon constitute parts of technosocial models that have been isolated, observed and integrated into human practices over many generations. With contemporary scientific sensibility it is easy to assert in shorthand that the movements of the moon are on a different cycle to the movement of the earth relative to the sun. A single orbit of the earth around the sun is not a whole number multiple of the cycles of the moon.

The context in which it seems important to consider these models together is in marking out the passage of the days, the seasons, months and years, basic functions brought into consciousness in the case of personal diaries and calendars, digital or otherwise. Various calendars reflect the irregularities between these celestial models and incorporate adjustments that have been agreed by different communities: hence the discrepant Gregorian, Islamic, and Hebrew calendars.[49] Months are roughly formulated around lunar cycles (28 days), seasons and days fit the solar cycles. Of course, there are at least two models based on the sun. The orbit of the earth around the sun (on average 365.2425 days) does not match precisely a whole number of daily earth rotations.[50] An extra day is inserted into every fourth year to avoid a kind of calendar drift.[51] Calendars based on the cycles of the moon, such as the Hijri or Islamic calendar drift by 11 days relative to the seasons, and the Gregorian calendar, causing interesting difficulties for people who fast in daylight hours during the feast of

Ramadan. The days are longer when the festival period falls in the summer and in regions nearest the poles. The earth, solar, and lunar models are calibrated through various practices, including the maintenance of calendars. As Mumford noted, the development of reliable clocks and standardized calendars was clearly important in obviating local variation, in overriding these discrepancies and introducing new ones.

There are interesting discrepancies between what sky watchers observe above them and the behavior of living organisms. Biologists Foster and Kreitzman note that without the daily alternations of light and dark, the social regulation of daily routine, and living by the clock, the human animal will tend to drift into a daily cycle that is on average eleven minutes longer than the twenty-four-hour cycle.[52] Workophiles and partygoers more happily stay up late and sleep in than retire early and get up early.[53] There are dozens of internal cycles that catch up at different rates in the event of major upheavals to the daily routine. The cycles of days and seasons, of the human organism and the animals and plants on which we depend are in a state of dynamic equilibrium, which is to say there are cycles that supplement, resist, interfere with, and push against one another.

Certain scholars advance a critique of pervasive communications media in terms of such cyclical dynamism.[54] Insofar as society depends on digital devices, it further inures itself against those intricate variations of place. In so far as place depends on local differences, the instant transportation evident among mobile phone users further emphasizes removal from place, or a situation in which people regard every place as the same, or treat places instrumentally. Local differences are reduced to time-zone differences that further instrumentalize labor to a twenty-four-hour cycle. While keeping to their own daily cycles, workers on the other side of the planet effectively perform tasks overnight and return completed outcomes the next morning.

Classical cosmologies seemed to conspire toward the suppression of discrepancies in favor of regular, circular geometries. Vitruvius described the laying out of a temple according to sixteen wind directions, easily derived from the movement of the sun.[55] The clock is divided into twelve units, the year approximates an ideal cycle of 360 days, divided into twelve signs of the zodiac. Circularity and centrality become emblematic of order and harmony, and become the means of understanding and ordering the cosmos. Plotinus, the ancient philosopher, spoke of a universe made of concentric spheres, with the earth at the center, inflecting premodern cosmologies with a "rotary motion."[56]

As if in resistance to idealized models, leap days are obvious manifestations of the discrepancy within temporal models. Contrary to idealized rotary motions, there is evidence that discrepant periodicities of celestial movements have been the focus and driver of both ritual and scientific practice. Were the configurations of the stars and the heavens as regular and obvious as the rotation of a wheel then they might have drawn less attention.

Music features prominently in thinking about order, discrepancy, technology, and cultural transmission.[57] Musical instruments precede clocks, and personal stereos were among the first mobile electronic devices. So music already pervades the way designers and consumers think about ubiquitous media. More profoundly, music was thought to provide evidence for the harmonious union of all things. But the so-called "music of the spheres," the ancient belief that the movement of the planets accords to harmonic ratios,[58] brings discrepancies further into relief. The seventeenth-century astronomer Johannes Kepler (1571–1630) is attributed with explaining the orbits of the planets around the sun as elliptical, and devising the mathematical means for calculating their paths. At the end of his extensive research and writing, and in a manner that accords less with contemporary science, he expounded on the complex relationships between planetary motions and musical harmonies.[59] He decided to calculate the ratios between the planets based on the average distance in degrees across the sky that each planet would traverse if seen from the surface of the sun over a given time period. He asserted: "The ratios of the apparent movements of the single planets approach very close to harmonies."[60] So Saturn and Jupiter, at the outer extreme of the known solar system, are an octave apart, and the interval between Jupiter and Mars is a minor third, almost. Kepler's model exhibits inevitable discrepancies when compared with other modes of observation, but also internally in terms of the model itself, which he details in terms of different scale units. For Kepler these discrepancies point to a "higher wisdom" that eludes him.

It is asked whether the Highest Creative Wisdom has been occupied in making these tenuous little reckonings. I answer that it is possible that many reasons are hidden from me, but if the nature of harmony has not allowed weightier reasons—since we are dealing with ratios which descend below the magnitude of all concords—it is not absurd that God has followed even those reasons, wherever they appear tenuous, since He has ordained nothing without cause. . . . God chose nothing without a geometrical cause of some sort, as is apparent in the edges of leaves, in the scales of fishes, in the skins of beasts and their spots and the order of the spots, and similar things."[61]

Kepler sought to preserve the ideal rotary motion of things by appealing to the symmetry and logic of harmonic ratios. By a slightly different reading, it is precisely the discrepant that motivates his metaphysical explanation, both in attributing the discrepancies to higher mysteries and the relentless quest to arrive at certain truth. Later astronomers of course abandoned explanations in terms of harmonic ratios, in part as the discrepancies between increasingly sophisticated models of observations and the musical model became so vast as to be uninteresting and unproductive. Of course, Kepler's abiding legacy lies elsewhere than in the harmony of the spheres, but in the more persistent mathematics of orbital movements, which in turn generated its own discrepancies, and later theories about gravity and the detection of new planets.

Philosophers of science such as Mary Hesse discuss such discrepancies between models in terms of analogy and disanalogy.[62] Kepler worked with an analogy between a model of musical harmonies and a geometrical model of the solar system. Hesse refers to other cases of the attempted alignment between the behavior of sound waves and light waves, which provided an obvious case of disanalogy. Sound and light are alike in many respects, and many of the calculations that are applied to sound waves can also be applied to light. The major disanalogy between these two models is in the issue of media. Sound waves are propagated through air particles, but an equivalent medium in terms of electromagnetic (light) waves is notoriously elusive, its absence requiring further sophistication in the development of the model of how light behaves. Two models are brought into line by new technique or are seen to deviate to such a degree that no amount of fine-tuning brings them into line. So the alignment between the models tends to be abandoned, as in the case of harmonic ratios and planetary motion. Philosopher of Science Thomas Kuhn describes this degree of irredeemable discrepancy in terms of incommensurability.[63] Two models eventually are seen to be on different scales and to use different variables, and do not compare or measure up. Over successive refinements, observations, and theoretical developments the models drift apart to such a degree that comparisons are no longer useful.

The identification and resolution of discrepancy is as much a motivator for developments in science as may be claimed of correspondences and similarities, the language of categories and standardization. More precisely, I would say that the developments of sociotechnical devices, which include pervasive media, are driven by discrepancy.

On the one hand the social historian may wonder at how such symmetrical contrivances as ideal harmonic ratios and orbital geometries gained purchase in the light of obvious discrepancies. On the other hand it may be precisely because of the discrepancies that the concept of ideal circular geometries has held sway. For the classical architect Leone Battista Alberti (1404–1472), "Beauty is that reasoned harmony of all the parts within a body, so that nothing may be added, taken away, or altered, but for the worse."[64] What is the assertion of this criterion but a presumption of the existence of discrepancy? Architectural historians Hart and Tucker relate Alberti's tendency to emulate Aristotle's quest for the mean, or mediocrity, away from extremes, to the rationale for decorous and polite architecture.[65]

Ideal geometries are the perfection that is only falteringly perceived and observed in an imperfect world. According to this view, it is the discrepant gap that holds together concepts of order. The discrepant fuels the conviction of a transcendent all-encompassing unity, Kepler's higher mystery. That the solar year deviates from the manageable geometry of 360 days provides further evidence that the world does not yet enjoy the perfection to be found in the realm of ideals. For cultural historian Adrian Snodgrass, awareness of this discrepancy motivated aspects of Indian temple architecture and symbolism. Discrepancy kept things moving: "As there is a remainder there is no end, the cycle recommences, and time continues on. The residue is thus the seed of the next cycle. . . . No further motion is possible without the discrepancy between one cycle and the next."[66] Hence, the *Vâstu* mandala building form is both a residence and a residue. The *Vâstu* is the place where the gods reside. It is also the residue of a sacrifice.[67]

The identification of the remainder is further support for the imperative to attend to the gaps, the place-filled thresholds in environments, and the ubiquitous technologies that open, bridge, occlude, and moderate gaps. It also suggests that designers should attend to operations around the gap, the stretching, the oscillations, the tightening and relaxation, the attention and listening through which tuning is accomplished.

The circle is a potent geometry for giving an account of space and time, but it is also a special case of a series, assuming regular periodicity. Circular geometries bring sequences back to the start and occlude certain variations. Periodic variations between models inevitably lead to drift, where events don't quite line up.

Temperament

The ways that people deal with sound provide interesting models for understanding pervasive digital media. As I shall show, sound is conspicuously discrepant. Considerations of sound provide a means of further unsettling the idealism at the heart of much thinking about the smooth melding of technology and environment. Music provides further evidence for the occlusion of temporal gaps and the battle between circularity and periodic variation. In keeping with my theme of digital devices as a means of tuning place, I need to attend further to the question of musical tuning.

The harmonies to which Kepler referred have a mathematical derivation that was well known from as long ago as the time of Pythagoras. I return to the string stretched across a table as described earlier. A second string with the same properties and end conditions but half the length will vibrate at twice the frequency. The difference between the two notes so produced is the octave. If successive strings are produced, each half the length of its neighbor, then this produces a series of octaves; in other words, each delivers a frequency twice its neighbor's in an increasing succession of octaves. Slight variations in this series produce the beats previously referred to, and introduce a kind of distortion, noticeable as a mismatch, or discord. Tuning involves making fine adjustments to be sure the intervals are accurate, or at least deliver the appropriate doubling of frequencies.

It is worth looking at musical intervals in a little more detail. There are of course other intervals than the octave in play in musical instruments. In fact, in Western music the octave is so called because it is divided into eight notes, or more precisely twelve notes (semitones) that are combined into eight divisions of one and two semitone intervals. How are these twelve semitone intervals derived? As is evident from inspecting the neck of a guitar or other fretted instrument, the intervals are not marked out as regularly as a linear thermometer scale. There are several methods of deriving the musical scale, one of which involves whole-number ratios to derive an exponential musical scale, the so-called Just scale.[68] Another, more mathematically consistent method attributed to Pythagoras is to work on the half octave. In order to produce a note that is half an octave higher you reduce the string to two-thirds its length, easily achieved by positioning a finger appropriately on a stringed instrument such as a violin. This produces an interval that fits well with the octave sequence. A single note that falls at the two-thirds point in the octave range vibrates sympathetically with the octave. This half octave note can be used to generate a further series of half octaves, each vibrating at one and a half times the frequency of its neighbor to produce simple two-note harmonic chords. The twelfth note in the half-octave series matches the eighth note in the octave sequence. The twelve-note scale is produced by bringing each note in the half-octave sequence within the range of the same octave, by successive doubling and changing their order from lowest to highest. This produces a series of divisions something like the fret positions on a guitar. The twelve-note scale is regarded as flexible and harmonious, and seems to allow for note combinations that exploit the natural harmonics of vibrating strings and columns of air of the kind deployed in musical instruments. The twelve-note scale is exponential and not linear. The half octave actually falls on the seventh semitone in the twelve-note scale, and is actually called the perfect fifth. The fifth note above C is G, followed by D, A, E, B, F#, C#, G#, D#, A#, F, and back to C. Musical scales and harmonies make use of this so-called cycle of fifths, which encapsulates important relationships. The cycle is a useful way of modulating between scales, that is, it demonstrates relationships between musical keys.

However, as is well known to classically trained musicians and musicologists, there is a discrepancy in the model. The seventh note in the sequence of octaves and the twelfth note in the sequence of half octaves only approximately match, and by an amount that can be easily calculated and detected as the beats that occur when two notes that are not exactly in tune are played together. Musical instruments that operate with a musical scale derived from the cycle of fifths may sound out of tune. Intervals that sound harmonious in one part of the scale may sound discordant in other parts of the scale. Melodies and harmonies that leap across octaves and that modulate between different scales will sound particularly discordant.

The discrepancy between the octave and half-octave sequences can be calculated, and has been named the *comma* (the Pythagorean or diatonic comma), a slight pause, or gap. This discrepancy or remainder is about a quarter of a semitone accumulated across seven octaves.[69] Contemporary tunings involve subtle "correctives" to ensure that musicians can move freely across scales and octaves and preserve standardized control over harmonies. Such tuning spreads the discrepant comma evenly across the scale so as to be scarcely noticeable. The musical scale has been tempered, the effects of the comma discrepancy rendered less extreme, and the widespread adoption of the well-tempered or even-tempered scale around the time of J. S. Bach (1685–1750) is one of the hallmarks of classical music.

Such even temperament is of benefit where standardized instruments are deployed.[70] Singers who can keep a tune without instrumental accompaniment can apparently perform without recourse to even temperament. They and their listeners can harmoniously migrate across complex melodies and harmonies, and modulate between keys, even ending the piece several semitones above or below the equivalent notes at the start of the composition. According to one musical theorist, if Mozart's opera *Don Giovanni* were sung unaccompanied, then the final pitch of the last phrases of the opera would drift five or six semitones flatter than at the beginning.[71] At no stage would the singers or audience be disturbed by this shift, as long as an orchestra with its evenly tempered, standardized instruments did not attempt to conclude the work by striking up the last chord of the score.

It is complex instrumentation and the ability to form ensembles of instruments that encourage standardization to the even-tempered scale. To this extent even temperament could be said to mechanize or even dehumanize musical production.

The defense of a musical scale that is not so well tempered has become a celebrated cause by certain practitioners of electroacoustic music who want to challenge the primacy of the octave and explore dissonance,[72] as well as by social theorists such as Max Weber. He saw the quest for even temperament of the musical scales as symptomatic of the unfortunate imposition of industrialization and standardization into the arts.[73] Consumers benefit in the age of industrialization from the transportability of music across national boundaries, but according to this argument, in the process music has lost regional nuance and color. In fact, even temperament represents a form of colonial domination and Eurocentrism. Music making outside of the Western classical tradition can exhibit other tuning practices, as in the case of the Indian sitar, that not only deploys a different scale system, but also different tunings according to the time of day.[74] Calibration and conformity come to the fore in the modern era. They pertain to measurement, mathematics, factory production, predictability, uniformity, control, and the paraphernalia of science and advanced technologies. The charge holds if I extend the criticism to pervasive digital media, which again promote and require standardization, glossing over local differences. Is the world being tuned and therefore being subjugated to the same scales, or does tuning provide an opportunity to adapt to a local condition?

It is interesting that the discipline that is so emblematic of order and harmony, namely music, is conspicuously infused with challenges to that order from within. Accordingly, the mathematics deployed to validate that order indicates discrepancy.[75] The necessity of the comma is further evidence of the compensations necessary to push order toward the geometry of the circle. It could be said that architecture and music have long focused on proportion and harmony, but in doing so have manifested the remainder, the excluded, the superfluous, and the deviant. The tuning of place could be seen as a restoration of the discrepant, of the local, a reversion to the unevenly tempered Just scale, or local, diurnal scales of other traditions.

The tuning of place need not insist on regularization. To the extent that they form part of the perceptual and social apparatus of place, contemporary ubiquitous media can enable subtle tunings without regularization, further evidence for which comes from an appreciation of the legacies of inconspicuous adjustment.

The naming of the comma, the discrepant, the remainder is perhaps one of the earliest recognitions of the central role of difference. Considering how important it is to calibrate, adjust, and tune equipment, then, the social historian might expect discrepancy to be a major factor embedded in other human practices, including architecture and art. The identification of early concepts of calibration and tuning, the subject of the next chapter, can inform contemporary design, urbanism, and the tuning of place.

3 Wedge

What is the archetypal pervasive device, the basic and ancient instrument from which portability, invisibility, everydayness, and participation in discrepancy might derive? It surely is an instrument of adjustment. The search for the prototypical device usually is overridden by the celebration of conspicuous buildings and structures that are thought to realize divine geometries. My argument emphasizes the existence of small-scale interventions into the environment that presage contemporary digital devices. I also emphasize the device ahead of the all-encompassing systems and infrastructure networks, of which devices might form a part. I also emphasize the material device ahead of some ubiquitous all-pervasive field of interaction. The key to understanding the relationship between pervasive digital media and place is in material, tangible, and nonconforming artifacts, outside of some abstract frame of reference.

Much is made in the ancient literature of the procedures for imposing divine order on the apparent disorder of nature,[1] or of identifying the order in the apparent chaos.[2] Certain rituals imply procedures for constructing symmetrical celestial geometries, the so-called pre-Copernican universe.[3] The detection of sunspots referred to in chapter 2 is emblematic of the apparent ancient sublimation of imperfection.[4] Sunspots have been observed on the face of the sun since ancient times but seemingly were ignored. They were difficult to detect, but more important, they suggested imperfection in the entity at the very pinnacle of a perfect universe—namely, the sun. In fact, even with the solarcentric conception of the cosmos, the invention of the telescope, and Galileo's recordings of the migration of sunspots across the sun's surface, there were those who maintained that sunspots were not discolorations on the face of the sun but must be the paths of planets.

There is covert recognition in the Western traditions of the fine adjustments that need to be made, the glitches in the process, the inevitable discrepancy between the ideal forms and the way things actually appear, which point to a "higher mystery." Negotiation of this gap between the ideal and the actual is a practical matter, less prone to regularization, order, and rule. Aristotle highlighted the practical virtue of *phronesis*, the ability to make appropriate judgments in everyday contingent circumstances.[5] There is wisdom in deriving rules of good conduct and forming them into laws and classifications, but the everyday application of those rules requires skilled judgment that is acquired by experience, learning from others, practice, and bodily engagement. Sculptor David Pye points to the need for such judgment in workmanship: "Some contrast and tension between regulation and freedom, uniformity and diversity, is essential."[6] The exercise of such contingent practices across the gap is evident in the way people would hold the stylus in calibrating the old-style touch screen, a subtle practice by which the user would negotiate the space between the device's demands for regularity and the free movement of the hand. Translating a regularized temperature reading into a decision to take a coat with you to the park involves similarly contingent practices, as is the case with the tuning of a violin, and laying bricks to create a wall. Making and constructing provide good cases of the human dependence on careful judgment and the ability to deal with discrepant conditions.

In an imperfect world, managing traditional building processes becomes a process of gap management. The master builder may claim to have the whole design in mind, but the trades people have the know-how to manage the intricacies and ameliorate the problems at junctions, where the ideal hits the contingent, where conditions differ from what they should be,[7] identified by architectural theorist and historian Colin Rowe as "the conflict between the absolute and the contingent, the abstract and the natural; and the gap between the ideal world and the too human exigencies of realization."[8] Successful architecture accomplishes a reconciliation of the mind to "some fundamental discrepancies in the program."[9]

Contemporary ad hoc adjustments on the construction site are anticipated by the classical tradition of arranging architectural elements. Vitruvius focuses on the ends rather than the means, but of necessity invokes adjustment: "The length of a temple is *adjusted* so that its width may be half its length"[10]; "Order . . . is an *adjustment* according to quantity" (my emphasis).[11] It seems that harmony, order, and symmetry depend on proper adjustment, as if things need to be brought into alignment from an initial position that is a deviation from the norm or the ideal. Adjustment is an active term, and resonates with activity on a construction site. Blocks of stone do not simply fall into place, but have to be maneuvered. The Latin word rendered as *adjustment* in English translations of Vitruvius is usually *temperantur*, a form of the verb *temperare,* to which temperature also relates, and which, according to the *Oxford English Dictionary* , carries connotations of dividing proportionally, combining properly, keeping within limits, regulating, and of course tempering. To temper is to modify something so that it does not go to extremes. The creation of even temperament in music is such an adjustment.

Vitruvius makes reference to visual correction in terms of adjustment. If columns are built with straight vertical sides they look insubstantial and hollow. This is an apparent fault of the observer's perceptual apparatus and must be compensated for: "Hence, we must counteract the ocular deception by an adjustment of proportions."[12] The visual world is subject to deviations that deny perfection, and requires the introduction of curvature (entasis) to the profile of a column.[13]

The necessity for adjustment is also explicit in the construction of war machines, such as catapults. That machines for destroying buildings are described in such a matter-of-fact manner in a treatise on architecture is also indicative of the recognition of a breach in the fabric of orderliness. In any case, Vitruvius describes a catapult in terms similar to the stringing and tuning of a musical instrument:

> Next, the loops of the strings are put through the holes in the capitals, and passed through to the other side; next, they are put upon the windlasses, and wound round them in order that the strings, stretched out taut on them by means of the handspikes, on being struck by the hand, may respond with the same sound on both sides. Then they are wedged tightly into the holes so that they cannot slacken. So, in the same manner, they are passed through to the other side, and stretched taut on the windlasses by means of the handspikes until they give the same sound. Thus with tight wedging, catapults are tuned to the proper pitch by musical sense of hearing.[14]

Among the various components that are named, Vitruvius makes explicit reference to the wedge, which he considers important in the process of adjustment. Circles and squares belong to the language of platonic perfection, but if you are looking for a shape that corresponds most to the existence of discrepancy then the wedge is the best candidate.[15] The wedge is the operative device for adjustment and tuning; it is perhaps the archetype of pervasive media. Wedges are bits of wood with a triangular profile, one side narrower than the other, which can be jammed into place with a mallet. In the case of Vitruvius's catapult, a rope passed through a hole at the top of a thick rod is wedged in place after being tightened by a rolling mechanism. The harder you hit a wedge, the further in it goes, but a wedge also pushes out to make a gap bigger or to fill it. Mumford references the wedge indirectly in his praise of wood, which has the capacity to be "split and split again with the simplest tools—the wedge and the mallet."[16] A wedge also increases traction and makes it harder for wheels and barrels to roll down hill, or for taut rolls of rope around axles and pulleys to unwind. The constructional and structural advantages of the wedge are apparent in the case of the stone arch,[17] formed by a series of wedge-shaped stones that gravity jams one against the other in succession, with the sharper end of the wedges pointing downward. The top of the arch often is completed with a keystone, a bigger wedge of stone that closes off the top. The keystone is an element that accommodates discrepancies.

The wedge is a means of adjustment and serves to hold things in place. Carpenters may deploy several wedges to keep a wooden frame aligned and in position. Two pieces of wood can be joined together by a mortise-and-tenon joint, which involves shaping the edge of one piece of wood into a series of wedges, which lock into the spaces between corresponding wedges in the piece to which it is joined.

Wedges were also used in the calibration of water clocks, according to Vitruvius: "The hours are marked in these clocks on a column or a pilaster, and a figure emerging from the bottom points to them with a rod throughout the whole day. Their decrease or increase in length with the different days and months, must be adjusted by inserting or withdrawing wedges."[18] Similarly, he says of pumps: "Over the vessel a cowl is adjusted, like an inverted funnel, and fastened to the vessel by means of a wedge thrust through a staple, to prevent it from being lifted off by the pressure of the water that is forced in."[19]

If astute observers of the manufactured and built environment allow their imaginations to run with the wedge, they will then see wedges everywhere. Teeth are in fact wedges. The axe, the most primitive of tools, is a form of wedge, as is a pick, a knife, an adze, a sewing needle or acupuncture needle, a nail, a skewer, a spike, and a rapier, all of which are instruments of reduced thickness in the direction of the force applied. The operations of the wedge apply to both swords and ploughs. An adze, which is a flat-edged pick for chipping at a surface, is "self-jigging," which means that its form acts as a template for the shape it produces and works.[20] The narrow side of the wedge goes in first and works the gap, translating a longitudinal force into an approximately lateral one, which is also the effect of a lever, or a ramp. The British idiom "the thin edge of the wedge" refers to the start of something of greater consequence. Once the point enters the material its splitting can be achieved with greater ease: a wedge-shaped military formation of tanks apparently achieves something similar, as a task force that is able to advance while simultaneously attending to its flanks. The wedge has evolved into more complicated apparatuses. For example, the screw is a twisted wedge that provides greater control and firmness of fit. Cogwheels, used in clocks and other machines, are made up of regularly spaced wedges that engage with the gaps between the wedges of an adjacent wheel. A ratchet deploys a rack with wedge-shaped teeth that engage with a pawl, a hinged and wedge-shaped component, to restrict mechanical rotation to a single direction. Wedges imply engagement, locking, and keying.

As for the keystone, significance is attached to the capping stone and ceremony is attached to the completion of a dome, and the accompanying capping-off ceremony. Capping off implies culmination, but also the final cover-up, the apparent gathering and occluding of all discrepancies, though in some cases this makes them all the more obvious, or at least draws attention to a disregard for precision. The wedge as keystone or inverted as a pyramidal capping element fulfills this role. It is an imprecise device for achieving an impression of accuracy, order, and neatness. There is more tolerance in the specification of a wedge than a wheel. The angles of the sides of the wedge do not need to be exact. Gaps are managed by the depth at which you drive the wedge. The workings of the wedge are apparent to anyone who has had to improvise a wedge of folded paper to slip under a table leg to stabilize a table in a restaurant.

Can we also build an understanding of idealized ordering on the tenuous foundation of the wedge? When formalized, the wedge gives birth to the triangle, a primary platonic form. Surfaces bounded by straight lines can be broken into triangles. Complex meshes and networks are shown as so many overlapping triangular shapes. Triangles are planar and stable. In buildings, triangles come into their own in elevation, in the distribution of gravitational loads, the shedding of water, and in buttresses and ramps.

There is psychological evidence for the primacy of the wedge in human cognition. Rudolf Arnheim demonstrates the obvious importance of the approximate circle in the drawings of young children. A circle delineates an object of as yet unspecified shape. Everything is drawn as a circle, but when the infant starts to introduce other shapes, then she starts to represent objects that she actually thinks of as round: faces, the sun, flowers. According to Arnheim, "A circle is a circle only when triangles are available as an alternative."[21] Wedges and angles are the medium of discrimination, including the appearance of scribbled "saw teeth" to represent hair drawn around the circle of a face.

According to this trajectory of investigation, the archetypal pervasive device is a wedge, not a wheel. The wedge is local and interstitial, compensatory, and apologetic. What is the relationship between the wedge and contemporary pervasive media? Designers and users deploy various words for a technological component or machine, such as *mechanism, apparatus, instrument, tool, device,* and *gizmo*. A common diminutive term for a machine component is *gadget,* which the *OED* suggests might derive from French *engager,* to engage one thing with another. A wedge facilitates engagement, and therefore is a kind of gadget.

Widget also is a common term denoting a trivially simple but perhaps essential apparatus whose name one may have momentarily forgotten. The *OED* suggests its origin in the term *gadget*. Widget seems to be a twentieth-century portmanteau (a word formed by joining two others, merging their meanings) and several dictionaries suggest it is a combination of *window* and *gadget*. The Online Etymology Dictionary suggests widget might be derived from "which it." Irrespective of a word's etymology its usage can persist due to connotations. The sound of "widget" is suggestive of fidget and digit, and indirectly of a key. It is also suggestive of wedge, though I know of no source as yet that refers to widget as "wedge it."

A discussion of wedges, cogs, ratchets, gears, and mechanical composites is perhaps apposite when we reflect on the history of computing (the Jacquard loom, Charles Babbage's Difference Engine, the Enigma cipher machine, old office adding machines[22]), and the popular romance with machinery in science fiction, fantasy, computer gaming, and steampunk culture. The differences between the idea of a wedge and a sophisticated item of pervasive computing such as a mobile phone are obvious. A wedge operates within the mechanics of adjustment, and is a long way from precision electronics, which is dependent on complex technological infrastructure. But diminutive terms are often deployed to account for the most complex and sophisticated organization: *plastic* for credit card, *hardware* for computer, *handy* (in German) for mobile phone, *widget* for a self-contained computer program. A simple characteristic is deployed to stand in for the whole complex apparatus—like the thin end of an ontological wedge, a metonym that stands for the whole, the tip of the iceberg connected to an invisible, uncharted, and unfathomable mass. Pervasive devices are often placed at the "cutting edge," and Internet blog addicts are on a slippery slope. Thus the alignment of sophisticated electronics with the wedge that works, fills, and creates the gap participates in familiar linguistic practice.

Colleague Dermott McMeel has examined the use of mobile phones on building construction sites in this context. Regulators often forbid mobile phones on building sites for reasons of health and safety, but where they appear they frequently are deployed as a means of stopping gaps: to make an emergency call to a supplier, for example, or get clarification of an instruction or a drawing. The contract documents (drawings, blueprints, specifications, shop drawings) and the line-managed passage of instructions provide the legally sanctioned framework for the project, but frequently it proves necessary to jump out of this framework and resort to unofficial lines of communication. Pervasive digital media provide conspicuous means of adjusting meeting times, schedules, and instructions. Of course it is not the devices in isolation that provide the adjustment, but the access, communication, and attendant social practices that they support or bring into focus on the construction site.

There are several aspects of ubiquitous devices that render them as "stop gaps," as ubiquitous, inconspicuous, portable, disposable, interchangeable, and incidental. They do not draw attention to themselves, but facilitate the operations of the network. They support something larger and more consequential. A structural wedge does not achieve much on its own, but supports the conspicuous edifice. It can also be replaced by something more secure or long-lasting. Like many cutting-edge electronic devices, mobile phones become obsolete within a year or two, but people hold on to them or pass them on. The device often fills a provisional role until the next model comes along. They are not only transient but also support and encourage transience, drift, slackening, and looseness in social relations. Think of the emerging casualness in appointment keeping. People might think less of running late for an appointment given they know they can phone ahead to explain. The device fills the discrepant gap in the schedule. It also adjusts and transforms the concept of schedule.

Sensory Wedges

The wedged profile features prominently in early accounts of architectural acoustics. For Vitruvius, the cornice is an ornamental detail that facilitates the transmission of sound. The cornice after all has the profile of a chamfer, an interior corner blunted by an angular edge. This wedge-shaped device covers over discrepancies in the junction between wall and ceiling, has an ornamental role, and serves to modify sound reflections.[23] The function is similar to that of the deflecting board above a pulpit that assists in the transmission of speech.[24]

Triangles also relate to lines of sight. Renaissance essays on perspective in painting draw attention to the importance of the pyramid, a three-dimensional wedge shape. In his treatise *On Painting*, Alberti relates the pyramid to the eye: "The vertex of the pyramid resides within the eye, where the angles of the quantities in the various triangles meet together."[25] Rudolf Arnheim writes about the importance of non-Euclidean, "pyramidal space" in the perception of environment.[26] The human understanding of space deals in convergences, and the perspective vanishing point constitutes the tip of a wedge.

Trinitarian symbols abound and feature within classical ideas of spatial organization. The triangle speaks of perfection and ocular dominance. But as its everyday forebear, the wedge does the work, including in visual perception. Philosophers of perception draw attention to the irregular trapezoidal nature of the visual patches that make up the visual field, which the human perceptual apparatus then processes into solid shapes and objects. According to philosopher John Hospers, perception of a tabletop begins with "a trapezoid with the acute angles on the nearer side,"[27] and a succession of variants that present themselves as one moves and which one learns to form into a continuous sense experience and thus a contiguous object. As is obvious in the crude graphical representations of early 3D computer games, the visual field can be construed as a collage of irregular wedge-shaped planes on the computer screen.

Cubist painting, the art of the Russian Constructivists, and the contemporary architecture of Zaha Hadid present as a celebration of fracture, rupture, and displacement realized often in terms of wedge-shaped, shard-like forms (more recently replaced in Hadid's work by fluid forms). So many acutely angled lines intersecting irregularly and according to site contingencies produce architectures that break with centrality and classical notions of symmetry.[28] Such forms are also artifacts of exaggerated straight-line-perspective geometries, as when simulating a wide-angled lens in a computer renderer that always draws straight lines as straight rather than curved as in a wide-angled photograph. Like straight railway tracks disappearing into the distance, wedges are ubiquitous in simplified ocular geometries. Sonic and ocular sense impressions converge on the wedge. Sound designer and colleague Martin Parker inverts the romantic metaphor of architecture as "frozen music" to inflect the dynamic of live performance: "Being neither frozen architecture nor liquid music, these live encounters are fractured and shard-like."[29] Sound structures often draw on the wedge.

Sound versus Sight

Attending to the relationship between the senses also highlights the role of the gap, as if there is a wedge driven between the senses. As I have shown, the scientific models that philosopher Mary Hesse invokes to account for analogy include the propagation of light waves with the transmission of sound. Sight is compared with sound in a kind of cross mapping. Calibration across the gap has a role to play in coordination between the senses. The senses are constitutive of different perceptual models, each carrying particular entailments. For example, some claim that sound requires visual confirmation of its source. For cultural theorist Steven Connor, sound "is experienced as enigmatic or anxiously incomplete until its source can be identified, which is usually to say, visualised,"[30] a requirement that is not necessarily reciprocated in the case of the visual sense. Whereas human beings appear to be adept at visual closure—completing an image consisting of four L-shaped marks such that the observer infers a square—human language for replacing sonic deficit seems to call for entities outside the experience of sound. In many ways sound is suggestive of incompleteness, and vision of completeness. Connor deploys the functioning of teeth to emphasize this incompleteness. After all, the voice, the major bodily sonic apparatus, involves the rolling volutes of the tongue, which are cut short by the abrupt operations of wedge-shaped teeth.

Wedges are devices for recalibrating structures and mechanisms so that they fit their environment and fit together, or interoperate. They also cleave, separate, and articulate the fissures between surfaces, rendering conspicuous the grain between devices and within networks. I have so far mainly considered calibration as a process involving two models that have to be aligned in some way under carefully controlled conditions. It only takes one wedge under the leg of a four-legged table to make it steady, but if the table surface is to be level or at a certain height then more wedges may be required. Making several interrelated adjustments is difficult. In some circumstances a complex measuring instrument similarly must deal with several interrelated variables such as temperature, air pressure, and altitude. The obvious procedure would be to isolate each variable and test them in turn. Procedures exist for *multivariate calibration*, the calibration of devices with many interrelated variables, typically involving rapid iteration through multiple readings and involving the adjustment of several variables. The readings can be handled probabilistically. Calibration therefore becomes particularly troublesome and interesting for ensembles of devices, or complexes of variables, none of which is entirely stable during the calibration process. Pervasive, ubiquitous, interconnected sensing devices might require calibration of this kind. Automated multivariate calibration is one of the elusive goals of pervasive digital media.[31] I will return to consider such calibration after a discussion of social tuning.

Social Tuning

The claim that clocks synchronize people's actions appeals to a standard, that of clock time. The clock provides a regular model against which to calibrate personal and group schedules and routines. Clock time ostensibly reduces reliance on negotiation and the subtle alignment of patterns and practices. Small, localized communities may be adept at organizing their routines by virtue of habituation and subtly nuanced signs and cues involving diurnal cycles, bodily rhythms, and informal communications: coming together or dividing their time for meals, work, recreation, and sleep. But it seems that commerce, trade, public transportation, and large-scale organization across distances involving large numbers of people require the externality of clock time, as an independent standard that people can share and against which they calibrate their actions. But even synchronization to the demands of the clock requires proficiency in the subtle, human arts of tuning.

Tuning as a human, interpretive activity seems to take place at the boundaries, the gaps between models, where calibration, recalibration, alignment, and measurement call on interpretation, judgment, and the visceral intelligence of human bodies. Musicians and computer users calibrate equipment to human particularities, such as tuning musical instruments to scales, or training voice recognition software to respond to the sound and inflection of a person's voice. But consumers and users also tune their faltering human practices and perceptions to equipment, at least as a kind of training. The calibration of a touch screen adjusts the equipment. It also provides a simple rehearsal for the user of the touch screen. It trains the device user to regard the process of drawing on the screen with a certain degree of care. The calibration of language recognition software and voice-activated devices operate in a similar way. The speaker trains the program to recognize words, inflexions, and usage patterns to refine its pattern matching and indexing functions and so convert speech to text. Users of such programs also report that they learn to adapt their speech to the program. They learn to speak "naturally" and clearly, and by pausing in the right places. Musical training is an elaborate and extended process of tuning muscles and nerves to align with the characteristics of a musical instrument. Technological implants and prosthetics also require extended tuning and retuning of bodily functions, as well as the calibration of equipment.

Recalibration implies resetting a device, model, or program so that it operates reliably, predictably, and with stability in relation to a reference model. Recalibration is required when the models drift out of alignment. But recalibration can be a dynamic process. Calibration is a special case of a process that is ubiquitous and constant within organisms and human relations. Cyberneticians explain the relentless processes of calibration and recalibration in terms of feedback loops. The organism moves in its environment, picks up signals that indicate some change, and responds with an appropriate action.[32] This produces further changes and responses. In walking, every step not only advances locomotion, but also provides feedback about surface, gradient, stability, and various resistances that contribute to the way the foot falls at the next step. Therefore walking on a pavement requires a different pattern of movement than does walking on a hot sandy beach. Dancing, ensemble playing, group working, sports, combat, and even conversation seem to require this two-and-fro movement that constitutes a series of complex, instantaneous, multivariate calibrations and recalibrations, tunings and retunings.[33]

Theories of embodied intelligence render such tuning processes inevitable and endemic to the way organisms are shaped and keyed to their environments (their morphology).[34] Tuning does not always equate to calculation or deliberative cognition. By virtue of muscle and nerve dynamics, and the general shape of things, creatures fall into stable patterns of movement (walk, trot, gallop) that require only minor adjustment by neural control. Neurologists Rolf Pfeifer and Josh Bongard describe such adjustments as "slight modifications." They also describe the way that an organism learns and develops as "an incremental and continuous process," by which the behavior of the organism alights on new "attractor states," stable moments of activity that are well suited to its physiology. From the perspective of embodied intelligence, tuning is less a cognitive labor than it is a process of letting things fall into or out of alignment.

It seems that similar tuning processes are in play as people interact with one another. Alfred Schutz places music at the apogee of social attunement. Music presents as a "mutual tuning-in relationship,"[35] indicative of all communication. Ensembles of musicians "tune" to one another's styles and expressive gestures: facial expressions, gestures in handling their instruments, posture. Practices that are in some way oblique to the task at hand are brought into play. Social activities seem to display something of the complex character of a multivariate calibration. Extended practice enables ensemble players to tune into and retune to each other's performances. Performers can be observed to participate in incessant retuning as they make microadjustments to their playing. A violinist makes small adjustments to finger positionings in order to compensate for a string that is slightly out of tune, or even an accompanist's slightly variant tuning.

The judicious use of glissandi (sliding notes) and vibrato enable vocal and instrumental performers to work around discrepancies in pitch, to inflect and calibrate as they go. In fact, the whole range of "expressive" musical moves, pitch, and rhythm play into the process of retuning in solo and ensemble work. As it happens, tuning is thought to have performance value in its own right, as proposed by the artist Marcel Duchamp: "Have a piano tuned on the stage . . . or make a movie of the tuner tuning and synchronize the tunings on a piano. Or rather synchronize the tuning of a hidden piano—or have a piano tuned on the stage in the dark. Do it technically and avoid all musicianship."[36]

Music also has an instrumental role in coordinating other activities. In his work on the history of technologies, Arnold Pacey notes how groups of workers use music and its rhythms to synchronize work.[37] In the Scots Gaelic traditions of textile production, women would sit around a table, grasp the sides of a length of newly woven tweed and beat it against the table in order to soften the wool fibers, all to the accompaniment of a repertoire of song, gradually increasing in tempo. These are known as "waulking songs." There are many examples where music seems integral to work processes, from cotton picking to warfare. The role of such practices in synchronizing the sociable aspects of certain activities are obvious cases of those secondary processes by which people align their practices, and tune their behaviors. Some practices apply to the short-term moment-by-moment performance of a task, but some abet longer temporal intervals, such as the ringing of bells in churches and monasteries, calls to prayer, and the observance of timetables and calendars.

People primarily think of synchronization, calibration, and tuning in terms of temporal coordination, but tuning also applies to space, being in the same place at the same time, and coordination of sensory experience: such that I see what you see, hear Mozart as others hear him, am repulsed by the scent of boiled cabbage as are my siblings, feel the touch of a guitar string as does my teacher, acquire the same taste for wine as members of my diners' club. Social calibration is temporal, spatial, and sensual and works through everyday practices.

As I have shown, commentators and designers often think of such tunings in terms of coordination and synchronization, in which machines and tools play a crucial role. Mumford's elucidation of the advent of the industrial era focuses on the central role of time keeping, through regular observances, sundials, water clocks, and mechanical timepieces.[38] By this reading, human societies deploy technologies to coordinate and synchronize their activities. Devices calibrate and tune the actions of people, to their environment, certainly, but also tune people to one another through their environment. As social animals, human beings use technologies to bring themselves into line with each other. According to cognitive scientist Edwin Hutchins, "the real power of human cognition lies in our ability to flexibly construct functional systems that accomplish our goals by bringing bits of structure into coordination" by deploying "artifactual and social interactional resources."[39]

If Mumford presented the clock as the pivotal technology to mark major social change, and the industrial, scientific, liberal age known as the "modern period," for his protégé, Marshall McLuhan, the operative technology was print.[40] It was language and its technologies that marked the transition into the modern, industrial era: sign systems (languages), texts, tables, dictionaries, encyclopedias, and indexes. For McLuhan these are visual technologies, amplifying the sense of sight, converting the aural medium of the voice to the visual media of writing and then print, able to be stored and mass produced. Language and its technologies of dissemination and preservation are the most conspicuous means of coordination and calibration within human societies. Electronic and digital technologies extend linguistic capability, but also amplify the range of sensory modalities. Writing in the 1960s and no doubt thinking of the incessant chatter of transistor radios, for McLuhan the electronic age returns human kind to the era of the ear, but we also have our eyes wide open.[41] Pervasive digital technologies are now implicated in this social tuning. The development of social network media seems to extend the means of disseminating, regulating, and monitoring shared practices.

Does this social tuning have as its end a process of harmonization, bringing social relations into a uniform, homogeneous, hierarchized whole? Social misalignment is commonly described in terms of a "culture gap," to be bridged by education, coming into contact with others, and exposure to the mass media, commerce, global capital, and the apparatus of the state. Contrary to such normative controls, liberal concepts of social tolerance imply looseness of fit, providing room to move, to disagree, on religious and other issues, as explored by the libertarian philosopher John Stuart Mill (1806–1873).[42] Liberalism implies openness to processes of alignment and misalignment, tuning and detuning. It is one thing to think of technical processes as working in concert in finely coordinated harmony, but human relations are more complex than machines, and benefit from friction and instability. To think otherwise is usually to appeal to some variant of utopian romanticism, idealism, or, worse, a return to feudal, bureaucratic, or dictatorial social organization. It is as well to attend to the gap as a palliative to social control. Tuning is a dynamic process that works the gap, at times amplifying, distorting, exaggerating, or diminishing difference, in order to bring two or more models into alignment with one another and see what interference patterns might emerge. As a dynamic process it implies restless change and adjustment in concert with, or in contrast to, moments of stasis.

If designers and social commentators think of the role of language in tuning human relations, then they could do worse than attend to the indeterminate operations of metaphor. If nothing else, the wedge is a suggestive and provocative metaphor for understanding the relationships between humans and their devices.

Tuning and Metaphor

As I have indicated, the most general formulation of the technical calibration problem is of the adjustment of one model with another, an adjustment necessary between two models. I have been dealing with technical models that involve interconnections and causalities. Such models concern physical objects, mechanisms, signals, and patterns. But I am also dealing with sociotechnical contexts. There has to be a context in which it makes sense to compare those particular models. Models have to be detected, identified, isolated, observed, and interpreted. What constitutes a model in any circumstance is open to interpretation, justification, and argument.

Models are created and not simply found. Calibration (and tuning) is a specific and instrumental case of the general problem of metaphor, and of language. One mode of experience is linked to another and reveals certain similarities and differences, as in the case of the water and light models of the propagation of waves. Such models are also metaphors or analogies, which Hesse describes in terms of contest, or *agon*: "Of course the description of similarities and differences between two analogues is a notoriously inaccurate, incomplete, and inconclusive procedure. Although we often feel some confidence in asserting the existence of a similarity and that some things are more similar to each other than to other things, we cannot usually locate discrete characteristics in one object which are positively and finally identifiable with or differentiable from those in another object."[43] Hesse is here describing models in science and other domains of measurement and their interpretive and conflictual character, an observation that can apply to all metaphorical interactions.[44]

The operations of metaphor therefore embrace ethical and political considerations. One model in the comparison is generally privileged above the other: the secondary model is calibrated against a standard. So the standard takes priority. Likewise a sentence is subservient to the thing to which it refers. A reference has to be adjusted to fit the referent. Any description language submits to the authority of the thing being described, the signifier adjusts to fit the signified, and the explanation adjusts to the explanandum. Calibration, or tuning, already implies a value is being assigned to models. The touch screen has to be calibrated against the visual display, rather than the other way around. It only makes sense to calibrate with the visual display, not the keypad, and the visual display has primacy. Recall Connor's observation of the incompleteness of sound until the listener can visualize its source.[45] Visual models are generally prioritized over the sonic. Tuning is therefore value laden. Metaphor involves similar entailments of priority. Depending on social context, some metaphors assume more importance, or greater currency, than others.

I mentioned "frames of reference" in chapter 2 in relation to standards. One problem with standards in the construction industry is that there are many players, professionals, and stakeholders, and each has a different view of the world, that is, a different frame of reference, or model. Political difficulties arise where the standards favor one frame of reference over another, or enable interoperability between powerful stakeholders (planners, developers, and contractors), but marginalize others, such as consumers, resident communities, and people working in minor trades. Certain players have to struggle to get into the tuning game.

The nature of calibration and tuning as implicating value is obvious in emerging metaphors of the city. So-called smart mobs suggest urban life in which individuals are empowered to contribute to something greater than the parts, a contribution that is socially redemptive. The autonomy of the urban crowd suggests the metaphor of the city as organism. Think of the properties of an organism: alive, self-determining, willful, growing, changing, sentient, in an environment, and in a complex relationship with other organisms. A city may suggest other entailments: a human construct, an overlay of models, historical, governed, subject to laws, which houses people, and has functions. What adjustments to these various metaphors are needed so that each is referring to the same thing? In other words, how are these concepts calibrated one with the other? How do critics, planners, and inhabitants calibrate organism with city and city with organism? This tuning is a two-way process. It is also a linguistic question, and an incremental linguistic operation. Terms are adjusted and configured to make sense of the comparison. Similarities and differences come to mind. Such tuning also raises a design question: how do you make a city more like an organism? What pervasive technologies facilitate this organic interaction, provide the variable ligatures in the complex network of human relations, and assist in the tuning and coordination of human endeavor? What technologies pull apart and reconfigure human relations?

Returning to the wedge as a particular metaphor: the wedge is emblematic of marginality in physical space. The wedge is the form of improvised constructions. The "lean-to" is an improvised structure formed by placing a less enduring construction, such as a wooden frame or a series of joists, against a solid wall to create a wedge-shaped structure, in other words, a planar frame that is neither horizontal nor vertical, but leans at an angle against a wall. Its roof sheds water as needed; its overall structure requires minimal precision. There is less of the ideal built into such structures, and less accuracy required in their construction. Such interstitial structures are themselves gaps in the order of the city. As well as emblemizing the forms of slum towns and *favelas*, there are parallels here with the way mobile phones have been adopted in poorer countries by a class of trader identified as the "microentrepreneur,"[46] who might minimize the cost of communications by adopting a hand-me-down mobile phone and using unanswered call tones as a code to signal that the milk delivery is on the way. Such interstitial practices lean on the expensive cell phone infrastructure designed for a richer clientele.

Organic metaphors of the city currently hold greater allure and currency among liberal planners than models that rely on hierarchical organization, where everything is master planned into place, a standardized, regimented city order. Such organic constructions can be contrasted to the obsolete concept of the ideal city, against which meager urban instances (London, New York, Paris) are supposed to be measured and calibrated. The formal, obsolete metaphors propose retuning as reparation.[47] Insofar as visitors and inhabitants experience real, contemporary cities so they participate in myriad social relations and interests governed by complex tuning practices.

Support for a politics of retuning comes from social historian Michel Foucault. Under the sway of the clock, society moves toward certain alignments and realignments, configurations and reconfigurations. Foucault talks of the role of repetitive practices in the assertion of rule in institutions.[48] So marching in time, exercise drills, and the regularization of times of sleep, ablutions, cleaning, meals, and so on have had an important place in the institution of military discipline, as in schools, hospitals, and prisons. Foucault's argument refers to the progressive development of the "modern era," where society opted to regularize itself and so bring practices into ordered alignment, rather than resort to ad hoc, brutal, and autocratic processing in the exercise of power. Historians may speak of increasing democratization, regard for verification and evidence, industrialization, freedom of thought, liberty, and enlightenment, but the modern era is also marked by the introduction of techniques for regulating the human body, its movement, comportment, and surveillance, processes readily associated with social tuning, desirable or otherwise, but according to Foucault essential in order to get things done.

Metaphors of the city based on tuning return us to the incremental, which at the pen of sociologist Michel de Certeau also becomes a political process involving empowerment. According to de Certeau, the users of the city make "innumerable and infinitesimal transformation of and within the dominant cultural economy in order to adapt it to their own interests and their own rules."[49] He said of the immigrant worker: "On the same terrain, his inferior access to information, financial means, and compensations of all kinds elicits an increased deviousness, fantasy, or laughter."[50] As for the microentrepreneur, this kind of retuning celebrates small-scale opportunism: "The tactics of consumption, the ingenious ways in which the weak make use of the strong, thus lend a political dimension to everyday practices."[51] These are processes akin to bricolage and "artisan-like inventiveness."[52]

Many everyday practices (talking, reading, moving about, shopping, cooking, etc.) are tactical in character. And so are, more generally, many "ways of operating": victories of the "weak" over the "strong" (whether the strength be that of powerful people or the violence of things or of an imposed order, etc.), clever tricks, knowing how to get away with things, "hunter's cunning," maneuvers, polymorphic simulations, joyful discoveries, poetic as well as warlike. The Greeks called these "ways of operating" *metis*. But they go much further back, to the immemorial intelligence displayed in the tricks and imitations of plants and fishes. From the depths of the ocean to the streets of modern megalopolises, there is a continuity and permanence in these tactics.[53]

De Certeau describes the resistance of certain indigenous cultures to colonization: "They metamorphized the dominant order: they made it function in another register."[54] Functioning in a different register alludes directly to processes of calibration and tuning. In his treatise on walking, *Step by Step,* the philosopher Jean-François Augoyard further celebrates the small change as perpetuated by residents of a large public-housing development:

Altering a partition, placing a flower pot on the window sill, or daubing some paint on a façade does not broach the geometric massiveness of the habitat-object. And yet these rare blisters and swellings, these secretive transformations, these sporadic scratches manifest, in an almost derisory way, a force that is perhaps more insistent than it might at first appear; this is a force neglected by our scientific knowledge because it is not of a stable nature, thetic, "essential," but rather a capacity for alteration, a mode, a way of doing.[55]

Tuning and Design

How does tuning mesh with issues of the urban environment and its design in the digital age? According to a common view, the designer identifies a gap between a desired condition and an actual situation. To offer an example: I need nutritious and palatable food, and technologies of food preparation and cooking are developed to fill the gap between my needs and starvation. A would-be traveler needs to meet with associates in another, distant location, and so technologies of travel come into being to bridge this spatial gap. Likewise the need for shelter from the rain is met by roofs; the need for instantaneous communication across distance is met by telegraph and the telephone. According to this view, machines address human needs. Discrepancies between desires and circumstances constitute gaps that devices fill. Of course, technologies open up further gaps or needs. Roofs need to be maintained, and cars need infrastructures. Those who can afford them fill the gaps with yet more devices. The gap features within common narratives of the insatiability of capitalist consumption. Technological development presents as a progression to finer grades of gap filling, the most recent stage of which is met by portable, personal, and customized ubiquitous devices. Concepts of pervasive digital media can perpetuate this trajectory, as if contemporary urbanites construct the need for their world to be filled with intelligent, interoperable, invisible computational devices. This model resonates with the early systems thinking of Christopher Alexander and the concept of fitness:[56] design enters to provide fit between goals and circumstances, as if there are complex structures of goals, needs, desires, subgoals, and the complex of environmental circumstances. The two models of needs versus circumstances require calibrating and recalibrating, aligning with one another, and devices do the job. A Darwinian version of this approach to design invokes concepts of the survival of the fittest. As for organisms, designs survive and thrive on the basis of how well they accommodate the exigencies of their environment, the design ecology: design as a complex adaptive system.[57] Perhaps I do not need to embark on a critique of these approaches here. Suffice it to say, needs and fitness are elusive, as contexts change.[58] It is sufficient to note that calibration and tuning provide interesting metaphors for formulating such approaches to design. In this case design, as the optimization of a fitness function, constitutes one particular take on the operations of tuning.

In summary, calibration and tuning feature as major design issues in the creation, invention, and configuration of pervasive digital media. There are several further design responses to the tuning metaphor.

First, calibration can be targeted as an undesirable characteristic of a fledgling technology that has to be eliminated during the design stage, or at least the device can be designed so that the user need not be involved in the tuning process. In this case the challenge is to make the calibration of the device invisible, as when I travel overseas and my mobile phone automatically searches and adapts to a new network provider.

Second, the challenge is to make the manual calibration task as simple as possible for the novice, or at least to ensure that the calibration constitutes an event that has meaning in terms of the use of the device. Calibration assumes the ritual significance of a musician tuning her violin. Detached instrumental calibration becomes meaningful ritualized tuning. My cell phone currently announces my arrival within the orbit of a different network provider in a subtle way that makes me aware of the change, and reminds me of the complexity and intelligence behind the device that supports my roaming communications. Tapping a touch screen on a handheld device to calibrate it (a process now largely obsolete) serves as a rehearsal and an inauguration ritual that relates to the context of use of the device, in the way that opening the back cover of a mobile phone to replace the battery or SIM card perhaps does not. Celebrated experiments into the coupling of electronics and organism point to the fusion of animal and machine, brought about by cyborg implants and prosthetics. Arguably, little attention is granted in the technical literature that celebrates the concerted human labor required in tuning, to successfully connect "biological neural tissue to technology."[59] The processes of tuning and such retuning are clearly subject to design consideration.

Third, a designer might think of a device as a means to facilitate adjustment and to fill the calibration gap, as in the case of the wedge. Devices can be thought of as enhancing fit, mapping territories to one another, or re-enforcing a standard. In this light a GPS device serves to calibrate visible landmarks with map coordinates, or my understanding of where I am with the map, or to tune hill walkers' movements relative to one another as they converge on the same landmark at the same time, much as timepieces synchronize "the actions of men."[60]

Fourth, tuning also features in a methodology of design that draws on templates, the selection of an appropriate type or solution from a set of templates, which is like designing by catalogue. As a model, the template has to be adjusted to fit the contingent circumstances. And so there are templates for web designers, the precise format and content of which may be adjusted for use by the retail or institutional client. Classical buildings and speculative house construction have often been produced in this way, from stock plans. The clever part of the design is in the adjustments that have to be made. There are now standard designs, operations, and shapes for cell phones and digital cameras. The fine differences between them can be understood in terms of adaptations and adjustments to different circumstances, market niches, and local conditions, as in the case of the

Ilkone cell phone that contains a compass for indicating the direction of Mecca. Tuning applies to market differentiation.

Fifth, bringing tuning to the fore goes some way in humanizing technology, or at least recognizing it for what it is, as dependent on adjustment. There is clearly a risk in the concept of a one-off calibration without recalibration. Media theorist Sean Cubitt highlights this in remarking on how remote-sensing scientists apparently calibrate the colors of the terrain on known "training areas," after which other correlations are extrapolated, which contributes to capitalism's "dangerous and damaging administration of global resources."[61] Could devices be designed such that they require periodic retuning to remind us of their limitations? Calibration and tuning procedures can be designed into devices as conspicuous processes that engage the user.

Sixth, tuning provides potent metaphors through which to think about the design process. Design is a venturing forth from a standard condition to an unknown contingent condition, with reference back to the stable home base. Attending to tuning can engender sensitivity to context and risk taking. The metaphor also invites a consideration of the effects of interference, where one model overlays another, and a discrepant condition emerges that is suggestive of something new. The new entity is a hybrid condition to be worked and developed through a generative process. Tuning points to the idea of design as an extended and iterative play of metaphors.[62]

Seventh, the function of the device is to reveal otherwise unrecognized structures and relations, the exposure of which can inform further design. A wedge works the grain, finds lines of least resistance, exposes fault lines, divides, and differentiates. The capacity of mobile camera phones to reveal sensitivities to privacy and security is palpable, and quite specific, in the case of school-yard bullying, for example. On a slightly different tack, Henrik Ekeus, colleagues, and I experimented with different means of interfacing physical interactions with the imagery of the three-dimensional simulations of the multiuser online role playing environment Second Life. One project involves pointing a camera at a physical room, some components of which correspond to shapes in a Second Life model. When someone enters the physical room they appear on a screen as if integrated into the Second Life world, surrounded by Second Life scenography, objects, and avatars. Such melding is usually accomplished by standing the human subject in front of a green screen. This turns out to be unnecessary. All that is needed is a means of filtering out those parts of the physical scene that are static. Humans invariably move, and so they appear visible. This is an interesting calibration issue. The computer processes are set up to detect and occlude static objects. In early trials of the process, the team noticed interesting behaviors from human subjects who entered the physical room. Once they knew the rule that static objects are invisible, they would then start pushing objects such as chairs around the space. This would make the chairs visible on the Second Life screen. To return the furniture to its original position would make it invisible again. It turns out that people are interested in threshold conditions, playing around with the border between visibility and invisibility, the calibration edge, the moments when things are in and out of alignment, and this can have startling and useful outcomes in creating and analyzing spatial experience.

Eighth, ideas about tuning contribute to public participation in design, as in various Web 2.0 developments. Usability testing is now live. Designers, publishers, and consumers take for granted that applications will be refined in time in response to user comments and reviews, as exemplified by reviews of third-party applications for the iPhone and other smartphones. The rapid rate of software release and rereleases indicates a responsive design environment involving various tradeoffs, and constitutes a kind of retuning. Design presents as a retuning to circumstances. If tuning involves adjustment of technical apparatus to context, then everyone is involved in this all the time. The processes of tuning reinforce the proposition of Castells and colleagues that "the more a technology is interactive, the more it is likely that the users become the producers of the technology in their actual practice."[63]

I hope this brief catalog provides a persuasive demonstration that the concept of tuning is helpful in explaining how people relate to pervasive technologies, and of tuning's role in shaping and defining the environment. Digital devices are complicit in tuning and potentially enable occupants to tune their environments, a means of modifying everyday experience. The tuning is the design. We are all designers, improvisers, collaborators, and calibrators.

Everyday

4 Habit

Two teenagers sit facing each other on a train. They are having a conversation, but they are also wired, each wearing an earpiece from a shared portable stereo. They are sharing a playlist, presumably enjoying an intimate and localized mood. Their split stereophonic union goes unremarked by the other passengers, several of whom are busy talking to friends and business associates many miles away via cell phones, others are viewing videos on their laptops, a child is playing a Nintendo game against a combatant in another country, and a student is having a video conference. People are reading newspapers and books as well. This scene says something about pervasive media. They are mobile, improvised, and unremarkable.[1]

That technologies might go unremarked is a major aspect of pervasive and ubiquitous digital media. Cell phones, smartphones, iPods, digital cameras, and GPS navigation are in use everywhere, and are widely accessible. They make extensive use of globally connected networks and interoperate with the Internet. The computerized components of these devices recede into invisibility, with some researchers predicting that the devices themselves will become less and less conspicuous, as microprocessing "specks" that can be inserted into fabrics and jewelry and scattered through buildings and across the environment.[2]

Whatever their size, the fact that pervasive media devices might go unremarked and unnoticed positions them among the ordinary, the habitual, the banal, and the everyday. As well as being pervasive, to the extent that they go unnoticed, such devices slip through the gaps in most people's awareness. They are technologies of the gap that nudge users and consumers into new modes of practice without them noticing. As such, ubiquitous devices are objects of habitual use and repeated encounter, as distinct from conspicuous, spectacular, exotic, and one-of-a-kind objects to which many people would accord special status: my first Blackberry, Babbage's Difference Engine, the CERN particle accelerator, Bill Gates's house. Professional adults whose business it is to reflect on technologies may make much of pervasive media, but it seems that young people (digital natives) who have grown up with mobile phones, Game Boys, and Wiis are more interested in the business of talking with their friends, playing video games, and exchanging files[3] than evincing wonderment at the pace of technological change and its implications.

Sigmund Freud titled his early work on forgetfulness *The Psychopathology of Everyday Life*.[4] Lest we rational individuals think that psychological disorders are the preserve of the clinic, his extensive work reminds us that everyday life and experience already are permeated by such conditions, or at least they contain the seeds of exotic clinical complaint. Similar everyday-oriented titles include Henri Lefebvre's *Critique of Everyday Life*, Erving Goffman's *The Presentation of Self in Everyday Life*, Michel de Certeau's *The Practice of Everyday Life*, Jean-François Augoyard's *Step by Step: Everyday Walks in a French Urban Housing Project*, Hakim Bey's anarchic chapter title "The Psychotopology of Everyday Life"[5]; and the examinations of sonic experience (Tia deNora's *Music and Everyday Life*) and design (Donald Norman's *The Design of Everyday Things*). Cultural theorist Anne Gollaway presents pervasive media in terms of philosophies of the everyday,[6] a notion that has surfaced repeatedly in reflections on human sociability and environment. A concern with the everyday suggests engagement with the simple things in life, but also indicates involvement with complex interconnections rather than a consideration of isolated, independent, and idealized objects. The study of the everyday highlights the importance of social contexts, practices, and cultures. It also foregrounds behaviors and artifacts unconstrained by divisions between high art and low art, between classical and pop, and between the sophisticated arbitration of taste versus mass opinion. To focus on the everyday deprecates the distinction between genius artist-designers and lay consumer-users.

The move to the everyday promotes methods of research that engage with narrative and socially situated ethnographic study, rather than the transportation of phenomena to the laboratory, or isolation into the calculative world of variables and quantities. Harold Garfinkel characterized ethnomethodology as the study of the methods that people use in accomplishing their mundane everyday activities "by paying to the most commonplace activities of daily life the attention usually accorded extraordinary events."[7] Objects seem to migrate between conditions of the everyday and the world of the spectacle. It is when unusual objects are accepted as the norm, taken for granted, that they pose the most interesting psychological, social, and political challenges, as technologies of the gap that nudge sociable beings into various modes of practice without them noticing. As I will show, to treat ordinary objects as strange excites similar challenges.

Habitat

Concepts of the everyday fit comfortably with the pursuit of pervasive digital media.[8] Ubiquitous digital devices are built into the world of everyday life, of social relations, places, and things. As mass-produced objects, such devices are becoming as commonplace as books, office stationary, sofas, and sports shoes. That there are at least half as many cell phone subsciptions in use as there are people in the world indicates substantial penetration of at least one paradigmatic pervasive medium.[9]

The everyday also poses a challenge to architects and the designers of structures, whose long traditions position buildings in the realm of the remarkable. Buildings are often designed to shout their presence and excite wonder, or at least, those buildings that historians and critics valorize and that fuel certain individuals' desire to become architects and engineers. In former times buildings were also deployed to connect with ideals and visions of perfection beyond immediate human experience,[10] ambitions that are often in conflict with the nonaspirational world of everyday things.

An emphasis on the everyday also affirms the animal in human nature, a kind of posthumanism that dispenses with human-centered narratives of progressive evolution, and engenders an intellectual position open to considering human intelligence in the same breath as bodily processes involving motor skills, physical movement, animal behavior, and patterned responses. The everyday concerns the habitual exercise of cognitive and motor skills other than those that distinguish the human species as remarkable.

The everyday relates to concepts of the unremarkable: everyday things go unremarked and people may even have difficulty talking about them, or at least they may be more adept in their use than eloquent in reflecting on them. In my own studies I have found that it is when everyday environments are rendered strange and unfamiliar in some way that users are able to be most expressive and vocal, as when our researchers provided a facility that enabled users to "log on" to a building as they entered it and thereby notify friends on their social network directory where they were. Thanks to the unusual nature of this scenario, users in our trials were able to articulate how they felt about moving in and out of buildings, what new routines they are prepared to adopt, and how they feel about privacy.[11] The inhabitants of spaces are sometimes more able to remark on the bizarre than the ordinary, or to remark on the ordinary when it is given a strange twist.

Much pervasive media is ordinary, pedestrian, commonplace, and regular—terms carrying multiple meanings that resonate with the use of such media, as in the title of Ito, Okabe, and Matsuda's book on mobile phone usage: *Personal, Portable, Pedestrian.*[12] Ordinary things relate to the usual order, where everything is in its place. The pedestrian relates to both ordinariness and mobility. Concepts of the commonplace relate to shared media and shared locations. Regularity implies a uniform series, a row of chairs in a lecture hall, with no individual chair demanding attention.

To promote the importance of the everyday can achieve political ends. According to BBC correspondent Americo Martins who reports on Cuba, autocratic governments are less worried about commentary that criticizes the government than online diary blogs by ordinary people that recount everyday life and that show indirectly how government policies affect everyday experience.[13] The writings of Lefebvre, de Certeau, and Augoyard that theorize about the everyday promote this potential to challenge the apparatus of the state.

The everyday also relates to the concept of habit.[14] In his analysis of the reconfigurations of intimacy encouraged by mobile phones, Michael Bull invokes "habitual everyday notions of what it might mean to 'inhabit' certain spaces such as the automobile, the street, the shopping arcade or indeed the living room."[15] House dwellers use everyday things habitually. Habits and the habitual derive from concepts of possession: having, to have, to possess. The equivalent words *to have* in German and French further emphasize the connection between having and habit: *haben* and *avoir.*[16] So people *habitually* seem to speak louder on their cell phones than they would when having a face-to-face conversation. This is a practice they possess and fall into without thinking. It is a habit from which they are extricated only by a conscious exercise of will, or after being berated by another passenger on the train. Mark Griffiths has observed that the Internet can promote "excessive, addictive, obsessive and/or compulsive behaviours."[17] A habit is also a demeanor, an outward appearance, a mode of clothing, or dress. The idea of habit is captured by the usage of the term to denote a clerical garment: a monk's habit. A habit is therefore something people take on, possess, as with clothing. To the extent that pervasive digital devices are objects of habit, they can be thought of as *wearables*. There are therefore many links between pervasive digital media and notions of habit.

Habit also invokes concepts of space. To *in*habit is to live habitually in a particular place, to occupy it with the same comfort and familiarity with which people wear clothing. According to the *Oxford English Dictionary*, to inhabit is to dwell in, to occupy as an abode, to live permanently or habitually in, to reside in a country, town, or dwelling.[18] Much hinges on the little word *in*.[19] There is a sense in which people wear the spaces they inhabit. They take spaces on, attire themselves with them, and immerse themselves in them, in ways that are presumably different from the experience of the traveler, someone who is just passing through, or a surveyor, or a person delivering groceries. Heidegger similarly relates the habitual to dwelling: "Building as dwelling, that is, as being on the earth, ... remains for man's everyday experience that which is from the outset 'habitual'—we inhabit it."[20]

According to most understandings, habits are *acquired*, even if unselfconsciously. To inhabit as having is to take possession of, or to take up. Social beings pick up habits. Biologists and students of animal behavior (ethology) often contrast habit with instinct. As if to emphasize the distinction, Charles Darwin qualified habits as *domestic* habits, and instincts are *natural* instincts. Animals reared in a domestic environment (e.g., canine pets) will expect to be taken for a walk at certain times of the day, will eat from a bowl, and coexist with the cat, as if resisting the instinct to run with the pack, forage, and hunt prey. According to Victorian author Samuel Butler in his book *Life and Habit*, a human baby acquires the ability to use a spoon by habit, but swallows by instinct.[21] Habits are aligned with the domestic. Domesticated animals have been trained to dwell amicably with their human masters in spite of, and building on, their instincts to defend and devour.

Animal biology also makes claim on habit through concepts of habitat.[22] A habitat is home to a particular organism.[23] In human communities, habitat supports the fostering of habits, the sedimentation of homely and domestic practices. Anthropologist Mary Douglas affirms the concept of home "as a pattern of regular doings,"[24] often peculiar to a particular houshold, as when the table is always set for breakfast before bed time, drawing the curtains at 5 pm, reporting on the day's events at the dinner table. I would add incorporating media schedules and digital communications into this list of daily routines, to be discussed later in this chapter. In so far as they occupy the world of everyday things, pervasive media become part of the regular way of doing things, the human being's habitual and everyday lifeworld.

Territory

Concepts of habitat are benign and domestic. Though we post-Darwinians are only too aware of competition and the fight for survival among and within species populations, concepts of habitat conjure up images of ecological balance, cohabitation, and belonging. Biologists refer to the concept of territory in addition to and in contrast with habitat. If habitat pertains to the unremarkable, ordinary, pedestrian, commonplace, regular, and everyday, then territory implies its converse. A territory is an area that an organism occupies and defends, usually to protect offspring and other members of the same species, or their breeding and living quarters. Territory has to be asserted and defended. If habitat is unremarkable, then territory is remarkable, concomitant with an assertion, with holding ground against a conflicting claim. Security guards, invaders, and rival football fans might use their voices to make assertions in language, and in so doing they assert territory. Social theorists and environmental biologists will rarely speak of disputes of habitat, but territory is nearly always about a claim. Territory is in the realms of the remarkable, extraordinary, and irregular. It is less about the pedestrian than the pageant; less about common places and more about conflict zones.

The contrast between habitat and territory is apparent in the earliest treatise on architecture. On the one hand, Vitruvius refers to an architecture encompassing subfloor heating, aqueducts, farm buildings, and the everyday world of comfort and function. On the other hand, he writes of an architecture of bastions and war machines: catapults, ballistae and siege machines, the paraphernalia of territorial aggression and defense—the architecture of habitat versus the architecture of territory.

Habitat and territory within the animal kingdom may be different ways of accounting for similar spatial phenomena, and they seem to overlap. Habitat for human beings generally is an issue of home, but by all accounts humans are the most predatory species of all in arguing, contesting and defending territory.

Repetition and the Everyday

Concepts of habitat and territory coalesce on the theme of repetition. Habits are generally acquired, reinforced, and realized through processes of repetition. Everyday things are commonly products of repeated craft processes or mass production, and are rarely one of a kind (except in so far as collectors attach significance to them).[25] Everyday occurrences happen *every* day, repeatedly, as when eating breakfast, brushing your teeth, switching on the television. Everyday things are complicit in such repeated events and encounters: eating utensils, implements of hygiene and grooming, and other daily necessities. Everyday things emerge from the production line, and they are also instruments in the production of everyday life. The ambition for ubiquitous computing is that digital devices not be recognized as remarkable but be secreted into writing implements, furniture and clothing, and other objects ordinary people use every day. Digital communications devices also become instruments of repeated daily use: the ritual phone call to home as the train pulls into the station, for example, or the selection of a playlist before the office worker hits the street. I use my cell phone today as I used it yesterday, and will probably do so tomorrow and in perpetuity across subsequent generations of such devices.

Everyday things fit within the cycles of each and every day: sunrise, sunset, the tides, the seasons. Another word signifying everyday is the technical-sounding *quotidian*, a term that persists in ordinary French as *quotidien*, or *everyday* in English. Le Corbusier's Unité d'Habitation at Firminy-Vert in France is one of the modernist prototypes of industrial-scale housing.[26] The large plinth at the entrance to the building has cast within it a diagram of two half circles positioned along a horizon line, one the inverted form of the other, and with two lesser semicircles at either end. The forms represent the rhythms of the twenty-four-hour day, showing the sky and earth, and the rising and setting sun, in recognition of the grounding of habitation in the diurnal cycles.

It seems that variation throughout the days and seasons is crucial for life. According to paleontologist Peter Ward and astronomer Donald Brownlee, life could not have started or developed were it not for the planetary tilts, pull of the moon, and orbits that provide daily and seasonal cycles of light, temperature, and tides.[27] Organisms, which is to say life, seem to require variations, and periodic oscillations between stress and comfort, which create the interstitial zones and establish habitat. Variation is born of repetition, of oscillations between conditions, and the oscillations in turn are enabled by irregularities, tilts, and eccentricities. Populations of organisms adapt on the basis of their interaction with habitat (involving other species as well), with traits from the survivors reinforcing the potential for survival of subsequent generations.

In so far as urban life engages with the everyday it participates in repetition. The everyday not only implies ordinariness, but also daily occurrence, as a rhythm. Ordinary everydayness is defined in terms of regularity and repetition. Lefebvre calls for an examination of urban life in these terms, as a "rhythmanalysis," highlighting the repetitions of everyday life "wherever there is interaction between a place, a time and an expenditure of energy."[28] Thought of daily rhythms also invokes circadian, biological systems tuned to the daily cycles: variations in bodily metabolism, digestion, hormone secretions, sleep, and blood pressure,[29] which receive attention increasingly from specialized pervasive devices.[30] Habits and habitat implicate repetitions, cycles, variations, and increments.

Habit and Everyday Cognition

Instincts are apparently acquired through inheritance, a repeated reinforcement of advantage over many generations, coded into the organism's physiology, neural structures, and intimate associations with others of its kind, other species, and its environment. At a step above instincts reside the habits in the behavior of the single organism, acquired through repetition, and by one organism mimicking another.[31] The acquisition of habits by domesticated animals often is equated with a rudimentary intelligence. An intelligent dog is one that is obedient to certain stimuli, will beg for a biscuit, and will walk behind its owner. Here the everyday invokes a certain triviality and mindlessness.

To the modern mind, habit often appears unthinking, unsophisticated, unreflective, and even animal in character, drawing on primitive processes of stimulus and response. In the context of human habituation, the philosopher Alain de Botton says of the familiarity of home: "We have become habituated and therefore blind."[32] In this light instinct and habit are born of repetition, and contrast with reason. Samuel Butler drew attention to the repeated performance or encounter that even causes people to forget what they know.[33] When people act out of habit they have lost the capacity to think matters through independently. Enlightenment concepts of human achievement suggest graduation from instinct to habit to intellect, a break from mindless repetition to sophisticated, singular, independent achievement.

The rehabilitation of the everyday advanced by contemporary theories of cognition seeks to break out of this Enlightenment narrative and shows intelligence to be no less dependent on repetition. Situated cognition suggests that human beings can never rise above the everyday. To promote the everyday is to emphasize the ordinary nature of the intellect, and its inevitably lazy dependence on repeated encounters. According to various theories of embodied cognition people use tools to "cheat" their way through calculation, navigation, and other cognitively demanding tasks. Measuring implements, calculators, and the tools of writing are obvious examples, but the habits and customs commonly regarded as "prejudices" also serve as shortcuts to understanding.[34] People don't so much construct chains of causal reasoning in order to solve problems as project solutions instigated by the recognition of patterns established from situations previously encountered. According to this reading, intelligence is born of repetition, repeated encounters, and patterns in the environment.

Philosopher Andy Clark discusses pervasive devices in the context of such models of cognition.[35] It is as if the cognitive scaffolding is in place, the resources by which the kinds of problems humans frame and resolve are readily to hand. The architecture and the artifacts within it provide the memories, the significations, the signs, the visual and spatial languages, and the sounds, through which all the other social, cultural, and linguistic components can operate. In other words, the ensemble that is habitat is conducive to the operations of thought, appropriate to the condition in which the human finds herself in that place. For the human being, a place is a space for thinking within, or, in the language of situated cognition, a space in which the cultural, social, and physical scaffolding is in place for effective thought to occur, by whatever agency.[36] According to Clark, a computational device is drawn into the "world of everyday objects and interactions where its activities and contributions become part of the unremarked backdrop upon which the biological brain and organism learn to depend."[37]

Therefore pervasive media seem to function as everyday media. The everyday brings to mind the role of repetition, which in turn relates to space through the homely concept of habitation and the more assertive posture of territory. The everyday also has a great deal to say about cognition, thought processes, and human achievement. Note that in this discussion I have emphasized repetition, with the emphasis on the fact of repetition in various contexts rather than on what is actually being repeated. This is a further extension of McLuhan's conflation of medium and content. There is a sense in which the medium of repetition is the message of the everyday.

Habit and Solidarity

How do pervasive digital media impinge on the habits of everyday life? A consideration of the mass media provides an obvious point of entry, as outlined by sociologist David Morley.[38] Sometimes people eat their main meal at the time of a particular television or radio program. People who live alone or are unemployed seem to welcome the regularity of the television schedule as a way of giving order to their lives. A change in schedule marks a significant moment of transition. Being allowed to stay up late to watch television programs marks a right of passage from adolescence to adulthood. People who do not own a television set sometimes miss out on the sociability that arises from being able to comment on last night's viewing and the shared anticipation of future programs. People also use their viewing and listening habits to define who they are, to identify with a particular group, now further instrumentalized through online services that enable people to share media files and playlists. The regularity of the news and weather broadcasts also helps support a sense of participation. All is well with the world as long as the news is being broadcast. The scheduling of broadcast media provides a way of synchronizing, of tuning, domestic and social life.

Pervasive digital media compound the operations of sociable scheduling. Many homes have more than one television set, and viewing habits vary throughout household. Video rental, satellite, cable, pay-per-view, on demand, and other modes of media delivery, including via the Internet, complicate the role of broadcast media in tuning sociability and domestic routine. Not least among these atemporal practices is peer-to-peer file sharing. Furthermore, portable media devices transpose media consumption into transport vehicles and life on the move. Podcasts and vodcasts introduce new routines. I can listen to *Digital Planet* (the BBC World Service digital magazine program) while walking to work, or at any time, though I have to wait until it is downloaded automatically to my iPhone on a Monday evening. Similar to many informational consumer products, the schedule of media delivery may operate outside the daily routine, as when I have to wait for the next release of some software. Such schedules may also depend on, or be nested within, longer cycles, as in the pattern of repeats within the regular showing of television series on satellite and cable television services. The terms *synchronous* and *asynchronous* have increasing currency in discussions of pervasive digital media. Emails do not have to be answered at the same time every day or even when they arrive, phone messages can be recorded and played back later, television programs can be recorded or are stored by the service provider for playback on demand. The negotiation of schedules is now more nuanced than suggested by the radio broadcasting of the 1960s to which Morley was referring—for example, media consumers currently might have to consider scheduled windows of opportunity when files can be downloaded, and messages retrieved before they are deleted automatically, and before offers expire. File sharing of commercial music and other media content also implicates tactics for evading detection.[39] Media schedules are now multiple and overlapping, and broadcast the promise of choice as well as content.

Pervasive mass-media devices are clearly complicit in a kind of temporal tuning, abetted by schedules, whether coordinating activities to bring people to the same place at the same time, allowing people to report to each other on events at which not everyone is present, or even working out how to avoid certain people and events. These schedules draw on repetition and cycles, and repetitions within cycles. Media consumers can be selective in the cycles they latch on to and, in a sense, invent. Schedules are not simply imposed but rather are detected, interpreted, applied, understood, and adopted. It is not just that the household coordinates itself by listening to the same radio program every evening at 8 pm, but also that the family deploys whatever means are at its disposal to assert its solidarity through repetition: meals, the weather forecast, when the heating system kicks in, the opportunities for file download. From this perspective, the disruption or compounding of a schedule does not necessarily lead to a loss in solidarity, or a breakdown in household operations, but solidarity will find other cycles to latch on to. The propensity to adopt and invent schedules to affirm solidarity applies to households, but also to any group that wishes to affirm its cohesion, to attune itself.

Presumably this is one of the many roles of ritual and song: to deploy repetition to enhance solidarity. When words fail, when sociable beings have difficulty articulating why they are together, then they resort to a chant, or share a playlist. Certain forms of music making render obvious such diurnal tuning processes. As introduced in chapter 2, for example, there are traditional Indian ragas that are played on a sitar whose form depends on the time of day when it is to be played, with different scales and tunings.[40]

There is ample support from among social historians for the role of repetition as a means of social enabling and social organization. According to Foucault, repetition is one of the major vehicles by which power, as an enabler of social transformation, is disseminated through society. Repetition is a major component in what he terms "disciplinary practice." The obvious cases are the emergence of practices involving repetition that seems to have only marginal functionality, such as requiring children to march in time into a classroom (a common practice in the United Kingdom until the 1990s), practicing musical scales, physical exercise, and the following of habitual daily routines. Such repetitive practices are not merely "arbitrary." Repetition is so endemic to the human condition that anthropologists and cultural theorists grace it with concepts of ritual and expression. Repetition is never "mere repetition." Repetition provides social order, coordination, synchronization, and tuning in various forms.

The repetition of human movement can strengthen muscles and imprint skills. Eugen Herrigel's famous book on archery describes the learning process thus: "Practice, repetition, and repetition of the repeated with ever increasing intensity are its distinctive features for long stretches of the way."[41] As any athlete or keyboard operator knows, repetition can also encourage one part of the body to work against another and induce stresses, the cure for which resides in further exercises. Learning, and unlearning, draws on repetition. But it is also fair to assert that learning serves repetition. People learn in order that they might repeat, and repetition is a means of perpetuating, affirming, and creating solidarity. Repetition also serves as a means of asserting difference from others and other groups: "marching to a different drummer," as the saying goes.

Pervasive media assist ostensibly in the alignment of the beats, ticks, and rhythms of individual lives, much as clocks serve to coordinate events, position people at the same place at the same time, regulate the work day, provide predictable transportation, ensure lectures begin on schedule, release goods to market, and secure the processes of production. Clocks as devices are ubiquitous and portable. They also perpetuate a temporal standard that applies across geographical distance. Portable digital devices substantially expand on this function, not least in abetting the coordination of schedules, broadcast media access, calendars, and personal diaries. These devices further disseminate the essential utility provided by networks of data stores, programs, and communications media to the immediate context of use. By such means the lives of individuals, households, and organizations are brought together for particular interactions, projects, and events. Groups use such means to partake of solidarity-building repetitions.

Such processes seem possible due to a substrate of shared practices. Clocks do not regulate people's lives but rather the shared practices by which people interpret and apply the operations of clocks, timetables, schedules, and calendars. If we need any reminding of this, it is a simple matter to note the experience of many professionals from highly industrialized countries trying to plan meetings within a foreign community far less dominated by clocks and timetables. In similar vein, people's lives are not ordered and coordinated by pervasive digital media, but by the practices that underlie them. People have had to learn from one another how to acquire the necessary habits, interpret, and apply the operations of pervasive devices. Complicit in this process of habit formation, learning, sharing practices, and social tuning are the devices themselves. The devices are both the vehicles of cultural transmission and its instruments.

At the time of writing this book, it is apparent that even in industrialized countries the practices by which ubiquitous devices are used to coordinate events are not uniformly shared. Practices and micropractices are emerging and changing. There are still many people who do not know how to use a cell phone to organize a rendezvous, plan a vacation with only the Internet and a credit card, exploit multiple modalities of communication, keep online diaries, or resort to readily available strategies for backing up information. Devices do not regulate and coordinate, but coordination occurs through the subtle, sophisticated, and emerging tuning practices by which people deploy various means to affirm their sociability, often opportunistically.

Habit and the Human Condition

Complicit in the preservation of solidarity is the role of repetition in communication. Language theorist E. A. Havelock indicates the importance of rhythm and repetition in primary orality,[42] in other words, speaking, using the voice rather than writing things down. In the absence of writing, repetition was the obvious means to provide continuity within a community. With its investment in the terminology of print, the culture of global capital treats repetition as concerned with the preservation, transmission, and remembering of information and knowledge. Repetition also implies redundancy—repeating the same communication over and over. Repetition and redundancy are necessary for a speaker to be understood, particularly in large gatherings. Not every word gets picked up by all members of the audience. Artful speakers often say the same thing more than once, or elaborate on a point, thereby introducing redundancy to increase the chances that someone will latch on that point. If the speaker is improvising, then repetition is an efficient way to fill the gaps while he thinks of the next thing to say.[43]

Extending Havelock's observation, it seems that in broadcast media much of the role of repetition as a means of communicating efficiently is taken over by the repetitive nature of the medium itself. A television commercial will be repeated over and over, thereby reinforcing its advertising message without having to restate information within the commercial itself. Mass advertising, propaganda, and viral marketing all work by repetition.[44] Similarly, many films and television programs are designed to be viewed more than once. Missed dialog due to a lapse in concentration is compensated for by the fact that the film has more to reveal on subsequent viewings. Thus repetition is endemic to communication, and according to Havelock, most occasions of enjoyment and engagement (ritual, dance, even sexual intimacy) implicate repetition and rhythm.

Advocacy of the importance of repetition also has support from Sigmund Freud's psychoanalytic studies. He described the repetitive fort-da game of the solitary child reenacting his mother's absence and return as a game of throwing something away (a cotton reel out of the cot) and bringing about its return (pulling on the piece of string attached to the cotton reel). The mesmeric operation hints of an anxiety that is in fact simultaneously relieved, enacted, and rehearsed through the ritual. Freud made much of such processes of repetition as if they were endemic to the human condition.[45] Repetitions in adult life further remind people of primal need and loss. When such repetitions touch people in a certain way they can be characterized as excursions into the uncanny: the peculiar, haunted, and "unhomely."[46] Adults sometimes are taken aback when an event occurs, such as a bizarre coincidence, that reminds them of their childhood condition, as if to reconfirm or reinforce a state of mind they'd believed to have outgrown. The repetition of events in this way presents as a kind of reversion to early adolescence when psychological dispositions were being formed. In this, repetition is both a comfort and a source of disquiet. Here resides the sense of the uncanny.[47]

Pushing Freud's observations to their limit, it seems that repetition per se is complicit in feelings of solidarity, identification, belonging, not belonging, or disquiet. A filmmaker could do worse, therefore, than to deploy repetition to activate emotion in an audience, not only through music, drum rhythm, heartbeat, chanting, and footfall, but also rhythm and repetition in the narrative. The film *The Blair Witch Project* provides an interesting commentary on amateur video production and the role of repetition. Film reviewers might attribute the sense of the uncanny to the mystery being investigated, the first-person camera view, and the pretense at verisimilitude, but potent among the narrative devices is the role of repetition. It is when the characters in this film all realize they are traveling in circles, lost, that emotions reach their peak. This repetitive structure is deployed to invoke the uncanny, a shared terror, solidarity in the trauma of repetition, and of course the potential for endless repetition of the experience in the video medium.

To focus on repetition might suggest a reduction of the complex array of human practices to something mechanical and instrumental. For Karl Marx, repetition features in processes of mass production, which ultimately dehumanize workers by turning them into replaceable machine components.[48] Critical theorists may invoke repetition, and one's place in the production line, as a cause, symptom, and symbol of relationships of domination. I hope by now I have dispelled any residual sense that repetition is a trivial matter.[49] There is further evidence of its importance. Philosopher Friedrich Nietzsche gave account of the "eternal return" or the "eternal recurrence of the same," the tendency within human experience to draw on the expectation of renewal, a mythology of cycles and reparations.[50] The philosopher Jacques Derrida asserts further the priority of repetition, maintaining that no one should be surprised by repetition so much as the idea of a first time.[51] Repetition is the norm. Authors and readers are caught in an endless stream of repetitions. For Derrida this is how language operates. There is no original referent of a language utterance, such as an actual object, a first move in a computer game, or the initiation of a phone call. Every utterance invokes reference to other references, which in turn have their referents. Every origin is preceded by something else.

In tracing the origins of pervasive digital media, the historian of technology is also referring to the concept of media, to writing about the media, to a panoply of authors, including Mumford and McLuhan, who have their own referents; and a particular technology is also a reference to other technologies from which it derives: cell phones, smartphones, telephones, telegraph, print, writing, hieroglyphics. Processes that designers might think of in terms of product development, product evolution, innovation, and mass production are imbued with and give expression to the impetus to repeat, and this is a shared compulsion.

Habit and Design

To focus on repetition has implications for the design of pervasive media devices. Their everydayness helps explain something of the challenge faced by architectural designers in incorporating the implications of pervasive media. Designers arguably are most comfortable, most at home, when dealing in the unfamiliar. In fact, designers sometimes deliberately present everyday phenomena as if strange: instead of designing a dining room they think about an eating house, instead of a bathroom, a bath house, instead of a cell phone a communicating camera. Design education commonly deploys strategies to rehabilitate the strangeness of everyday situations, devices, and scenarios—rendering the familiar strange as a pedagogical strategy. Innovation often is born of looking at things in a fresh and unusual way. Design therefore involves a play between the familiar and the unfamiliar, the everyday and the extraordinary, the sequential and the singular, the series and the one-off, the same and the different, habitat and territory.

The home similarly is brought into relief when considered as a site of otherness. Nothing elevates the importance of home so much as its violation, the incursion of alien and unhomely elements. Concepts of homeland emerge in periods of conflict or threat rather than peace.[52] Designers could do well to contrast concepts of homely and comfortable digital devices that blend into the fabric of everyday habits against the territorial, agonistic, and invasive role of digital devices.

In summary, pervasive devices participate in the human propensity to repeat, through habit. Digital devices serve to coordinate and tune human interactions, through fixed and varying schedules, and their connections to the repetitions of body and environment. As part of this synchrony, devices also embody cognition. There is a sense in which people think through their artifacts, machines, and environments. Digital devices are both the vehicles of cultural transmission and its instruments, and are complicit in design as the tuning of place. Repetition is also amplified through rhythm and sound, the focus of chapter 5.

5 Rhythm

"Rhythm is one of the most fundamental formal means of composition in classical music, poetry, and architecture," according to architectural historians Alexander Tzonis and Liane Lefaivre.[1] Think of colonnades, window placement, and the stacking of office floors. Regular repetition provides a tool of spatial organization. This much is obvious, but repetition is also an affirmation of habit, inhabitation, habitat, and home.

What I describe as repetition pertains closely to Henri Lefebvre's notion of rhythm. For Lefebvre, repetition pertains to mechanical processes, production processes as well as capitalist machinery that treats everything the same. And for Lefebvre rhythm pertains to "the relation of the Same to the Other."[2] Rhythm is a contextual matter, involving variation and memory. He offers the case of the movement of the waves on the sea, which constitutes a rhythm rather than a mere repetition because it involves counter movements and complex overlays of movement, with their pattern relying on a range of contextual factors such as the shape and materials of the shore, the tides, and weather conditions. The body too operates rhythmically, its movement depending on the body's size, shape, strength, condition, and context. Rhythm is repetition with modification. Every stroke need not be exactly the same. For Lefebvre, notions of sameness are subordinated to difference.

Of interest here is the role of sound in repetition. There are other obvious modes of repetition, such as movement, dance, display, color, and visual pattern, but sound and repetition are intricately linked. Sound is, after all, a vibration (an alternation of air pressure intensities) and often is presented through rhythm: the beat of a music track, the sound of machinery, the insistence of a ring tone.

In the child's mesmeric fort-da game, described in chapter 4, repetition is an expression of "out and in," a spatial schema given prominence in linguist Mark Johnson's account of the embodiment of thought,[3] and echoed in Walter Ong's account of orality, the use of the human voice, as it pertains to interiority.[4] According to Freud, the "in" condition is the object of yearning, the enveloping condition of comfort to which the child wishes to return. The comfortable condition is that of the mother's presence, an enveloped, undifferentiated condition of psychic immersion in a state of bliss or innocence. The game as described by Freud is already a sonic phenomenon. In his account the child says "fort" as the cotton reel is cast from the cot, and "da" as it is returned, as if mesmerized by the sound and the action.[5] The "in" condition is ubiquitous in human experience, as when a person participates *in* an experience, or is *in* a state of agitation, *in* rapture, *in* debt, or immersed *in* sound; hence the importance of the repetition of movements in and out.

Urban life is saturated by sound, as if lived in continuous immersive soundscapes: the sound of a crowd, the hum of machinery, the roar of traffic. The ambient sound compositions of Iannis Xenakis, Steve Reich, and John Cage give expression to this sense of sonic immersion. Even raw, unedited field recordings made without special microphones and visual cues commonly sound noisy, reverberant, muffled, and are elucidated through spatial metaphors of being in a hollow tube, a mysterious place, or the sea. But such metaphors of continuity and smoothness also seem to depend on repetition. An ocean of sound is composed of repetitive waves. In one of our studies we invited people to explain, through writing and drawing, their experience of particular sonic environments. In trying to describe a space on the basis of environmental sound recordings, there was common recourse to metaphors of immersion and of being consumed. As if to corroborate Lefebvre's characterization of context-rich rhythm, one of our respondents put vividly the repetitive nature of the sonic experience: "It just seemed to be a plane in which one—something would sweep over you from one direction and then something would sweep back across from another and you just seemed to be in the middle of these things kind of sweeping, and you were moving in and out of them. They were sweeping over you and then off into the distance again and something else would sweep in from another direction, and back out again in a tidal-like way, almost being swamped in these sounds."

The overwhelming, immersive qualities of sound come in sweeping waves, and their repetitive motion calls to mind the arrhythmic but nonetheless repetitive musical soundscapes of Pauline Oliveros and Pedro Rebelo.[6]

Returning to the theme of chapter 4, a home's inhabitants are reminded of its cave-like, immersive, submersive, and nurturing character through the constancy of repetitive sounds, coming from heating units, air conditioning, fans, the hum of the refrigerator, their sonorous rhythms suggestive of the heart beating.

Therefore the home also sustains certain biological rhythms. Neurophysiologists Foster and Kreitzman explain how human and animal physiology operates through overlaid temporal cycles. Rhythms vary according to the age of household members. It seems that the cycle of attentive activity for adolescents reaches its peak late in the afternoon and for adults in the late morning, an important consideration in the coordination of mixed-age households, athletic activity, and education.[7]

Repetition, rhythm, and reproduction are also linked to habitat through memory. Memories are embedded and reinforced through repetition. Cultural historian Frances Yates explains that prior to the widespread adoption of writing, a skilled orator would recall the points of a speech by spatial mnemonics.[8] The orator would associate each point of the speech with an item of furniture in the room or some architectural feature, and use these to reconstruct the outline of the speech during its delivery. The facts of a speech are recalled by association and the appropriateness of the association. Similarly, the repetition of domestic routine and the constancy of encounters with the same rooms, objects, and people amplify and reinforce the home's role as a repository of memories and associations. Such memory processes are abetted by the home's infiltration by machines, media, and pervasive digital devices that serve to jog and nudge the occupant's recollections and make place.

Rhythm and Territory

Chapter 4 introduced concepts of territory. If repetition is complicit in the establishment of habitat, it likewise is in the assertion of territory against predators, and in defense of the organism's turf, breeding ground, and food source.

The spatial operations of pervasive digital media seem unconstrained by the usual geopolitical boundaries and architectural artifices of rooms, walls, and floors. Pervasive digital devices are among the various means that homebodies have at their disposal for venturing out of their habitat. People can configure themselves in open spaces (plazas, malls, fields) without the aid of space-defining structures. Individuals, groups of people, and activities form space, abetted in no small part by portable devices.[9] It is a common observation that you can "be with" someone on a mobile phone while in different geographical locations. Such formations may be fluid, transient, invisible, overlapping, and transgressive, all terms that apply conveniently to territory, as do negotiation, conquest, surrender, and assertion.

Territorial assertions are apparent in the case of animal behavior. The birdcall provides an obvious example of territorial claim by sonic means. According to ethologist William Etkin's standard account of territorial behavior in birds,[10] a songbird takes a conspicuous position on a tree and sings loudly and persistently. If another bird of the same species comes near, and is able to withstand the aggressive posture of the current resident, then they divide the territory in two: "Each bird keeps strictly to his own territory, clearly recognizing and respecting the invisible boundaries separating it from that of its neighbors. Each bird frequently sings from his display area in his territory and behaves as a self-confident, dominant."[11] The enthusiasm and energy with which the territory is preserved varies with the seasons.

The usual means of indicating territory are aggression, threat, and the marking of boundaries.[12] In survival terms, animal populations balance the high cost of patrolling territories against the benefits of having a predictable food supply. Mammals usually mark out territory by leaving scents, but also by means of sounds. In their account of sonic environments Augoyard and Torgue assert that in the case of birdsong, "territory is defined by a certain number of repetitions, and perceived by others as a spatial shape,"[13] and it is not the first or second occurrence of the birdcall that marks the territorial claim, but the occurrence of a "significant series."

Birds and other creatures may define territory through the repetition of sounds, but is there evidence for similar spatialization within human communities? Think of the newspaper seller on the street who repeats the cry

"Evening Standard." Any passerby hears the call more than once, as if it is the repetition that draws attention to the territorial claim and the possibility of a transaction. The call also excludes other potential vendors from the immediate vicinity. Furthermore, calls repeated with less regularity, and with arbitrary variation, seem to assert less of a claim on territory. Our study into the sounds of market stallholders reveals nuanced definitions of space. Competing callers modulate, synchronize, and generally negotiate their spatial claims with great subtlety, in situ, and for the moment. The process is one of a dynamic tuning, an instantaneous calibration of complex rhythms that defines spaces of overlap and territorial borders.

The territorial nature of repetition is also evident in the case of team sports. For example, in the popular UK game of touch football, which is an informal version of rugby (not to be confused with American touch football), players use calls and other sounds to indicate game territory and team solidarity, thereby claiming turf in a public space and distinguishing their play from any other matches going on in the same neighborhood. (Informal pickup basketball games are a similar, North American example.) One of our observational studies in London's Hyde Park revealed ample instances of sporting platitudes ("well-played, Batty"), affirming phrases ("right, right, right," "yep, yep, yep"), naming each other ("Jim"), and claiming the territory of the ball ("mine"), all repeated assertions, concomitant with the game action, and perhaps amplified by virtue of being in a public space and on shared ground. Similar observations apply to the incessant repetition of sound in other spaces of contest, such as the open outcry on the bidding floor of the stock exchange,[14] and the call of the auctioneer in the auction house. Bell towers have also exercised this territorial function in towns and villages, with the bells sounding repetitive signals at different times of the day and for particular events. In an essay on auditory markers in traditional villages, Alain Corbin draws attention to the correlation between "bell and boundary and between bell ringing and processions."[15] The loudness of the bell also related to the extent of the parish or community's boundary.

During the political demonstrations in Tehran in July 2009, there were poignant videos on Youtube of the cityscape redolent with the cries of "Alah-o Akbar" from ordinary citizens on rooftops. The sonic repetitions supplemented the ceaseless flow of messages on Twitter, the Internet-based short message service. By coincidence or by design, the claim on the space of the city was permeated with sound: from the metaphor of the "tweet" to the open outcry of invisible voices.

Repetition duplicates or copies what went before. As such, repetition is an aspect of reproduction, or mimicry. Mimicry features in territorial assertions in several ways. In our studies we observed how groups of friends deploy vocal mimicry when they enter each other's company. Repeated listening to field recordings of a group of teenagers speaking loudly on the London Underground (subway system) highlights repetitions of phrases, such as "you're a genius," a kind of arbitrary (deictic) banter in terms of communicating meaning, but one serving to define the subarchitecture of the group as it moves through the crowds. It is the reiteration of an in-joke deployed in humor, and as a means of gaining the upper hand, imposing exclusion and territorial definition. As Augoyard and Torgue assert, "teenagers' conversations seem to be filled with onomatopoeia, interjection, and deictic words borrowed from the media or cartoons . . . the imitation effect activates a feeling of belonging."[16] Deictic utterances are those for which the listener needs to know the context in order to ascertain any meaning. Such exclusive uses of terms in language, whether spoken in groups or into mobile phones ensures that if the conversation is overheard it is not understood. Thus the loud conversation can be deployed to stake out and claim territory independently of the overt meaning of what is being said, and by deliberately occluding meaning.

Technologies of Repetition

Cultural theorists have drawn attention to the role of mechanical reproduction in art and design.[17] Sounds have to be repeated in any case if they are to persist. Whereas the contents of the visual field are commonly available for repeated inspection (the view of the city from the hilltop persists), sounds have to be renewed, regenerated for the occasion, reproduced. In one of our studies we presented human subjects with photographs of building interiors to analyze and discuss. It seems that people are adept at examining, describing, and using photographs when in company. Undertaking similar studies with recordings of sounds without pictures reveals different capabilities. Sounds require listening, without speaking, with comment following. Whereas a picture just presents itself inert for scrutiny, sounds have to be replayed. Repetition is endemic to the interpretation of sounds. In a different study we shadowed two sound designers assembling a sound installation. They had created an installation in which shapes on a computer screen responded to the playback of sound recordings. One of the designers said: "I think those recordings are so interesting that they justify multiple listenings. And every listening will be a different experience because there is so much in them, so much sensible for analysis." Sounds require and encourage technologies and practices that facilitate repeated playing and multiple listenings. The urban commuter with an iPod need think only of the looped playlist to be convinced of the complicity of mobile devices in the imperative to repeat. Personal stereos are instruments of repetition.

Our analyses of cell phone conversations also reveal the presence of repetition through mimicry. Recordings of conversations make apparent the way participants imitate one another's style of laughter and tone of voice. When two participants in a conversation have difficulty hearing each other, one will commonly repeat the other's statement as a question, for clarification. As in the case of Havelock's characterization of improvised public speaking (chapter 4), there is a need for repetition due to noise and distortion. In conditions of poor transmission and reception, casual conversationalists also resort to repeated platitudes and clichés: "how are you?," "yes I know," "I'll call you back," "we got cut off." For unwilling listeners nearby, a cell phone conversation is only half there. A meager grasp of the conversation's content causes its formal structure to dominate, amplifying the flows and breaks in repetition and mimicry.

The current trajectory of pervasive media sometimes seems to increase the role of repetition. Contemporary digital media raise repetition to the *n*th power. Computers and networks constitute machinery for repetition. The operations of their circuitry are governed by clocks that tick inexorably at millions of bit-processes per second. Digital devices deploy internal calendars, which facilitate record keeping and communication following everyday cycles and rhythms. Time-bound and clock-watching workers use these functions every day to coordinate, consolidate, and communicate schedules.

Digital devices deploy information and databases that can be displayed in tabular form. The rows and columns of any tabulation effectively are exercises in repetition: records and fields, data organized by type, as in calendars, schedules, lists of addresses and phone numbers. Visual displays process rows and columns of pixel values and do so iteratively, pixel by pixel, in imperceptibly fast, repetitive operations. The most common structure in any computer program is the loop, the repetition of the same operation over and over, and with incrementally different values inserted into memory locations or variables with each iteration. Computers repeat tirelessly, and with fewer consequences with regard to wear than human limbs and mechanical components.

At the time of writing, pervasive digital media are most conspicuous as a range of familiar portable functions: phone, camera, calendar, electronic diary, web browser, email device, and location-aware navigation, abetted by various forms of cabled and wireless connectivity involving Bluetooth, phone networks, and Wi-Fi connections to other devices and to the Internet. These functions converge and interconnect. Consider the journey of a visual image through this network of capabilities and how it is subjected to processes of repetition. An image of Edinburgh Castle taken with a digital camera will be date-stamped automatically, and, with GPS capability, marked with locational coordinates. Image formats include provision for the automatic recording of time, date, and place. The image can be dispatched to a friend's cell phone via the phone network and downloaded to my Facebook web pages and other social network sites. In turn, the image can be attached to a location on a publicly accessible map (Panoramio) for private or public consumption. If the image is in fact a moving image, then it can be loaded into YouTube, or other publicly accessible video archive. My social network page may dispatch emails to friends telling them to look at my images. For web-enabled mobile devices, my social networking page, complete with images, can appear on someone else's handheld device.[18]

It takes little effort to see the role of repetition in each of these functions. Digital cameras deploy arrays of pixel values. Digital images can also be captured as videos, which are subject to operations that repeat at a regular number of frames per second. Wireless networks deploy communications protocols that involve the regular dispatch of packets of information. Phones emit repetitive call signals; digital diaries repeat events; web browsing and search iterate through vast databases and indexes to display tables of hits; movement through space records GPS coordinates in succession; tabulated email correspondences cascade down the computer screen. Processes of repetition permeate the creation, dissemination, and archiving of even a single image.

Sound and repetition are commonly linked as I have shown: the ticking of a clock, footsteps tapping, sirens, alarms, waves on the seashore, bird calls, ring tones, in-store music, work songs, a playlist of World Music on a personal stereo. But repetition is also integral to the visual image. Amateur photography features in an interesting and domestically oriented exchange economy, as a means of remembering and sharing experiences, associating people with places, relating me to you through shared leisure destinations and business travel, comparing conduct at special occasions, offering reminders of mutual friendships, being initiated into someone's personal circle, turning spaces into habitats. Digital photography differs in many respects from film-based photography in the plethora of imagery it encourages. It costs as much to take twenty images as to take one. Digital photography emphasizes processes of collating, sorting, editing, and archiving large numbers of pictures, abetted by functions integrated into image-capture software. Digital photography makes explicit the repetitive nature of amateur photography. Images are produced in vast quantity and channeled into arrays. Rather than residing unsorted in envelopes, boxes, and slide trays or lovingly folded into bulky and half-completed photograph albums, digital snaps are immediately organized by date and displayed as thumbnail images to be scanned visually and searched. Digital snaps do not come in ones and twos, but in the hundreds. The digital tourist need not be restricted to one precious picture of the view of Edinburgh Castle from the bridge, but a dozen, with friends in the foreground and without, with a lot of sky and with a little, when the sun is out and in shade. Amateur digital photography is an art of permutations and cherished misjudgments. Nothing need be thrown away. The photographer's fixation on repetition is evident in the practice of constructing time-lapse portraits. YouTube contains many video presentations showing a series of photographs of the face of an individual, from the same camera position and at the same time of day. The rapid sequence of images records changes in attire, skin tone, state of health, facial expression, and hair growth—day after day after day.

Fetish

Such repetitive practices soon fold into the operations of ritual. According to cultural theorist Christy Desmet, there is a relationship between personal web pages and concepts of the ritual fetish,[19] a practice evident in certain cultures involving the construction of shrines and memorials adorned with personal effects. A comb, handkerchief, concert ticket, lock of hair, defunct cell phone, or bracelet serves as a reminder of someone, or some occasion, and such objects may be arranged on a wall, table, or cabinet. The arrangement is improvisational and personal, and has the character of a bricolage, presenting strange juxtapositions, that in turn suggest special (deictic) meanings known only to those with intimate knowledge of the situation. Such assemblies are attempts to grapple with meanings (love, loss, adoration, fortune, reverence) that transcend the mere monetary or use value of the parts.

The concept of the personal webpage has been largely displaced by the standardized branding of social network sites. But earlier manifestations revealed the fetish character of the web. Arguably, the prototypical web page was not the well designed and controlled corporate site, but rather the personal web page—the instinctual (and habitual), improvisatory page made up of its creator's favorite color schemes, fonts, personal details, pictures of loved ones and pets, and favorite links. In this light, the web page as fetish gives expression to transcendent aspirations of freedom, self-expression, participation in a community, and asserting one's place in the world. Personalized cell phones may now serve a similar function. Not only are they designed to be populated with personalized images and customized with "wallpaper" and "skins," but the way the phone is used (in terms of its user's posture, gesture, mode of speech) can constitute a certain fetishistic theatricality, tantalizing others with a view into the owner's private life, according to social theorist David Morley.[20] Pervasive devices are media for circulating this tendency toward fetish, and for transforming and taming it. By this account the corporate web portal, and the corporate-packaged presentations of social networking, are extensions of a primal and domestic mode of fetishism.

The fetish also suggests a preoccupation with repetition. To fetishize is to elevate the status of a component object rather than to take account of the whole, as when developers and planners make a fetish of the idea of the palm tree, one of the symbols of the city of Dubai, construct a huge island complex in the shape of a palm tree and then plan to repeat the same along the coastline. Rather than ennoble the idea of the palm, such use can diminish it, or render it ludicrous (or "mannerist" in architectural terms). Such overindulgence is one of Karl Marx's complaints about the fetish of consumption.[21] Mass production and mass consumption reduce everything to the commodity. Unlike the fetish of the devotee, here the fetish results in an apparent trivialization. Alternatively, the fetish acts as overstatement, an exaggeration that brings a spatial condition to light in a certain way. The fetish can operate as an ironic move, a gesture that shifts spatial experience into a different register.

Printing processes encouraged the multiplication of images: wallpaper, fabric patterns, and gift-wrapping paper, for example. The concept of the "multiple" continues as an art form as illustrated in the artist Damien Hirst's colorful wallpaper designs consisting of repetitive arrays of pills and biblical quotations, or rows of pharmaceutical products on ordered shelves. Edward Tufte's seductive books demonstrating principles of information display similarly explore the logic of repetition, of "visually enforcing comparisons of changes, of the differences among objects, of the scope of alternatives."[22] The organization of digital images continues this fascination with ordered arrays of graphical information.

The World Picture

Repetition and place converge on the issue of the world picture presaged by the philosopher Martin Heidegger: "The world conceived and grasped as picture."[23] Here Heidegger is referring to the aspiration of contemporary technoscience to have everything within its grasp, available for inspection, represented and amenable to control. This is a territorial imperative, expanding one's boundaries to take in as much as possible. This propensity toward the all-encompassing embrace of technological control relates to repetition, as exhibited in the processes of the digital scan.

To scan is to inspect a surface systematically, and in detail.[24] It is also to emit a ray onto a surface, as in the case of scan lines on a cathode-ray picture tube. Devices commonly scan from a single point, and direct their attention elsewhere, either projecting signals, or receiving them, or both, as in the case of radar and sonar.[25] Scanning relates to panning, which is in the repertoire of camera technique. The camera sweeps across a scene to take in a larger area than enabled by the single-frame shot.[26] Examples of panned images include the panorama as a composite image derived from a sequence of views, as in Google StreetView, and images from satellite and aerial reconnaissance, manifested now as the potent presentation media of Google Earth and GoogleMaps, also available on handheld devices. You now have the "whole world in the palm of your hand."

Concepts of repetition are revealing when examined through the lens of the panorama. As already discussed, anyone with a digital camera and Internet access can post and tag images on publicly accessible websites. Many of these images are related to places and record aspects of the transient visual experience of the visitor. Microsoft's Photosynth system[27] sifts and stitches apparently random images drawn from social web pages of canonic tourist sites and redisplays these automatically as large-scale composite images.[28] The promise here is not only of a complete pictorial representation of the whole earth, but also of joining these images to produce a giant mosaic of life on earth. There are now several such projects. The Geograph British Isles project declares that it "aims to collect geographically representative photographs and information for every square kilometer of Great Britain and Ireland, and you can be part of it."[29]

Photosynth, Google StreetView, the panoramic stitching function on digital cameras, and other compositing applications are technologically sophisticated developments of several imaging traditions. For example, the panorama developed in the eighteenth and nineteenth centuries as a means of presenting painted views of cities and environments in large-scale installations for public consumption.[30] Historians often position the panorama in the company of dioramas, periscopes, optical illusions, and other ocular apparatuses and devices that presage 3D cinema, wide-angle projection, and immersive virtual reality games and environments. The panorama persists in some 3D computer games where players are immersed not so much in a three-dimensional model but move through a series of fixed positions, each position presenting a near-360-degree panoramic view of a highly rendered animated scene.[31]

Many digital cameras incorporate a panorama function that allows the photographer to take a series of photographs that are "stitched" together automatically, based on the detection of areas of overlap near the junctions between the images. Most three-dimensional software provides a facility for generating panoramic images of a computer model, such as the interior of a building. Panoramas also structure the spaces of urban advertising, as in the luminous cylindrical displays in and around the O2 Pavilion at London's Millennium Point. Contemporary artists such as Sanford Wurmfeld have capitalized on the allure of the panorama as physical public spectacle. The panorama—traditional and contemporary—is emblematic of the attempt (through elaborate ocular constructions, mechanically and now digitally) to turn visual images into instrumentally interactive public experiences, a process that involves inevitable repetition. They also represent attempts to command and master space, presenting it for viewing in controlled circumstances, and from a fixed point. The panorama presents as a phenomenon of the Enlightenment, purveying the ocularcentrism of command, control, and progression to bigger, faster, cleaner, safer, and more spectacular commodities and environments.

The operations of the panorama photographer bring to light the role of repetition in interpretation. Machine operations repeat, but when humans and animals scan they do so with purpose. The operations of the intentional human scanner constitute a search: picking up cues from the environment and preparing for the next step. The digital photographer with multiple images at her disposal does not scan as a machine, but as an active interpreter of place, projecting and receiving stimulus through the viewfinder, and of the wider context. In their explanation of how organisms relate to their environments, Humberto Maturana and Francisco Varela draw attention to the scanning operations of the frog, whose physiology is tuned to the perception that moving black specks—flies—are food.[32] The frog sees what is essential for its survival. The scanning capabilities of the human being are no less motivated, seeking out what one wants to see. Scanning can be a richly interpretive, which is to say projective, process.

Everyday digital devices manifest further panoramic functions: scanning for radio signals, surveying, reaching out, projecting, defining, and appropriating. A photographer may set his camera to video mode and scan across a scene in an attempt to take in the totality of the view. Technologies even exist for taking the frame sequence from a video source and converting it into a panorama. The process uses smart pattern-matching algorithms to identify areas of overlap between frames in a continuous video sequence, selecting and stitching the frames together to produce a single-strip panoramic image. The panorama is generated automatically from a continuous sequence of video frames rather than a sparse number of still images. Such capabilities are becoming more common with 3G, Wi-Fi, and other ubiquitous high-speed network technology, with the added capacity to stream video in real time to another phone user or to a server able to further process the image stream. By such means the human agent works in tandem with the medium to influence the way the urban environment is perceived and defined.

Pervasive devices amplify the scanning function. Think also of a simple torch with a built-in beacon that indicates location by virtue of a regular pulse. On a larger scale the lighthouse and the beacon serve a basic spatial function. The regularity of the pulse serves to rise above the background "noise" of stars and other luminous objects. A repeating siren or a church bell serves a similarly hegemonic function. Technologies that monitor the environment also deploy repetition, such as laser-based land surveying equipment, radio telescopes, and aerial reconnaissance technologies, that scan earth and sky through inexorable repetition.

The single-eye view, particularly as a scan directed from above, comes under criticism as a means of unifying and controlling space, and potentially ruling out difference. Technologies of combination, averaging, and overlaying blur out moving objects, subtle differences, choices of viewpoint, foreground subject matter, and people. The scan of the surveillance camera operates as a similar means of apparent control.[33] Repetition and the scan converge to promote the world picture. Scan technologies reveal the world by showing what is there, systematically and in an ordered, totalizing way. There is also a sense in which scans can create the world. Certain artificial landforms and structures, such as Dubai's Palm Island, are to be viewed from above, from a great distance, and via satellite imagery.

Scanning can also reveal the world by highlighting differences. For example, there are interesting side effects to the panorama function: panoramas so constructed can obliterate or blur moving objects; objects can appear more than once if they are in motion across the field of the scan; scanning the camera across the horizontal plane while sweeping it from side to side generates an ethereal kind of visual flow and new visual languages. There are also programs that will do the following: pattern-match panoramas against similar images held in a database to identify where the sender is located or identify someone who has been at that location before; return a visual or audio cue to the sender's viewfinder as he pans across a scene to identify a particular target (e.g., help the sender identify the library building); and provide techniques for blocking out common content in a series of images. Google StreetView displays sequences of street level panoramas of major cities, and presages such interactive and mobile functionality.

Pervasive digital devices are products of the repetitive processes of global capital and mass production. This much is obvious, although it seems many advocates also maintain that pervasive media are harbingers of nonconformity, individuality, and autonomy, providing user-consumers with greater control over their lives and interactions with others. In this chapter I considered how, as technologies of the everyday, pervasive digital media appear within the panoply of devices and machines for the perpetuation of repetition and rhythm. I have focused on the primacy of repetition rather than considering content. Repetition is always present, occasionally flicked into a different cycle, or kicked into another orbit. Repetition highlights further the complicity of digital devices in the tuning of place.

6 Tags

Tags are small labels attached to bigger things, such as address labels attached to luggage. Passengers with luggage and buyers of clothes probably think of the tag as of secondary importance. It supplements the thing it is attached to, the host (luggage, goods, garments), making the host identifiable, able to be found, more usable, and useful, and without getting in the way of its usual operation. Computer users post static and moving images onto Facebook, Flickr, and YouTube web pages and tag them with descriptive words. Here tags are "subject key words" that are apart from the image and assist in online searching. If you search the Facebook, Flickr, or YouTube image databases for the word *steampunk* you will receive a list of images or videos tagged with the word *steampunk*. Shared bookmarking sites such as del.icio.us add the further capability of retaining information about the tag's author and enable you to trace tags as links, as in a thesaurus or bookmark manager, to find what else any particular author or editor labeled *steampunk*. Tags can be so linked and clustered. Social-networking websites have multiplied and instrumentalized the role of the humble tag.

I began chapter 4 with an observation about the unremarkable—that which people do not regularly remark upon. Tagging deals with those things people have little difficulty remarking on, which is to say that can be marked, and remarked, with tags.[1] Tagging is a simple, everyday idea. Tags seem to work well now, while web users await the development of algorithms that classify images and sounds automatically according to subject matter or content. Tags used with digital media are not much more sophisticated conceptually than the name tags handed out at conferences, or ownership labels—small strips of cloth with names printed or written on them—like the ones attached to children's gym wear. To the extent that pervasive digital media deploy tags, their role in small-scale adjustment can further an understanding of the tuning of place. Tags are unpretentious, instrumental, and can be deployed in calculation. Like bits and bytes, tags champion no overt utopian or technoromantic claims to transform human cognition or sociability.

Tags are endemic to many computer operations. HTML and XML facilitate the tagging of blocks of text, a process also known as markup, which involves supplementing a body of text with tags to indicate formatting.[2] As any web designer knows, HTML tags can be deployed to indicate complex formatting, and in the case of XML they help structure documents.[3]

Pervasive computing draws substantially on concepts of the tag. Tags are both ubiquitous and emblematic of ubiquity.[4] Sticky labels bearing printed barcodes adhered to consumer goods, QR (quick response) printed tags, fiducials (symbols that provide location and orientation information in image processing), and passive RFID (Radio Frequency IDentification) tags are examples of digital tags.[5] A passive RFID tag is a cheap, battery-less microchip attached to goods. When the tag receives a radio signal from a nearby RFID reader it emits data in return, such as an ID number. RFID tags assist the progress of inventoried goods and components through a warehouse or factory. RFID tags implanted under skin are now a common means of tracking wildlife, pets, and people. The ID is the tag, which such technologies attempt to secure unambiguously to the object. Physical or behavioral characteristics of the organism also are deployed to secure the link between the tag and its host. Fingerprints, iris scans, DNA tagging, the peculiar way a typist strikes a computer keyboard, or a person's distinctive gait all constitute identifiable signatures to aid recognition, identification, and tagging, even "at a distance."[6]

Tags of any level of sophistication help identify and indicate ownership. They facilitate tracking and mapping. The pervasive digital media world is one pervaded by electronic tags. As this chapter unfolds, I hope to show that tags form colonies, ecologies, or "clouds" that occasionally come into contact with collections of hosts—objects to which they might be attached.[7] The main objective of this chapter is to show that tags are temporal before they are spatial, which is to say tags are of the moment. Tag users don't need to think of tags as permanent markers of the way things are forever, but rather as signaling a change in state.[8] Tags mark time ahead of their role in indicating ownership or territory. In this tags connect strongly with the senses, in particular with sound. At the very least, thinking of the temporality of tags opens them and the media that deploy them to new possibilities in the world of the tangible and sensual.

Hidden Languages

I suggested that tags might form colonies, ecologies, or clouds. As communications media tags also form languages. Tags rarely exist in isolation. I also want to extract tags from their purely instrumental role, as if the primary function of a tag it is to label the way things are, incontrovertibly, mechanistically, unambiguously, and logically. Logic needs to give way to the role of social convention as we think about and deploy tags.

There are conventions for assigning, reading, and interpreting tags. RFID tags are brought into service through mass production and are designed to be read by specialized devices, RFID readers, in the same way that HTML tags utilize a specific tagging language, the interpretation of which is embedded in web browsers and conforms more or less to the W3C standards. The tagging of airport baggage entails several sets of conventions. There are the official tags supplied and attached by the airline to map luggage to passenger information. The components of this tagging language usually involve a mass-produced and easily identified strip of tape adhered to the suitcase handle. The tag has a unique code printed on it (perhaps in QR format) that corresponds to a code on the ticket, in the computer database, and on boarding lists (manifests). It is unlikely that the average traveler pays much attention to this language, unless something goes wrong, for instance, if luggage gets misplaced. At the very least, the presence of the tag signals to the traveler that an instrumentally useful process is in hand. Then there is the tagging language belonging to other conventions, such as attaching a leather, plastic, or paper label bearing the name and contact details of the luggage. These languages are less standardized, but any seasoned traveler inspecting an item of luggage, for example, is likely to know where to look and how to interpret the address tag. Furthermore, people often tag their luggage with a strip of colored tape or a sticky label to make it distinctive and easily identifiable on the baggage carousel. Suitcase owners are adept at adorning or marking items of luggage to distinguish theirs from the rest. Then suitcases can bear the scars and peculiar features of use that also help in identification. This is a deictic, private tagging language, created accidentally, on the fly, idiosyncratically and opportunistically. However sophisticated the technology, tagging languages seem to fall within such categories, each of which depends on the establishment of a set of human practices. Tags are useless as tags without an interpreter and a set of conventions and practices by which to interpret them.

Tagging conventions, or languages, tend to be highly redundant. As in the case of luggage tags, conventions overlay one another. There are official, legal, and dispute-minimizing conventions involving printed codes, databases, and safeguards against fraud. There are also folk-oriented and idiosyncratic conventions.

The concept of a tagging *language* is more helpful than that of a tagging system. A system implies there is some overarching logical organization that takes priority over the practical. Linguists generally accept that language requires ambiguity, and looseness to fit the context. There are rules to language, such as grammar, but linguists acknowledge that these are dynamic and changing, and people engaged in conversation still understand one another even when the rules are not adhered to.[9] Which rules apply is a matter of context. Some politicians, intellectuals, lecturers, and arts critics can deploy the most "correct" language usage when in a formal setting, and lapse into informal language, and even street slang, when it suits them, with no apparent detriment to their reputation or authority.

In fact tagging derives much of its contemporary potency as a phenomenon of the street, as a bottom-up, noninstitutionalized, antiestablishment idiom. The term *tag* is often applied to the signature of someone who produces graffiti, and sometimes the tag is all there is—for example, someone's name: Spike, Sivel, Jase,[10] invoking hip hop, rap, and beatbox references. As for other languages, tagging extends from the legal to the illegal, the formal to the folk, and the popular to the esoteric, the transparent to the deictic.

Tagging brings the issue of attachment into focus, and in this respect invokes debates within language theory. Regular tag users might commonly assume that tags have to be attached to something. Certain theories of language, notably the theories of Structuralism as derived from Ferdinand de Saussure, sought to dispense with the notion that a word might attach incontrovertibly to some object, as if objects preexist as isolated entities independently of language.[11] Both objects and their supposed linguistic attachments are subject to questioning. For my purposes here, a single tag might attach to a single object (host), but also to another tag, clusters of tags, or clusters of hosts, or be free-floating.[12] By virtue of their detachable nature, tags exemplify well the Structuralists' proverbial floating signifier.

Language theories accommodate the possibility that in certain contexts words attach to particular things and thereby function as tags. The binding of a word to a thing in this way is captured by the idea of the indexical, a concept strongly related to the tag.

Floating Indexicals

Indexes are ubiquitous in digital media, involving linkages, cross-referencing, and lists. According to the early linguist Charles Sanders Peirce, an indexical is a sign that "signifies its object solely by being really connected with it."[13] Words such as *home, suitcase,* and *ubiquity* are general. They account for an indeterminate number of things. But indexicals are words that supposedly denote specific one-to-one mappings, such as *this, that, you,* and *I.* These more commonly are known as pronouns. Pronouns seem vague but are used nonetheless to make specific reference in particular contexts. The indexical is not the tag, but the means of attachment. To say "this belongs to John" is to use "this," the indexical, as the glue or the piece of string that attaches the label "John" to the thing, the suitcase. Indexing makes specific connections.[14]

In everyday speech animated conversationalists make the connection between the thing and the tag even stronger with gestural pointing for emphasis and clarity. If I say "this is my suitcase" and touch the suitcase on the word "this," and thump my chest on the word "my," you will have little doubt as to my claim of the strength of connection between the thing and its tag. In this respect, the human senses, including touch and sound, are complicit in the fixing of tags to objects.

Pronouns are everyday and inconspicuous, and as is often the case with everyday devices they draw attention to someone, something, or some place. Pronouns such as "this," "that," "you," and "I" obviously recur in people's speech. In so far as they constitute the glue that binds a label to its host they are fluid. The indexical changes role depending on context, and contexts change. So "this" today will probably refer to a different "this" tomorrow, or in the next sentence. Indexicals are not fixed, and indicate further the fluidity of language and of tags.

Indexicals are ubiquitous in people's ordering of the world. The relationship between your home and its street address, or the entries in a cell phone contact list and the individual phones to which they connect, are also indexicals. Indexical mappings are specific in an index to a book or in a database on a computer. Needless to say, databases are designed to be flexible. As anyone with an electronic contacts list knows, friends move to new addresses, out-of-date data gets replaced. Tags change.

Electronic and mechanical systems are infused with changing indexicals. In computer memory management, data types known as "pointers" refer to data stored in memory. In some programming techniques the data stays where it is while the program operates on the pointers. It is more efficient to manipulate a pointer[15] (a kind of indexical) that stands in for the data than to keep rewriting the data into different memory locations. This is not unlike the processes by which a caterer might organize place-cards at a dinner party. It is easier and more polite to test the arrangement of people at the tables by juggling the cards around than it is to move the guests once they are seated. Tags and indexicals are good stand-ins, or surrogates, with which to test relationships and solve problems prior to dealing with the things themselves.

Tags can also be designed with change in mind, in other words, what they indicate can change. Indexicals and indicators share the same etymology (*indicem*, a pointing finger). Indicators can entail complex mechanical connections. In this respect, gauges, dials, and alarms have an indexical function. The speed indicator in a car registers changes in voltage from a small generator attached to the transmission and presents them visually on the dashboard. The speed indicator is an indexical, as is the station indicator on your digital radio. In this light, electronic and mechanical mediation appear as a further commerce in tags. Tags can be any variable or static component that signals something about its host at a moment in time. Warning lights and alarm bells call attention to a specific fact or event (for example, when a driver exceeds the speed limit). Alerts highlight the temporality of the tag. A fire alarm, flashing signal, or other warning is a case of an activated tag that is otherwise dormant.

Stretching the temporal tag metaphor further, avatars are at another end of the indexical spectrum from pronouns. Avatars are elaborate digital surrogates for the human beings who may be playing computer games or MMORPGs. These three-dimensional indexicals or tags that appear as human forms have properties and attributes that may or may not accord with the hosts who possess them. As if to reinforce their role as tags, avatars in Second Life walk about with name labels hovering over their heads. In fact, the avatar even presents itself as a representation of a mobile tag with the image of a body suspended beneath it. In the heyday of virtual environments, one of the intrigues about the avatar as tag was the extent to which people might play around with identities, change and multiply their avatars, and even exchange them with one another. One of my colleagues relates how he left his computer while still logged on to Second Life. When he returned, his partner had changed the form of his avatar from the generic shape to that of a frog, which he then never bothered to change back. In some cases the Second Life population bears the traces of shared and exchanged ownership and access. Author Tim Guest begins his novel about his Second Life experience by describing how a community of people with limited mobility would share an avatar, controlling different aspects of its movement and taking turns at operating it.[16] To the extent that avatars are tags, they are complicit in a temporal game of exchange and alteration. Like avatars, mobile devices such as cell phones host personal profile information. The user profile on a SIM (Subscribed Identity Module) card is a surrogate for the phone user, and can be transported from an old phone to a new one. The tag can be detached and reattached to a new host.

Locational Tags

If tags are flexible, changeable, and temporal, then they are also a powerful means of identifying locations. Tagged locations often constitute landmarks that aid navigation.[17] Survey markers are tags attached to the ground at certain points indicating property boundaries, ownership, elevation, the position of services, and land features. A tag indicating numerical geographical information is often referred to as a datum, a primary component of mapping. Geographical coordinates are commonly identified with tags. Ubiquitous digital media make increasing use of geotagging, attaching information to specific geographical locations, made possible in particular through satellite GPS technology, or multilateration from cell phone masts, or local navigation systems.[18] As indicated in chapter 5, with such locational technologies it is possible for photographs taken with a GPS-enabled camera to be tagged with coordinates and later inserted into digital maps. Particular points or regions can also be tagged with information accessible via a digital device such as a cell phone. When you are near to a particular geographical point then you see the tag as a message or a map reference on your device. The display on the device indicates where you are on the map, where the nearest coffee shops are, or if you are near a Facebook friend. Geotagging merges into a suite of sophisticated location technologies and applications.[19]

Locational tagging is most evident at the thresholds, which further emphasizes the temporal aspects of the tag and of spatial experience. A threshold is a moment of change or transition. Tags mark moments on a map, many of which pertain to lines, contours, and edges, and moments of transition, the crossing of which constitutes a change in state: being inside to being outside, resident to trespasser, dry to wet.[20]

There are other digital means of tagging the environment than GPS coordinates. One such approach is to use visual information to position a tag, not through coordinates but by taking advantage of the physical features of an environment, such as the appearance of a particular wall surface or building façade, or various visual cues in combination.[21] Using rapid image-matching algorithms, pictures of such surfaces taken with a cell phone camera can be dispatched instantly to a server and then matched against a database of images and their tags. The server matches each photograph to its approximate equivalent in a database.[22] This technology assumes that someone with a networked digital camera has been to that place before to pick up its visual "signature." Experimentation with such technology deploys image matching to detect where you are in the environment, a capability that could be extended to other modalities, such as sound, which also consists of matchable patterns. Any tagging based on image matching technologies would of necessity present as dynamic, temporal, and contingent, as opposed to relying on fixed GPS coordinates. Furthermore, such contextual locational technologies could function as supplemental to GPS, or operate in interior spaces or other areas where GPS does not function well. Positioning via image matching also suggests the dissemination of locational information according to what someone

has regarded as significant, rather than drawing on blanket GPS coverage which ostensibly treats every location on the planet the same.

Real-time video streaming from mobile devices enhances positioning via locational cues. You sweep your camera around a scene and receive information on the camera's display specific to that location.[23] Various locational technologies combine to place and view digital tags in the environment. To the extent that such operations involve scanning, sweeping, and the identification of change and transition using time-based media, they reinforce the temporal and dynamic characteristics of the tag.

Locational tagging draws on the compulsive way that urban environments come ready-tagged with signs, posters, and graffiti that contribute to the identification of place. In the same way that luggage tagging merges labels, brand marks, and scuffs, the physical brandscape of a place constitutes a means of identifying where you are, where you are looking, and to whom things belong. The changing tagscape provides inadvertent locational cues.

Tags not only bind labels and hosts; their positioning also signals relationships. This is particularly apparent in the case of labels on drawings, such as maps and anatomical diagrams. Tags on maps can tell shoppers that the post office is next to the supermarket, that the cafes are clustered around the city square, that the petrol station is near the junction with route 12. The label is not only a way of indicating what something is, but also to what it relates.

The concept of locational tagging suggests that tags might move. If a place is tagged with information about which of your Facebook friends are in its vicinity, this information will probably change over time. Tags move, and can be visualized on a display screen as moving. The objects to which they are attached also change position, and tags can attach themselves to different places and objects.

The Temporality of Tags

Tags cue complex activities. Names as tags trigger complex social practices. The invocation of your name kickstarts a personal introduction, a conversation, a memory of who you were with yesterday, and the process of booking a room in a hotel. Tags shift circumstances from one state to the next: for example, when you pass custody of your suitcase to an airline. Sometimes these tagging conventions enable potential antagonists to avoid and settle disputes, such as when passengers are processed through passport control and customs. Tags can be deployed to signal and formalize contractual obligations, and changes in obligations.

Thus tags are of the moment. When a traveler gets home or to her hotel room, she probably removes and disposes of the tag that was attached to her luggage on check-in. Tags are relatively inexpensive to move and dispose of, and the objects to which they are attached remain largely intact. But tags can also be exchanged, multiplied, and collected. In fact, lots of everyday objects people take for granted can be thought of as tags in this respect: passport stamps, coupons, raffle tickets, checks, IOUs, postage stamps, business cards, credit cards, money. Seen in this light, tags are a basic form of ubiquitous mobile media. Tags proliferate, multiply, and accrete. Such is the temporality of the tag.

Tags reference each other and can be duplicated in lists. In fact, it is helpful to think of items in lists as tags attached to storage locations. Items in a grocery list attach to cupboards, shelves, food departments, stores, collections of items, and categories. Attempts to "tag the world," as in the case of location-based tagging and tags attached to online media, are easily understood as entries in databases. Tags belong within the realms of inventories, bookkeeping, indexes, lists, and other mundane paraphernalia of everyday organization and bureaucracy. The compilation of calendars, diaries, and events lists constitutes a conspicuous commerce in databases of tags, revealing their temporal nature. Shared digital calendars and negotiations over appointments constitute commerce in tags. Tags are time-dependent, but concepts of time are strongly dependent on tagging as well. The inexorable march of time is often characterized as an ordered succession of tags marking the hours, days, and years. A timeline is a graphical presentation of a sequence of events tagged with words and other details, marking great events and epochs: the Battle of Hastings, the period of the Tudors, the end of the dot.com boom.

So-called time-based media rely on tagged timelines or channels and sequentially processed files. Computer animations are constructed from temporal sequences calculated on the basis of regular "frames," some of which are tagged as key frames. Key frames are important moments in the animation of an object or character. Other actions are calculated from the positions of objects at the key frames. Tags are important in synchronizing time-based media. Tags indicate key moments to help align channels and media, such as animation and sound, and are vital for editing and mixing sequences. A tag may indicate when a sequence is to start and stop. Tags can reference one another and are used in searches. In fact, tags feature in most communications systems, not least in conventional musical notation. Dynamical markings (*p, mf, f*), quarter notes, glissandi, embellishments, numbering of bars, and indications of fingering are so many markers on musical timelines. If notes are thought of as tags, it is apparent that in communications media tags progress from incidental markers to constituting the nature of the thing. Communication is all tags, and time-varying tags. Tags are markers of so many ubiquitous small increments.

Tuning Tags

Tags feature in processes of calibration, which emphasizes further the tags' dynamic and temporal character. Instrument specialists identify stages to processes of calibration, such as "yet to be calibrated," "calibrated," "out of calibration," and so on. Instrument specialists might tag a device with its calibration status, recording the date the next calibration is due, the authority that performed the calibration, and the standards applied. The tag might be date stamped and designed to be removed and replaced, sometimes with a seal to ensure it is not tampered with.

Tags are used in measurement and in the calibration of measuring devices. In his detailed account of ship navigation, Edwin Hutchins explains how early navigators would estimate the speed of a vessel by use of a long piece of rope, a so-called log line, which had a paddle at one end and was marked out with regularly spaced knots. The navigator would time the rate at which the knotted markers raced over the edge of the ship as the log line unfurled and the paddle end was dragged along in the water. The line needed to be marked out accurately: "Log lines can shrink with use, so it is important to check the length of the segment between the knots. . . . Decks don't stretch and shrink as ropes do. Putting the calibration nails into the deck is a way of creating a memory for the lengths between knots in the log line."[24] As in this case of a nail in the ship's deck, a reference datum serves as a calibration tag.

A reference datum is a tagged location used for making comparisons between data, and for checking the alignment of sets of data. Cartographers and surveyors enlist geographical reference points against which map locations can be calibrated, analogous to the deployment of standard weights and measures. Locational reference points are important for accurate GPS coordination, the accuracy of which can vary by tens of meters. Some GPS services involve transmission of a signal from a known location on earth to help fix the location as calculated from satellite signals. Extra information from the stable and local transmission point is deployed to compensate for discrepancies in the GPS signals. GPS reference stations act as calibration points.[25]

Elevation data provides particular problems to surveyors, with or without GPS. Mean sea level is difficult to determine and standardize. The geometry of the Earth does not help; distances from the center of the Earth are significantly greater at the equator than at the poles. In addition, the information on the maps available for any particular site may only be accurate to within a few meters. Therefore, a surveyor may set a reference datum on a site as a standard against which the elevation of the ground and the height of buildings can be measured. The cast-iron cover of an inspection hole or other relatively stable and identifiable surface may provide the reference datum. Once the elevation above mean sea level of that surface is known, other elevations can be determined with reference to it. Surveyors and builders do not always need to know elevation information relative to some stable earth datum with great accuracy. In the case of building construction it is often only the heights of things relative to one another that are important. The use of a reference datum is significant in most areas of geographical mapping.

Tags are employed in many mapping and alignment processes, including in printing. Tags identify registration and control points for the alignment of surfaces, as in the case of printer's marks used to align plates when printing in color. In time, repeated machine operations result in misalignments. Tagging helps resolve, and is prone to, the peculiarities of calibration drift, the gradual misalignment of tags as their hosts drift and slide over time.

As an exercise in calibration, tuning inevitably resorts to tags. It is likely that your digital radio provides a means of assigning a radio frequency to a particular button for quick access. Aligning buttons, frequencies, and station IDs fixes cross-mappings and their tags. Tagging operates in all directions in information networks. Which parts of the network constitute the hosts and which are the tags depends on how you think of the network at any particular moment. That tags can be assigned to locations furthers their relevance to musical tuning. The divisions of a vibrating string to give musical intervals can be tagged, not unlike the log line used for determining the speed of a ship. The various notes—C, C♯, B♭, and so on—are tags, as are the positions of the frets on a stringed instrument. Tuning musical instruments is a subtle process that relies on sound, touch, and the positioning and alignment of tags.

Tags and Sociability

Tags are complicit in the means by which technologies "synchronize the actions of men." Sociable human beings employ tags to align calendars and diaries, and check these to ensure arrival in the right place at the right time to encounter one another. Social networking websites fulfill similar roles in coordination and collaboration. According to blogger and web commentator Adam Mathes, the creation and deployment of user-defined tags on social network sites can contribute to community formation.[26] Tags contribute to a culture of sharing and are a means of making information instantly accessible, lowering barriers to cooperation. One of the advantages of user-ascribed tags on social networking sites is that they evoke instant feedback. Your tags become active as soon as they are attached, and can be modified in response. They can also be processed, compared, statistically analyzed, and visualized as clouds of greater and lesser density of connection, relevance, and frequency. As dynamic entities tag clouds drift and float in response to changing meanings, usages, and contexts.

Tags fit within in overall economy of social signs that includes brands, flags, and insignias. As such, tags feature in our rich and variegated experience of the urban environment and the "semiosphere."[27] Tags accompany brands as marks of modernity. Branding is a modern, postindustrial phenomenon, relying on mass production, commerce, marketing, corporate management strategies, and mass media, though it also draws on the legacy of cartouches, signatures, seals, and heraldry. Contemporary businesses project brands, labels, and tags to consumers, but are also in negotiation, or competition, with one another. Nike, Apple, Amazon,

Prada, and Waitrose do not have monopolies on branding. Brands do not only belong to the companies that create them but are also the property of consumers. Naomi Klein's influential book *No Logo* captures this sense of shared investment in brands and tags, their subversion through culture jamming, their détournement for unintended uses, and the strength of feeling they engender.[28] Tags have a social and political aspect, aided and abetted by the possibilities of digital social networks. Tags get contested, negotiated, and altered. According to Saussure and the semiotic tradition,[29] signs are socially and subtly negotiated, and as such are implicated in the play of power.[30] Pervasive media invest substantially in the humble tag as both signifier and signified.

Tags and Habitat

As further evidence of their social and spatial role, it seems that tags are used to assert claims on territory. In chapter 3, I labored over the role of repetition in defining habitat and territory and showed the complicity of sound and mobile media. What is the role of tags in the articulation of space? The tags of graffiti artists can be thought of simply as claims on the spaces in which they are placed. As such, graffiti tags are analogous to the trail of scent left by animals to mark territory, or the territorial call signs of birds. Imposing one's own tags on an environment is a way of claiming space. There are many ways to mark one's territory: settling into a public place with a laptop or a mobile phone, or simply wearing earphones is a means of putting a claim on space, more so when such activity involves broadcasting and reinforcing that claim through gesture, sound, conversation, and repetition. Though they may not persist, temporary squatters and sitters tag spaces with their gestures. Territorial claims by whatever means relate to tagging.

Inserting one's private tagging language, which is recognizable as such by others but cannot be interpreted by strangers, adds potency to territorial claims, as one's presence is noted but without the transfer and distraction of overt meaning. One of the ways that novelists and filmmakers induce a sense that the protagonists are encroaching on alien territory is to suggest the presence of inscriptions, marks, sounds, and other alien tags, the code of which is unknown to the protagonists. In Joseph Conrad's novel *Heart of Darkness*, the travelers found that: "At night sometimes the roll of drums behind the curtain of trees would run up the river and remain sustained faintly, as if hovering in the air high over our heads, till the first break of day. Whether it meant war, peace, or prayer we could not tell."[31] In the film *The Blair Witch Project*, the discovery of twigs fashioned into obscure signs contrives similar menace and uncertainty about territory. Territories are defined as much by secret conventions as they are by walls and boundaries. As explored in chapter 5, the technical term for such sign conventions is *deictic*. Deictic tagging is complicit in the conflictual, agonistic, and territorial aspects of spatial experience. The prolific, promiscuous, and instantly accessible jungle of the World Wide Web forms its territories as much by esoteric subject matter and languages as by overt structures. It is simply the case that much of what is churned up by a search engine is beyond the comprehension and grasp of most net surfers. Not many could claim to apprehend what most web pages are about. Tagging intentionally clarifies for some and obscures for others.

Tags can be exclusive. Tagging is complicit in critiques of hegemonic control, where one group or class is identified as asserting its power by labeling, branding and tagging the world in ways that are conspicuously its own, as when an invading or colonizing nation changes all the street signs of the subjected territories into its own language.[32] The introduction of brand signs (Coke, Nike, McDonald's, for example) serves a similar purpose, and features in Klein's critique of branding. Tagging also represents a bureaucratic attempt to avoid and settle disputes, or subjugate dissent, whether by colonizers, capitalist hegemony, or pragmatic and consensual social ordering.[33] The infrastructures and products of pervasive digital media are of necessity sourced by large corporations in tandem with governments and regulators. Much has been said about the hegemony of the Internet, as the purveyor of Western, capitalist values, and the complicity of service providers in supporting regimes with poor records in human rights and civil liberties.[34] Much of this criticism resides in the way that corporate interests lay claim by tagging and branding spaces, services, networks, and people.

In spite of deictic differences, one of the claims made of global capital and bureaucratization is that they label everything, and in so doing tend toward making everything the same. Or at least they suppress difference. For Lefebvre, the spaces of capitalism are "homogeneous so that they can be exchanged, bought and sold, with the only differences between them being those assessable in money—i.e., quantifiable—terms (as volumes, distances, etc)."[35] This tagged homogeneity applies to habitat. Gaston Bachelard draws attention to the kind of homes where inhabitants of the city "live in superimposed boxes,"[36] indicated by "the number of the street and the floor."[37] In keeping with a familiar critique of modernity, the imposition of addressing and stacking, the mass production, and the regularized tagging of places imply that everything is interchangeable and disposable.[38] Pervasive digital devices seem to extend this uniformity. Everyone has to have a mobile phone and a mobile phone number, to be contactable everywhere and anywhere. Places thereby become disposable. It matters little to the caller whether you are at home, in the street, at work, or on the bus. Places, as well as labor, are subject to the rules of exchange, commoditization, and capital.

Contrary to such narratives of hegemony, there is a certain autonomy that disregards homogenizing organizational structures, or at least works to exploit them. For Augoyard, the operative term is *appropriation*. Inhabitants are capable, through their micropractices that cut across the grain of the grand design, of taking over a place. Not least among the citizens' methods for this is the phenomenon of naming: "the inhabitants carry out a veritable *process* of place naming."[39] In fact, they may purvey a kind of un-naming, a willful removal of labels, in other words, not recognizing the names supplied by the developer, and misusing the official appellations.

Renaming practices are explicit in digital media, as in the use of aliases, file names that refer to other files, made-up names as login IDs, address book names, chat room aliases, and avatar names, though here the software requires and encourages such renaming. Claiming and registering domain names in order to sell them is a form of appropriation for gain. Then there are (or were in the early days of web search engines) more tactical strategies for claiming space through naming, such as naming one's own web page, and lacing the page with key words in an attempt to influence the hit rate from search engines. Naming is so much under the hegemony of code in digital media that, unlike Augoyard's advocacy of renaming places in order to take them over, renaming someone else's web pages requires hacking skills beyond most computer users.

There are other methods of appropriation that implicate tags. For Bachelard, a domicile within stacked apartment blocks is a diminished version of the authentically prototypical house, which is particular, idiosyncratic of its time and place, and connects with stable symbols and values: "A house constitutes a body of images that give mankind proofs or illusions of stability."[40] Tags, as signs, have a role in this apparent stability. Residents of the house might think of the home's spaces as tagged with personal signs, given expression by personalized labels on doors, as in John's room, Jane's cupboard, or the wood shed. Photographs, ornaments, and souvenirs are among the means by which the home's occupants tag habitat. Placing an object in a space leaves a mark and personalizes the environment. For Bachelard, the reality of the house is thereby subject to constant "re-imagining."[41] Populating spaces with personal objects sediments memories, perpetuating the recollections of the occupants and of the former occupation of spaces. Tagging still exhibits this strong temporal aspect, whether deployed territorially or habitually.

Personal web pages and pages on social network sites provide similar opportunities for personalizing and claiming space. The deposition on personal web pages of images, personal facts, messages, links, and playlists expands this domestication of space into information space, through tagging.

As I demonstrated in chapter 4, habitat is distinguished by cycles of use. If the proliferators of tags are prepared to expand tagging from paper labels and database entries to other means of marking space, such as personal effects and indicators of human presence, then habitat is imbued with temporal tags indicating that these are the places where people sleep, eat, prepare for work, return—where toothbrushes are kept, keys deposited, food eaten, television programs saved and viewed, and files downloaded. Habitat bears the tags and traces of temporal cycles, and different households adopt their own tagging languages, dialects, and deictics of temporal habitation.[42] There is a sense in which personal web pages, social network pages, and public photo galleries expand the temporal nature of habitat and seem intent on rendering public the private world of the fetish.[43] By this account the display of database content, online collections, and the web portal are recent extensions of a more primitive and domestic mode of expression that originates with the home.

Thus tags are linguistic, social, locational, temporal, territorial, and habitual. The presence of tagging in the context of habitat provides further evidence for the primacy of the small move, the temporal shift, the nudge by which pervasive digital devices and their spaces operate, further support for which comes from theories of cognition.

Tags and Cognition

Contrary to the idea of placement in a received taxonomy, digital social networks demonstrate the distribution and tagging of images and sounds, clustered as so-called user-created metadata or "folksonomies."[44] Folksonomies are emergent taxonomies that are loose, varying, and even inconsistent. Simply attaching keywords to photographs generates loose categorizations, as if by consensus rather than some official, imposed, and rational schema. Tags are complicit in the supposed democratization of knowledge, and seem to amplify the observation that language is, after all, a "social contract," fluid and contested.

Early theories of cognition suggested that the objects of the world present as ready for labeling, if not already tagged. To name things is one of the human animal's higher cognitive functions. It is as if custodians and teachers encourage language facility in a child by naming individual things, by attaching labels to them. When an infant sees a chair, she recalls the label "chair." The mind is an index and works on correspondences between words and things. In his early critique of such theories of language, Saussure asserted, "a linguistic sign is not a link between a thing and a name."[45] From that premise he went on to develop a theory of language in terms of concepts, sound patterns, and social agreement. Computers seem to be good at looking up indexes relating names to things, but humans are less adept. In fact, the human incapacity to think by establishing and manipulating correspondences might be precisely why societies have invented increasingly sophisticated tagging technologies. Tags are complicit in organizational practices extraneous to human cognition rather than representative of it.

As a variation on tagging, the concept of taxonomy involves assigning objects to agreed categories according to some rationale, such as assigning a plant specimen to a class. What a gardener informally identifies as a red oak falls within the species classification of *rubra*, within the genus *Quercus*, which is part of the family *Fagaceae*, in the order *Fagales*, in the class *Angiospermae*, and so on.[46] Taxonomic classifications form hierarchies, and are in fact tree-like, with no branches rejoining. The tag on a specimen in a laboratory, museum, or botanical display case indicates the place of the item in its taxonomy. Tags put things in their place in ways that the technician, museum visitor, and plant lover would find difficult if they had to depend on thought processes, memory, or cognition alone.

Rather than emulating human cognition, the tag is emblematic of participative moves to adjust the environment by means of small-scale local interventions. In so far as human cognition is a distributed process that implicates context and environment, tags are part of the cognitive scaffolding. They can also be thought of as hanging from the scaffolding. Human beings are used to thinking about tags as describing what is, what belongs to whom, and what things mean, but it is also helpful to think of tags as triggers, nudges, or cues put in place to initiate certain practices. Your name does not only say who you are, but its invocation also sets in train a series of actions and reactions, of complex social practices. A login name can grant access to a wealth of interactions—a diminished form of the power of an introduction at a committee meeting or dinner party.

Tags are easier to manipulate and organize than their hosts. Baggage handlers might think little of hauling all the luggage bound for Manila over here, and that bound for Rome over there. Baggage gets moved around and sorted, and tags serve in cross-checking that things are in the right place. In order to plan, solve problems, and reason about the world, physically able individuals might similarly think of hauling objects (hosts) into their required categories. Moving specimens around in a botanical garden is more difficult. Baggage handlers, gardeners, and furniture movers adopt different classification schemes for different purposes, and in any case it is unlikely that arranging things spatially according to diverse classificatory schemas is going to be convenient for all contexts of use.[47] Where classification is important, paper tags are the quintessential tools. They are easier to manipulate than their hosts, and in some cases operate as extensions to their hosts. The symbols and tokens of digital media expand further on the economy of tags as substitutes for people and things.

Without tagging, and positioning things together, party hosts and schoolteachers would have to rely on their capacity to recognize faces, shapes, bodies, people, and things unassisted. In certain contexts a host may think it sufficient and even more gracious to recall the names of the people she has invited to the dinner party without issuing nametags.[48] How do people recall without tags? The art of mnemonics, introduced in chapter

5, provides a more subtle and spatially engaging means of identification than tags. In fact, the techniques of mnemonics are the main contenders to tagging. But mnemonic practices can also help the reflective designer understand the way tags work.

Mnemonics are spatial and temporal. An orator recalls points in his speech by virtue of their relationships to one another and with space.[49] In preparing a speech at a wedding, for example, to impress on memory the fact that you will need to mention the groom's sporting interests, you might try imagining him pole vaulting over the buffet table. When it comes to delivering the speech, the setting thus provides the reminder of what you need to say. Nowadays, few public speakers are practiced in the deployment of this kind of mnemonics, or brave enough to attempt it, and prefer to use written notes. Yet even when delivering a speech in full swing, experienced orators do not always need to read every point in their notes to know what to say. Looking at the paper itself sometimes suffices as a reminder, in noting the general layout of the page, or picking out a key word. Visual aids in lectures (slides, PowerPoint, and interactive digital media) give the speaker a similar mnemonic advantage, especially if the presentation medium is rich in sensory images, as opposed to simply bullet points.

It is also helpful to think of tags as a form of mnemonics. They are reminders rather than hard data, or at least they are reminders that there is something of significance here, before they are hardbound, instrumental markers of objects, facts, and data. Items on a to-do list are not the tasks, nor are they complete descriptions of tasks but rather reminders that something is to be done. This applies to many digital symbols, markers, and tags.

Mnemonics work by unusual associations—such as vaulting bridegrooms. Frances Yates explains the Roman orator Cicero's understanding of exceptional occurrences as a means to memorization. Whereas even the most nostalgic individuals will not easily recall a particular sunrise or sunset, they will certainly remember solar eclipses, which "are a source of wonder because they occur seldom, and indeed are more marvelous than lunar eclipses, because these are more frequent."[50] Mnemonics work by association involving the insertion of something unusual into the otherwise usual scheme of events: "We ought then to set up images of a kind that can adhere longest in memory."[51] Tags can serve this end. A tag can render an object unusual or special in some way and bring it into the world of remembered things. There is a hint here also of the potential of discrepancy. It is where the cycles fail to align in the accepted, predictable, and regular way that memory secures a foothold. Cycles, gaps, and memory converge on the tag.

To summarize, the unassuming tag is emblematic of ubiquity, and it is ubiquitous in digital media. Tags embody discourses about the desirability—or otherwise—of organization and control. At one extreme, tagging is complicit in the reduction of the world to taxonomies and labels. But tags also feature in discourses that seek the liberalization of knowledge, in recognition that people can create their own taxonomies on the fly. Observant individuals might label the world as they see fit, but solidarity and community require that social beings adjust their tagscapes to enrich communication and interaction. It seems that people tune their environments through tagging. They adjust and manipulate their tagging languages. In all this it is helpful to think of tags as temporal, which is to say in time, as so many floating signifiers. There are other metaphors to account for unmoving solidity, not least of which are: idea, knowledge, category, home base, center, and ground. Tagging captures the possibilities of temporality and impermanence, and as such provides a helpful metaphor for the role of pervasive digital media in the tuning of place.

In the creation of devices that exploit tagging, designers might do well to attend to the overlay of tagging languages and their dynamic interaction. In so far as design is abetted and stimulated by hybridity and the crossover of languages, it is a play in tags.

The existence of tags provides further evidence for the presence of small moves, temporal shifts, and nudges by which influences and potentials ripple through social organization and social practices, processes abetted in no small part by the presence of ubiquitous digital devices.

In chapter 7 I will explore the physicality of the tag, to further understand the senses. As long as interaction designers and programmers focus on digital tagging as a database exercise, they deprecate the importance of hearing, touch, and the other senses. In implicating time, the idea of the tag also engages with issues of embodiment.

7 Taps

This chapter continues the discussion of tags and draws insights from the tactile and material character of tagging technologies, from paper based to electronic. The investigation amplifies further the role of digital tags in the tuning of place by attending to touch, attachment, and the voice, and to the provocative role of tags as potential parasites.

Insofar as ubiquitous digital media engage with the senses, they implicate touch. Think of the touch phone and the touch-sensitive display of smartphones such as the iPhone. Tagging, introduced in chapter 6, connotes touch, as deployed in the game of tag in which one player pursues the others in order to pass on the role of pursuer. According to the *Oxford English Dictionary,* the word *tag* may derive from the northern UK dialect word *tig,* meaning a kind of light touch.[1] The concept of the tag, as I have presented it, enjoys close association with *tig,* tap, and touch. There is something light and transient about tags, ostensibly inconsequential unless people construct practices around them that bring them into significance. A tap on the shoulder is time-bound and can be inconsequential, or it can indicate a significant change in status, the conferring of an honor, for example. Though physical, a tag does not leave a mark, as might a slap or a blow, nor does it draw pain. Touch screens involve this kind of ephemeral contact, or tagging, as attested by the deposition of so many fingerprints and smears on glass and plastic.

I have alluded to the way that indexicals, as pronouns, can be reinforced by touch and gesture, as when pointing at something on naming or claiming it. The communication of touch via pervasive digital media is an important goal of research into tangible media.[2] In creating play out of the avoidance of contact, the game of tag also brings physical touch into prominence. Of course there are variants of the game, not least as a sport of pretending to shoot your opponent, as in paintball and first-person shooter computer games. Armed with the appropriate technology, some of our students developed a variant of the tag game that avoids both physical touching and pretend shooting. In the students' version, tagging is done by photographing one's opponents with a cell phone—specifically, by capturing on camera the image on the front or back of another player's t-shirt, as evidence of a successful tag. Who has been photographed by whom is arbitrated by image-matching software invoked as the game is in progress, and the scores are compiled automatically. Trials with the game indicated the emergence of new tactics for avoidance, such as running at an angle to avoid exposing one's front or back to an opponent's view and wedging one's body between obstacles.

Image tagging resonates with the tag game dynamics. Part of the language of tagging involves laying claim via touch. Passengers feel uneasy about physically handling each other's luggage from the carousel. The tactile history of the host object (the suitcase or other tagged object) implicates a sequence of putative events, each of which has consequences for its life and legitimacy. Touch-sensitive surfaces at an airport that register your fingerprint institute the formal digital traces of your touch.

To further align tags of the kind discussed in chapter 6 with the senses, think of the superfluity of tags. A surplus piece of fur, wool, hair, or fabric that is ready to be removed is also known as a tag. A torn piece of fabric or a shred of tissue rent from skin are also referred to as tags. The incidental bits around the seams and edges of metal or plastic casting are also tags, to be broken off, shaved, or otherwise removed. Such superfluous appendages survive as tags, tabs, and stubs. Tags are the result and the trace of a process; a tag is a further sign of temporality and embodied action. Traces of unpurged tags populate non-W3C-compliant HTML code, like inactive DNA. Computer programs frequently contain unused routines or variables declared but never used.

Rags are forms of tags and are emblematic of supposedly marginalized social groups.[3] People dressed in rags are presumed to be somehow superfluous. The humble tag and its grassroots role in the democratization and socialization of information resonate with the idea of rags. The accretions of labels, scuffs, and repairs are among the tags by which travelers identify their luggage. Dissatisfied occupants of virtual 3D environments attest to finding it hard to identify the unique and the personal in a pristine world.

Such incidental identifiers are emblematic of the contingent nature of the physical tag, which is very difficult to replicate in digital environments, should anyone want to.

Attachment

The issue of fixing draws attention further to the physicality of the tag. Tags invite attachment and detachment. There is a difference between a tag firmly adhered to the surface of a jar in a pathology laboratory and a place card at a dinner party. The strength of bonding between tag and host says something about the character and importance of the host and the context. A brand logo as a tag on the cover of a box of breakfast cereal connects loosely with the contents, governed by marketing conventions.[4] The same logo on a web page can be connected by code to other information, mediated by a click.

The security-conscious might think that tags need to be locked in place, but tags can also lock other entities together. A piece of protruding metal or plastic that enables another component to be joined to it operates as a tag, much as a latch secures a closed door to the door jamb. Recall from chapter 3 the wedges of interlocking gear wheels. Wedges function as so many enmeshed tags. A model maker might also consider to be tags the extensions (tabs) to a cardboard surface that aid in the construction of a miniature house: insert tab A into slot B. To tag is also to buttonhole someone, to engage and fix their attention, as one would insert a flower in a buttonhole, or attach two parts of a garment by inserting buttons into buttonholes. Bootlaces are obvious tag-like fixing devices. In digital media, social networking tags provide a kind of glue or matrix that adheres images and media to their owners/authors and to one another.

Throughout this catalog of tagging tactics note that the fixing of a tag is contingent. The bond between the tag and the host is only as firm as human conventions and technologies allow and require. Think of tags as floating, secured for the moment by various pragmatic contexts. Floating tags can also signify. Like "dead links" on a web page, floating tags indicate a work in progress, that a page needs repair or the server supporting the page has detected an error, or that no one cares about this page any more.

Techniques of biometric tagging are significant in digital security and indicate moves to fix the tag to the host permanently. It seems that every means of permanent tagging has limitations and is prone to manipulation, with concomitant risks to civil liberties.[5] Criminologists and urban sociologists have observed that security measures in gated communities reduce the traffic of people and the usual means of watching out for one another.[6] Like the pursuit of absolute security, permanence can harden the resolve of others to extract, break through, or at best move the sabotage elsewhere. The specter of misidentification of a biometric ID has been explored in science fiction. For example, in Danny Cannon's 1995 film *Judge Dredd,* one of the characters is shot in the neck. The automated security guns then turn on him because his voice is no longer recognized. Security with online banking seems to rely on the escalation of measures and countermeasures against the increasingly sophisticated means by which hackers and hacker "bots" impersonate other users.

In some security cases it is sufficient to establish that the agent accessing the information on the website is in fact a human being and not a computer program. With interactive websites that encourage user-generated content come attempts by individuals to post their own extraneous information, or insert links to their own sites to improve hit rates. Automated programs that tirelessly search for and blitz websites with spam (unsolicited) messages seem to pose the greatest challenge. Website developers have introduced techniques to reduce the chances of intrusions from spam bots. A page so protected will contain a distorted image of a sequence of keyboard characters that only a human being should be able to recognize. Before a user can dispatch an on-screen form she will be required to correctly enter the string of deliberately distorted but readable (by humans) characters into a special text field. Such CAPTCHA (Completely Automated Public Turing tests to tell Computers and Humans Apart) procedures are widely used to prevent spam on websites.[7] Hackers are deploying even smarter OCR (optical character recognition) techniques that break through these security measures.[8] The challenge to incontrovertibly link the human being to their actions is caught in such escalations of sophistication on the part of both the site developer and the intruder.

Attempts to fix tags permanently to their hosts are tantamount to codifying the subtle cues by which humans and animals negotiate their sociability and security. I need hardly say that the propensity for human beings to exert influence on one another by subtle cues and nudges, let alone edicts and constraints, is not always benign. The obvious lesson here is that the circulation of incremental cues and nudges is a distinctly human-animal affair not easily or happily relegated to machine surrogates. Tags and hosts seem to require a looseness of fit in any case, as amplified further in the role of the voice as tag.

Tag Lines

Narration captions or speech balloons in comics and graphic novels are conspicuous as temporal tags. Before the advent of sound recording media, spoken words were depicted graphically as scrolls, ribbons, or blocks of text loosely attached to the speaker, as commonly seen in stained-glass windows or woodcuts incorporating dialogue from plays or religious texts.[9] Intertitles in silent movies and subtitles in foreign language films continue this tradition. Text messaging and Twitter feeds are variants of the short textual tag.

According to certain commentators the voice has this supplementary, transient character anyway, different from the substance of the host to which it is attached.[10] As discussed in the introduction to this book, the dominance of the visual tradition in modernity presents sound as a supplement to vision. It seems that tags provide an important way of giving visual expression to the voice and to sound.

Telephone users are accustomed to depositing and retrieving time-stamped recorded messages via voicemail or automated answering systems. The term *voice tag* is often assigned to commands or key words that can be picked up by automated voice-recognition technology. Many computers and smartphones have this software built in and can be instructed to respond to your voice, and to open and close files and windows, activate a call from your address book, and perform other operations. There are telephone services that respond automatically, though in a constrained way, to spoken requests. The usual paraphernalia of personal organization, to-do lists, diaries, calendars, memos, and email come with the capability to accept spoken input. Thus events and other data can be tagged with voice messages. These spoken tags can also be converted automatically to text. Voices return to the textual tag.

The nomenclature of the tag also borrows from the domain of publishing. Taglines are catchy phrases, titles, or slogans, often produced as part of an advertising campaign, which turn readily into clichés. Some taglines are so familiar that they lend themselves to distortion while still retaining the connotations of the original. Such derived taglines are sometimes called "snowclones,"[11] and demonstrate the metaphorical, loose-fitting, and contingent side of taglines. Snowclones should not need to be explained, and if the cultural reference is missed then the phrase still carries some cachet: "Vinyl is the new black," "The virtual taxman cometh," "All the world's a tag." There are websites dedicated to such tropes,[12] which clearly evolve and change. The point here is that the more firmly a community adopts certain literary taglines, the more readily the taglines are adapted. Taglines reference other taglines. Place names get similarly adapted and corrupted, such as naming a corner of a housing estate "Red Square,"[13] and other neologisms. Taglines feature as design elements in websites and in cell phone text messages.

Tags are inconspicuous but can communicate power. Switching a label can bring about a substantial change or at least can be complicit in tipping a situation from one state to another. Such is the power of a new slogan or tagline: "Workers of the world unite," "A house is a machine for living," "Change we need."[14] Such slogans are the thin end of a metaphor, or a shift in metaphor—a complex, indeterminate, and contingent perceptual structure or paradigm. People seeking to influence others hope that the humble tag will trigger a major shift in public opinion and behavior. Where they occur, such tag-induced changes result from the complex of human practices already in train. In this sense, tags provide a means of mobilizing human action and mutual forces of persuasion and influence already present in communities. Pushing this proposition to its extreme, tags imbue the formulation of substantive policies, the complex designs of structures and networks. Tags run all the way through design, as a manifestation of the tuning function.

Parasites

It seems that computer programs and databases are populated by incidental, redundant, and superfluous bits of code that are not always benign, sometimes operating as so-called *computer viruses* and *malware* propagated deliberately through networks. The philosopher Michel Serres provides an extended treatment of parasitism as an allegory for the social relationship between the host and the guest, the gift giver and the recipient, major interests and minority groups, production and consumption.[15] In the remainder of this chapter I will attempt to recruit Serres's position to align the incidental tag with the parasite. His basic proposition is that the terms *host* and *guest* are in various senses interchangeable. He alludes to the riskiness of his project: "It might be dangerous not to decide who is the host and who is the guest, who gives and who receives, who is the parasite and who is the *table d'hôte*, who has the gift and who has the loss, and where hostility begins with hospitality."[16] Concepts of parasitism reinforce again the role of the small element in influencing the whole, the small increment that aligns or maligns the tuning of place. As bloggers Joseph Weissman and Taylor Adkins ask in their account of Serre's work: "How much (r)evolutionary capability are we going to assign to minor elements—to parasites, tiny fluctuations, minimal differences?"[17]

The link between parasitism and ubiquitous computing has not escaped theorists of embodiment. For example, Rolf Pfeifer and Josh Bongard note that cell phones "are parasitic on humans for moving about and do not need their own locomotion system. . . . Phones exploit their users by hitching a lift with them!"[18] They argue that this affiliation between phone and human carrier typifies the symbiotic relationship between humans and machines.

Standard biology texts describe the parasite as a smaller organism or colony of organisms that feeds on a larger host. Some parasites keep other parasites under control so as not to overwhelm the host, which may in turn be parasitic on other creatures. Animals higher up the food chain may suffer from parasites that carry other organisms from one host to the next. Some parasites are visible as appendages, hanging from or clamped to their hosts: leeches, for example, and barnacles. Some parasites are like so many tags attached to the bulk of their host, having to go where the host goes, fixed at one point and vulnerable to external forces, be it rain, wind, or current. Parasites are complicit in both benign and malevolent intermingling. In the words of the poet John Donne: "It suck'd me first, and now sucks thee, And in this flea our two bloods mingled be."[19] Parasites are complicit in mingling the attributes of one host with another.

Thus tags can be thought of as parasites, moving from host to host, having no merit other than what they extract from their host or transmit between hosts. As well as the obvious example of computer viruses, digital tags sometimes display this opportunistic character. A luggage tag is useless without the luggage it is attached to. But then sometimes the surrogate becomes the thing it represents or tags. The digital avatar is a case in point, assuming the characteristics of and becoming synonymous with its host.[20] The capacity of the tag to exceed its role presents as a kind of parasitism, for example, by assuming greater significance than the host, by stealing the limelight, by swapping positions to take the one more powerful.

Logos—such as the familiar Microsoft, Apple, Lacoste, and Nike symbols—are a kind of tag and seem to participate in these parasitic processes. Cultural critic Naomi Klein says of clothing labels, "logos have grown so dominant that they have essentially transformed the clothing on which they appear into empty carriers for the brands they represent."[21] She goes on to describe this as a literal consumption, thinking of the Lacoste label in particular: "The metaphorical alligator, in other words, has risen up and swallowed the literal shirt."[22] This crossover of functions is not uncommon as reflective consumers think of how the symbol exceeds the thing symbolized, which has often enough been said of money, the value of which sometimes increases beyond what it is supposed to represent: hinting at the acquisition of money for its own sake.[23] To the extent that economists and critics identify credit notes and IOUs as causal elements in economic recession, they are perhaps complaining about the overvaluation of tags,[24] with the parasitic tag displacing the host.

Protestors who desecrate or hack brand symbols are practitioners of the art of culture jamming or *déteurnement*, forays into parasitism. For Klein: "The most sophisticated culture jams are not stand-alone parodies but interceptions—counter-messages that hack into a corporation's own method of communication to send a message starkly at odds with the one that was intended." This is a process that forces the target company to pay to have the intrusion ejected, in other words the company has to "foot the bill for its own subversion."[25] Of course, ad campaigners also play on the culture of subversion: "there are no rebels who cannot be tamed with an ad campaign or by a street promoter who *really speaks to them*."[26] The old campaign by Apple that aligns the brand with the relaxed, slightly subversive creative innovator against the corporate, distant Microsoft user trades in such ambiguities, especially in light of Microsoft's fightback campaign. The culture jammer as parasite becomes the host to corporatism.

Continuing the organic metaphors, many organisms "advertise" themselves through colorful tails, extended plumage, and conspicuous appendages. Such spectacular accessories have little function other than as a lure, distraction, or decoy for prey, a mate, or to initiate a parasitic relationship with a host. Here the tag does little more than call attention to its main object. The lure flashes and flickers, and is effective because most organisms are better adapted to detect movement than stasis in the visual field. Savvy website developers now apply judicious visual advertising ploys, including the insertion of high production value videos in neat rectangles into web pages, aloof from the rest of the page content, perhaps with some interaction and a link to further advertising content. Here advertisements bear something of the character of the tag as lure.

As lures, tags may also invite attention to themselves and invoke more curiosity than the host to which they are attached. A tag may make the host more interesting than it would be otherwise. Tagging something with a ribbon, flag, or other fluttering attachment generally draws it to the attention of otherwise indifferent passersby. A tag on something seems to indicate significance and attaches value, suggesting that the tagged object has been through a process, approved, legitimated as an object of concern. It also shows that the object has a place: it fits within a schema, and it is linked. In our digital media classes we often conduct an exercise requiring students to create an animated computer model of a found object, a piece of junk to be displayed in a museum. To help the student take seriously the arbitrary piece of circuit board, broken arm of a toy, or pinecone found on the ground, we attach a specimen label to it. Almost anything assumes value if it is tagged appropriately. Not only can the tag add interest, it also can excite interest by virtue of the relationships that it sets in play. One of the tricks of social network sites is to ensure that pages look busy, in use, and visited even if the owners of the pages do not regularly attend to, edit, or update them. There are automatic processes in play by which pages get updated with messages, invitations, images, and applications. Tags that link the website to people, events, and places seem to indicate connectedness and engage the viewer. Social websites are animated by such subtle forms of subterfuge, with arrays of tags and links to sites with which they are in parasitical relationships.

Tagging on social websites attracts attention and curiosity: what key words have people used to label this image, sound, video, or blog, and why? Sites such as de.licio.us publish lists of the most commonly used tag terms. Tagging encourages web users to know more. The artist Yoko Ono is fond of inserting what she terms "wishing trees" in galleries and other places of significance.[27] Following various ancient traditions, people are invited to write a wish onto a paper tag and attach it to the tree. There are always those who are drawn to the task, who will attach their own tag wish, and there will be some who read them. Tags draw attention as much by requiring close attention as by their flickering allure, or their effect en masse. You want to zoom in to the tag. I recall visiting such a wishing tree and reading tags at random, one of which invoked a death wish on the artist. The tag as parasite sometimes turns round to bite the artist.

Mistagging

In computer programming, a common and fatal cause of error occurs where pointers are directed to incorrect storage locations. Indexicals become dysfunctional when they point to objects other than their usual referent, as when an inhabitant of a computer game switches avatars, deliberately confuses who the avatar is standing in for, or has to manage multiple identities. Away from computer games, identity theft constitutes a kind of illegal trade in indexicals and tags.[28] Similar to the confusion that arises when labels are moved around at a banquet table or pathology laboratory, a host or lab technician will readily equate mistagging with the introduction of chaos.

Through error, malice, or adventure, the switching of labels provides a primary means of subverting the order of things, of changing a condition from one state to another. That tags can be portable already invites disruption. But then perhaps tags are primarily illusory, misleading, or even deceptive. They are a way of securing a false sense of order. Given that the world does not come pre-tagged, that language is more than fixing names to things, then attaching tags to hosts presents as provisional, contingent, and problematic. Tagging, like language in general, can be a mischievous process, participating in Plato's denigration of speech as an exercise in "trickiness."[29] Pervasive digital media that depend on the proliferation of tags serve to amplify this tendency to deceive, with cunning and tactical ambiguity.

Tagging inherits the mischief endemic to various linguistic tropes, such as metonymy. A metonym is a small or incidental aspect of a thing that tends to stand in for the whole, as when blue-collar workers talk of "the suits" when they mean the company executives, or customers offer to pay with "plastic" when they mean a credit card. Metonymy constitutes a play on the trivial, treating the minor as if it were major. Tags as metonyms become their hosts. Login names, aliases, avatars, and links become the objects ahead of the things they point to. Tags are meant to be inconsequential in themselves; the significance lies in what they mark. But then the tag can become the thing.

Insofar as tags are also lures, they have the capacity to deceive as if insubstantial and transient flashes of light and sound, or an insincere touch. As decoys,[30] tags are common in the hunt, in war, courtship, and digital communications. Tags can lure and distract by pointing to something other than their usual referent, or by being mistaken for their referent. In his work on mimesis, Roger Caillois attends to the nature of transient seductions, recounting the cunning way insects use mimicry to lure prey and repel predators.[31] Darwin maintained that deception is part of the "natural order," and has a sonic manifestation. He speculated on the vocal ability of monkeys to impersonate approaching predators as a warning to the rest of the group.[32] Ethologists Naguib and Wiley show how certain animal species are capable of mimicking their own sounds as if made a long way off, to buy time when encroaching on a neighbor's territory.[33] Ruse, deception, seduction, and parasitism are written into the natural order, and also constitute the surreptitious aspects of ubiquitous devices, not least as attributes with which or against which to design.

All these material and contingent properties and peculiarities indicate the importance of tags, as devices or tools, and as metaphors for ubiquitous digital media. As argued in the previous chapter, rather than emulating human cognition the tag is an adjunct to thought processes and is instrumental in moves to adjust the environment by small-scale temporal interventions. The way designers think about tags can reflect back and inform their views of the technologies that perpetuate them: smart phones, digital cameras, websites, the panoply of ubiquitous digital media. The digital tag is complicit in a series of adjustments by which people refine their social interactions. Attending to the materiality of the tag highlights further the place of tags in the repertoire of measures by which people tweak and tune their environments.

Commonplace

8 Tactics

How do mobile technologies affect the way people position themselves and their artifacts?[1] Not all movement involves navigation, but focusing on how people find their way around highlights the issue of space and sociability. In this chapter I will explore how navigation is a social practice rather than an individual, private process. Movement through space is also opportunistic—often drawing on arbitrary reference points, cues from the environment, and devices to hand—and is therefore tactical as well. Tactics for moving about amplify the role of mobile media in exploiting the small increment and tuning place.

Operational Practices

Many developments in communications technologies entail successive improvements in speed and accuracy.[2] Historians and critics of technology offer similar accounts of the instantaneity and precision of transportation and technologies of navigation.[3] Improvements in speed and accuracy mean that many operational practices, processes, and procedures, such as calibrating and operating navigational equipment, are invisible or unnecessary. Only specialists or enthusiasts need think about how GPS signals convert to a point on a map indicating where one is located.[4]

Communications technologies provide obvious examples of the occlusion of certain operational practices. Couriers traveling to outer reaches of an ancient empire by foot or on horseback would convey important letters to distant governors. The courier might well have known the content of the message. The Roman historian Tacitus recounts how "panic-stricken couriers" brought to Fabius Valens the news of the threat to the province of Narbonese Gaul.[5] Such was the integration of message, messenger, sender, and recipient that couriers were attacked for bearing bad news.[6] Increasing automation in postal services today conflates processes of transmission, processes largely invisible to consumers, who have their own local operational practices. In the office and at home the consumer might have to locate stamps, organize paper copy and envelopes, and schedule the day to accommodate mail collection and delivery, queue at the post office, or employ others to carry out these operations. It is not that communications processes become seamless, but rather that the seams move about. Over time, the consumers of postal services have directed their attention other than to the means of transmission.

The processes of transmission are mostly invisible to users of email, SMS (the text-based Small Message Service via cell phone) and MMS (the Multimedia Messaging Service for exchanging photographs), which invoke local operational practices that differ from regular mail services.[7] Enthusiasts for new technologies are often known as "early adopters."[8] In the early days of the Internet, many users were interested in the way email was routed, how the packet-switching protocol worked, and who controlled the networks. They may even have monitored the flow of Internet traffic. Users of email now probably think more about organizing, filtering, deleting, synchronizing, and archiving an ever-growing flood of correspondence in multiple mail accounts and mail-handling programs than they concern themselves with how the messages get through. The target of concern changes and new tactics emerge, as in the case of text messaging via cell phone. Whereas the Roman correspondent might have had to assess the reliability of the courier, organize bribes, and plan for the long wait before a reply, contemporary cell phone users apply themselves to the problem of when to switch on predictive text to help with spelling. Users have also developed strategic linguistic practices, in the form of abbreviations, to minimize the effort of keying words into a small handheld device. These practices constitute improvised tactics by which workers survive, and some thrive, in the world of rapid communications, but worrying about the transmission protocols by which the message gets from sender to receiver is not usually part of their plan.

Navigation provides a similar story of changes in operational practices and a redirection of effort, of which J. E. D. Williams gives a helpful account in the book *From Sails to Satellites*.[9] Early navigators rarely had difficulty working out their general direction of travel. Before the compass was invented there were cues from the position of the sun, moon, and stars, as well as wind directions.[10] Travelers also had reliable means of calculating the distance of travel from the north and south. As travelers move toward the equator, the sun appears higher in the sky at noon. The rate at which it climbs in the sky over a succession of days can be correlated with distance, and hence position. As well as the sun, the relatively constant centers about which the sky rotates—the North Star in the northern hemisphere and the South Celestial Pole in the south—provide further references for calculating latitude. The calculation of where you are in terms of longitude, the grid lines of the earth's coordinate system that run north-south, are a different matter and require accurate clocks to determine time equivalence for relative positions in the directions of east and west. By most accounts, the story of navigation is a saga of the quest for accuracy in calculating longitude, especially at sea.[11]

Navigational practices had to fit the contingencies of life on the move. Williams notes how the techniques of astronomy and mathematics provided little benefit to fifteenth- and sixteenth-century sea explorers. Such procedures were beyond the abilities of many seamen. The records show that even Christopher Columbus was "greatly in error" and didn't understand how to interpret his readings.[12] Navigational practices had to account for conditions at sea, the types of provisions and supplies carried on board a vessel that pitched and yawed, the differences between nighttime and daytime conditions, the occlusion of stars and horizon by cloud and haze, the difficulty of looking at the sun with the naked eye to get a bearing, and the aptitude of seafarers in measurement and calculation. It is the case now, as it was for the early explorers, that navigation requires a repertoire of methods and tactics, including the default strategy of "dead reckoning," which involved setting off in the right direction, as decided from a map, and calculating position based on speed of travel and allowances for wind direction and wind changes.[13]

Anyone educated in the history of exploration knows that the sky provided the most useful datum for calculating position. Visible celestial bodies move across the sky on trajectories that can be predicted from tables or calculations made on the fly. At any moment, every celestial body is positioned precisely overhead at some point or other on the surface of the earth. The North Star will always be above the North Pole (the point at which all longitude lines meet). The sun, moon, planets, and stars move in predictable patterns that can be observed and determined from calculation. The development of increasingly sophisticated models of celestial orbits, methods of observation, correction, tabulation, printing, publication, and distribution converged on the production in 1767 of the first reliable tables of celestial positions by His Majesty's Nautical Almanac Office in the UK. Along with the US Naval Observatory this organization now publishes nautical almanacs showing the latitudes and longitudes of key celestial bodies at regular intervals, past, present, and future. These positions are also published or fed as instantaneous calculations to websites and through other electronic media.[14]

Nautical almanacs can be used in several ways to determine location. The simplest is to measure the angle of two or more celestial bodies above the horizon, using a sextant or quadrant.[15] Subtract this angle from 90 degrees to give the angle from the vertical. This angle tells how many degrees distant you are from the position on the almanac for the celestial body under observation for that particular time. Latitudes and longitudes on maps are also angular positions. If at the moment Venus appears 30 degrees from the vertical, then that angle is also a distance in degrees on a longitude line passing through the almanac position; in other words, it provides a radius. My boat must be somewhere on the circumference of a circle scribed onto the surface of a globe with the latitude and longitude of Venus marked as its center. If I can do the same for other visible planets or stars in the almanac, then my position will be the point at which two or more circles intersect.

In his detailed account of navigational practices, ethnographer Edwin Hutchins shows how the deployment of such methods is a highly collaborative exercise, involving teams of people with special skills (quartermaster, lookout, helmsman, pilot) observing, measuring, corroborating, and cross-checking. Complex technosocial practices combined evidence from the sky with data from astrolabes, quadrants, line logs, clocks, charts, and almanacs to converge on a determination of a ship's position and direction of travel. In practice, the procedures might be difficult on paper, but nowadays, thanks to onboard computers navigation can be accomplished with a modicum of training. With the introduction of satellite navigation (Sat Nav and the use of GPS), the navigator of a modern sailing vessel accomplishes in seconds what in the past might have taken hours of observation, calculation, charting, and cross-checking. Of course, older operational practices survive as backup and linger in the terminology. Some procedures are retained in the tactics of sole adventurers or deployed as a last resort in a crisis. Some practices, such as sniffing the wind or tipping log lines into the water, are rendered obsolete by new technologies and practices. This foray into navigational practices confirms the dependence of humans on fine-tuning their relationships to one another and to the spaces in which they move.

Arcane Practices

Humans are rarely content to leave the control or navigation of their environment to machines, and are not averse to tweaking, fiddling, and intervening to exercise genuine, vicarious, or imagined command over machines. Many contemporary technophiles still wish to retain the vestiges of machinic fine-tuning, adjustment, and control.

Though their operations may elude the contemporary traveler, navigational technologies that predate electronic communications involve practices and processes that would have been relatively transparent to sailors and navigators in their day. Even now, such older technologies present as comprehensible, even if not fully understood by the layperson. Some enthusiasts retain an intrigue with earlier, apparently transparent embodied processes and technologies, and seek to continue them, or retain memories of them. Ignorance can fuel the technoromance, as if knowing these archaic and arcane practices might draw the adventurous and intrepid into a world of secrets, which perhaps explains the perpetual romance with procedures and processes in computer games, science fiction, fantasy films, and the romance with Victorian machinery of steampunk devotees.[16] It is not enough that a technician of a science-fictional future taps a screen or presses a button on a control panel, but the elements on the screen have to move, lights flash, gauges spring into action, and sounds emerge as if the operator is going through a process of consequence. Such archaic references persist in computer interaction design, with menus and windows on screen that operate like roller shutters, or time-lapse films of flower petals, as in the case of the iris shutter effect on the iPhone camera. Clever interaction design typically makes reference to appropriate previous technologies, metaphors, mnemonics, and usability, but also to technoromance.[17] Handheld navigation devices that indicate the traveler's position with a mobile blue navigation beacon or concentric circles pulsing along a map nod in the direction of former locational technologies, such as navigation buoys and radar.

Contemporary artists, designers, and activists may seek deliberately to expose the otherwise occluded components of a technology.[18] The early days of wireless networking saw an interest in mapping the contours of Wi-Fi reception. Wi-Fi became emblematic of public accessibility, and before rigorous security protocols were instituted savvy operatives could free ride on other subscribers' networks. The codes of Wi-Fi operation constituted a medium and language for creative exploration and social commentary. Wi-Fi was new, relatively transparent, potentially subversive, or able to be used tactically, with practices and legislation trailing behind. *The Free Network Visible Network* project, for example, advocated free access to networks while implementing "actions in the urban landscape as a way to create new meanings in the public domain."[19]

Retaining, exposing, and monitoring operational practices provide practical benefits, not least to enhance people's confidence in technological and organizational processes. Putting a letter in the mailbox yourself enhances the sense that you are contributing to its safe delivery. Some smart ecommerce applications tap into this desire to engage with operational practices. Such is the case with online sales where you track the progress of purchases from the warehouse to home. Announcements in planes and trains indicating the causes of delays, the speed of travel, the approach to one's destination, and dynamic maps charting progress serve to enhance the traveler's engagement with the travel experience, albeit remotely, and on a voluntary basis. Within reason, many travelers would like to know what is going on, to be aware that others in charge of the journey are informed, or that crucial information is available if passengers want it. Sometimes passengers are reassured simply knowing that someone cares enough to keep them informed.

The revision history in Wikipedia fulfils a similar role to travel announcements and journey charts. Academics have criticized this collaboratively constructed online encyclopedia as unreliable and too easy to corrupt with spurious information.[20] But it is not only the authority of the encyclopedic entry and the cross-referencing that decide the net surfer's level of confidence, but also the trace of the process. Anyone can access the revision history of a Wikipedia entry. In the case of transportation, there will be those who want to probe the progress of the journey. In a similar manner there will be those who want to probe the journey of the encyclopedia entry, the story of how it was constructed. In any case, scholars rarely rely on just one Internet source. It is a simple matter to cross-check with other sources listed as alternatives in a web search. Knowledge that enthusiasts can carry out such checking procedures might at least decrease the likelihood or longevity of rogue information. Thus there are varieties of practices and procedures by which communities of users activate trust in technological processes and navigate their way through space and information.

Designers might also revive and amplify operational practices, whether current or archaic, treating them as alien encounters that are disclosive of the context or phenomenon under study. Architectural design teachers are fond of encouraging in students an appreciation of operational practices. If, for example, students are to design a building for the food processing quarter of Cadiz in southern Spain, they might be encouraged to investigate processes of salt production, historic and contemporary. This is not only an expression of sensitivity to heritage, but also an encounter with a technology removed from that of building, which somehow intersects with it and informs the design process. A study of navigation practices might similarly inform computerized interaction design, or the design of spaces for ubiquitous digital media. Interaction designers might similarly invoke understandings of contemporary navigational technologies to inform the design of pervasive devices and the spaces they serve and create.

Location Aware

Digital processing supports many methods of determining location,[21] with GPS currently the most prominent. GPS provokes interest in what it can achieve and what its widespread use implies. The fixing of a GPS position is still a conspicuous process, though faster and more reliable computation, data transfer, and smarter interaction design will probably render GPS operational processes invisible and more ubiquitous in time. Increasingly, GPS and other locational technologies are being incorporated into pervasive devices to render them "location aware" without us even noticing. Data is stored (tagged) with locational information. In addition to text browsing through hyperlinks, researchers are able to sift through information according to where it is located or to which places it applies—a kind of "geobrowsing."[22]

The move of GPS into the public realm is emblematic of ubiquitous media and late modernity. Combined with remote sensing and satellite imagery[23] available from services such as WMS (Web Map Service) and WFS (Web Feature Service),[24] GPS further promotes in an obvious way Heidegger's "world picture"[25]: "a domain given over to measuring and executing, for the purpose of gaining mastery over that which is as a whole."[26] Interlaced world maps and imagery that can be observed at any scale combine with publicly available GPS to allow anyone to locate themselves in coordinate space via smartphone, cell phone, digital camera, and other handheld devices. Researcher Arnold Sharl summarizes the condition: "Geobrowsers promote the 'planet' metaphor by providing users with an accurate visual representation and allowing them to browse geospatial data from a satellite perspective."[27] Such ubiquitous mapping seems to test people's faith in the world picture. The proliferation of folksy and personal participant observations, reviews, and interventions attached to online digital maps brings the pretensions of the putative world picture down to earth.

GPS highlights society's difficulty in balancing security with hypersurveillance. The prospect of knowing everyone's location supplements the world picture and adds to people's anxieties. GPS is also at a stage where an understanding of its operations highlights shortcomings and discrepancies in attempts to determine a global picture. Developers put substantial effort into ameliorating error, and processes by which corrections are made feature prominently in any textbook on GPS. Product reviews and blogs by GPS users highlight further the importance and awareness of GPS error correction. GPS is supported by the Global Navigation Satellite System (GNSS). Selective availability (SA) is the feature introduced into the GNSS to degrade the accuracy of civilian GPS and reserve accurate readings for military use. May 1, 2000 features prominently in GPS lore as the date when selective availability was "turned off," giving ordinary civilians access to high-resolution GPS.

The results of errors in navigation are often obvious and carry conspicuous and dire consequences, as in the case of Columbus's apparent miscalculations in reaching America. There is also the case of the Korean airliner shot down in 1987 when it strayed over Soviet airspace, its journey apparently compounding an initial error of a few feet. At the time there was no suitable means of cross-checking navigation data in flight by which the error might have been corrected.[28] Travelers become aware of navigational error as they cross-reference to other methods of ascertaining location, not least visual identification. Navigation amplifies discrepancy, destabilizing our usual satisfaction with approximate regularity and certainty. Apart from human error, precision navigation highlights that non-uniformities exist in the gravitational field around the Earth, the ionosphere slows the transmission of radio waves in ways that are not constant, continents drift apart up to 10 cm per year, and the earth is about 42 km wider at the equator than it is at the poles. The variability of sea level and other matters of detail loom large when trying to fix a position from orbiting transmitters positioned 20,200 km above the Earth's surface. These features, well known to geologists and other specialists, are brought to bear on a technology that purports to tell you, the individual, where you are in your car or on the street. If society is moving closer to a totalizing world picture then GPS highlights how delicate that picture is. There seem to be no limits to our pursuit of precision, which takes ever-increasing degrees of technological sophistication to achieve. As with many modes of scientific and engineering representation, the quest for precision results in an infinite regress. The uncompromising navigator, cartographer, or surveyor is never satisfied. The acceptance and amelioration of error, imprecision, and concomitant risks are there to be managed and factored into certain navigational operations.

As well as taxing the limits of the world picture, GPS exercises our taste for the technological sublime. The GNSS is one of the great megastructures. It arrays devices at about the largest scale human beings can deal with, in outer space, and at the most local scale, that of the personal mobile device.[29] GPS satellite navigation operates as a giant machine, with components positioned in a sphere of radius of over 26,000 kilometers (sliced by approximately six virtual wheels centered on the Earth's core), distributed and coordinated in orbit around the Earth, and involving control stations on the ground, synchronized atomic clocks, and vast communications networks. (The GNSS is eclipsed in scale only by the so-called "Interplanetary Internet."[30])

In its scale, scope, claims, and conceits, GPS connects with our ontology. It deals in the matter of positioning, addressing a primordial concern with where people are, which in turn touches on who they are. The traveler's experience of positioning arguably feeds concepts of an independent physical reality, further amplified by GPS. GPS is arguably a highly technological response to the desire to orient ourselves: "thrownness" or "being–in-the-world" in Heidegger's terms. Orientation in the world relates to human practices of pointing, positioning, placing, connecting, naming, and tagging. Positioning is a convenient architectural metaphor, alluded to in Vitruvius's accounts of the primary architectural moment, the placement of the pole or gnomon into the ground that forms the center of a circle and defines the orientation of the city[31] and its relationship with the sun, the winds, and the constellations. Positioning presents as an assertion, as staking out, defining, orienting, and grounding. In this GPS is an audacious move, supplanting the constellations and transposing the operations of social practices and sacred geometries to overtly instrumental ends. As well as amplifying our sense of an independent reality, through its scale and hegemony GPS illuminates the issues of error and imprecision by working with and exploiting temporal discrepancies and corrections.

Getting a Fix

In chapter 6 I discussed fixing coordinates to objects as a tagging operation. Here I will examine what the processes by which the fix is derived reveal about pervasive media.

GPS involves a series of procedures that supply a receiver on the ground or in the air with a positional fix in terms of coordinates relative to the Earth's reference frame (latitude, longitude, and altitude). GPS deploys signals broadcast from a fleet of satellites orbiting the earth on known trajectories. GPS positioning deploys synchronized clocks located on satellites and on receiving devices. A satellite emits a signal according to regular codes that are then picked up by the receiver. The receiving device is busy playing its own version of the same signal. The inevitable microsecond delay between the satellite signal and the device signal provides a means of calculating the distance to the satellite. The device contains information on the satellite's position relative to the Earth's reference frame. The position of the satellites is contained in an almanac (ephemeris data) stored in the receiver that is updated periodically via satellite signals.[32] Knowing the distance from four or more objects with known positions is sufficient to secure a fix, within a certain range of accuracy, through quadrilateration.[33] Specialized handheld GPS devices commonly come with instructional guides explaining these processes. A user's engagement with these automated processes entails certain navigational and other operational practices, many of which deal with the issue of accuracy.

The GPS device, therefore, is fed with a model of the position of the moving satellites and can compute their position relative to the Earth's reference frame at any moment. The momentary configuration of satellites constitutes a constellation of about twenty-two known positional points surrounding a volume of space that contains the Earth and its surrounding void. Signals from most of the satellites are blocked by the planet itself.[34] As long as you stay in the same location, a reading a few minutes later will bring a different configuration of satellites into view, and the software's judicious calculation can increase the accuracy of the fix. For a device that is stationary relative to the Earth's reference frame, a succession of readings can improve further the accuracy of the locational reading. Additional readings supply more points from which to quadrilaterate.

There are interesting similarities and differences between celestial navigation (in other words, navigation by viewing the stars) and GPS. The celestial bodies are where you find them, but GPS satellites have been planted in the sky in known and controlled configurations on orbital planes. Taking a fix from stars requires that you are able to observe their positions in the sky as an angle: the angle above the horizon and the angle from north. You cannot see satellites, as you can the stars, and measuring the angle of a satellite in the sky is too cumbersome a process for handheld devices. Satellite navigation works with calculations of distance.[35] Navigation by the stars and GPS both depend on almanacs of the positions of objects in the sky.

Because handheld GPS devices are not able to provide information on the angle of view to a satellite, their accuracy resides in the calculation of distance. It is worth reflecting briefly on this process to tease out the role of discrepancy. A satellite emits a pulsing signal that can be picked up by any GPS receiver. The device has its own signal that is configured to replicate the coded pulse sequence of each of the orbiting satellites. The device and the satellite are calibrated, and periodically recalibrated, such that they run the sequence at precisely the same time. Were the device and the satellite in the same room, they would be in perfect synchrony. Move the satellite 20,000 km away and there will be a slight discrepancy in the signal as received and the signal as generated in the device, registered as a time delay. The device measures this delay. The delay multiplied by the speed of travel of radio waves is the distance between the satellite and the device.[36] The calculation of this time delay is crucial for accurate GPS positioning, a process hampered by blocking from buildings and landforms, refraction and reflection of signals, conditions in the ionosphere, and errors and noise in the device. It can also take time to get a reliable fix, tuning into signals and waiting for up-to-date almanac (ephemeris) information to download.

Information derived from satellite positions is often augmented by data from cell phone base stations (towers) that do some of the hard work in relaying information from the satellite, such as the almanac of satellite positions. Cell phone base stations are of fixed known coordinates. Any discrepancy with what the GPS might be delivering can be used to send correction information to the GPS-enabled phone. The GPS position can also be checked against coordinates derived from triangulation or quadrilateration with cell base stations. Cell phone signals provide a good estimate of distance from base stations.

In chapter 2, I noted how small discrepancies in the positioning of two identical overlaid grids or sets of parallel lines are amplified as a series of moiré patterns. For overlapping patterns of concentric circles these interference patterns are configured as parabolic curves. If the patterns are moved slightly in relation to each other, the parabolic curves move dramatically. Small differences have large effects, a feature exploited in calculations from the tiny phase differences in the transmission of radio waves. There are several methods for calculating distance from a radio transmitter (such as a cell phone base station). The most interesting and accurate is multilateration, or hyperbolic positioning. A cell phone transmits its signal in all directions at once in concentric circles. Two cell phone base stations located a few hundred meters apart receive the same signal from the same phone, but with a time difference of a fraction of a microsecond. The points within the range of the two base stations at which that particular time difference could be detected will lie on a surface shaped like a three-dimensional hyperbolic paraboloid, in other words, a dish-shaped *hyperboloid*.[37] The shape of these hyperboloids can be derived from formulas and basic trigonometry. The parameters that determine its shape are the distance between the two base stations, which is known, and the time difference, translated to a ratio of the distance between the two base stations. If the time difference were zero, the hyperboloid would in fact be a flat surface perpendicular to a line joining the base stations. The introduction of a third base station generates another series of time differences and two further hyperboloids. These hyperboloids will intersect one another and, barring errors and noise, determine that the emitting source must be located somewhere along a single curved line in space. Information generated by the presence of a fourth base station, or some assumptions about the ground plane, fixes the location of the phone source in three-dimensional space. Readings at other base stations in the vicinity can be deployed to further increase the accuracy of the positioning. A similar process applies if the phone is the device making use of signals from base stations, in which case the phone detects phase differences between identical signals generated by nearby base stations. The time difference from transmitting signals of precisely the same frequency produces an interference pattern, where the shape of the interferences follows the hyperboloids, analogous to the moiré patterns formed by overlapping plates of concentric circles.

The calculation of distance therefore relies on the geometries of interference. The effects of small differences are amplified to calculate distances, and the discrepancies between distance calculations are ameliorated by multitudes of readings, which effectively home in on a fix. The pursuit of an accurate fix does not necessarily follow a simple linear trajectory to greater and greater accuracy. Extraneous factors enter into the calculations. The processes are palpable when looking at a screen-based map displaying a positional fix in real time, and the estimated position floats around on the screen, as if the device is moving about in space: at one moment the traveler appears to be twelve meters from her assumed position, then three meters to the north, then some distance to the west. There are GPS tracking services that enable you to see the position on a web-based map of your own or someone else's movements. The person being tracked may appear to be moving when in fact he is stationary.

Software designers who program GPS devices can control what happens to the data from the satellites and other media to secure a fix. The suppliers of GPS services compete to provide the most effective design of algorithms, interactions, and supplementation to enhance accuracy.[38] Essentially, GPS calculation involves iteration and equation solving to determine the volume created by four spherical surfaces that are supposed to intersect, ideally at a point. The data rarely comes in quickly or accurately enough to give a speedy and reliable fix on the ground. What the user might be aware of is an initial operation of locking onto signals, noticeable as a delay, an approximation, a search operation, and subsequent revision, with varying indications of the degree of accuracy. The early versions of publicly available handheld GPS devices presented coordinates on a small screen and perhaps derived information about direction of travel and speed. Such a device might also show a visual trace of where you had been, but with no map and only rudimentary reference points. The display of your return journey might erroneously show that you had returned to a point fifty meters away from where you knew you really were. Such drifts typified the inaccuracy of early, public GPS.

Some devices enhance the sense of engagement with GPS operations by plotting the position of the satellites across a map of the sky. Today a handheld device (for example, a smartphone or iPhone using Google Maps) might show its position as a blue dot on a full-color display of an aerial photograph complete with street names and land features. GPS for air, sea, and some land navigation will use specialized navigation maps. GPS for hill walking and trekking show Ordnance Survey map data. Clever interaction designers turn the complexity of fixing a location into an interesting and instructive visual operation, albeit simplified. In some devices the traveler sees a circle showing accuracy grow or recede, and the blue dot pulse and shift as if to catch up with your current location. Different symbols may be used to indicate whether the fix is being calculated from cell phone base stations or satellites. With vehicular-based Sat Nav (for satellite navigation), the graphic display is simplified for the driver, as a rudimentary perspective view of the road ahead, and interfaces with detailed information assembled from databases about roads, ramps, junctions, and traffic signs. The information is transmitted as vocal instructions guiding the driver to her preprogrammed destination.

GPS and other navigational technologies are in the public domain. Travelers can see where they are on a map on the handheld device or on a desktop or laptop computer screen. They can also map where they have been and where they intend to go. Custodians and parents can track the position of their children's cell phones to identify their locations. Drivers and passengers new to Sat Nav are bemused or disturbed by the insistent voice of the digital navigator and the indefatigable way the program attempts to direct you back on course if you willfully or accidentally deviate from the designated route.[39] Such are the emerging navigational practices invoked by GPS.

Walking

Navigation is opportunistic and tactical and accompanies technologies of long-distance travel on sea, land, and air. Contrary to highly technologized travel, the study of walking entails concepts of navigation and roaming as ordinary practices that increasingly draw on digital mobile devices. According to some commentators, what travelers really want is an efficient and safe means to get from A to B. Peter Morville expresses this objective in a book on how people find their way in the world of information: "Wayfinding remains an inefficient and even dangerous activity. At best, we waste time and endure needless stress. . . . After eons of bumbling around the planet, we're about to take navigation to a whole new level."[40] In his commentary on the emerging urban condition William Mitchell concurs that those with the resources can now travel very lightly: "with credit card and passport, some portable electronic equipment, and a carry-on bag; you can take full advantage of the world's highly developed network infrastructure to access whatever you want, wherever you may need it."[41] But walking is not only motivated by efficiency and access to information. Geographer Doreen Massey regards such discourses as transcendental narratives that persist in characterizing space in terms of distance, and distance as a constraint: "The constraint of distance, rather than, perhaps, the pleasure of movement or travel."[42]

Studies that philosopher and urbanist Jean-François Augoyard conducted prior to the existence of ubiquitous mobile devices expose the navigational practices of the pedestrian to detailed scrutiny.[43] Sometimes pedestrians want to get from A to B by the quickest and safest route, to attend a meeting, to cover ground, to see everything they want to see as in a museum, or to deliver or receive goods or information. But walking need not always be thought of as self-consciously intentional. In fact it is helpful to think that walking inheres in what it is to be human.[44] Occasionally walking is deflected to some purpose or other. Most of the time people are simply under the compulsion to walk, compelled by ambulatory practices, and walking connects them to their basic grounding as human beings. For Augoyard walking is a lot like talking: both are "fluid, prone to digressions, capable of forgetting what is apparently essential and of lingering over details."[45] As with language, the ordinariness of walking becomes a means of asserting one's presence, a "tactic of everyday life," a "mode of being."[46] Attending to walking is also instructive on the subject of mobile and ubiquitous media.

By this reading, day-to-day, habituated walking through the streets rarely is just an exercise in navigation. Rarely is it a process of covering all bases efficiently, as it might be for the person delivering the mail, for finding the right address, rushing to meetings, or keeping appointments. In terms of navigation, walking typically occupies the interstitial position of uncertainty, the refinement of the fix, or homing in. There is an interstitial component to navigation, and this is the process of finding those precise fixings or corrections, those maneuvers that get you back on course. Day-to-day walking has the character of the operational praxis of Hutchins's navigation team rather than that of moving from one known position to the next.[47]

In these respects, walking, roaming, and navigation are suggestive of the primacy of bodily movement, of mobility ahead of stasis, of evading the fix. According to Augoyard, in the modern era, as exemplified in Newton's theories, spatiality commonly assumed fixity, as if space is a static container, albeit of infinite extent. Contrary to the celebration of walking, the modernist tradition elevates the static pose, as indicated by the architect Le Corbusier's scheme of the "Modulor," "of the basic postures of everyday man (reclining, seated, standing)" according to Augoyard. Modernism, he states, presents "static architectural thought" as the norm. Augoyard claims his study of walking highlights gaits rather than postures: "a style and quality of movement." He proposes that cultural observers attend to pauses "rather than poses . . . and the characteristic possibility of stopping."[48] He joins with Deleuze and Guattari in displacing sedentary metaphors with concepts of nomadic wandering, drifting from one concrete situation to another without relying on maps of the whole.[49]

What is the character of walking? Taking a lead from Augoyard, walking involves stops and starts, backtracking, lingering and rushing; it is occasionally time limited or time filling, and frequently leisurely. It is easy to think of these as activities of the individual. Group many individual movements together and you get crowd behavior. As new media theorist Lev Manovich reminds us, the experience of the walker is "determined by his interaction with a group—even though it is a group of strangers" characterized by "an exchange of glances."[50] Expanding on Augoyard's account, by an alternative reading the motion resides with the crowd, from which individuals occasionally break away. Something similar has been said of conversation and thought.[51] Private introspection has the character of a conversation, and theorists posit that thinking is social before it is individual. Sociable beings are in conversation incessantly, and private thought requires that individuals imagine what they would usually do in company, or in breaking away from group conversation. The pervasive use of mobile phones suggests that absence from one's ken constitutes only a minor absence from conversation, readily restored by a phone call. So too, walking is a walking together, before it is walking alone. It is the tribe, the herd, the group, the mob that walks, a practice from which individuals break out from time to time for solitary ambulation, or to consort and flirt with members of a different clan.

Navigation can provide an excuse for and a focus of social activity. Two people can sometimes find their way better than two individuals alone, or at least they may find their way to a different place than either would alone. Navigation is negotiation before it is private, an aspect brought to light as the traveler reaches for her phone to warn of impending or late arrival or train delays, or to clarify navigational instructions. The sole navigator in any case is negotiating with mapmakers and the people who erect the street signs. GPS brings the developers of handheld navigation devices and the promoters of various sociotechnical legacies to the ship's bridge, the negotiating table, or the planning meeting.

Walking provides an opportunity to meet people. If you don't want to linger, people will assume you are rushing to get somewhere and are constrained by time. Walking with a companion establishes rhythms and punctuates the conversation in ways that are different from sitting at a table. Increasingly this sociability takes place over a mobile phone. Many nuances of social relations can be acted out in walking, such as lagging behind or requiring your companion to keep up. Walking is a way of offering or forcing hospitality. Walkers can take turns in the role of guide, pointing out items of interest, demonstrating local knowledge, using the sights and sounds of the street to illustrate points in an argument, using spaces to think with, getting caught up in the thought of the place. In some cultures people new to an area are not expected to walk unaccompanied. They need to be in the company of someone who is local, a personal guide. The guide is also someone in touch, phoning ahead, negotiating adjustments in the itinerary, and preparing the way.

Walking can of course be augmented by technologies, involving bus, train, taxi, ferry, car or bike pool, or private vehicle. Walking sometimes involves synchronization with schedules belonging to other modes of travel: will I be at the bus stop in time for the next bus? Walking can be provisional: will I catch the bus or keep walking? Walking blurs into the deployment of other personalized techniques for getting about: the use of wheelchairs, power-assisted personalized transportation devices, skateboards,[52] scooters, rollerblades, trainers with heel wheels, strollers, prams, bath chairs, shopping trolleys, and bags with wheels dragged along the footpath.

Walking features in the habitual, repetitive cycles of the day. The constitutional is a daily walk taken for health and wellbeing. Walking or running for exercise is generally conducted on a regular basis, and formal training for fitness conforms to routine, assisted in many cases by pedometers and other digital monitoring devices. People also use walking to break out of daily habits. The office worker might go for a stroll as relief from sitting at the desk.

People deploy media to extend or modify the sociable aspects of walking. People connect to the vicarious sociability of radio, podcasts, and media streaming of various kinds. Walkers use personal stereos to block out other people. The phenomenon whereby people indicate their desire to be left alone by keeping headphones or earpieces in place has been well documented.[53] Walking can also entail media production. Sketching and painting are rare and specialized activities, usually undertaken while sedentary, but the use of a camera and audio recording offer instant image capture while on the move.

Most walking involves leaving a trace of footsteps, dust, scratches, or litter. Pedestrians deliberately or inadvertently tag the environment with markers of various kinds. Individual walkers may leave negligible traces, but so many negligible footfalls in time wear a perceptible indentation in the stone treads of a staircase. Locational technologies provide increasing access to the traveler's trace, not least through the automated geotagging of digital photographs, trails on maps, and surveillance.

Artist Hasan Elahi has combined the trace with his own reaction to the menace of surveillance. In response to apparent mistaken identification by the FBI as a terrorist, and to advertise his innocence, he claims to provide a web record of his movements for all to see stretching back to 2002.[54] Surveillance turns walking into spectacle.

Everyday walking can contribute to the spectacle, the promenade. People walk to watch, to gather and combine sensations, as in the case of the bricoleur or the flaneur. Walking also enables the traveler to be there, to say he was present for some occasion, or encounter, to construct narratives, to form memories, and to revive memories. People walk to lose themselves. People walk to search, and even good citizens will seek to evade detection. Reports from early experiments with active or "smart badges" and other location-aware tagging indicate the propensity of workers within an organization to find dead spots where the signals can't be picked up, and to exchange badges with other workers or even attach them to pets for fun.[55] Such is the tactical resourcefulness of the contemporary flaneur. Walking provides a primary example of the exercise of tactics in everyday life, increasingly moderated and abetted by the presence of ubiquitous digital media.

Walking Nowhere

Do pervasive digital media diminish the pleasures and benefits of walking, uprooting human kind from its grounding in ambulatory practices? I argue that technologies of navigation, mapping, surveillance, tracking, and location awareness provide little threat to the formation and persistence of spaces with meaning. To address the issue it is helpful to examine the way walking encounters and even creates remaindered spaces, or so-called non-places.

Walking has a territorial aspect as a way of claiming the street, or reclaiming the street, of keeping pathways open by frequent use. Walking is also a way of avoiding spaces. As Augoyard asserts: "Tell me what you avoid, and I shall tell you what kind of inhabitant you are."[56] His studies hint at the existence of remaindered spaces: "These discontinuities exist only upon a background of absence, of 'blanks,' of 'holes,' as the inhabitants say."[57] The housing estate in Augoyard's study looks like a prime candidate for anthropologist Marc Augé's designated non-place.[58] Non-places are someone else's places, and visitors are there as if under sufferance, never knowing for sure if they are guilty of trespassing.[59] Aesthetically rich locations of interest from the point of view of heritage or tourism are dominated by issues of meaning and a "sense of place." Insofar as non-places are ordinary and uncelebrated, they provide an opportunity to think of walking as involving "the almost-nothing, the inconsequential dross of life."[60] Arguably GPS extends further Augé's characterization of non-places. Abetted by globalization, the world picture, rapid transportation, ubiquitous communications, and digital processing in general, GPS potentially renders alien earthbound human beings' cherished views of the heavens and place long embedded in sociocultural navigational practices and architectures.

But rather than look to advanced navigational and communications technologies as the perpetrators of remaindered places, non-places, I'll return to the humble tag of chapter 6. Interactions with pervasive media seem increasingly to rely on negotiations between how individuals are constituted in any particular circumstance and who they choose to be, and whether they want their identities visible or invisible. Badges feature prominently in the arsenal of tags to negotiate identity. As well as the smart badges I alluded to previously, the badge category can be expanded to include medals, badges of office, honor, and shame, and other signs bestowed and worn to indicate extraordinary affiliations within a community. The relationships between shame and guilt provide useful headings under which to consider badging. According to Bernard Williams, shame is manifested significantly as a desire for invisibility.[61] If only I could disappear from view I would be relieved of my sense of shame.[62] Avatars, digital tags, and other surrogates feature among the means available for dealing with such anonymity. The cloak of anonymity provides opportunities to engage in activities of which some people might be embarrassed, were they to be visible doing them. A tag also serves as a means of exposure. A badge of shame is a mark, stigma, or other public indication of activity conducted in private that would at least cause embarrassment if widely known. "Outing" someone in print or a blog attempts such branding and shaming. According to Williams, in contrast with shame, guilt is a condition in which people feel that even were they to remove themselves from the shameful circumstance then the guilt would go with them. For guilt is something people carry wherever they go. Guilt is a heavy kind of tag, an encumbrance that gets in the way, and a burden.

Shame and guilt have their correlates in walking. According to the *Oxford English Dictionary*, the phrase *walk of shame* has no particular historical grounding other than as recent college slang, but the allusion is clear: the actual or pretended desire to be invisible while returning home from some activity about which one may have some regrets. Walking that is encumbered by guilt suggests the stooping posture of John Bunyan's pilgrim[63] weighed down by the burden of his own wrongdoing.

It seems that environments can also place on hapless citizens the burden of guilt by virtue of their tags, labels, and signs. Think of encounters at the customs or security area at an airport, a place in which a traveler rarely feels at home, where posted signs suggest she is automatically under suspicion. Digital simulations amplify such encounters. To the extent that the Second Life online community presents as a series of immersive 3D spaces, it implements elaborate protocols to tell players and visitors where they may and may not go. Depending on how permissions are set by the "land owners," labeled barriers will appear around properties. In any case, spaces decked with clusters of signs advertising products and activities can appear to exclude as well as welcome the newcomer.

In everyday walking people encounter spaces that are conspicuously weighed down by signage, designed as if to accuse rather than inform: don't wait here, have your passport ready, this is a quiet zone, no entry. The charge of trespass and violation hangs heavy through visible and invisible reproach and censure. A person is there under sufferance, and avoids any charge simply by dint of a legal technicality. You are in such places on someone else's terms, and vulnerable to eviction. Pedestrians have to bear the burden of upholding their innocence. Whereas breaking into the liquor store or someone's home leads to incontrovertible guilt, in security zones, multistory parking garages, pedestrian walkways, and loading bays pedestrians are never even sure whether they are trespassing or not. These and other places occupy the vexed threshold between innocence and guilt, assisted in no small part by ubiquitous technologies of automatic signage, alarms, remote-controlled doors and gates, and of course surveillance cameras. The pedestrians' uncertainty is amplified by what they carry or do in such places and how they appear, including their gait, comportment, and dress. To the extent that commuters carry cameras, recorders, Wi-Fi-enabled laptops, and palmtop computers, they are reminded of the presence of invisible zones under the governance of other people's networks.

Courthouses and prisons arguably are the site of guilt, as are confessionals, sexually explicit websites, and certain peer-to-peer Internet sites. Spaces for innocent perambulation might include gardens, hospices, daycare centers, the home, charity shops, and the CBBC (the Children's BBC television channel) website.[64] But it seems that nowhere affords pure innocence or complete guilt. At best people are neither entirely innocent nor guilty by virtue of the spaces they occupy, but the charge against them is simply "not proven," in other words, the case has "insufficient grounds."[65]

Many ambulatory practices occupy this interstitial condition between guilt and innocence. For office workers and academics the retention of confidential emails, files, and assessments presents as a source of guilt-innocence. Making the news are those high-profile cases when laptops or memory sticks containing confidential records from the British National Health Service, major banks, or the military were left in public places or on public transport. But in fact, many commuters daily carry around information that they or their organization absolutely would not like to be made public: assessments of clients, colleagues, or students, personal notes, copies of personal emails.[66] Often we nervously ask ourselves: Did I delete that information? Did I delete the backups? Is it still on the mail server? In this sense the laptop draws the traveler or mobile worker into this condition of guilt-innocence. Nervous travelers carry the weight of putative guilt-innocence with them.

The condition of not proven, or guilt-innocence, is identified in French legal parlance as a condition of *non-lieu*, the literal translation of which is "non-place." From this coincidence of terms derives the subtlety of Augé's theories of place and non-place.[67] Non-place has emerged as an obvious category to account for environments that are unhomely, alienating, blighted, and heavily mediated by technology. It is not difficult to identify non-places with surveillance and other pervasive technologies. But non-places are not just places drained of meaning. Neither are they only the left over, overtly commercial, or systematic sites of instrumental interaction and bureaucratic processes. Non-places are tagged, labeled, and signed with communications that contribute to a sense of guilt-innocence. They are defined subtly by signs. Updating Augé's characterization, travelers and workers in transit carry many of these signs with them as pervasive mobile media, or the signs enter their awareness through display screens. Not least in this array are the links to those rarely read "conditions of use" contracts encountered when visiting websites or downloading software. To the extent that people think about them, such legal tags, labels, and signs serve as reminders of the walker's and computer user's ambivalent condition in non-place.

Non-places are also those environments in which an institution, official, or individual has insisted on rendering the implicit obvious with a label. Sociologist John Urry draws attention to the problematics of display design, museology, heritage, and tourism,[68] where curators attach labels to cultural artifacts that indicate significance, as if to tell visitors what to think. The labels explain the object. Once the visitor has imbibed this explanation, he can move on. Handheld audio guides in heritage and tourist sites are further ubiquitous contributors to the labeling of places and things, as are palmtop electronic guides and technologies that channel local contextual information to cell phones.[69] As well as supposedly enriching the traveler's experience of a place, such technologies are answerable to the charge of perpetrating non-places.

Of course the existence of the automobile and its infrastructures contribute substantially to the sense of non-place and the scales of encounter it requires, which often are out of scale with the activities of walking. Thus the signs that appear beside highways, indicating what is to be found some miles away, appear as "texts planted along the wayside that tell us about the landscape and make its secret beauties explicit . . . the traveler is absolved of the need to stop or even look."[70]

Signs also remain in non-places as traces, in the same way that the Internet is populated by many dead links, unlinked sites, out-of-date pages, and remnants in caches and proxy servers. To elaborate this category further, in the depths of non-places there are corners that retain the vestiges of old announcements and out-of-date rules. Visitors sometimes have to guess from the state of the sign whether it still strictly applies. For many years I used to walk past a sign baked onto the wall tiles of a major railway station. It read "do not spit," the usefulness of which had gone along with the custom of chewing tobacco. In another case, the sign "bathing caps must always be worn in this pool" apparently only applied during the holiday season when numbers in the water exceeded fifteen, caveats not displayed on the sign. Interactions with computers provide further reminders of semiotic redundancy. Digital media often carry obsolete instructions, warnings, and exhortations that have not caught up with best practice. Such outdated practices include requests to log bug reports after a program crash, having to eject a peripheral device by dragging it to the trash can before removing the plug, being required to read an instruction manual before operating new software, and having to click on pop-up advertisements to delete them from the browser window. Some reckless individuals will ignore signs unless they are reinforced by strong evidence that the rules stated on these signs will be upheld. The lesson here relates to the contingency of signs, the unsteady and unsettling condition in spaces and technologies that are dominated by them, and the tactics of the savvy user, consumer, and pedestrian to evade intimidation.

The casual and unsanctioned tagging of spaces provides a potent means of diminishing the authority of signage, highlighting its temporal and contingent aspects. Streetscapes of busy cities are littered with small signs advertising furnished rooms, clubs, tanning services, and special offers. The elements of this microecology adhere to lampposts and even bigger signs. They are too small for anyone to think of prosecuting the purveyor or for city councils to be bothered to remove them. The urban tagscape presents as non-place in microcosm, or perhaps a foil to the non-place of official signs and notices.[71] The urban tagscape links to the Internet through the publication of web addresses, and shares in the promiscuous mixing of the official and the unofficial, the signs of the powerful and the tactics of the tagger.

In some spaces there are no labels. Augoyard draws attention to urban places that are "unnameable because they lack any imaginable name."[72] These are the vestibules in front of elevator doors, the place where the corridor turns a corner: "these unnameable and unappropriable places are given over to accidental and erratic uses," such as play, a place to store furniture, momentarily, until others complain,[73] and in the larger urban context a place for skateboarding and *parkour*.[74] Such spaces are also useful as somewhere to retreat with a mobile phone, away from where people normally congregate, where you can pace about. There are more things than there are labels with which to identify them, were it not for the richness of language and human invention.

Digital environments amplify the problem of unnamed spaces. There would seem to be little in digital space that is unnamed, uncoded, its use undesignated, but pervasive digital media feature as tools with which to organize the tactical possession of unnamed spaces, not least in helping to arrange intimate and group assignations and rendezvous.[75] But there are new characterizations of dead and unnameable spaces. These are the interstitial zones where you cannot get a phone, Wi-Fi, or GPS signal. The environment presents as an overlay of visible and invisible, surveilled and private, named and unnamed, networked and blanked-out zones.

To the extent that digital technologies, from GPS to handhelds, might abet the transformation of places into non-places I maintain that such technologies are in the company of signage. Signs, labels, badges, and tags populate the world of walking and other ambulatory practices. But the making of non-place is not simply a negative condition to be resisted. For Augé place and non-place are "opposed polarities: the first is never completely erased, the second is never totally completed."[76] The tactics of walking already implicate remaindered and leftover spaces and places through encounters with difference, the subject of chapter 9.

In this chapter I have attempted to align tuning with the tactical processes of technological navigation and the low-tech practices of simply walking about. Human societies invent new technologies and practices in tandem. Navigational practices are acquired socially, even though their sociable aspects may be buried or hard coded into the design of devices and the environment.

Tuning involves correction, fine adjustment, modification, and accommodation, operations brought to light in technologies of navigation. As brought into focus by GPS, navigation illuminates the issues of error and imprecision by operating on the basis of temporal discrepancies and corrections between frames of reference. The calculation of distance relies on geometries of interference. The effects of small differences are amplified to calculate distances, and the discrepancies between distance calculations are ameliorated by the multiplication of readings, which effectively home in on a positional fix.

Similarly, the prosaic practices of walking about typically occupy the interstitial sites of uncertainty, where positions are refined, and deviations compounded. Sociable beings tune their relationships to place and others by adjusting their positions, and the simple act of walking implicates tactics. Human beings are tactical creatures, evident in their investments in unassuming as well as conspicuous technologies. Movement through space is opportunistic, drawing on cues, tags, labels, and devices to hand. Tactics for walking highlight the role of mobile media in exploiting the small increment in negotiating non-places, and in the tuning of place.

9 Threshold

Contrary to the expectation that ubiquitous devices might auger "smoother and more natural forms of interaction and expression,"[1] I press the case for their capacity to defamiliarize and even alienate. Mobile devices render the environment strange in various ways, and this process can be recruited as a tactic in daily living and design. Ubiquitous devices tease the fine line between familiarity and unfamiliarity. As such they work the thresholds of the urban environment and assist the tuning of place.

Emerging Mobile Practices

As explored in chapter 8, GPS seems to introduce new factors into ambulatory practice, or at least it modifies, amplifies, and inflects current practice. To the extent that GPS advances monitoring and surveillance it expands non-place into the enterprise of walking. It also advances the cause of the world picture, reliance on maps, the aerial view, coordinate geometry, and Euclidean space. Furthermore it pushes these schemas to an extreme, perhaps revealing their limitations, in what is an emancipatory process, provided that people have the means to opt out of these schemas, or at least to redeploy them knowingly. GPS technologies and gadgets assert their place within narratives of utility and the satisfaction of needs: the visitor "needs" to know how to get to the hotel; pilots "need" to know where they and their passengers are; suppliers and customers need to track goods; parents require knowledge of where their children are, or at least that they are safe. The use of these communications and navigation technologies blurs into public and private motorized transportation, and into the waiting for transportation.[2] There was a time when the only activities while traveling were socializing, reading, or playing games. Now the whole panoply of media delivery is available on shared and private devices. You now can see where you are while traveling by train, and if so inclined you can wile away your traveling time in checking and rechecking your position.

Apart from their apparent utility, these technologies introduce new ambulatory and mobility practices. New walking practices, or at least modifications to current practices, are emerging, which in turn reveal something about current routines. People may set out from the suburbs to socialize with friends in the city without a clear understanding of where the various parties will meet.[3] The meeting is negotiated by cell phone calls or text messages. Groups may be primed and ready for instruction to implement social action or protest, their meeting abetted by a nudge transmitted by text messaging or phone calls. Such human "swarms" and "flash mobs" reveal further the communality of walking, as well as its tactical character.

Pervasive media introduce new and strange practices as loose variants of existing practices. For example, geocaching is a treasure hunt played with GPS navigational tools. It is an organized pastime targeting concealed collections of objects sealed in watertight containers. Participating players seek out these caches, the locations of which are published as GPS coordinates. Players may then take items from the container and leave others. They put an entry in a logbook in the container and discuss their adventures on the Internet.[4] There is usually some mystery involved or instructional narrative about finding the cache. That GPS coordinates are rarely precise enough to pinpoint the cache in all terrains and environments enhances the quest. The activity tests the players' sense of trust, that other players, or anyone else who happens on the cache by chance, will not plunder it. The social aspect is further manifested as a commitment by geocachers as a group to preserve this trust.

Mapping provides a further example of new, variant practices. Access to online maps and aerial photographs is taken for granted now and seems to have an impact on how people think of place and navigation, providing previews of destinations in ways that proprietary brochures and guidebooks cannot. Vacationers commonly talk of checking out holiday destinations, properties, and journeys through Google Maps, Google Earth, Google StreetView, and their successors, on desktop, laptop, and handheld devices. Dynamic map resources are increasingly interfaced with other programs and applications. Maps are proprietary objects involving investment in keeping them up to date, and most maps and map services are protected by copyright. Arguably, maps only show information that the owners, investors, sponsors, and regulators want people to see. Maps are also selective in what they display. As if to emphasize the contingency of maps, online resources such as Wikimapia enable regular users to tag locations on publicly available maps and modify these tags in a manner similar to a Wikipedia entry. These tags include unofficial, personal, noncommercial, and idiosyncratic information about locations.[5] Related innovations include the creation of open-source maps online; by this means, for example, users of OpenStreetMap can edit graphical map information. The copyright of such maps is regulated through a creative commons not-for-profit license.[6] More interestingly, amateur cartographers can draw in walking trails, property lines, and other features considered of interest to users but omitted from mainstream maps. In *How to Lie with Maps* Mark Monmonier calls such grassroots mapping practices "folk" or "lay" cartography.[7] These initiatives emphasize, if it needed emphasizing, that "a single map is but one of an indefinitely large number of maps that might be produced for the same situation or from the same data."[8] Open-source maps introduce new mobility practices that highlight the consensual and contested nature of map creation and usage, and hence navigation.

Putative hazards are the kinds of features that people might want to see on maps, such as strong sources of electromagnetic radiation: cell phone base stations. Telecommunications regulators in many parts of the world require that the positions of cell phone base stations, or towers, are made public, and there are websites that map their positions, indicating heights above ground level. Many towers are now concealed atop new buildings, within church steeples, domes, and statuary, or camouflaged as trees. They are even disguised as or concealed within and behind lamp posts, the chimneys of heritage buildings, Georgian rainwater downpipes with rain hoppers, replica ventilation louvers on church towers, and restored clock faces.[9] These maps provide a different view of the city, especially considering commonly held views about the possible health risks of living close to communications towers. The distribution of these towers forms a kind of anxiety map,[10] and their mapping introduces new practices of exercising and ameliorating anxieties about the safety of places in which people live and work.

Mapping radio sources provides a dynamic constellation of reference points, and such data can help in mapping other points of reference. Internal and external environments are permeated with Wi-Fi and cell phone carrier signals of known frequency. Any point in the city will have a characteristic spatial signature detectable by a suitable radio receiver. GPS signals are weak and in any case are readily occluded or distorted by the presence of buildings and geological features. The stronger Wi-Fi signals generated deep within buildings can often be detected outside. The mobile phone user subscribing to peer-to-peer positioning moves around and goes about their day-to-day activity, and as they do so their phone or other personal device automatically monitors signal strength from various transmission sources, then sends this information to specialized servers to determine the positions of those sources.[11] Other phones without GPS, or phones unable to locate GPS signals, can then use this information about the locations of such sources to calculate their own positions. In this manner, privately owned indoor Wi-Fi sources located arbitrarily by their owners can be deployed vicariously to provide positioning for others.

In this light, radio sources form ecologies of dynamical codependencies. By a variant reading they highlight navigation as a trade in parasitical relationships, which is the character of navigation anyway. You derive your position from a fix in relationship to another position. Navigation presents as a journey through a series of successively derived reference points and way stations. There is no final moment that decides or arbitrates your position; every fix is relative to some frame of reference or another, which is to say, some pragmatic consideration. For example: I have arrived at my friend's house when we can converse, share a cup of coffee, browse his CD collection, and position ourselves within a certain sociability script or reference frame. I'm also there when I can cross reference this script with a set of navigational practices involving street names, house numbers, directions, and coordinates.

Such emerging locational practices introduce or amplify certain positional vocabularies. Walking or positioning operates as an adjustment, finding or negotiating your place among a series of overlapping frames. Positioning presents as an optimization process, searching for the best position in lieu of an overview of all relevant factors. Positioning is akin to nudging, moving things into view or out of the way. Settlers and nomads nudge themselves into position, discretely and opportunistically attaching themselves to other mobile agents. To position oneself is also to drift. Drifting recalls the problem of calibration, as reference frames move out of alignment, and mobile devices become complicit in wayfinding and wandering.[12] And so people tune their relationship to place and each other by adjusting their position, a process abetted by phones and GPS.

In summary, locational devices are complicit in the emergence of new practices, which is to say new ways of understanding the environment. They bring to mind processes of navigation as processes of tuning. These devices also suggest movement out of one's comfort zone, to spaces that challenge our trust and draw us into unfamiliar realms.

Excursion and Return

To what extent do such pervasive, location-based technologies diminish the experience of walking by turning it into a highly technologized, clock-bound instrumental process? Perhaps tracking, mapping, speed, efficiency, precision, and *knowing where* replace *being there* and engagement with the primal act of walking for its own sake. Architectural theorist and colleague Adrian Snodgrass explains further the basic propensity to wander, and the remnant of this tendency in various social practices. For example, it is common to ask a fellow traveler, "How are you going?" or "How goes it?" The inquiry is as much about the other person's state of health or state of mind as it is about their mode of travel. Such ambiguous exchanges resist the usual imperative to give and expect reasons for the journey. That walking does not require a reason is given more obvious expression in the case of certain practices in India, according to Snodgrass.

> In Tamilnad in South India, when you meet someone on the path, he will ask, "Where are you going?" It is good manners to reply, "I am simply going," or, "Simply" (*summa*), with a vague gesture with the hand in the direction you're going. That is sufficient. It is enough that you are simply walking on the path. You aren't required to give reasons.[13]

Snodgrass draws attention to the ubiquity of concepts of "the way" in Asian cultures. Taoism, "way-ism," suggests, "those who aimlessly walk a path are walked by the path."[14] You don't just follow where the path leads, but "the path and she who walks it are one; they move along together."[15]

The job of the wanderer is "to keep moving, keep the eyes (and the mind) open, be aware and receptive."[16]

Participation in such wandering is itself a sign or symptom of peaceful coexistence, of bonhomie, and comfort in one's habitat. Way-ism is a further recognition of the primordiality of walking-with, walking with the tribe, roaming with the herd, of comfort in one's homeland. But way-ism also gives space for encounter with the unfamiliar. The home is the place of familiarity from which the traveler embarks on a journey to unfamiliar territory. Home and the traveler's view of home are not the same when the traveler returns. The circumstances may be different from when she left, and she may have a different view when she returns. The adult returns to the home of his youth only to find that his bedroom has been turned into a sewing room, the front door that once loomed large now looks small, and the aroma of cooking has turned stale. As well as changes in the home, several years of new life experiences have passed that color the homecomer's understanding of what he once took for granted. The duality of the familiarity of home and the unfamiliarity of being "abroad," away from home, in alien circumstances, constitutes a process of *excursion and return*.

Everydayness seems to be characterized by this cycle of excursion and return. The journey from home to work or the shops and back again may not present as alien an encounter, or as transformative, but then it is often against this background of the everyday that the character of the excursion cuts through: where the traffic is particularly bad, the sun strikes the trees in an unusual way, the newspaper seller is not at her usual stand, or I receive an alarming text message on my cell phone. The familiar and the unfamiliar can oscillate and embed themselves in any aspect of the journey. Another way to think of the journey is as a series of way stations—instances of home I encounter along the way, echoes of home, or moments of familiarity interspersed with the unfamiliar. Home has this transient character anyway, as experienced by the migrant arriving at a new "home." According to social geographer Jane M. Jacobs, this homecoming is where you have to reorientate yourself to your "old home," as well as to your new circumstances.[17] According to Snodgrass: "One's prior home is now understood not as a final homestead, a home where one stands steadfast, but a way station, a starting place for entry into the alien; and what was alien is now one's own."[18] Any journey can be understood as a progression through a series of way stations, or temporary homes, homes that refer back to the home that I left, homes transformed.

To cross a border into foreign territory epitomizes the encounter with new, alien, and unhomely experiences. In this respect the pilgrim epitomizes the individual undertaking a transformative rite of passage.[19] Studies in tourism amplify this process. For John Urry: "Like the pilgrim the tourist moves from a familiar place to a far place and then returns to the familiar place."[20] Part of this encounter involves the provision of a new backdrop to the ordinary aspects of a person's life, such as physical activity, shopping, eating, and drinking. The experience implicates the senses. Urry thinks of this backdrop as primarily visual, as if a stage setting. The gaze of the tourist "renders extraordinary, activities that otherwise would be mundane and everyday."[21] There is pleasure in eating as I usually eat, even from the same menu, but at a café on the beachfront rather than my own dining room or in front of the television; or to walk as I usually walk, but in the mountains or on the streets of Paris. Yet tourist destinations can be "sensuously 'other' to everyday routines and places."[22] Some tourists seem to gravitate to enclaves that remind them of home, but even the most adventurous will inevitably carry home with them, making comparisons with what they know. The traveler might also trespass or infiltrate the patch or habitat of others. Strangers may move into or invade the traveler's habitat. Conflicts over territory characterize moments of alien encounter. In addition to danger and threat, such incursions can focus the journey and expose the traveler to otherness, the alien, and the unfamiliar.

Of course, tourists and other travelers increasingly carry personalized electronic devices for listening to their own music and movies as podcasts. In this manner they carry around prepackaged accessories of home. For sociologist Michael Bull, on the one hand, listening to personal stereos takes the traveler away from the mundane aspects of domesticity; on the other hand, such practices render the potential hostility of the urban jungle safe and homely, albeit in ways that are highly commoditized.[23] Networked media invite further experimentation that brings distance to play in rendering the familiar strange. For example, Jeff Mann and Michelle Teran have conducted social picnic events at a distance, described in their website as reimagining "the familiar objects and utensils of our everyday social spaces as an electronically activated play environment, capable of transmitting over distance the physical presence and social gesture that comprise such a vital element of human interaction." The activity requires coordination and calibration of gestures and actions at a distance, centered on ubiquitous wireless Internet access points: "Nomadic groups pack mobile feasts of sensors, antennas, robotics, food, and music, and head out on the town . . . wherever bandwidth is plentiful and security guards scarce."[24] Such activities, though not widely practiced, serve to defamiliarize the activities of walking, socializing, and moving about, to the practitioners, observers, and those who read their accounts.

The traveler's experience of territorial incursion and defamiliarization commonly draws on the antagonisms between the sense of sight and sound. Vision is often associated with commoditization and consumption from a distance, as in the case of the fleeting glimpse of a landmark from a tourist bus.[25] Vision is here equated with a particular appropriation of otherness, where the alien encounter involves the identification of something to look at, without engagement, and often from a position of superiority or envy: the privileged tourist visiting the quaint spectacle of the local economy of the poor, or gawking at the homes of the rich and famous.

If sight implies distance and disengagement then sound might invoke its opposite, including the threat that comes with proximity. If regular residents want to characterize tourists as invaders, they might refer to them as boisterous or noisy, as in the common identification of "rowdy" young tourists, or mobile "stag" and "hen" parties. For Augoyard, gangs of youths roaming the streets seem to constitute a major specter in the imagination of responsible citizens. Such groups are innocuous during the day: "By day, small youth gangs *are seen*, . . . At night, most of the inhabitants sense the irruptive presence of these gangs only through their *hearing*."[26] Threats are amplified at night with the occlusion of vision and heightened sensitivity via sound.

Travel has a transgressive character anyway. Urry recounts the "modest acts of rebellion"[27] evident in the eighteenth-century popularization of rapid transportation and even walking as a leisure pursuit. The newfound freedom instilled a sense that you were overturning conventional social hierarchies. Extreme sports and adventures, and the acting out of hedonistic fantasies provide contemporary demonstrations of this encounter with the other. For Urry such activities constitute a pursuit of pleasure, and implicate the body, through the "touch, of the feet on the pavement or the mountain path, the hands on a rock-face or the steering wheel."[28] As well as pleasure, such bodily exertions introduce an alien element constitutive of the traveler's embeddedness in the cycles of excursion and return. The defamiliarization of the city arguably is at the center of the tactics deployed by the Situationists, those artists who in the middle of the twentieth century drew on the traversal and playful mapping of cities in an attempt to communicate a politics of freedom and a world "without frontiers." The leaders of the movement included Guy Debord, Constant Nieuwenhuys, and others who responded to the legacies of Dada and Surrealism by elevating the concept of the *dérive*, or drift, wandering without purpose.[29] Their "psychogeographical" methods, images, models, and built interventions in cities and landscapes were intent on provoking new understandings of place. Some contemporary works in this vein can be subtle, including Richard Long's "A line made by walking," which is simply a series of lines across English meadows created by the trampling of grass.[30]

Sound is complicit in people's awareness of territory and their encounters with the unfamiliar. Animals use sounds and other sensory modalities to define territory, as do street vendors, auctioneers, lecturers, tour guides, phone users, and conversationalists. For Schafer, "The definition of space by acoustic means is much more ancient than the establishment of property lines and fences."[31] As I discussed in chapter 5, the voice asserts and defines territories by as primitive a means as issuing a repetitive call or sound. The assertion of a repetition provides the most basic claim on territory, a means deployed by crowds of sports fans, and drunken and disruptive bands of tourists. Sounds can serve to define territories, but also to break through and redefine them. According to Augoyard, "the auditory sense comes to undo the territorial limits that had been set between private and public."[32]

The company they keep also introduces an unfamiliar element into people's travels. The comments and insights, enthusiasms and indifference of a traveling companion present aspects of a familiar journey in a new light. The philosopher Alain de Botton expresses it well: "Our responses to the world are crucially molded by whom we are with, we temper our curiosity to fit in with the expectation of others."[33] The introduction of portable objects into the journey also renders the familiar strange. Things to be carried, pushed, pulled, and worn, mobility aids, and even a shopping bag represent a class of objects that impinge on wandering, not just by impeding or assisting movement but also in providing a new view of the world. Some years ago I encountered a male fraternity initiation rite that required new students to carry a building brick, displayed in plain view, around with them for a week: going home, on the bus, at social occasions, and to lessons. The world takes on a different cast when you have to negotiate the day's journeys around the presence of an arbitrary, useless, and inconvenient object such as a brick. People look at you differently. You are self-conscious, anxious about being watched by classmates, and fall into a new regime of solidarity with other brick carriers. Portable electronic devices have more use-value than a brick, but similarly provoke encounters with the unfamiliar, which has the potential to reveal something new, and inform the journeying. As if to amplify this point, Urry highlights the way that technologies extend the engagement of the body to create "hybrid assemblages" of "humans, objects, technologies and scripts," which "roam countrysides and cities, remaking landscapes and townscapes through their movement."[34] For the tourist such technologies include the car, bicycle, hiking shoe, sailboat, snowmobile, personal stereo, and camera.[35] Technologies present the world in particular ways. For some, technologies of speed and cameras conspire to render the world a vast domain of unlimited potential and suggest participation in an "endless futurity."[36] Sometimes these transformations engender sociotechnical milieus such as the age of steam power, the communications revolution, the digital age, the smartphone generation, and the age of location-aware computing. The new view of the world invoked by technologies can also appear as an effect of the moment on the local traveler with a cell phone or iPod.

Thresholds

Journeying involves transitions from one condition to another, a repetition of processes of excursion and return, an encounter with the unfamiliar which then assumes familiarity to some degree, or becomes subsumed within a world view. Journeying may also involve taking the familiar and rendering it unfamiliar, as when visiting the city with a small child, or using GPS to navigate. The movement between a position where things are familiar and an unfamiliar setting constitutes negotiation across a threshold that separates so many connected waypoints. Journeys are permeated with thresholds. Pedestrians pass over the thresholds of doorways, cross over from the footpath to the road, from inside a building to the street, from one precinct to another—encountering changes in spatial configuration, surfaces materials, and levels. But not all threshold encounters are visible as lines or marks in space, though travelers may detect their effects.

Yachters talk of the "no-sail zone," an invisible area in the direction of the wind in which mobility ceases. They report on the transition into a zone. Everything is running smoothly; then the sails start to flap and the vessel stops or even reverses. Air travelers might pass through "choppy air" in clear blue skies. Mobile phone users become increasingly aware of electromagnetic fields as they pass through zones providing different qualities of reception. In any case, the cell phone network is designed to pass the control of communications from one base station to the next while people are on the move. The traveler crosses the threshold from one mobile phone cell to the next. As interaction theorist Ann Light has observed, mobile phones also introduce practices for managing transitions, not only spatial but also in terms of moving from one space of activity to another.[37]

Walking through the city, pedestrians pass through zones of microclimatic variation, areas of light and dark, into and out of the shadows. The architectural historian and theorist Colin Rowe describes urban spaces in terms of transparent overlays, in plan, elevation, or section, which overlap and distort one another in the manner of the patches of color and grain in a cubist painting, creating areas of ambiguity and richly textured meaning.[38] But the simple geometry of a space also reveals transitions that are not necessarily marked out in the fabric of the environment. Imagine a precinct of a city with buildings, streets, and public squares. In some parts of the precinct you will get clear vistas down to the town hall. At the same spot, if you turn to the right you will get a clear view into the city square. Behind you will get a view to the forecourt of the library. If you move 200 meters to the left you might find yourself in a small side street, which provides a much smaller area of view, that is, the extent of your view is reduced. With a plan of the city and elevation data, a computer program can calculate the area on the ground that you can see from any position. Such a map constitutes an isovist, viewshed, or visibility graph. If you could plot the isovist values for the whole precinct you would get a shaded or contoured map showing those areas from which you can see a lot of the city, and those awkward corners where you can see very little, with many spaces in between. Spatial researchers Alasdair Turner and colleagues have explored the calculation of such maps from the geometry of a city precinct, or inside a building, and their spatial implications.[39] They argue that such maps help in understanding spatial perception, such as wayfinding, movement, and the uses of spaces. The areas with the largest viewshed are not necessarily the centers of squares or the middle of busy streets, but can be street junctions and the edges of public spaces. Therefore people might tend to gather informally in such spaces. Thresholds are those areas where people make "movement decisions" at moments of "rapid change in isovist area values."[40] If your view is extensive, it is likely that you are also highly visible.[41] The thresholds between areas of high and low visibility therefore do not necessarily correspond to doorways, entries, or changes in materials, but rather to lines that cut across spaces. Such thresholds also move around, as doors are opened and closed, new structures erected, with changes in vegetation, and the viewer adjusts her height.[42] Viewshed thresholds are different from a wheelchair than they are from the top of a double-decker bus.

Such viewshed configurations are also distorted by the use of mobile technologies. Digital cameras can be held at arm's length, high above your head to expand the range of view, like a periscope. With each explosion or other spectacular moment on the stage of a pop concert or public spectacle, the audience turns into a sea of arms reaching skyward, supporting a constellation of digital cameras, and distorting the viewshed landscape.

Sound is also complicit in the formation of urban overlays. Acoustic thresholds are characterized by leakages and an even greater dynamism than the strictly formal and visual. In an essay on sounds in the city, urban theorist Jean-Paul Thibaud calls on people to think of public spaces in terms of sonic "thresholds, knots and configurations."[43] The traveler with a personal stereo crosses a threshold when leaving the house, and encounters knots of concentration when negotiating the interfaces between ear, footstep, and built environment. Moving around the city involves the configuration of various "lived itineraries." In their study of everyday sounds in the environment, Augoyard and Torgue explain sonic thresholds in terms of the cut, which they describe as "a sudden drop in intensity associated with an abrupt change in the spectral envelope of a sound or a modification of reverberation (moving from reverberant to dull spaces, for instance). This effect is an important process of articulation between spaces and locations; it punctuates movement from one ambience to another."[44] Here a sound space is characterized as an ambience. The correspondences between visual and acoustic spaces are only loosely formed, and characterized as so many leakages across each other's thresholds. In a journey along a street the walker experiences the sound of someone operating electrical equipment in a side street. The sound increases in intensity as she moves toward the side street and recedes as she continues on her journey. The sound is interrupted by the buildings lining the streets in ways that views are not. Sound is subject to dissipation effects, reflections, and leakages. It also operates obliquely. You don't need to face the side street to experience the sound emanating from it. As with vision, the sound transitions can be abrupt, but unpredictable, and of unidentified source. Sounds can travel over and around obstructions.

The consideration of sonic thresholds further highlights an important aspect of travel: the overlay of zones, spaces, fields, and thresholds. If such encounters can be mapped then they are maps overlaid one on the other, fading in and out of prominence, moving in and out of focus, and prone to interference effects between maps.[45] Occasionally the traveler reaches a "calibration point," where fields correspond, or there is visual corroboration or verification. We see the source of the sound, identify the tower of a cell phone base station, hear the street vendor, and tune in to a location.[46] The traveler can be thought of as a disturbance in various fields, or a mobile creator of these fields. The traveler is also a catalyst, irritant, parasite, disturbance in the fields, a portal or permeable moment within a field: the creator, distributor, and perpetuator of thresholds. Of course it is never the traveler alone that is the cause, but a mobile army of movement. Think of "waves of tourists" descending on a historic site, sometimes made obvious by uniforms and colored hats, fluid fields of disturbance disgorged from buses and trains. Even independent travelers congregate. They arrive and leave, and follow the seasons: the ebb and flow of uniform seas perforated by small differences.

Cognitive Horizons

By a certain reading the symbolism of excursion and return is also embedded in architectural forms and sacred practices, such as the form of the sacred mandala, the highly symmetrical building based on a geometry of nested squares and circles seen in Indonesia and elsewhere. Snodgrass discusses the form of the traditional mandala in this light, as charting a journey of excursion and return: "an expansion from the centre to the periphery, and a contraction from the periphery to the centre, an alternating centrifugal and centripetal movement which relates to such rhythms as the exhalation and inhalation of the breath and the systole and diastole of the heart's action." The journey reference is temporal as well as spatial: "It relates to the coming and going of the heavenly bodies, the rhythms of the universe, the passage of the sun, birth and death."[47]

Cultural historians recruit theories of excursion and return, defamiliarization, and way-ism as so many metaphors to account for cultural encounters of various kinds, and for how people interpret and understand the world. Wayfaring provides a metaphor for thought. The familiar habitat is the human being's place of accepted preunderstanding, norms, and prejudices—their comfort zone. Those difficult aspects of the place or text under study, the artwork, the building, the landscape, the new piece of software, the screen image, the digital installation, the music, or the sound piece may constitute unfamiliar territory. What a person encounters might constitute a challenge, which she takes on board or rejects, or in any case accommodates in some way to a frame of reference. Interpreters, readers, and critics form judgments, which later are brought to bear in other encounters. Interpretation involves a negotiation across the space between the familiar and the unfamiliar, and revision of what constitutes familiarity, revising the boundaries of our comfort zones.

Someone who is accommodating in this way is usually identified as tolerant or nonjudgmental, but the process by which a judgment is formed and revised is at best one of movement, and in flux. At worst, the interpreter is subject to blind prejudice on all matters of substance, and unable to learn from difference. The prejudiced traveler is unable or unwilling to move into new territory, or he sees that new territory after all as his own, or only as it appears on his own map.

Tolerance and tuning are related. The issue of toleration as a process of tuning presents as a means of accommodating disparity between frames of reference as discussed in chapter 2. Thoughtful human beings could not interpret without their capacity to prejudge, and artful and lucid thinkers are those able to nudge, align, and realign their maps of preformed opinion, reregister or deregister to the maps of others and other circumstances.

Toleration is a well-used catchword of liberal reformers and politicians, exemplified in Barack Obama's self-confessed rethink of issues pertaining to human sexuality: "I must admit that I may have been infected with society's prejudices and predilections and attributed them to God."[48] But this capacity to shift and remap one's own prejudicial landscape is a feature of thinking in any case. Without it understanding could not take place.

The idea of the changing shape of the traveler's viewshed is instructive. The field of view from where I stand now can be defined as my horizon. For Gadamer: "The horizon is the range of vision that includes everything that can be seen from a particular vantage point."[49] If I shift my position I get a different horizon. Traveling is a collective enterprise that also entails encounters with others. If horizons are so many perspectives and traces from a plethora of journeys, the metaphor can be expanded to the fusion of horizons. For philosopher Hans-Georg Gadamer "this process of fusion is always going on, for there old and new are always combining into something of living value."[50] In this light, to interpret something—a book, a message, a building—is a collaborative process involving various fusions between viewpoints, the way a journey involves shared and compared vantage points, traces, and memories of varying horizons.

The edge emerges as a prominent condition within this mixture of hermeneutical metaphors, as the threshold between one understanding and another. Reflective individuals do not readily encounter situations that suddenly demand they replace one frame of reference with another, or teleport instantly to a different horizon, as might a Second Life traveler. As suggested by Thomas Kuhn's theories about revolutions in science, the process is rather a nudge in the direction of a new position.[51] Such small moves can still tip the scientist into a brand-new horizon; the reflective pedestrian steps forward to a suddenly expanded viewshed, seeing past the wall, where the line of columns no longer occludes but frames the view.

The architect Peter Eisenman's Berlin Holocaust Memorial involves an array of regularly spaced blocks of concrete as faux tombs, or steles. From certain positions you are only aware of walls of gray. If you move your position a little you may suddenly be aligned with the space between the rows so that you encounter long, uninterrupted vistas. Visitors are fascinated by moments of minor and tentative transition that can produce maximum effect, and tend to linger at such thresholds. Art historians and theorists have noted the techniques of romantic landscape painting where the viewer is positioned on the edge, under the tree canopy, at the edge of the cliff, and looks out to the inhospitable landscape beyond.[52] It seems that people like to view and listen from the secure vantage of the edge or threshold.

Lingering at the threshold is an important component of the travel experience. This is where active tourists take their bearings, survey the terrain, read the map, check a GPS reading, make a phone call. I have elaborated at length elsewhere on the prominent role of the liminal condition in design and commerce.[53] The condition can be applied to travel too. Lewis Hyde characterizes the occupant of the boundary condition as the trickster. The trickster is the one who crosses the line and confuses distinctions: "Trickster is the mythic embodiment of ambiguity and ambivalence, doubleness and duplicity, contradiction and paradox."[54] The trickster is the lingerer in the doorway and at the crossroads: "He is the spirit of the doorway leading out, and of the crossroad at the edge of town (the one where a little market springs up). He is the spirit of the road at dusk, the one that runs from one town to another and belongs to neither."[55] The trickster does not wield a sword, kidnap, or threaten the traveler. His mode of intervention is incremental, flirtatious, obsequious, and altogether ambiguous, Machiavellian, "cunningly confusing men"[56] rather than conquering them.

Ubiquitous digital devices seem to amplify this functioning too. Whereas much of the discourse on pervasive media focuses on the putative "deeply transformative nature of our biotechnological unions,"[57] and other metaphors of blurring and merging, my exploration here of navigation and threshold encounters suggests that much of the transformative power of digital devices resides precisely in their otherness and the estrangement they promote. It is not only that machines are like people, extensions to human capability, and may become intelligent and sentient, but also that they complement, supplement, and provoke cognition. They may irritate by their defective functioning, but devices also act as catalysts and stimulants by expanding spatial experience, provoking and nudging their users, as well as critics and commentators, to behold new horizons.

You may object that cars, airplanes, and rocket missiles do not exactly nudge societies into new states of understanding. Arguably, they brazenly and spectacularly transform horizons by flattening them. But even these over-scaled technologies are composites of devices, not only of mechanical parts, but also ancillary technologies of schedules, calibrations, tags, navigational apparatuses, and other devices that serve to tune and "synchronize the actions of men." Without the attendant fields of devices and sociotechnical practices, they would not have their transformative effects. Hence my repeated appeal in this book to attend to the incremental operations, the subtle shifts secreted within apparently bold moves. Apart from their overt utility, ubiquitous technologies serve as a means of rendering the familiar strange, of defamiliarizing, in their day-to-day use, in experimentation, in art, and on reflection.[58]

Ubiquitous devices do not only meld invisibly into walking and navigational practices. Sometimes they also present as alien and alienating artifacts, rendering the environment unfamiliar. Their power resides in their capacity to distort the landscape of everyday encounters, and in this way they are instrumental in the tuning of place.

10 Aggregation

Configurations of pervasive digital media now constitute active laboratories and studios for innovation and experimentation requiring modest outlay on the part of the innovators. Enterprising software architects can aggregate services, data, programs, and templates from diverse sources to customize new and useful crowdsourced innovations, mashups, and media mixes. Expansive infrastructures are already in place to support the convergence of designer, user, and critic. Whether or not such developments lead to socially useful products that are widely adopted, or reach markets, they test and reveal something about the contexts in which they operate. The lessons may be technological, revealing which avenues to investigate further, or which technological avenues to abandon. There may also be lessons that pertain little to the development of digital media, but rather to greater understanding of the nature of society, including marginal social conditions as well as major movements. The development and review of pervasive technologies test our attitudes toward privacy, surveillance, access, participation, dependency, personalization, conformity, and dissent. The immediate beneficiaries of this learning process may be the experimenters and developers, participants in the experiments, or those who review their work and read their articles and reports. The experimental aspects of pervasive digital media seem to contribute to the current pervasive atmosphere, the *Stimmung,* or entunement, of the social milieu, in the same way that the publicity surrounding the CERN particle accelerator, stem cell research, cloning, and Mars landings feed into our worldview, even though the experimental findings are inconclusive or the general population is unconcerned about the details.

Of course, the market of this experimentation is not value- or cost-neutral. The ready availability of support and funding for pervasive digital media research, development, and dissemination indicates that there is scope currently for experimentation in this area. In keeping with the priorities of the Information Age, the license to experiment with digital media is generous. Though profligate and sometimes wasteful, digital experiments are also constrained. Their revelations are skewed in the direction of what the technology can accomplish, and experimentation is channeled in the direction of what is technically feasible. In this book I have highlighted these directions of inquiry pertaining to tuning, through calibration, the everyday, tags, and location. Though inevitably there is much that such inquiries leave out, the consolation here for the critic is that the exaggerated embrace of technologies and devices need not lead inevitably to a reliance on automation, technological dependence, and thus the legitimation of technorationalism, but in fact can exaggerate awareness of an opposite condition. Concepts of craft, environment, nature, sustainability, sociability, presence, and being-with have emerged in tandem and in complex dialectic with major technological developments. Armed with an understanding of the purpose and outcome of research into pervasive devices, I wish to illustrate and consolidate the theme of the tuning of place with reference to a series of four experiments inevitably reflecting the material limits of the technologies at the time of writing this book.[1] My intention here is to enlist worked examples of digital design in action to bring the arguments of this book into sharper focus.

Location Services

Our first experiment involved aggregating various online services and innovations to collect and display images that are already uploaded to social network sites by communities of computer users.

Social network websites that invite membership and formation into groups of "friends" were commonplace as this book went to press. The developers of such sites have successively tuned them to the emerging practices of large numbers of people for whom the sites are instruments to maintain personal profiles, keep in touch with friends and family, locate long-lost friends, reunite families, leave messages, manage email, and deposit photographs and other files for general or private viewing. These sites also attract another category of users, including politicians and other public figures such as musicians and actors, who use them to encourage favorable commentary and expand their influence and popularity.[2] MMORPGs such as Second Life have a similar aspect, in that they enable individuals to present profiles and identify groups albeit in an overwhelmingly 3D setting meant to encourage role-play and commerce. Digital cameras and cell phones with cameras are among the panoply of pervasive digital media devices,[3] and provide resource material to be uploaded to social network websites and specialized photo-resource sites such as Flickr. Access to location services such as GPS is available on most smartphones, cell phones, digital cameras, and laptops. InstaTracker is one of a range of applications downloadable to a mobile camera or other GPS device that dispatches your current location to a website that can then be visualized as a datum on a map, for anyone to see if you so wish. You can plot your journeys across the surface of the earth as a series of points and lines. Increasingly, cameras and camera phones deploy georeferencing. Digital images are tagged with location information as metadata; the images uploaded to websites such as Flickr and Panoramio then appear positioned on digital maps at the location where they were taken. There are thousands of such images available on these websites for public scrutiny for most cities, landmarks, and areas of interest to tourists. In many cases the imagery is not of the place but of people and artifacts, the locations of which are incidental in the general scheme of the city. Such snapshots may be of the interiors of peoples' homes and gardens.

It is possible to interoperate between these various online services. For example, a group of artists at the Exploratorium in San Francisco built a web resource that plots the journeys of taxis across the city. Their site involves processing a stream of GPS coordinates made available by a taxi company, mapping these and disseminating outputs through the World Wide Web. The developers claim on their website: "The patterns traced by each cab create a living and always-changing map of city life. This map hints at economic, social, and cultural trends that are otherwise invisible. The Exploratorium has invited artists and researchers to use this information to reveal these 'Invisible Dynamics.'"[4]

The project also invites further experimentation with the same data, building on the original development of the Exploratorium artists. For example, Henrik Ekeus and Mark Wright, researchers and programmers at the University of Edinburgh, gained permission to access the data stream of the taxi locations, then used it to harvest geotagged images from Flickr and display these on a website of their own creation. This website displays a matrix of images garnered from each sample point in the journey of a designated taxi in San Francisco. Those images were posted by people unconnected with the taxi journey, days, months, or years earlier, and depicting planes landing, people on the beach, someone giving a lecture, or a garden party. The images happen to be tagged with location information close to the points on the taxi journey. According to Ekeus, "It's like the taxi is sweeping through the city tossing up memories of past events." This exercise is interesting in its own right, but served as a stimulus to further development.

Ekeus and Wright then adopted this idea to the movement not just of taxis but of any cell phone user. The traveler with a cell phone or smartphone registers his current position with InstaTracker and dispatches a text message to a special phone number, which connects to the researchers' file server. In fact, the traveler simply dispatches a text message requesting a certain number of images—three, for example. The traveler then receives a text message with WAP (Wireless Application Protocol) links to three images harvested from Flickr that are the closest to the recipient's current location. The traveler sees Flickr images relevant to that location. A tourist might find such a feature helpful in homing in on a particular attraction, or seeing what the attraction looks like under different weather conditions. There are unusual consequences however. One of the testers of this application reported the uncanny effect of being in a room and then seeing an image of it on his cell phone screen; he had uploaded that geotagged image to Flickr some months before. The traveler using the application on his mobile device receives images in areas where there is a high concentration of geotagged Flickr images. So the traveler can get a sense of what other people have found interesting about that particular location.

The services deployed in our application include InstaTracker, InstaMapper, Flickr, the Internet, the cell phone network, and GPS. The aggregated service also leverages off others' applications, visible on the web and readily accessible. In this way we tuned an application developed by an independent organization—to deploy the everyday journey of a fleet of San Francisco taxis—to suit our own needs. The authors of the cab-spotting website suggested other topics of research: "Examine the points where cabs rarely or never visit and explore why this is through photographs, interviews and historical research." Ekeus designed our version so that the nearest images are harvested. If you happen to be at a place where there are no uploads to Flickr, then the images are harvested from further afield, because the program always selects the nearest images however far away they are. If you are in the middle of a field miles from anywhere, it is likely that you will receive images on your phone from the nearest village, suggestive of a kind of telescopic vision. The content of higher-density areas spills over into less-populated areas.

In a further adaptation we expanded the idea of locative media to any digital medium, such as text documents, videos, sound files, and web links. The peripatetic worker subscribing through Facebook to our group uploads geotagged files to our central server, which then displays their positions on Google Maps. Anyone in our group will then receive access to those documents if their GPS device is nearby. Files can be uploaded to the server through a GPS-enabled phone, webpage, or email, or as text messages on a cell phone. To make the system as general as possible and work across different platforms we exploited the locational capabilities of Google Maps. If you are uploading files from a device that does not have automatic geotagging, then you need to type the area code of the location into the subject line of the email, or in the SMS message. The Google Maps applications programming interface (API) then tags the file with its approximate GPS coordinates.

Active Branding

Our second experiment worked with the theme of branding. The applications described so far fit within a suite of projects. I maintain that the projects' trajectory and methodology are as revealing as their tangible outcome or deliverables. The projects began with the general aim of deploying the current milieu of pervasive digital media to aid the conduct of business meetings—that is, meetings that are scheduled and in which people transact, plan, and reach agreement. Such meetings might include an encounter between a client and consultant, a department meeting, or a meeting of researchers and designers intent on moving a project forward. We presumed that such meetings take place not only in offices and meeting rooms, but also in public places, while in transit on planes and trains, and in local cafes, coffee shops, and bars as well as at globally franchised places (Starbucks, Club Med). It made sense to think of these improvised, uncontrolled places as "branded" meeting places.[5] Researchers have directed considerable attention to the social uses of public spaces, and the impacts of communications technologies on the social field.[6] Here we were interested in transposing some of these insights to business meetings. Such meetings generally take place in comfortable, social spaces that combine the right level of privacy with hospitality and catering. As such they are also places of commerce and inevitably are branded places: with signs, advertising, and logos as part of the paraphernalia of their ambient sub-architectures. We thought we could use the ubiquitous signs that populate these places instrumentally as accessories of the meeting context. Brand-marks are, after all, tags of a kind.

We had access to a technology that could instrumentalize such brand images using mobile phones developed by our industry partner, Mobile Acuity Ltd. You photograph an image with your cell phone and send it as a multimedia message (MMS) to a special phone number,[7] where software attempts to match that image against images in its database. A successful match can trigger a range of responses: it can send an MMS or SMS in return, phone you and play you a sound file, or activate a web page. Mobile Acuity had used this technology previously in advertising and promotional campaigns. One of its campaigns involved the production of small sheets of cardboard folded into cubes with a photograph of a celebrity printed on each face. These simple, 3D advertising objects were deposited as brochures in pubs and cafes. The cubes also had printed on them a multiple-choice question to be answered by photographing the correct face of the cube and sending this back to the server. Anyone who guessed correctly won a digital coupon for a free soft drink. Mobile Acuity also invented a treasure hunt game, in which participants received clues on where to look for a particular visual element, such as the pub sign above the Wayfarers Arms. If you found the sign you took a photograph of it with your cell phone and dispatched this to the server. The reward was an MMS with a picture of the sign that had something added: a gremlin sitting on top. In selling the technology to potential clients, the original developers of the technology deployed metaphors referring to depositing and unlocking ambient data, and suggested that the world could be its own tag. We took this capability of image matching as raw material to be fashioned into new applications. Could we deploy the same technology for tagging documents at meetings?

Much could be written on advertising as an ambient activity as part of the fabric of daily life, and the advantages of advertising that is targeted, relevant, and close to people's putative needs, oriented to activities, and engaging. As examined in chapter 6 on the subject of tags, some advertising can act as a nudge, a way of deflecting what you were going to do anyway toward particular products and services.[8] Smart campaigns seek to influence people's choices as a subtle tuning process, directed at individuals and groups. Advertising as a process of tuning is perhaps best exemplified by the case of an election campaign in which the desire is to tip the balance, by targeting the undecided voter, or voters in marginal electorates. Campaigns often are targeted to niches where small changes will make a major difference. For our project, however, the workings of ambient advertising are a diversion. We were interested in seeing how such technologies could facilitate meetings.

The project followed our research by design strategy,[9] involving teams of designers whose activities were monitored and recorded. We presented the cell phone image-matching technology to teams of designers to see what uses they could invent for it. They were supported by a programmer who was able to implement software changes to help them develop their projects. The projects did not begin with detailed specifications, but rather involved rapid prototyping and iteration. We did not steer the inception of the applications in order to see what emerged. The marketability of the final outcome of each project was of less interest to us than what the outcomes revealed about the tuning of place, and the potential each opened up for further investigation. How can the visual image be deployed operationally, to enhance, challenge, or bring into relief aspects of meeting places? The initial focus of the design team was not business meetings but game play, and not GPS but the relative locations of everyday objects identified by visual images.

Culture Jamming

Culture jamming involves the overt or covert subversion of a brand message.[10] More positively, culture jamming involves the appropriation of brand for one's own use, often political. The term *jamming* here suggests blocking, but also play, in the way that musicians might improvise around a theme, pass the theme to each other, and make the theme their own.[11] Assuming a brief that suggested the ability to leave digital graffiti on public surfaces, one of our design teams developed and implemented an "invisible art" exhibition, in which a cell phone user visits designated locations around the city and photographs particular wall surfaces. The viewer then receives prepared images via their phone of the same surface but with a "hidden" graphic revealed on it. It is as if the phone has rendered visible a hidden artwork.

How does this safe, digitally mediated culture jamming relate to the tuning of place? Needless to say, the play of such imagery has the character of graffiti. Here it was deployed to demonstrate the potential of sabotaging the neat surfaces of significant buildings. In one case the designers targeted a prominent Edinburgh department store and daubed one of its walls with their own virtual art. One team member developed this idea and superimposed images of chicken carcasses over the local storefront of a popular fast-food chain, and the logo of Gamblers Anonymous on the shop front of a local bookmaker. Of course the system could also be deployed to enhance brand imagery, unlocking brand messages and artifacts around the city, or enhancing existing brand support. The system can provide users with links to websites with further information, or messages and information about others who have visited the same location.

Researchers Mark Wright and Henrik Ekeus have since developed this capability to adjust image inserts to match the angle of view. Thus if you photograph the facade of the local department store in order to receive the hidden art, then the visual art is returned to you mapped onto your original photograph, with the same angle of view and lighting conditions. Image matching of this kind presents as an exercise in calibration: detecting the angle of view, deriving the necessary transformation, and applying this geometric transformation to the image insertion. It is an attempt to enliven or animate the everyday world with provocative interventions. The technology is also unusual. In early field tests it was apparent that people are surprised when the modified image arrived, wondering: "How did it know what image to send me?" This is of course a tamed, safe, and legal form of "graffiti art."

Such interventions relate to location. In fact, the locations where the process operates have to be prescribed, and there is an interesting challenge in working out how to notify people to direct their camera phone to a particular wall. There are technological and algorithmic constraints in play here, but it would be interesting to expand the process so that anyone anywhere could select an image from their phone's database and deposit that on any surface for anyone else to view. One could imagine a world populated by such signs, subversive and otherwise.

Brand Play

Our third experiment focused on play. Consumers can play around with brands, mixing, matching, and distorting them in ways similar to how storytellers create their own versions of other writers' plots and characters. Cultural theorist Constance Penley provides compelling examples of the subversive aspects of certain consumption practices in the context of popular television programs,[12] such as those individuals who publish their own unofficial and eroticized versions of *Star Trek* stories. While brand and copyright owners have initially objected to these activities, they now recognize such appropriation as a key motivator for their most loyal fans and customers.[13]

Brand play is ubiquitous. Conventional game play frequently involves the manipulation of tokens with which one identifies, such as the famous metal dog, thimble, ship, and other player pieces one moves around the *Monopoly* board, or the character profiles (Colonel Mustard, Mrs. Peacock, etc.) adopted by players in the game of *Clue*. MMORPGs are sociable game media involving similar identification with an avatar. Mobile phones also support games—including multiuser games—that can be played on small screens. Mobile game consoles support multiuser play and are also used for communications.[14] There are also games that deploy cell phones as portable devices. As described in chapter 7, one design team produced such a game based on tag that also bears similarities to the "paint ball" game and "capture the flag," and could take place in any setting where there is a cell phone network. Such a game has commercial potential given that the players can wear brand marks from any source, tapping into the long tradition of branded clothing.

The designers made a video of their game play that attests to the unpremeditated adaptive tactics of the player. Players wore individualized logos attached to their chest and back. To avoid being tagged (i.e., captured on camera) you need to be far enough from your opponent so that she cannot take a clear picture of your logo. Once you are photographed that image constitutes evidence that you've been tagged. When the image is sent to the server it registers the hit and keeps score. Players adopted various tactics to avoid being hit (photographed), including running in circles and wedging their bodies between surfaces so that opponents cannot get a clear picture. Of course, if you choose to assume a safe position it is unlikely you will at any stage tag your opponents. As well as the overt reference to tagging, there is the subtle calibration of practices between players. This version of tag also amplifies the sociability of play outside the context of a specific play space. Any everyday environment can be turned into a site of play. As a game the application amplifies the potential for contest in the use of pervasive devices.

Social Network Sites and Physical Network Sites

The GPS locational applications I have described derived from the work of one of our design groups that recognized and acted on the potential of social networks. Digital networks further emphasize mobility and nomadic practices. It is apparent that many people now rely on informal contact via cell phones in order to decide where to meet up, deploying techniques for alerting one another with their locations. Online social networking sites now constitute major social venues. Think of the computer user at home or at work, whose presence is registered through messaging networks that signal availability and provide a log and commentary on everyday activities. Social network sites such as Facebook, Plazes, or Twitter provide information through a user network, including users' current activities, locations, and moods. This capability seems to mirror aspects of everyday sociability and spatiality as workers, pedestrians, travelers, and friends enter and meet in different physical places, or pass one another in the corridor or street.

These experiments amplified the notion of covert branding, play, and access, and prompted further synthesis and experimentation. To explore some of these ideas further we connected these functionalities to the online community of Second Life (SL), which supports similar operations in a three-dimensional, ludic world context.

Cross Mapping Sociable Media

Our fourth experiment developed as a hybrid of these approaches and deployed the SL environment, image matching, and location identification. It is possible to port messages in and out of SL via cell phone SMS and text fields on web pages. This opens the channels of communication to include visual images, including those produced while people are on the move, outside the office and about town. As the images are projected onto the walls of the SL "virtual" room they also have the effect of evoking an atmosphere. This is not intended to replicate an everyday environment, but it provides a series of images that are suggestive of a meeting's location.

A further innovation was to introduce a simple capability for identifying locations. We created a series of locational "brand markers" and positioned them on the floor of eight different rooms in our workplace. Each marker indicates roughly where to position a mobile phone camera in order to take a photograph identifying the room. When entering the room the visitor would take a photograph as indicated and dispatch it to the server. The image matcher would then compare that image to the contents of its database to determine where the visitor is located. That locational trigger would then signal a change in the SL environment. We wrote software that provided a means of identifying at which of the eight locations the visitor is positioned. These location triggers are date stamped and the history of movement kept as a record for later inspection. For this test we only considered the location of a single visitor on the move.

The findings of this experiment are largely negative. It seems that it is not necessary for virtual meetings to take place in persistent environments. SL and similar environments purport to present a unified worldview that is the same for everyone. SL as meeting environment is a further manifestation of a highly technologized, instrumental, and mathematized one-world view. When communicating, people do not need to occupy 3D coordinate space and other representations of everyday spaces in order to conduct online meetings. There is no inevitably strong relationship between three-dimensional practice and the narratives people develop in meetings. According to urban theorists Stephen Graham and Simon Marvin, in the world of communications "there is no single, unified 'cyberspace.'"[15] 3D online social networks attempt individually to homogenize the communicative experience. In any case there are many such environments, all competing with other modes of communication.

The major advantage of conducting such studies in the SL environment is that SL provides a means of inviting people to demonstrations. At the time of the experiment, SL was populated by curious researchers interested in new ways of deploying the medium. SL is widely accessible. People can be encouraged to attend (virtually) informal demonstrations and provide feedback. This is certainly possible in other shared environments, but in this case the common access, novelty, theatricality and spatial references of SL work in favor of the promotion and progression of a research project. Accordingly, visitors leave traces when they inspect demonstrations. Persistence works in favor of the study because the experimental environment is accessible to all users of SL, even when the researchers are not present.[16]

SL has provided a new and unfamiliar context for testing ideas about sociability. Contrary to the notion that it provides a physical world simulation in which anything can happen (for example, you can fly), the new resident finds she has to adapt her social practices to the environment and to the uncomfortable circumstance of meeting other people through this medium. New practices have emerged in SL, such as signaling that you are in conference by sitting your avatar on a surface, though this is really nothing like actually sitting down to have a conversation. The encounter highlights the extent to which meeting participants, acquaintances, and friends can be elsewhere while in conversation. Not only can the people in conversation multitask on their computer (reading emails, for example) without detection, they also detach their vision from their avatar to zoom in and out of the scene, or even to target areas outside of that context, as if to multiply the putatively out-of-body experiences of virtual reality. Our own interventions compounded these complexities of practice. It seems as though the more so-called residents attempt to turn the SL experience into the everyday or "natural," the more removed from reality it becomes. If we ever needed any convincing, SL shows us that the world really is not as Cartesian geometry would suggest. No matter how much sensory data and putative realism it offers. SL draws people back to the affirmation and enjoyment of the everyday, and back to pervasive media.

Typical of any project of this kind, various changes occurred in the environment that deflected the project in different directions. Social networking was not as prevalent when we started the project, nor were its implications so apparent. APIs were introduced to Facebook and placing pictures on maps; interest in Second Life grew and waned, blogging emerged as a medium for creating and disseminating records, followed by the advent of video blogging and easy access to the creation of podcasts.

Then the iPhone appeared on the market, followed by the development of third-party applications for mobile phones and GPS and APIs for interoperating between programs and networks.

This changing climate represents an important shift in the ecology of devices and network developments. The scope for experimentation with pervasive media has grown. With a modicum of resourcefulness it is possible to produce and test complex innovations. The laptop and handheld have become the laboratory for doing so. The evolution of our project brings to mind the character of innovation in the context of pervasive digital media. Experimentation and innovation require stable infrastructures and networks, though these can be modified and tuned, and in turn undergo transformation.

In order to function as a source of useful feedback, an innovation has to provide something that people consider useful, returning pleasure, satisfaction, or a sense of participation. Even if its creators are not seeking a place for such an innovation in the commercial market, it still needs to find a place in human practices. People need to be able to adopt it and adapt themselves, their practices, and the devices to its use. One avenue we explored proved less productive. This was the deployment of voice for registering protest, for ranting over the phone against some intervention in the environment, an idea that emerged from one of our workshops and which we implemented as best we could. This involved sending a text message by cell phone to our server, a key word only, such as *election*. The server would then call that texter back and invite him to leave a voice message on that topic. Another person who sent the same text message (*election*) would also receive a phone call and be invited to add their voice message to the first. Messages would accrete over time. The first texter would only hear the last few messages on the phone, but at any time could hear the full set via a website. As it happens, technologies for leaving voice messages are not well developed or reliable, but more importantly we discovered that people do not like being telephoned by a machine and then expected to voice an opinion on the spot. The positive side of this experiment was the confirmation that people's voices constitute a special human capability that they do not readily deposit or abandon for others to make use of.[17]

Innovations are also called on to fit within an ecology of other networks and devices. There are marketplaces of devices and ideas, and competition among them. In keeping with the ecological metaphor, such marketplaces are prone to incremental change and adaptation. There needs also to be a critical mass of users and innovators. Although our experiments were in media that could be accessed by anyone, they were never conducted online long enough or well publicized or sufficiently reliable and robust to enjoy a global user base. Scalability emerges as an important concept in the innovation of pervasive digital media. Much product design assumes a relatively modest and localized investment in innovation and testing. Eventually the production of the device or application is scaled up, mass produced, distributed, and serviced worldwide. In the case of digital media the worldwide distribution comes much earlier in the process, and for free. The scale issue enters in terms of consumer volume.

With many users of an online application you need robust servers and software. With many interoperating applications reliability is less assured. Consumers demand trouble-shooting services and updates from developers and online publishers. Then there are issues pertaining to privacy, program security, and data,[18] especially if money changes hands. Various development platforms provide much of the robustness and security needed, but in the case of some of our own development work the innovations stretched the capabilities of the platforms that supported them, such as integrating analog voice-messaging services.

The operations of such incremental innovations are illustrated well in the case of the iPhone applications store. Apple has opened a marketplace for rapid development and user testing in ways that seem both to promote the Apple brand and to encourage innovation. The environment also supports versioning and customer reviews. It is tempting to think that the requirement for robustness points to a development norm that is highly regularized, organized, and outside the philosophy of subtle tuning advocated in this book. Perhaps serious, commercial, accountable design requires processes that differ from the relatively free-form experimentation of innovation outlined here. I propose that the processes are the same. To reiterate an argument I presented in chapter 1, the most rigorously articulated plans for design, development, production, distribution, and support, are after all artifacts; they are designed objects—charts, tables, diagrams, and spreadsheets that aid in communication. The real work is done by the complex network of social actors who interpret and draw on such artifacts, and use them to synchronize, calibrate, and tune their actions to one another in order to produce additional artifacts. Rather than eschewing rigor, concepts of tuning accord to their rightful place the artifactual nature of plans, actions, and things.

Regularized design brings to mind its converse in capricious and chaotic creation, or the workings of noise, a study conducive to a closer understanding of aggregated services, data, and programs—and the subject of chapter 11.

11 Noise

Claude Shannon's seminal essay on communication theory provides a model of communication that assumes a sender and a receiver. A signal passes between the two.[1] The sender and receiver can be two people in conversation, the interlocutors at either end of a telephone line, a computer server and client, a transmitter and mobile device, or any subcomponent of these and similar configurations. Shannon deployed a now familiar diagram, which in its simplest form shows the sender and the receiver as two rectangular boxes aligned horizontally, labeled *sender* and *receiver* and connected by an arrow progressing from the sender to the receiver.[2] One of the main innovations of this model was to theorize the problem of noise intervening in the passage of the signal, and to ascertain the capacity of a noisy communication channel to transmit information.[3]

Noise is an obvious consideration as designers, users, and theorists reflect on ubiquitous media and tuning. Hisses, crackles, and distortions are among the first symptoms of an out-of-tune analog radio receiver. Computer users are not so aware of noise in the transmission of digital information, that is, when they transfer files or receive text or graphic data through the Internet. Digital bits are discrete and can be error-checked and re-sent instantaneously under control of network firmware and software.[4] Noise enters computer users' awareness of digital transmission if they have to invoke compression algorithms to reduce the size of a file so it will fit through available bandwidth in reasonable time; when they have to change the sample rate settings of a sound or image. Many graphics programs allow you to adjust the compression of JPEG- or TIFF-formatted images. The file size of a highly compressed image will be smaller than an image with low compression. The cost of this reduction in file size is that a highly compressed image may be less clear than an uncompressed image. It will tend to blur or smooth details in the picture or you will see some side effects (artifacts) of the algorithm that restores the image from its compressed state.[5] Creators of digital multimedia content may have to trade file size for image clarity. Similar processes are at work with sound compression, as in the case of the MP3 compression format.[6] Sample rate is a relatively simple way to think of sound compression. Sound waves propagate as variations in frequency and amplitude. When converted to digital signals they must be converted to sequences of binary numbers indicating amplitude at each microsecond of the sound's duration. Shannon has shown that a sample rate of twice the maximum frequency of a source is sufficient to accurately reconstruct the original signal.[7] Much lower sampling rates produce the audible distortion characteristic of telephone communications. The benefit of low sample rates is that more channels can be passed along the wire and more signals transmitted within a particular bandwidth. Lower sample rates produce smaller files and hence more efficient transmission through networks. Higher compression produces noisier data. The process of trading compression for sound or image quality has to be "tuned." How much noise will you tolerate for the convenience of being able to store and transmit sounds and images through portable media?

Noise also has a bearing on people's ability to communicate and on their comfort. Cultural theorist Emily Thompson provides a telling history of early modernity in terms of its generation of and responses to the increasing din of industrial production and motorized transportation: "the Roaring Twenties really did roar."[8] In 1930 the New York Noise Abatement Commission identified a range of noise sources, most of which were machinic in some way: traffic, transportation, building operations, harbor sounds, collections and deliveries, and airplanes. These competed for prominence with loudspeakers and radios in homes and on the street, and musical instruments, late parties, and barking dogs. In the contemporary context, cell phone ringtones and conversations constitute noise that disturbs reading, listening, viewing, quiet contemplation, and conversations. The ability of people engaged in conversation to block, exclude, or ameliorate the effects of noise also presents as an exercise in subtle tuning. People are adept at identifying and targeting noise. They object not only to loud and raucous sounds or the deep bass from the neighbor's surround-sound entertainment center but also to the high frequencies generated by personal stereos that leak into the environment, the quiet pings from other people's game consoles, and taps on a computer keyboard. The use of noise-blocking technologies, such as personal stereos and special noise-cancellation headphones, present an obvious means of adjusting and tuning environments to suit an individual's personal requirements. The designers of open-floorplan offices install speaker systems that transmit white noise in order to raise the threshold of hearing: while the human aural apparatus attends unconsciously to the white noise—selected sounds that people find neutral or pleasant—office workers trying to concentrate on the task at hand are less aware of other intermittent and potentially distracting or disturbing sounds.

People often think of noise as random and unattributable sounds. More technically, and as defined by Shannon, noise is any unstructured or random signal. Noisy signals are those with high entropy. Like the molecules of a heated liquid or a gas, noise contains a lot of energy and random movement. Shannon identifies noise with distortion and the introduction of errors,[9] but the most interesting aspect of noise is that it introduces ambiguity, which he calls "equivocation": "the average ambiguity of the received signal."[10] A noisy signal is not only full of errors, but it contains *a multiplicity of signals*. Sound theorist Douglas Kahn captures this definition with his claim: "Noise is the forest of everything."[11] Shannon distanced himself from a concern with the meanings of messages, but in human terms it seems that listeners and viewers can read lots of messages from a noisy signal. Think of a mistuned FM radio, or a poor telephone signal. It is not only that determined listeners can't hear what is being said, but also that they hear too much. They don't only hear "the train is delayed," but "the rain is delayed," "the train is derailed," and other phonetic variations. Listeners get the message thanks to repetition and their capacity to derive meaning from context.[12] In fact, in so far as communication is the passage of a signal through a conduit, it invariably involves a multiplicity of filters that transform the noise into something intelligible.

For a while one of the top-ranking YouTube clips was of an excerpt from a popular UK television program (*Songs of Praise*) showing a church congregation singing a well-known hymn, but apparently to absurd words displayed as subtitles. "Blessed city, happy Salem" became "Yes I'm sitting, happy sailor," and other arbitrary phrases.[13] The noise and ambiguity in the sounds from a large gathering of voices, viewer's underdeveloped capacity to accurately read lips, and the clever manipulation of textual cues all conspired to filter the noise into something at extreme variance with what a worshipper expects to hear sung or said in a church. Filtering is so much sensory tuning of the ambiguity of noise.

Noise enters Shannon's diagram from below as a third box with its own arrow pointing at right angles midway along the line connecting the sender to the receiver. His mathematical theory of communication extends beyond the limits of this diagram, but already noise comes across as something alien, from the outside, an intrusion. As the theories indicate, noise is in fact commonly a product of the communication system itself. But as the diagram indicates, noise presents as extraneous, as intruding from beyond the edges of the frame. Noise may eventually emerge center stage, and its source is revealed, but its origin in fact and conceptually is off stage. Murray Schafer captures this sentiment in less technical terms: it is as if noise "descends from God."[14]

The UK Living TV channel runs a popular ghost-hunting program entitled *Most Haunted*. Much of each episode is recorded using a night-vision camera, and the production team's usual indication of paranormal activity as they move through the darkness is a team member exclaiming in an agitated voice, "Did you hear that?!" There is a flurry of excitement and anxiety as presenters and camera crew turn in the direction of the sudden tap, bang, or knock. The popular nineteenth-century parlor séance, and its depiction in fiction and film, is characterized similarly by the excitement generated by noises from outside the current setting, which then assume the character of sounds from beyond, and from the deceased. The idea of disembodied sound has long connoted access to ethereal otherness—sounds from without. According to Kahn, the earliest days of the electronic recording and transmission of sound were accompanied by the notion that listeners could now hear the voices of the deceased.[15] Detecting such subtle sounds from without requires tuning in to the glitches, crackles, and blips in the environment, and those occurring outside the frame.

Not all sounds from without are noises, but attentive listeners are content to call them such until they identify or corroborate the source, often by visual means. "I heard a noise" is nonspecific. It could be water running in a pipe, someone walking up the stairs, a timber structure creaking, a car passing. With a stronger hypothesis or greater evidence a listener might simply say, "I heard a car," which settles the matter. Until listeners are satisfied that they have identified it, the noise presents many possibilities—too many possibilities, in fact, including spirits. In Stephen Spielberg's film called *Poltergeist,* the white noise from a television set that has lost its signal after station shutdown becomes a medium for the communication of messages from beyond. The hisses and crackles become distant whispers. The movie audience soon tunes in to a specific hypothesis from a plethora of possibilities. Tuning and filtering are closely related. Listeners filter noise. The corroboration of a sound also operates as a type of tuning, aligning the visual with the aural, calibrating expectations to the evidence, and filtering the evidence to suit expectations.

Noise effects are not only subtle. The externality of noise suggests its potential for intrusion and violence. Like a blow to the body, noise has visceral effects.[16] The word *noise* shares its etymology with *nausea,* which means sickness in the stomach and also disgust. Noise has similarly been deployed as an emblem of protest and resistance. Think of the sounds of the angry mob. The appeal to noise acts as a foil against the language of order and harmony. I referred in chapter 1 to the way that uneven temperament has been deployed by theorists such as Max Weber to characterize the premodern, when musical tunings were prone to produce effects that strike modern listeners as discordant, which is to say noisy. Luigi Russolo's 1913 manifesto, the *Art of Noises,* listed the sounds of machinery and animals: roars, thunder, explosions, bangs, booms, creaking, rustling, humming, crackling, rubbing, shouts, screams, shrieks, wails, and hoots in its typology of sounds for composition. He was in the company of other Futurist composers who celebrated machine noises, the "nonsymbolic" and the "alogical."[17] The Dadaists too, such as Kurt Schwitters, explored the potential of the repeated recitation of letters of the alphabet or syllables, at varying speed and volume, to create a babble that he would have been content to hear people deride as noise. Jacques Attali's polemical book *Noise: The Political Economy of Music* advances similar provocation: "Work noise, noise of man, and noise of beast. Noise bought, sold or prohibited. Nothing essential happens in the absence of noise."[18] He contrasts noise with the musical and social imperative toward harmony and order, or "code." In this polemic, notice the reference to the interplay between the unsubtle effects of loud noise and stark silence: "Our science has always desired to monitor, measure, abstract, and castrate meaning, forgetting that life is full of noise and that death alone is silent."[19]

Noise might appear to present the converse to a philosophy of fine-tuning, nudges, and increments. But the subtle aspects of noise that I want to relate to the tuning of place here pertain to noise's relationship with silence. The theme of silence provides a means of explaining the ambiguity and externality of noise.

Silence

Noise is close to silence in any case. For Attali there are three modes of controlling people through the emotive power of music: you can try to make them forget, to make them believe in something, or you can silence them.[20] To be silenced or exposed to silence constitute modes of subjugation. Noises in everyday life corroborate the power of the contrast between noise and silence. The cessation of noise can be alarming at least. Augoyard reports the experiences of people inside an elevator in a housing estate: "Dramatic evocations are set in gear on the basis of *noises*." Noises invoke haunted castles, but "the most dramatic images arise with the *halt of the noise*, at the point where one no longer knows whether one is moving or if one is stuck."[21] Silences bounded either side by noise are more potent that silences alone, as are noises interspersed with silence. Silence has boundaries, which contribute substantially to its character. For film theorist Michel Chion, the impression of silence in a film requires preparation. It is the result of the contrast to a previous very loud moment: "Silence is never a neutral emptiness."[22]

The composer John Cage reinforces the point that "there is no such thing as silence."[23] Absence is noisy and ambiguous. After all, it is a trivial truth that there are more things that can be off screen at any moment than in the frame. Eavesdroppers picking up on someone's conversation on a mobile phone have to infer from half of the conversation what the other party is saying, which is to say, to discriminate from a range of possible remarks. Hearing nothing at all of one half of an exchange relates to noise in extremis. Think of silence not as nothing but as so much white noise containing every possible signal. This is also one of the lessons of silent film. Chion suggests that prior to talking movies, "Garbo in the silent era had as many voices as her admirers individually conferred on her. The talkie limited her to one, her own."[24] It is helpful to think of absence as noise, as providing infinite possibilities of what could be, a space of rich potential, of high entropy, in which to exercise the imagination. It is in the silences and gaps that possibilities reside.[25] There are also situations in which people do not speak, will not speak, or cannot speak: as in the case of the silent musician or dancer. Silent commuters on public transport, clients at the gym, or a phalanx of security police speak with voices of the listener's own choosing, until these otherwise silent companions are actually heard to speak. Silent and obsequious attendants and servants further tarry on the edge of inscrutability, which is to say their silence carries a multiplicity of voices.

Silence is also a response in the face of the indescribably grand, beautiful, horrific, glorious, or profound: that which aestheticians commonly describe as unspeakable, or ineffable. In their detailed study of the acoustics of renaissance churches in Venice, Howard and Moretti note that "Most people respond almost unwittingly—with softened footsteps, perhaps, or hushed voices—to the special sound qualities of a religious interior."[26] According to architectural theorist Juhani Pallasmaa, "A powerful architectural experience silences all noise; it focuses our attention on our very existence, and as with all art, it makes us aware of our fundamental solitude."[27] Certain architectures at times take our breath away. The sublime is also that which escapes the reflective observer's capacity to imagine or describe: the extent of the constellations, the size of an atom, pure transcendence, complete silence, the Big Bang, ceasing to be, the terrors of nature, the power of the machine, the global navigation satellite system (GNSS), the implausibility of flight. It is as if in the face of such wonders there is after all nothing that can be said.[28]

For Immanuel Kant, the response to the beautiful in nature is calm contemplation, but in consideration of the sublime one is "moved." According to Kant, "This movement (especially in its inception) may be compared to a vibration, i.e., to a rapidly alternating repulsion from and attraction to one and the same object."[29] Human imagination, the capacity to represent or describe, and words fail us in the face of the sublime: "What is excessive for the imagination . . . is as it were an abyss."[30] The concept of vibration, which is readily ascribed to sound, comes to the aid of the acoustic aesthetician in giving an account of silence, the gap, and the tuning of place.

So this space, silence, gap is not nothing but is instead a vibration, an oscillation. My colleague and architectural theorist Adrian Snodgrass describes the Japanese philosophical concept of *ma, No-Mind,* in terms of the gap. *Ma* is both spatial and temporal: "It is a stop or pause in a sequence of actions or events, . . . the pause that interrupts the flow of narrative, sound or action."[31] In Japanese arts these spaces are regarded as highly productive. In his investigation of cultures of sound, cultural theorist Steven Connor explores concepts of the gap through clapping, which involves the conjunction of two surfaces of flesh, generated collectively or in private, prolonged or brief, to signify approbation or censure, as interruption multiplied. Clapping "creates a space, a shape in time and space."[32]

Certain spaces also invoke respectful silences in response to institutional apparatus, the means by which bodies are encouraged to be docile or placid. This is one of Foucault's main observations about the development of modernism toward progressively ordered practices and institutions that encourage quiet, well-comported, and docile bodies.[33] The expression of state power is transformed from brutal punishments, public ridicule, quashing of rebellion, and strident repression, to confining people in corrective prisons; ordering people's days by the clock; disciplining inmates, soldiers, and children with arbitrary marching drills and recitations; and subjecting the sick and socially marginalized to hospital routines. According to Foucault's theme of the panoptical prison, society orders space so that people are aware constantly of the presence of the reproachful gaze, of their superiors or each other. As in Thomas More's *Utopia,* citizens have a tendency to behave themselves because "Everyone has his eye on you."[34] Silence is abetted by the hegemony of vision.

Expanding further on Foucault's panopticism, building occupants may be inured to the sublime aspects of spaces that support mezzanines, glass elevator shafts, communicating bridges, escalators, large-format display screens, and other trappings of modernity, but such devices ensure they are always under the gaze of others. Contemporary panoptical architecture invokes a sense of seeing and being seen, hearing without being heard, which engenders a kind of docility and quiet. Technologies are further grafted onto such spaces, such as closed-circuit television (CCTV) and other surveillance technologies, to abet the inducement to acquiescent silence.

Silence shares with noise the operations of ambiguity, a multiplicity of signals. Silence also draws on outside sources, externally generated noises, to define and fill it. In this respect silence and noise are two sides of the same coin, polar opposites in a dialectical tension, players in a game or contest (*agon,* as introduced in chapter 1). Each infuses and distorts the other. Such play pertains to philosophies of the gap.

Gap Filling

According to Snodgrass, the *ma* is manifested in Japanese music as "the rest that temporarily stops the melody in order to evoke the power of silence; in the Kabuki, it is the 'pose' (*mie*) that freezes action for dramatic effect; it is the core of an actor's 'timing' or the comedian's delay before delivering the punch-line."[35] Twentieth-century occidental musical composition has made much of silences: John Cage's *4′33″*, in which the performer or ensemble does nothing for the duration of the piece,[36] or Arnold Schoenberg's *Erwartung,* which opens up a moment in time, extending an event of one-minute duration to half an hour. Matt Rogalsky's *Two Minutes Fifty Seconds Silence* captures the silences between the words in a speech by President George W. Bush; Rogalsky's work is prosaically described as "a reduction of address to the world by President George W. Bush 8 pm EST, Monday March 17 2003."[37] The resultant drone, intakes of breath, and exhalations are likened to the sounds of the drums of war. The listener reads much into the noise of the gap (*ma*) between words.[38]

The sublime also implicates echo, the interreflection of sounds across and between surfaces that occupies the "silences" between notes. Unreflective spaces seem unresponsive and absorptive, as in the case of Howard and Moretti's description of a church interior: "In the very dry acoustic of the nave, the singers could hardly hear their own voices, which seemed to evaporate into an unresponsive, absorbent void."[39] Conversely, spaces with highly reflective surfaces can generate such interreflections as to amplify the tiniest sound, which then gets lost in the noise of its own reflections, even favoring certain frequencies over others depending on the nature of the space.

The effects of interreflected sounds have long been a concern in architecture, as indicated in Vitruvius's advice on the design of theaters[40] and the placement of large vases to prevent disturbing resonances.[41] Howard and Moretti describe the qualities of the church of San Francesco in Venice in terms of such resonance: "The direct sound was followed by some reverberation from around the nave, giving a satisfying roundness. Further away, the sound was less vigorous, but its mystical, devotional character proved equally emotive."[42] In San Martino: "The mellifluous sound seemed to envelop the listener in the nave, as if rolling along the ceiling and floating down from above."[43] Reverberation relates to noise in that it can "muddy" the otherwise pure sound of a choir; it can introduce ambiguity, occlude the effects of error, fill the silences, transport the listener and the performer, and invoke the sublime. As if to underline this point, Blesser and Salter in their book on aural architecture speculate that prehistoric ancestors would have thought of caves as homes to powerful spirits due to the reverberations therein. A cave would seem to respond to the sounds of a person's approach with living voices.[44]

Singers and instrumentalists adapt their style to the nature of the performance space, and composers take into account the characteristics of the space or medium in which their work will be performed. Music written for a cathedral will differ from that composed for a salon. Performers and composers tune their works to place. Resonance, the residue of sound decayed, muffled, and distorted, has been abstracted as a performance medium in its own right. Alvin Lucier's sound piece *"I am sitting in a room"* (1970) involves repeated recording and playback of a spoken sequence.[45] This recursive recording process eventually occludes the original spoken words and reveals the hollow, booming quality of the space in which the recording was made. As recounted in chapter 5, the soundscapes of Pauline Oliveros deploy reverberant sounds from hollow plastic tubes and Pedro Rebelo's work in Lisbon exploits the spatial resonance of water cisterns. The dark ambient music of Robert Henke also presents as a droning resonance in which the listener is scarcely able to detect the sounds of machines and of nature. The musician David Byrne turns old buildings into musical instruments by strapping solenoids, switches, and motors to plumbing fixtures, girders, and pillars and cabling them to a keyboard.[46] The sounds produced are deep, resonant, industrial, and reverberant.

Needless to say, spaces are also tuned to accommodate the requirements of sound, often remedially, with wall hangings and baffles, for example, and electronic sound systems and other technologies are put in place to alter the sonic characteristics of spaces. Pervasive digital devices in the form of personal stereos further expand the reaches of space, as personal, mobile sound sources that overlay and interact with the sounds of the environment, fill some gaps, and create other gaps. The tuning of place involves the subtle manipulation of noise and its complicity with silence.

Absent Others

I have alluded to the ambiguity inherent in noise, its putative source from outside the frame, and the complicity of noise with silence. The externality of noise and its relationship with silence invoke thought of absence. To the extent that the clock and by extension ubiquitous digital media "synchronize the actions of men," most of the agents of this coordination are outside anyone's particular horizon at any time. Would-be companions are inevitably in different times and places, conspicuous by their absence, as people say sometimes. For Urry, with mobile phones: "Absent others are only a call or text message away so people can be in communication with significant others while moving through a sea of strangers."[47] Michael Bull highlights the pathos of so many pedestrians distracted by mobile phone communications: "In a world where most of us are talking to 'absent others' the street becomes a potentially lonelier place."[48] Absences are rendered sadly obvious through the sound of a ringtone to which no one responds, the static or silence when the person on the other end of the line hangs up, the empty voice message, or the ethereal noises the phone owner receives when a friend accidentally triggers the automatic dialer of his phone. Silences muffled by clothing pockets or handbags are so many reminders of potential communications beyond the would-be interlocutor's current horizon: reminders of absent others. The single footprint on the shore provokes such an awareness of an "absent other," the discovery by Robinson Crusoe, Daniel Defoe's castaway. De Certeau uses Defoe's story to demonstrate the extent to which such a singular sign can disturb the individual's sense of mastery, assuaged only "when the absent other shows himself."[49] Concerns about absence fold into disquiet over anonymous others whose goals are unknown, but who nonetheless exert influence. For philosopher Alfred Schutz, with rapid communications individuals are "potentially subject to everybody's remote control."[50] These absent others can become agents of control.

Absence connects with ritual, not least in cultural theorist Jean Baudrillard's assertion that certain rituals and attendant images mask the "absence of a profound reality."[51] For the dialectical materialist (following Karl Marx), so much religious ritual is thought to occlude the fact that there is, after all, really nothing there. But there is no need to foreclose on the issue of who or what lies behind the ritual.[52] Classicist David Gill explains Greek sacrificial ritual as an extension of table-fellowship. The host might set a place at the common table for a god: "The fact that an extra place was apparently made at table for the god (the trapezomata)—seems to indicate that the god was thought of as himself being present at the meal in some way."[53] That the god is present at the table of the meal-sacrifice points to the importance of communion with an absent other, an invisible guest. This ancient notion of communion, being at table, the session (séance), resonates with the concepts of noise as ambiguous, external, and with the invocation of otherness. A detour on the ritual aspects of the meal will further illuminate the subject of noise and its ambiguous and external aspects.

Sitting down for a communal meal carries connotations of communality in any case.[54] The meal is sanctioned and elevated by certain rituals and practices, and is also brought into service as a pointer to other, apparently transcendent truths.[55]

What is the character of the communal meal? The image of the traditional communal meal is of a noisy, animated affair, but noise also enters the frame insofar as the meal draws on externality, concepts of absent guests. In a "traditional" family meal the order in which people get served, the apportionment of the best cuts and quantities, indicates something about the relationships among the people present: host and guests, parents, children, elders, with differing seniority, status, and roles.[56] Lewis Hyde explains how the Greek idea of sacrifice amplified such ritual apportionment: "The way the Greeks divided an animal made a map of the way their community was divided."[57] Accordingly, the best cuts would go to the master of the house, with the slaves having to be content with leftovers.[58] Modern consumers have transformed such traditions to accommodate takeout meals, fast food, TV dinners, fridge raids, bachelor meals, leftovers, microwave cooking, snacking, dieting, bingeing, catering for allergies and asynchronous meal times—but the role of apportionment in the communal meal is far from lost, and persists for some at least as representations in television programs about food preparation.

Noise also enters the frame of the meal as a factor that ambiguates the social order. The god Hermes plays a major role in stories about food, consumption, and sacrifice, and is characterized as the one who subverts categories and messes up the social order. Hermes "invents the trick of reapportionment, some sleight of hand by which the thigh of an ox ends up on the plate of a slave."[59] Hermes the trickster god recurs in various ritualized forms. According to Gill, there was the "the custom of placing small bits of food on top of the piles of stones (hermai) that dotted the countryside and in which a deity, later called Hermes after the stone piles, was thought to be embodied."[60] Travelers and pilgrims frequently recognize the presence of someone or something whose physical manifestation they do not detect. The other has come and gone, will follow after, or is invisibly present. Dinner in front of the television reveals this trickster function to great effect: the media celebrity assumes the role of the absent guest and ambiguates the customs of the meal.

There is a trace here in various rituals and practices, ancient and contemporary, of an absent other, someone—or something—who is offstage, who disturbs understanding, a role often associated with mischief. Frustrated computer users attribute the failure of an electronic device to a gremlin in the works, the bug that creeps into the circuitry. In an extended series of oblique metaphors on the politics of noise, Michel Serres relates noise to the role of the rodent or parasite. The home occupant never knows for sure whether the parasite is guest or host: "The host, the guest, breathes twice, speaks twice, speaks with forked tongue, as it were."[61] As for noise, Serres inserts the parasite in the communication channel between the two interlocutors and conjectures a three-way relationship: "The guest becomes the interrupter; the noise becomes interlocutor; part of the channel becomes obstacle and vice versa."[62] The provocation here seems to be to think of noise as confounding the distinctions between sender and receiver: "The noise, through its presence and absence, the intermittence of the signal, produces the new system, that is to say, oscillation."[63]

There is much that could be said about absent others, or invisible guests, but I here attribute to this invisible entity the characteristic of noise. For my purposes here it is worth seeing this absent entity in its noisy, ambiguating, and provocative aspect, as the entity that enters the communication channel from the bottom of Shannon's diagram, from outside the frame.

Like noise, it seems that sociability draws as much on absences as it relies on those who are present. Digital social media such as Facebook and Second Life seem to provide unlimited opportunity for interacting with others, but have inevitably developed protocols for dealing with who is in and who is out of one's social orbit. It seems that there are limits regarding whom users of social networks will accept into their circle as "friends." The willful breach of such protocols is sometimes referred to as "griefing." The visitor is not only uninvited but also unwelcome, bent on messing up other people's interaction and role-play.

People's relationships with the other can also be accounted for as a tuning process. Viewers tune in the television set, and tune into the channel, the vicarious presence, at the TV dinner. The other also invokes concepts of conversation and dialogue. There is always someone else present in any individual's deliberations. According to literary theorist Mikhail Bakhtin, "verbal discourse is a social phenomenon—social throughout its entire range and in each and every of its factors, from the sound image to the furthest reaches of abstract meaning."[64] Social practices, human culture, and private thought consist of a multiplicity of languages and voices: "As a living, socio-ideological concrete thing, as heteroglot opinion, language, for the individual consciousness, lies in the borderline between oneself and the other."[65] Words and ideas are always "half someone else's."[66] Before I appropriate an idea and call it my own "it exists in other people's mouths, in other people's contexts, serving other people's intentions."[67]

The externality that is noise is endemic to thought processes. Psychologists such as Hubert Hermans have expanded notions of the ubiquity of dialogue into theories of the "dialogical self": "One person is like two persons in dialogue."[68] Sometimes the communicants in this internal dialogue are in a destructive relationship, where one voice, a negative voice, dominates the rest. Some psychoanalysts express what I am calling calibration and tuning as the formation of coalitions, positioning and counterpositioning.[69] It seems that one of the tasks of psychotherapy is to reorganize the "self-system."[70] The idea of the divided self, the parts of which need to reach some kind of coalition, is not new. Freud's concepts of the id, the ego, and the super-ego, Lacan's concepts of the fractured self, and Deleuze and Guattari's elevation of schizophrenia all point to the resolution or provocation of internal differences and competing voices.[71] The human psyche is a noisy forum of ambiguous voices. Silence and noise give space to any of a number of voices. Foucault's prison warden who can see but barely be seen has a homologue in invisible dialogue.[72] The controller at the security console is mute. The authority here of the other resides in the multiplicity of vocal possibilities from which listeners make instantaneous choices. The voice they hear is of their own devising, the inner voice of authority, or in Freud's terms, the voice of the censor or super-ego.

Echoes and reverberations are the traces of a sound source that is terminated or exhausted, or of someone who has just left. Noisy silences are akin to absence. The friend of a friend who was invited to the party but never showed up can be the subject of endless speculation. Waiting guests fill the void with conjecture. Samuel Beckett's play *Waiting for Godot* highlights this potential, as the characters reflect on the human condition while waiting for someone who may never show up. The absence of the other reveals much about those who are present. There are several traditions that celebrate the absence of an ambiguous other, such as deliberately setting a place at table for an invisible guest. That noises have their origin outside the frame makes them close companions to the absent other.[73]

The concept of multiple selves is not new to digital media. Much has been written about how role-play in digital social networks and multiuser games reveals how ready people are to display themselves as multiple and complex.[74] The multitude of voices that make up the self are voices off, noises from beyond the frame,[75] and they are voices-noises that can be tuned into or tuned out.

Noises Off

That noises enter the communication channel as interference from outside recalls the proposition that sound is extraneous, subservient to vision, and enters the viewer's field of vision from outside. Film stresses the externality of sound. Sound was introduced late in the history of the medium. More importantly, sound serves as a means of extending the action contained within the visual frame to what might lie beyond it. Michel Chion articulates the role in film of the voice that appears from outside the frame, which he identifies as the acousmêtre. He draws attention to three such voices that it is appropriate to relate to the functioning of noise and everyday conditions.

First, there is the already visualized voice whose face is known but currently not seen, and generally projects reassurance.[76] The voiceover from a recognized celebrity in a television commercial might serve this function. The voiceover connotes a standard against which the viewer calibrates the content of the frame. The advertisers want the content of the frame to inherit, absorb, or otherwise tune to the standard set by the personality and authority of the voice. The voice of a friend or a familiar voice on the telephone can have this reassuring function. The externality of noise has a reminding and reassuring function, as in the familiar sound of the ventilation fan, rain on the tin roof, waves on the seashore.

Second is the voice of the commentator who has no personal stake in the scene. Comparable to the narrator of a news item or nature program is the public address announcement, whether live or recorded. The occupants of waiting rooms at bus stations and airports generally take such announcements in their stride, though passengers are sometimes surprised to discover that the source of the ubiquitous voice is in fact the check-in clerk in front of them. The commentator voice is also close to Chion's "radio" voice, the voice heard over the radio that has no possibility of showing itself, and therefore does not participate in the uncertainty or choice of visibility. The externality of noise can also project such indifference, as in the case of the routine public announcement, the sound of traffic, a jackhammer, or someone else's choice of music in a public space.

Third, there is the completely absent voice, to whom no one can yet attach a face, "but who remains liable to appear in the visual field at any moment."[77] The completely absent voice is a potent element in cinema. The voice can be from within the frame or outside it. Film directors make play with the possibilities of revelation at any time, and the suspense this builds, which Chion calls the "epiphany of the acousmêtre." As in Alfred Hitchcock's film *Psycho*, "the completely absent voice brings disequilibrium and tension."[78] The surprise ending of *Psycho* in which the voice is matched to its particular source requires a recalibration on the part of the viewer of the entire movie. Events that did not quite make sense are now reconfigured in her review or subsequent viewings of the film.[79] The voice at the other end of a cell phone conversation has a similar role to Chion's characterization of the completely absent voice, and the occlusion and revelation of the voice constitute a repeated epiphany. The externality of noise can function in this way, where the distant roar is revealed as the sound of a low-flying aircraft, the rattling sound in the forest is a great spotted woodpecker, and the shuffle at the front door is the arrival of the mail.

Public spaces are not so dominated by the frame as cinema, though it is difficult to divorce media-savvy individuals' experience of space, and the expectations it engenders, from the experience of cinema, cinematic collage, and amateur photography. Furthermore, public spaces in global cities are dominated by advertising imagery that inevitably adopts the conventions of framing, and presents to the visual field as so many overlapping framed images. Increasingly, such spaces are dominated by at least one animated video screen, showing Sky or CNN broadcasts. Insofar as environments are presented as framed, they share with cinema the potency of the externality of noise, vocal and otherwise.

The rectangular frame may not shape the everyday world, but there are spaces from which people may be heard but not seen. Howard and Moretti describe Venetian churches in which orphan girls were recruited to sing from concealed positions in "singing galleries" high overhead, as if off stage or outside the frame. The congregation would not see the choristers arriving, singing, or departing: "The sense of mystery was enhanced by the ornate metal grille, which screened the singers from view." Howard and Moretti report how congregations of the time were transported by these delightful celestial sirens' "voices from paradise."[80] Such is the impact of the voice outside the frame and that harbors the potential to reveal its source at any time. The externality of noise participates in these vocal, cinematic effects of reassurance, indifference, and expectation, the three voices of the acousmêtre.

Calibrating the Voice

So the externality of noise brings us to the human vocal apparatus, the most obvious source of sound and noise, and a source of ambiguity. The operation of the voice from outside the frame highlights the need to coordinate (calibrate) the voice with other sensory modalities. Cinema rarely deploys the voice as recorded by the actors while they are being filmed. Voices are added afterward by the actors and engineers in a sound studio, and adjusted and placed with the image as part of the editing process. This overdubbing, or post-synchronization, further indicates the disjunction between voices and bodies, sounds and visual images. In some cases the connection can be disengaged deliberately, as in the case of Federico Fellini's use of voices that "hang on the bodies of actors in only the loosest and freest sense, in space as well as in time."[81] The combination of dance and song in the Bollywood musical exhibits a similar detachment.

Ventriloquism likewise emphasizes the externality of the voice and the necessary calibration of voice and interaction. Connor's seminal work on the history of ventriloquism, *Dumbstruck*,[82] highlights the legacy of throwing the voice, making it appear to come from a different part of the body than the throat, projecting it across space, disguising the voice, and grafting the voice onto other bodies. The control of the voice in a way that suggests action at a distance shows a command over space,[83] but like the video of the church congregation singing incongruous words, the trick depends on tolerance to different sensory cues, and the performer's ability not only to synchronize her vocal projections with the movement of the lips on a puppet, but also to effect an appropriate calibration and recalibration of sensory cues in the audience.[84] John Logie Baird's early experiments with television involved the projection of the face of a ventriloquist's dummy.[85] The powerful lights required were too hot for a human being to endure. But the necessity to use a dummy hints that the ventriloquial aspects of these media were apparent at a very early stage. Now there are myriad ways of throwing the voice, through television broadcasts, projecting persona into mobile devices through ventriloquial proxies, and talkative avatars. The ambiguity and externality of voice maps onto the character of noise.[86]

Cinema draws on the false attribution of vocal agency, the simulation of the vocal apparatus (overdubbing, post-synchronization, Foley editing) continuing the Rebalesque tradition whereby comedians and impersonators artificially graft words into the mouths of public figures. The tradition continues with algorithms that simulate the voice, digital devices that deploy a synthetic voice to advise on the progress of software processes, and satellite navigation systems that vocalize directions and warnings to motorists on the ground.[87]

Like noise in Shannon's diagram, these sounds enter the frame from without. In this respect the voice and all sound have the character of noise. Sound is external before it is present. Sounds are grafted onto entities in various visual and interactive media. The art of sound design, and the design of pervasive media that deploy sound, is to filter these relationships and to facilitate the tuning of place.

A straightforward reading of Shannon and Weaver's theories about noisy transmissions and entropy might lead media consumers to think that communication is impeded by noise, a type of signal distortion. But I have attempted to demonstrate that noise has two important characteristics that can inform an understanding of pervasive digital media. Noise purveys ambiguity, a plethora of messages. Metaphors of noise also suggest an external source beyond the frame. From ambiguity and externality I further conjectured an understanding of pervasive media in terms of silences, and a kind of sociability that assumes an absent other, including the voice from outside the frame. I explored understandings of the absent other as complicit in a series of ritualized practices that continues in the development of fully featured smartphones and pervasive digital media. Insofar as noise enters from outside, it presents as interference, the theme of chapter 12.

12 Interference

Visual or aural signals from outside the frame can operate as interference. In this chapter I want to develop the concept of interference in its enabling aspects as a source of innovation. I introduced the concept of externality in chapter 11 as a characteristic of noise. It seems that pervasive digital devices are complicit in bringing people together and in synchronizing and tuning their interactions. Therefore this chapter begins by considering interference within gatherings of people or at meetings. Meetings of any size can be noisy affairs, with participants sometimes talking over one another, enduring interruptions, and purveying misunderstanding and ambiguity. Yet, typically, meetings also depend on interference from absent others, invisible participants operating from different places and in different time frames.

Meetings and Interference

Business meetings rarely only involve the interlocutors present at the table on a single occasion, but often make reference to people not present as well. In many cases, such participants are brought to the committee or business meeting through video conferencing, phone calls, and tabled notes and memos. Notes and minutes are recorded for those unable to be present. In certain respects, the meeting is similar to the sacrificial feast introduced in the previous chapter, and in turn to the traditional meal around a domestic table. Aspects of the meeting constitute a kind of performance for people not present: What would Bob say? What would the boss think? If Jane were here she would support the proposal. Recorded minutes, notes, and video blogs of meetings highlight further the presence of the other, to whom participants disclose their views, addressing someone external to the proceedings who may or may not be reading, listening, or watching.

Much of the business of any meeting is in fact conducted between meetings. Meetings rarely exist as isolated events, but come in series. There are important pre- and post-meeting activities often involving people not scheduled into the gathering. Meetings move around to different venues, are sometimes conducted on the move, and participants may be present or remote in both time and place to varying degrees. Meetings are often abetted by electronic audio and visual communications, sometimes taking place online or supplemented by online presences. And of course there are meetings in putative cyberspace, in chat rooms, online worlds, the Second Life community, and multiplayer game environments. The concept of the meeting diffuses into a multitude of modalities by which societies and individuals perpetuate their proclivities to establish and sustain networks of contact, and to get things done.

Video diaries and blogs share in the ethos of the contemporary meeting. Anyone can create and store a video and aural account and post it on the web for anyone or no one to chance upon.[1] Many aspects of ubiquitous technologies are concerned with addressing the absent other.

Therefore, many web pages and text message and email archives represent traces of people who have left the frame—the absent others. As I showed in chapter 10, the deposition of digital files can have a spatial and geographical aspect. It is a simple matter to send files to a server from a laptop or other mobile device from anywhere in the landscape, which are geotagged automatically with the GPS coordinates of their place of origin. Photographs from cell phones are often geotagged without the user knowing. When received by a file server such images are stored with the geotag references and their positions displayed on a map. As explored in previous chapters, the Flickr photo-archive service facilitates this process for photographic images, but other file types can also be uploaded in this way. It is as if geotagged documents are deposited across the landscape and, using other locational technologies, within buildings. Users can be notified when they are in physical range of relevant documents via a cell phone message or an email generated automatically by the server. There is the possibility here of leaving behind a geo-located document trail, in preparation for or following a meeting. One can harvest public and private image files and other documents in this way. These technologies amplify the idea of the absent other, of leaving a record for someone who might follow, even physically, who may eventually appear at the same place and contribute to the proceedings in distant, vicarious, and only loosely synchronized ways. The means by which absent others can contribute, intervene, and interfere seems to expand with the growth in communications technologies.

The temporal synchrony required of meetings occurs across several dimensions implicating calendars, diaries, and appointment schedules. Business people may have trouble with meetings where people do not show up, or are unpredictably late or leave early without notification. In the life of a meeting series, such discrepancies are the norm. Organizers sometimes have to convene meetings that key players cannot attend. So meetings are noisy affairs in several ways. Communication is not always clear. But, more importantly, meetings are constantly invaded by considerations from outside the frame. They are invariably haunted by noises off, Chion's complete acousmêtre multiplied. The communication of the meeting is characterized and even assisted by noise and externality.

Cut-Continuance

Noise enters as interference from outside the frame. Interference interrupts the flow of communication. The experience of much electronic communication, for some of the time, is of interruptions, cuts, disruptions, glitches, leakages, and breaks in the network. Interference pertains to the relationship between the continuity and discontinuity of flow, continuity and the cut.

As presented in chapter 11, Adrian Snodgrass presents the pivotal relationship between continuity and the cut in Oriental art. He explains "cut-continuance" as a property of the Japanese concept of *ma*. The Japanese literature on aesthetics compares the cut-continuance in art to the rhythms of human life: "It corresponds to the moment at which inhalation of the breath ends and exhalation commences . . . the pause between one step and the next in walking; and the mid-space between life and death."[2] In ikebana, the art of arranging flowers, the flowers are cut, "which is tantamount to ending their life, but they continue to live on, their life-force and beauty continuing to shine forth with greater intensity in the arrangement."[3] Similarly, the dry landscape gardens of rocks and gravel cut away the natural landscape but reveal the "dry bones of landscape beauty." Dealing with this "middle space" requires subtlety and sensitivity and for "those who are attuned, forms and emptiness interlock in fusion."[4] The subtle relationship between continuity and the cut folds into theories of the sublime to which I referred in chapter 11.

Concepts of sound draw continuity and the cut into further prominence. Composer Martin Parker and I contributed a chapter to a book, *Mobile Understanding,* describing two theories of sound[5]: that which draws on smooth, consistent, reverberant ambience on the one hand, and that which participates in the presence of clipped, truncated flow or interruption on the other. Here I bring this distinction to bear on the problematic of noise and the tuning of place.

How does sound give expression to concepts of continuity? Designers and aestheticians commonly think of acoustical shapes in terms of the spiral, horn, shell, volute, curved wall, and amphitheater, and the shapes of musical instruments and auditoria. Such shapes are also suggested by the folded form of the outer ear and the spirals of the inner ear.[6] Sounds radiate and emanate and there are shapes that abet their reception and concentration. In his theorizing about the human senses, Stephen Connor adds the shape of the tongue to this spatial morphology, and its continuous rolling action during speech.[7] All of these curved shapes do not necessarily guarantee effective acoustic transmission or amplification, but are readily associated with it. They also carry with them connotations of the natural and the welcoming. Earpieces, headphones, and even the smooth pebble-like shape of the handheld cell phone are suggestive of acoustic properties. John Dewey related the hand-drawn curved line to sound and cultures of the ear.[8] The celebration of the smooth and the curved is not limited to sound. The nineteenth-century aesthetician John Ruskin praised naturalistic, ornamented, curved, and voluted forms and details, in contrast to the sharp-edged adherence to proportion and repetition evident in neoclassical architecture.[9] His advocacy of Gothic naturalism in architectural style was easily aligned with his support of communitarian and socialist ideals.[10] Folded and voluted spaces suggest informality, welcome, and democratic engagement. Think of the enfolding arms of Bernini's Baroque forecourt to St Peter's Basilica in Rome, and the folds of Frank Gehry's Guggenheim Museum in Bilbao, Spain, both in their own formal ways intent on an exaggerated language of participation. Curves and folds are also subtle, suggestive of fine-tuning. Much research into responsive environments involves the delicate distortion of shapes and wall surfaces, in their conception or as dynamical components on site,[11] taking account of fluid flows and animated by servomotors. Tuning a curve by slightly changing its shape can leave the overall form intact.

A further advance on this theory of the curve is to regard sound not only as comfortable with the curve, but also as requiring a looping process to function. Sounds return.[12] I referred to the myth of Narcissus and Echo in chapter 1. Theorist of the senses Mladen Dolar elaborates on the story.[13] In offending the god Hera, Echo had already been consigned to a communicative life of repetition: merely repeating what others say. Her love for Narcissus goes unrequited, and she eventually fades away, leaving only her voice.[14] She persists in acoustic form, whereas Narcissus dies in his reflection. Despite its obvious transience, sound has a persistent quality, even before the advent of recording technologies. It is implicated in processes of looped repetition: in the echo. The same can be said of the human voice, and the importance of hearing oneself. The voice projects. It emanates from the human vocal apparatus, but it also returns, through a kind of instant feedback. People are so familiar with hearing their own voices that it comes as a shock to hear the voice as others hear it, returned by other means, and without the body's inner reverberations. Speaking in an anechoic chamber for the first time has a similar effect, where the speaker's echoless voice seems to be smothered by silence. Much attention to the tuning of the acoustic properties of a space deals in reverberation, the repeated return of sound, an excess of which produces incessant noise and distinct echoes, amplifying every footfall and breath. Baffles and fabrics are put into place to moderate and tune the effects of reflection.

The loop is also implicated in modes of transmission. Connor draws attention to the early intrigue with electronic transmission of the voice.[15] The miracle of electronics was not only that communication could be achieved at a distance, but also the fact that the voice was passed into a wire, which could be bent, stretched, and coiled. On the one hand, the wire suggested the voice could be propagated by a vector, along a line, rather than just radiating from a point. On the other hand, the wire suggested coiling, compression, storage, and amplification. As indicated in the establishment of Pythagorean harmonic ratios, adjusting a wire or string is the archetypal tuning task. The surplus of wire finds its way into a coil at the end of the instrument and winds round a tuning peg, with a further length released of tension trailing in random curls from the peg. The tightly or loosely coiled surplus has no particular acoustic properties. In fact, the wire has to be taut in order to vibrate. Tightly bound coils of wire have a key role in electronic amplification and in the conversion of electronic signals to vibrations, and vice versa, as in the loudspeaker, the variable potentiometer, the electric motor, and the solenoid switch—the knobs, dials, and sliders by which sounds and electrical signals are fine-tuned and calibrated.

Therefore sound is a looped phenomenon. Sounds do not only project, but also are returned, in echoes, reverberations, vibrations, repetitions—features of sound that can be exaggerated or resisted, but are ever present. The concepts of ambience, ambient sounds, or ambient music commonly invoke such ideas of smooth continuity: for example, the background hum, waves on the sea, rain on a tin roof, or other comforting and relaxing noises.

Counterposed to this theory of continuity is a theory of cut sound. For Connor, if the human voice is modulated by the rolled tongue, it is also torn apart (macheted) by the teeth.[16] Voices are punctuated by glottal stops, cuts, discontinuities, and breaches to the rhythm and flow of the loop. The metaphor is that of the circle and the cut. As indicated by an inspection of Frank Gehry's voluted buildings, Peter Cook's Graz Kunsthaus, the digital organic forms of Greg Lynn, Marcus Novak, or Marcus Cruz, the socially articulated scroll is characterized by so many disjunctions of surface. Curly shells and petals do not stack seamlessly, and much of the intrigue of organic architecture resides in the ingenuity of the junction as much as the smoothness of the acoustic surfaces. The smooth articulation of sound gets disturbed. The rolling volutes of ambient sound are inevitably punctured by the crackle that disturbs the hum, the shrill birdcall above the waves, and the intermittent rattle of the loose metal sheeting as rain pounds the roof. In this book's introduction I attempted to show how sound is capable of inducing a sense of apartness that reinforces so many aspects of separation: message and medium, mind and body, body and soul. The punctuation of the cut also points to the ubiquity of noises within noise.

An interruption is also an inflection in a unified field of flows, a break in a repetitive sequence. Inflection carries the connotation of a flick, an incidental movement. The philosopher Gilles Deleuze captures the idea of inflection as "the ideal genetic element of the variable curve or fold. Inflection is the authentic atom, the elastic point set in motion by an exterior force."[17]

Noise and interference impede communication, and the cut is an extreme case of impediment to flow. Certain devices deliberately halt or resist the flow of otherwise seamless interaction between organism and world. The body of an athlete in training works against equipment in the gym. The variable resistor as volume control is a basic electrical component, the performance of which is measured in terms of impedance, the degree to which the flow of a current is inhibited. Circuits and machines have to be slowed down as well as powered up, and various regulators limit the flow of current, power, and fuel, or otherwise resist the propensity of the machine to burn out under its own momentum. The control of impedance, rather than its elimination, is a major function in mechanical and electronic devices and their design.

Impedance is part of everyday human practices. It is well known that the qwerty keyboard was configured to even out the operations of the fingers by positioning the most commonly used letters in the least accessible parts of the keyboard, issues that resurface in the design of handheld touch-sensitive keypads. Material, nondigital, analog musical instruments that are plucked, bowed, struck, and blown, offer resistances that are inevitable in the production of high-quality sounds and contribute to the virtuosity of performance. Performance is not all flow but also the overcoming of so many impediments. These observations further work against the presumption that good device design must enlist seamless, effortless, and even invisible interaction. Devices, like musical instruments, need not be designed to blend into the background. At best their operations are characterized by so many cuts between continuities, interferences in the flow, the noise of interaction.

Impurity

To the extent that noise represents interference from outside the frame it also constitutes an impurity in the network. Noise is commonly described as a pollutant. Anthropologist Mary Douglas has examined the question of impurity in detail, societies' designations of what constitute the pure and the impure, and their attitudes toward them. It is tempting to think that entities designated as polluting are somehow impure, disgusting, and unhealthy in themselves: dead animals, excrement, and fetid water, to give examples. But anything can invoke disgust simply by being out of place, in the wrong place, assigned to the wrong category. It is worth quoting Douglas's characterization of the impure as "matter out of place," and examining what it suggests about sound, noise, and pervasive media.

> Shoes are not dirty in themselves, but it is dirty to place them on the dining-table; food is not dirty in itself, but it is dirty to leave cooking utensils in the bedroom, or food bespattered on clothing; similarly, bathroom equipment in the drawing room; clothing lying on chairs; outdoor things indoors; upstairs things downstairs; underclothing appearing where over-clothing should be, and so on. In short, our pollution behavior is the reaction which condemns any object or idea likely to confuse or contradict cherished classifications.[18]

Through this homey exposition Douglas explains that disgust arises as an affirmation of human societies' commitments to the categories they form, and need, in order to survive. Individuals and groups commit to a framework, a schema by which they organize the world. Items that do not fit are excluded. She describes this as a sifting process: "We share with other animals a kind of filtering mechanism which at first only lets in sensations we know how to use."[19] Of course, adventurous individuals and groups do admit incongruity, things that do not fit their schemas from time to time. Without this capacity people would not learn. Any student of biology or sanitation engineering can train himself or herself to accommodate objects and situations that might initially invoke disgust, or more accurately they adapt to the juxtaposition of certain objects. They shift their schemas to accommodate animal dissections and the study of excrement moving through pipes. People tune their schemas to the world as they encounter it.

How do people adapt to the impure? Douglas outlines a range of responses to the anomalous, to things that do not belong together. People can correct the disorder by moving things around: move the dirty dishes out of the bedroom and into the kitchen sink. Considering the Internet as a source of impurities: as an update of Douglas's examples, the concerned custodian could move the computer out of the child's bedroom and into the living room.[20] Communities can also set up rules and procedures to prevent any impurity from interfering with social operations. Think of laws governing what may be viewed in the media and on the Internet. Signs, alarms, and tethering objects in place prevent certain categories of violations. Cautious individuals might also label anomalies as dangerous, in an attempt to put them beyond dispute. For example, custodians may advise building residents in their care of the danger of keeping a free-standing electric radiator or a toaster in the bathroom. The World Wide Web is pervaded by signs advising on age restrictions as well as tethers in the form of firewalls, logins, locks, and disclosure protocols.

But Douglas outlines a further response to the impure: more adventurous groups and individuals may also seek out and deploy the misplaced matter as a deliberate provocation. Homeowners and residents might derive stimulation from and even enjoy putting bathroom scales next to the fireplace, a carburetor in the bedroom, an artwork in the lavatory. Douglas describes such provocations as a function of art: "We enjoy works of art because they enable us to go behind the explicit structures of our normal experience."[21] People might also deploy anomalies in ritual, "to enrich meaning or to call attention to other levels of existence."[22] There is something of this tarrying with the misplaced object and its categories in rituals of animal sacrifice, passing the communal cup, and the persistence of blood references in church services. Of course, the alert reader has only to think of the cadaverous and sexually explicit motifs of artists such as Francis Bacon, Jeff Koons, Tracey Emin, and Gilbert and George to recall how concepts of the pure and the impure, of innocence and complicity, interweave and interact one with the other.

Something analogous to disgust accompanies interference by loud mobile phone conversations overheard in restaurants, public places, and railway carriages. Following Douglas's typology of responses, to deal with such matter out of place fellow occupants or passengers might encourage the offender to move to another space. Since the inception of the mobile phone, and under public pressure, regulators have designated quiet areas on public transport to engender consideration to fellow travelers. Warnings have also been posted about the dangers of prolonged cell phone usage and close proximity to strong radio signals. It is unlikely that people in a train compartment would be provoked in an interesting manner by the out-of-place conversation, as they would to a work of art; however, in a different context they might. Adopting a stoic response, the reflective passenger might think of the noisy passenger as a test of fortitude and tolerance. Here Douglas does not develop the possibilities of humor as a way of coping.[23] Bothered passengers in a noisy train compartment might respond to such matter out of place by ridicule, as a public display or private joke, applied at the time or later in recounting the experience.

In this context it is useful to remember that noise, nausea, and defilement are related. To the extent that noise comes from outside the frame it constitutes matter out of place. More accurately, noise is a category, similar to danger, which human beings deploy to deal with impurity. Noise is a useful label for unclassified and disturbing sound. Douglas conveniently equates impurity, anomaly, and ambiguity.[24] An anomalous condition is that in which an item does not fit an assumed category; ambiguity relates strictly to situations for which there are two or more interpretations, which I have already associated with the character of noise. For Douglas there is no practical difference between anomaly and ambiguity as they both draw attention to a boundary condition, a vexed relationship between categories. For example, Douglas notes how treacle gives ambiguous sense impressions. It is both solid and liquid; it is also anomalous to the system of classification in which people distinguish solid from liquid. Extending Douglas's insights to the media, a mistuned and noisy radio station could present similarly ambiguous messages. Was it "train delayed" or "train derailed"? The noisy utterance also trades on anomaly. In fact it is often the apparent incongruity of the announcement that alerts people to a possible explanation: they are encountering noise.

Douglas also makes reference to perceptual filtering. Tuning-in is a process of filtering out the noise, or more accurately, filtering through the noise to reduce ambiguity. But human beings are not only agents who filter noise: they are capable of deliberately introducing anomaly, surplus channels of information, of inserting noise to excite the senses, to learn, to defamiliarize, and to provoke.

Entropy

As if to reinforce Douglas's articulation of cultural responses to noise and pollution, noise also has instrumental value in certain calculations. Noise features in computational processes that require iterative calculation: small incremental adjustment to many interconnected variables, as in the simulation of neural networks, or the stresses in structural frames. The objective might be to find some optimal configuration of values. In fact, finding the "best" in any situation involves many comparisons, trade-offs, and compromises. It often happens that in trying to find the best solution you have merely encountered something that is better than all the other, similar solutions, but is substantially worse than the very best result. An applied mathematician or engineer might say that the current solution is suboptimal. To find the very best you sometimes have to shake things up a bit; explore beyond the current solution. The computational processes that abet this strategy are often referred to as "stochastic." They require randomness, noise, testing adjustments, and improving on initial approximations. Paradoxically, the introduction of randomness, increasing the entropy or adding noise, can bring a computational process to a more satisfactory, and even accurate, conclusion. Pounding a heated bar of metal with a mallet increases a metal's strength by a similar process. The heat raises the entropy of the sample so that it will be stronger on subsequent cooling and as its molecules order themselves into a more stable and robust configuration.[25] Concepts of heat help explain noise as entropy. There are further examples where the controlled introduction of impurity improves some material process. Think of the development of a vaccine to improve resistance to disease. In any case, the development of immunity within communities requires the exposure of human populations to "safe" levels of microorganisms, the controlled introduction of organic noise.

The deployment of noise, even to shift a computational process into a new state, is a subtle endeavor. Too much noise and the process flies off into an unstable condition in which nothing is resolved or it kills off possibilities. A little randomness, judiciously applied, can tip the process into a usefully new condition. Think of this requirement for noise as providing space to move. Noise and its accommodation involve flexibility. Any structure needs to accommodate looseness. Rigid structures tend to be brittle; they fail catastrophically. Bridges have to move a little in response to the vibration of the traffic, the wind, and seismic vibrations through the judicious use of gaps and tolerances. Structures don't only need to be specified and built with accuracy, but also with an accurate assessment of tolerances, of where and how elements can move in relation to each other. The variability that is noise can require precise science, precisely controlled interference.

Entropy and Community

Entropy has a social dimension. The composer and architect Iannis Xenakis developed an approach to musical composition that harnessed the power of "stochastic laws," which he explained in terms of a crowd's violent protest. It is worth including an extended quotation here, as it touches on many of the themes of this book, including noise, interference, rhythm, voice, sociability, agonistics, and of course sound.

> Everyone has observed the sonic phenomena of a political crowd of dozens of hundreds of thousands of people. The human river shouts a slogan in a uniform rhythm. Then another slogan springs from the head of the demonstration; it spreads towards the tail, replacing the first. A wave of transition thus passes from the head to the tail. The clamour fills the city, and the inhibiting force of voice and rhythm reaches a climax. It is an event of great power and beauty in its ferocity. Then the impact between the demonstrators and the enemy occurs. The perfect rhythm of the last slogan breaks up in a huge cluster of chaotic shouts, which also spreads to the tail. Imagine, in addition, the reports of dozens of machine guns and the whistle of bullets adding their punctuations to this total disorder. The crowd is then rapidly dispersed, and after sonic and visual hell follows a detonating calm, full of despair, dust and death. The statistical laws of these events, separated from their political or moral context, are the same as those of the cicadas or the rain. They are the laws of the passage from complete order to total disorder in a continuous or explosive manner. They are stochastic laws.[26]

We readily associate noise with the behavior of the crowd, which is seen here to exhibit structure and movement.

Communications between people are inevitably and desirably noisy. It is tempting to think that any group of people working together on a project needs to share common terms, and agree precisely on what to accomplish and how to go about it. If groups had to settle on a common vocabulary before they could communicate, nothing would get done. People working together commonly just get on with the task and leave the definitions to emerge in the course of their interactions. The one group member who insists on being precise about terms, definitions, and objectives before starting work is usually sidelined. But groups do not only accommodate flexibility in order to avoid arguments; flexibility is how things get done in any case. Meanings emerge by virtue of the context of the task. Rigid definitions inhibit the opportunity for meaning by suppressing the context, the task at hand, and the complex social relations of the group. In this sense noise is essential for the functioning of the group, and the creation of meaning. Wittgenstein said, "The meaning of a word is in its use."[27] Insofar as the completion of a task draws on ambiguity and flexibility I would add: meaning is in the noise.

Noise can also be introduced into the group as a tactic. A rigidified community or meeting can be enlivened by the introduction of a person or theme that creates a condition of ambiguity, incongruity, and anomaly. The new entity ambiguates a situation in which everything is otherwise taken as clear-cut. Prejudices are challenged, new aspects of the task are brought to light, and new questions are opened up. This process may be enlivening or frustrating. It may be just what the task calls for or it could debilitate. Noise can enable and disable, reveal and conceal, clarify and occlude. In any event, noise contributes a major component in the arsenal of communication, interaction, and tasking, to be tweaked and tuned by the group.

I have suggested throughout this book that devices can have this disclosive function as well. As much has been said in the case of the incursion of consumer products such as skateboards into the public realm. For architectural theorist Iain Borden, their marginal position allows skateboards and their practitioners to function as a "critical exterior to architecture," helping critics and urbanists to "rethink architecture's manifold possibilities."[28] Mobile phones also contribute to the noise of human sociability in more ways than one. The audio signals they transmit occasionally succumb to noise and interference. Mobile phones contribute unregulated, extraneous, and often bothersome noise to the ambient environment. But such devices also present as alien and incongruous entities that challenge categories and render social interactions and social relations ambiguous.

Lest people become inured to their unusual character, it is worth noting that mobile devices are also carriers of change. Electronic devices currently exhibit multiple and amorphous functionality. My possession of any single mass-produced device involves participation in a sequence of devices, an ever-developing product line, new releases, versions, and improved models. In this sense electronic devices are conveyors of incessant renewal and change. As smartphones and programmable computers they are also media for delivering a regular stream of newness. Just when societies think they have come to terms with the cell phone, adjusting their schemas and ontologies to fit, they find that the objects in their hands are not only phones but also interlinked locational devices, with maps. Then I download a third-party application that further transforms the device into a phrasebook, a game console, a means of dispatching photographs to a web-based photo display service, a planetarium, or a seismometer.[29] Participation in this newness—as consumers, users, critics, developers, investors, publishers and designers—keeps the incongruity alive, refreshes the noise potential of the device, and sustains entropy in the marketplace.

Detuning and Innovation

If the removal of noise is a filtering process then the introduction of noise constitutes a kind of detuning. As any one who has adjusted a stringed instrument knows, the process of tuning sometimes involves first slackening or tightening the string beyond the target position. You might make the string tighter or looser than it needs to be in order to test the results of working the tuning peg. You may also expect the string to snag and slip across the bridge and nut, and an initial exaggerated movement tests whether the tension is in equilibrium along the length of the string. Therefore the process of tuning is not a smooth progressive development that takes the instrument closer to its tuned state at every step. Tuning inevitably involves detuning.

Conventional even-tempered classical tunings present as a deviation from tunings according to Pythagorean ratios in any case. In this sense, even-tuning is a case of detuning outside the regime of "natural harmonics." But then a musician might deliberately detune his instrument outside any conventional tuning practice. More than for any other art, people burden music with the expectations and promises that it will enhance their well-being, induce harmonic states, and excite the emotions.[30] Music is ready to be personalized and tuned to moods. It is little wonder that there are those composers and performers who would willfully break from such conventions in an attempt to decouple music from expectations of order, harmony, pleasure, euphoria, sentiment, or other classically authorized aesthetic outcomes. To abrogate responsibility for conforming to these expectations is a form of detuning, which may even involve a deliberate detuning of the instrument, or ignoring the usual convention of tuning instruments before a performance, just to see what the instrument produces. Contemporary experimental musicians and composers can operate in this way, exploring different aspects of their instruments, playing them in ways contrary to their classical usage: using wind instruments in a way that is percussive, amplifying the sibilance of a saxophone or flute, exceeding the normal range of the instrument, ignoring conventions of scales, harmonies, and rhythms. Where computers are involved in such contemporary composition and performance, the sounds of the instruments may in fact constitute raw samples that are manipulated electronically as part of a composition or performance.

How does musical detuning translate to the everyday world of pervasive digital media? This emphasis on sound, noise, tuning, and detuning amplifies further the nature of pervasive digital media invention and innovation outlined in chapter 10. Much design and development is noisy, which is to say it is permeated by ambiguity. It trades in successes and failures, the useful and the useless, the meaningful and the meaningless. In this experimental context the possibility of defamiliarization undergoes constant renewal. The richly experimental milieu of pervasive digital media may or may not produce good products. But the devices may reveal something about the social contexts with which they interfere or that they perturb, those aspects of the human condition they bring into relief, much as Douglas proposes that an artwork provokes and reveals insights into a social or cultural condition. The surrealist art of Marcel Duchamp has been described in these terms, as operating in terms of the "in-between," according to art theorist Craig Adcock.[31] Duchamp's sculptural "readymades" were mostly everyday objects (a bicycle wheel, a large glass, a rattle, a ball of twine) elevated to the status of artworks by virtue of being installed in galleries. Duchamp also created sound compositions, which he regarded as "musical readymades." He spoke of his first readymade, the bicycle wheel, in these terms. In his studio he would spin the wheel and play it with a plectrum. Such work "reveals a mysterious objectivity" according to Adcock.[32]

This art function is evident in many experiments into the uses of mobile and pervasive media: community-based games with oceans of tagged balloons followed by their release over Greenwich Park, London; using the logic of the phone game Snake as the basis of an urban intervention[33]; or the CoMob public artwork organized by colleagues for the FutureSonic Festival at Manchester, UK, in which an army of participants with iPhones followed instructions to sketch huge emergent geoforms and shapes.[34] Insights from one project may inform indirectly other innovations. Thus an experiment in the use of cell phones for transmitting images of documents to a central server for later access on web pages may fall short of a useable product, but its invention and deployment in some context or other may inform the researchers about what people in meetings actually seem to want, or provide insights about the commercial marketplace or the adequacy or otherwise of the communications infrastructure. This understanding may enable the development of further innovations, some of which achieve commercial success. Thus there is no real failure within this subtle ecology of innovation. The noise of pervasive innovation informs and reveals, in much the same way that Douglas attributes to certain incongruities the ability to provoke and inform social conditions.

If innovation is noisy and pervaded by interferences, then so are the teams that produce it. Researchers, designers, and users constitute ensembles of media innovators.[35] The media they develop are pervasive, and so are the talents that pervasive media call on for their development. Opportunities for innovation are diffused into communities. Formalized R&D departments and universities are not the only places for innovation, but they indicate something of its character, conflating the roles of researcher, designer, artist, and manager. The introduction of so-called "living labs,"[36] users as designers,[37] research by design, public-participative art production, and open-source software development strategies amplify something of the democratization of development and expertise, the ambiguation and contamination of roles.

Shannon's model of communication draws attention to the pairing of transmitter and receiver, but networks involve legions of such connections. Pervasive digital media deal in distributed networks, which are both the products and media of development. The media in which development and experimentation take place are also the media of communication among designers and innovators. The medium is a hotbed of rapid communication, development, review, dissemination, critique, testing, and revision. Such networks are prone to the workings of noise and interferences in communication, and the way meanings develop through the noise.

A modest incremental investment in resources can produce powerful effects for a developer or member of a development team, thanks to the leverage available from the networks and infrastructures already in place. It takes minimal resources to produce a website that is instantly published to the world. The innovation can be lost in the noise, or be of such crucial significance that it has a wide impact independent of the resource investment.[38]

As I explored in chapter 10, pervasive media provide scope for testing in use. In fact, much software and hardware development now factors user testing and market-led innovation into the period after product launch, and during the product lifecycle. A developer may expect feedback from the base of early users who serve as initial testers of the software. The developer may follow reviews and complaints with new releases and patches to correct discrepancies or introduce new features. Though they are unlikely to be introduced deliberately, minor design flaws can provoke useful responses from the marketplace that prompt further innovation. Some noise in the development cycle of a product produces benefits.

The everyday constitutes the context of use of much pervasive digital media. Networks extend into every area of life, and contribute to the noise and ambience of the environment. Ambience and noise are related after all. Everyday digital media are also pervasive, ambient, and noisy. The processes of innovation diffuse into ordinary life. Much of this everydayness involves communications among heterogeneous families of devices. Development and innovation draw on the interoperability among devices and among media. So mobile media, web-based environments, digital sensors, and affectors constitute a rich canvas for research and development. Web applications now have to accommodate a range of platforms in any case. It is not enough to design for a web browser, one must also create a feed to other devices and services, including phones and other handheld, portable, and ubiquitous devices. As a pervasive media user, you might want GPS locational data from your cell phone for inspection and manipulation on maps on your desktop computer, or to be able to access your home security system by phone.

The leveraging and appropriation of networks and infrastructures provide pointers to political engagement. By some readings the impetus for the development of many sophisticated communications systems has been primarily to gain a strategic military advantage, secondarily to enhance capital, and only lastly to enhance user/consumer participation.[39] On the one hand, the expansion of the Internet, remote sensing, and global positioning systems presents as a marvelous appropriation of forces of domination for the common good and grassroots innovation.[40] On the other hand, perhaps societies are acquiescing to and sanctioning agendas set by the dominance of global capital. Furthermore, it is likely to be the techno-elites who have the advantage in forming such innovative teams. In any event, participation in pervasive media innovation is inevitably a form of political participation, and an agonistic one. In his account of the displacement of Philippine President Joseph Estrada by a civilian-led coup in 2001, Vincente Rafael highlights the role of the crowds of people communicating by cell phones: "The power of the crowd thus comes across in its capacity to overwhelm the physical constraints of urban planning and to blur social distinctions by provoking a sense of estrangement. Its authority rests on its ability to promote restlessness and movement."[41] The crowd emerges as a technology activated by the capabilities of mobile devices. Note Rafael's reference to estrangement. These technologies do not only bind, unite, and ensure accurate flows of information, but they also render the familiar strange. Mobile phones and social media can provoke and intensify difference. What digital designers and developers produce is easily construed as social and global and therefore pertains to what Plato termed the *polis*.[42] Pervasive digital media are political. In this and other respects they participate in the political economy of noise.

In this chapter I showed how communication commonly assumes or invites an absent other. I also referred to two theories of sound. One relates to a smooth kind of enveloping ambience; the other refers to the cut, the gap that severs continuity. Against this background I explored noise as an impurity, a pollutant, an interference, a breach in the flow, and a source of entropy and innovation. In his revision of Shannon's cybernetic model of communication, the anthropologist Gregory Bateson provides a useful summary: "All that is not information, not redundancy, not form and not restraint—is noise, the only possible source of *new* patterns."[43] Noise, impurity, entropy, and interference are variants, multiple symptoms, and enablers of so many dealings in incremental change. Small change is the currency that enables innovation, and the tuning of place. By these various means pervasive digital media tune places: via the rhythms, tags, and habits of the everyday; and commonplace tacties, thresholds, and noises.

Notes

Preface

1. Richard Coyne, *Cornucopia Limited.*

2. Richard Coyne, *Technoromanticism.*

3. Richard Coyne, *Designing Information Technology in the Postmodern Age.*

4. The identification of architecture with frozen music is attributed to both Johann Wolfgang von Goethe (1749–1832) and Friedrich Wilhelm Joseph Schelling (1775–1854). See Johan Peter Eckermann, *Conversations of Goethe with Johann Peter Eckermann,* 303.

Introduction

1. Lewis Mumford, *Technics and Civilization,* 13–14. He posited this view contrary to the popular conception that it was the steam engine that augured the Industrial Revolution. Mumford's (1895–1990) sentiment echoed that of Georg Simmel (1858–1918), for whom "the technique of metropolitan life is unimaginable without the most punctual integration of all activities and mutual relations into a stable and impersonal time schedule." Georg Simmel, "The metropolis and mental life," 352.

2. Manuel Castells et al., *Mobile Communication and Society,* 89. They reference the work of R. Ling, *The Mobile Connection.* See also Heesang Lee, "Mobile networks, urban places and emotional spaces," 53. For a discussion of the significance of clocks and timetables in the context of mobility see John Urry, *Mobilities,* 95–100.

3. Cloud computing typically involves the provision of a software application such as a word processor as a service accessed through a web browser. Software and data are stored outside the desktop or palmtop environment, to be accessed from anywhere where there is a network connection. See Brian Hayes, "Cloud computing."

4. William Mitchell has made extensive use of the informational metaphor in accounting for the contemporary urban context and pervasive media: "a whole city

becomes a vast, collectively constructed memory palace that divulges its contents to inhabitants as they circulate through it." William J. Mitchell, *City of Bits*, 128.

5. They assert that: "Animals produce future most dramatically by anticipating seasonal processes, and regulate their annual breeding, migration and hibernation to chime with them." Russell Foster and Leon Kreitzman, *Rhythms of Life*, 133.

6. See Martin Heidegger, *Being and Time*, 172; and Hubert L. Dreyfus, *Being-in-the-World*, 171. See also Martin Heidegger, "What is metaphysics?," 100.

7. Alfred Schutz, "Making music together," 177.

8. Henri Bergson, *Time and Free Will.*

9. Schutz, "Making music together," 176.

10. I elaborate on these positions further in relation to concepts of cyberspace in chapter 4 of Coyne, *Designing Information Technology in the Postmodern Age.*

11. Edward Relph, "Spirit of Place and Sense of Place in Virtual Realities," 18; Lee, "Mobile networks, urban places and emotional spaces." Also see E. C. Relph, *Place and Placelessness.*

12. My considerations of place draw on the substantial literature on the subject: Marc Augé, *Non-places;* Edward S. Casey, *The Fate of Place;* Joshua Meyrowitz, *No Sense of Place*; Mitchell, *City of Bits*; Robert Mugerauer, *Interpretations on Behalf of Place*; Kristóf Nyíri (ed.), *A Sense of Place;* Relph, *Place and Placelessness.*

13. R. M. Schafer, *The Tuning of the World*, 5. He sees tuning as a more subtle modification of environment than the crude barrage of sound that assaults the ear. He refers to Robert Fludd's famous illustration of "The Tuning of the World": "in which the earth forms the body of an instrument across which strings are stretched and are tuned by a divine hand. We must try again to find the secret of that tuning." Schafer, *The Tuning of the World*, 6.

14. Doreen Massey, *For Space*, 9.

15. See Nicholas Negroponte, *Being Digital*; and Bill Gates and Collins Hemingway, *Business @ the Speed of Thought.*

16. A trend evident in reflections on architecture as well as digital media. See Jonathan Hill (ed.), *Architecture: The Subject is Matter.*

17. Malcolm McCullough, *Digital Ground*, 92–94.

18. Brandon LaBelle, *Background Noise*, x; R, Banham, *Architecture of the Well-tempered Environment.*

19. Mark Wigley, "The architecture of atmosphere." Sociologist Michael Bull links mood and place (atmosphere) in iPod culture through synchronization: "the

syncing of mood to place." Michael Bull, Sound Moves: iPod Culture and Urban Experience, 126.

20. Bruno Latour, *A Cautious Prometheus?*, 6.

21. We can draw on lessons learned from sociological study into ubiquitous devices that focus on mobile telephony. See for example Manuel Castells, *The Rise of the Network Society*; Castells, "An introduction to the information age"; Castells, *The Internet Galaxy*; James E. Katz and Mark Aakhus, *Perpetual Contact*; Nyíri, *A Sense of Place: The Global and the Local in Mobile Communication* ; Mizuko Ito, Daisuke Okabe, and Misa Matsuda, *Personal, Portable, Pedestrian*; Castells et al., *Mobile Communication and Society*.

22. Urry, *Mobilities*, 173.

23. See Garrod and Pickering on theories of interactive alignment in conversation: Simon Garrod and Martin J Pickering, "Why is conversation so easy?"

24. See Thorstein Veblen, *The Theory of the Leisure Class*; Michel Foucault, *The Order of Things*; and Erving Goffman, *The Presentation of Self in Everyday Life*. McCarthy and Wright provide a helpful account of the nature of human practices and the debates surrounding a pragmatic approach to the design of computer systems. See John McCarthy and Peter Wright, *Technology as Experience*.

25. Foucault in particular promotes the role of institutions and disciplinary routines in purveying power relations, under the rubric of "bio-power." See a summary of Foucault's writing on this topic in Michel Foucault and P. Rabinow (ed.), *The Foucault Reader*.

26. See for example Richard Coyne et al., "Co-operation and complicity."

27. See also Roger N. Shepard and Jacqueline Metzler, "Mental Rotation of Three-Dimensional Objects; Richard D. Freedman and Stephen A. Stumpf, "Learning style theory; Jessie Lovano-Kerr, "Cognitive style revisited"; Stephanie Shipman and Virginia C. Shipman, "Cognitive styles"; David Kolb, *Experiential Learning*.

28. Lovano-Kerr, "Cognitive style revisited."

29. Perhaps "spatial experience" already presumes too much, as if space is there to be experienced without dispute, and in the way I have introduced the subject, as if space incontrovertibly exists as an object of experience. For that matter "experience" is also limited as a concept. Spatiality is about not only the experience of space, but also the whole immersive configuration through which people construct space and concepts of space. *Spatiality* is the most general term we can apply to this phenomenon. See Casey, *The Fate of Place*.

30. Hiroshi Ishii and Brygg Ullmer, "Tangible bits,"

31. See Julian Holland Oliver, "The similar eye"; and Michael Rymaszewski et al., *Second Life*.

32. See for example Stephen Kline, Nick Dyer-Witheford, and Greig de Peuter, *Digital Play.*

33. See Mark Weiser, "The computer for the 21st century"; Mark Weiser and John Seely Brown, "The coming age of calm technology." For my own contribution to the critique of cyberspatial narratives, see Coyne, *Technoromanticism.*

34. This critique often develops from the theories of Henri Lefebvre, *The Production of Space.*

35. Geert Lovink, *Zero Comments,* xxiii.

36. See Thomas P. Moran and Paul Dourish, "Introduction to this special issue"; Bradley J. Rhodes, Nelson Minar, and Josh Weaver, "Wearable computing meets ubiquitous computing"; Steve Mann, "Smart clothing"; Rolf Pfeifer and Josh C. Bongard, *How the Body Shapes the Way We Think*; Adriana de Souza e Silva, "From cyber to hybrid." Such technologies have also been described as persuasive as well as pervasive. See B. J. Fogg, *Persuasive Technology.*

37. See Weiser, "The computer for the 21st century," and Weiser and Seely Brown, "The coming age of calm technology."

38. Matthias Rothensee, "User acceptance of the intelligent fridge."

39. Pfeifer and Bongard, *How the Body Shapes the Way We Think,* 270.

40. See for example J. David Bolter and Richard A. Grusin, *Remediation.*

41. Claude E. Shannon and William Weaver, *The Mathematical Theory of Communication.*

42. Harold A. Innis, *The Bias of Communication*; and Marshall McLuhan, *Understanding Media.*

43. "The medium is the message" is a suitably ambiguous tagline that has resounded through forty years of computer interaction design and media theory, apparent in Alan Kay, "User interface." I examined the legacy of McLuhan in Coyne, *Designing Information Technology in the Postmodern Age.*

44. J. David Bolter and Diane Gromala, *Windows and Mirrors.*

45. Bolter and Grusin, *Remediation.*

46. Marc Langheinrich et al., "As we may live."

47. Nicholas Negroponte, *The Architecture Machine*; Aart Bijl, *Computer Discipline and Design Practice.*

48. See McCullough, *Digital Ground*; and William J. Mitchell, *Placing Words.*

49. Yvonne Rogers, Jenny Preece, and Helen Sharp, *Interaction Design.*

50. Francesco Careri, *Walkscapes*; Anthony Vidler, *Warped Space*.

51. See George Lakoff and Mark Johnson, *Metaphors We Live By*; Mark Johnson, *The Body in the Mind*; George Lakoff, *Women, Fire, and Dangerous Things*; Donald Schön, "Generative metaphor" in *Metaphor and Thought*; A. B. Snodgrass and R. D. Coyne, "Models, metaphors and the hermeneutics of designing"; Richard Coyne, Adrian Snodgrass, and David Martin, "Metaphors in the design studio"; Coyne, *Designing Information Technology in the Postmodern Age*; Adrian Snodgrass and Richard Coyne, *Interpretation in Architecture*.

52. Such promiscuous associationism has many adherents, and draws on several legacies. Perhaps Deleuze and Guattari best exemplify this cross-disciplinary approach, which has appealed greatly to designers and artists. According to some commentators, Deleuze and Guattari's organicism, their enthusiasm for naturalistic, rhizomic, geological, and machinic metaphors is drawn from Stoic writing, including that of Marcus Aurelius. See Gilles Deleuze and Felix Guattari, *A Thousand Plateaus*; and John Sellars, "The point of view of the cosmos." I would add to this list of Stoical legacies the writing of the Roman architect Vitruvius. See Vitruvius, *The Ten Books on Architecture*; Indra McEwen, *Vitruvius*.

53. Adilkno, *The New Media Archive*, 100, quoted in Lev Manovich, *The Language of New Media*, 270.

Chapter 1

1. Gottfried Wilhelm Leibniz, "The relational theory of space and time."

2. We explored these issues of devices that disclose in two articles. See Richard Coyne, Hoon Park, and Dorian Wiszniewski, "Design devices." The Surrealist's concept of the *objet* is also relevant here. See Richard Coyne, *Technoromanticism*.

3. Don Ihde, *Bodies in Technology*, 106.

4. David Bolter and Diane Gromala demonstrate the power of the design experiment in their analysis of several digital artworks at the SIGGRAPH 2000 exhibition. According to Geert Lovink, "new media" are characterized by "disruptions, anomalies, failed attempts, unnoticed remakes, comebacks, and rare instances of the new." Lovink, *Zero Comments*, xxviii. The predigital experiments of pioneering cybernetician Gordon Pask provide examples of earnest inventions that exhibit obscure utility, but nonetheless inform further research. See Peter Cariani, "To evolve an ear."

5. As does "tweaking" according to Malcolm McCullough. See McCullough, *Digital Ground*. For accounts of the contingent and sociable aspects of computer programming see Adrian Mackenzie, *Transductions*; Adrian Mackenzie, *Cutting Code*. Note the "Technicity of Time" chapter in *Transductions*.

6. Scott Fullam, *Hardware Hacking*. Also see Nicolas Collins, *Handmade Electronic Music: The Art of Hardware Hacking*.

7. David P. Jordan, "Haussmann and Haussmannisation."

8. In a different case, the designs of Albert Speer for Hitler's Berlin dominated planning in that city only to be cut short at the end of World War II. The grand plans of his department were not in the company of the interpretive practices, political contexts, financial systems, and myriad contingent relations that would be necessary in the construction of a city. The shorthand way of saying what happened is "his plans were not adopted," but it is also the case that the practices were not in place by which the plans could have a role. The drawings of Speer and his draftsmen do have a place of course. They feature in histories, and their models appear in museums and on film. See Paul B. Jaskot, "Anti-semitic policy in Albert Speer's plans."

9. Christopher Alexander, "A city is not a tree." Some of Alexander's ideas on architectural and urban design have been taken up by software designers. For a discussion see Stephen Rank et al., "Software, architecture, and participatory design."

10. There is much that could be said to support and refine this bald statement. The simplest advocacy against ideas in this sense comes from arguments about meaning and language: "When I think in language, there aren't 'meanings' going through my mind in addition to the verbal expressions: the language itself is the vehicle of thought." Ludwig Wittgenstein, *Philosophical Investigation*, 107. For a full discussion of the idea of "ideas," see Richard Rorty, *Philosophy and the Mirror of Nature*. Neil Silberman provides an apposite critique of the quest for faithful and essentialist digital representations of historical buildings and artifacts. See Silberman, "Chasing the unicorn?"

11. Tom Inns (ed.), *Designing for the 21st Century*.

12. Charles Darwin, *The Formation of Vegetable Mould*, 9.

13. Jonathan Sterne, *The Audible Past*.

14. J. C. Jones, *Design Methods*.

15. Robin Williams and David Edge, "The social shaping of technology."

16. Malcolm Gladwell, *The Tipping Point*; Malcolm Gladwell, *Blink*; Richard H. Thaler and Sunstein Cass R., *Nudge*; Joseph L. Badaracco, *Leading Quietly*.

17. The forays into understanding the city advanced by the avant-garde Situationists are recounted by Catherine de Zegher and Mark Wigley (eds.), *The Activist Drawing*.

18. P. Markopoulos and G. W. M. Rauterberg, *LivingLab*.

19. Michael Bull, *Sound Moves: iPod Culture and Urban Experience*.

20. For an example of a project involving digital devices for "actual and situated interaction with ambient sound" in the countryside, see Elisa Giaccardi, "Cross-media interaction for the virtual museum," 118.

21. I summarize some of the issues under the heading of "technoromanticism." See Coyne, *Technoromanticism.*

22. I borrow the term from the theorist of language, Walter Ong, who described aural culture as agonistic. See Ong, *Orality and Literacy*, 43–45.

23. Aristotle, *De Anima*, 176. For an explanation of Aristotle's theories of the senses, see T. K. Johansen, *Aristotle on the Sense-Organs.*

24. Steven Connor, "The help of your good hands," 68.

25. See, for example, Donna J. Haraway, *Simians, Cyborgs, and Women*; Kevin Robins and Les Levidow, "Soldier, Cyborg, Citizen." William Mitchell also invests heavily in the cyborg metaphor and the proposition that we are undergoing "a fundamental shift in subjectivity . . . I link, therefore I am." (*City of Bits*, 62.)

26. Matthew Chalmers, "Seamful design and ubicomp infrastructure." Also see Anne Galloway, "Seams and scars"; Andy Crabtree and Tom Rodden, "Hybrid ecologies"; and Richard Coyne, Pedro Rebelo, and Martin Parker, "Resisting the seamless interface."

27. See Constance Classen, *Worlds of Sense*; Joy Monice Malnar and Frank Vodvarka, *Sensory Design*; David Howes (ed.), *Empire of the Senses*; Caroline A. Jones, *Sensorium.*

28. Martin Heidegger makes much of this sense of breakdown as an event that brings objects into consciousness. See Heidegger, *Being and Time*; Hubert L. Dreyfus, *Being-in-the-World;* and in the context of computing, Terry Winograd and Fernando Flores, *Understanding Computers and Cognition*; and Richard Coyne, *Designing Information Technology in the Postmodern Age.*

29. David Howes, "Hyperesthesia."

30. Roger Caillois, *Man, Play, and Games.*

31. See for example Robin Evans, *Translations from Drawing to Building.*

32. See Vitruvius, *The Ten Books on Architecture*; Indra McEwen, *Vitruvius.*

33. As explored by Leon Battista Alberti, *On the Art of Building in Ten Books.* For an account of the obvious ocular bias in architecture, see Juhani Pallasmaa, *The Eyes of the Skin.*

34. See Rudolf Wittkower, *Architectural Principles in the Age of Humanism.*

35. See Johan Peter Eckermann, *Conversations of Goethe with Johann Peter Eckermann*, 303. Also see Deborah Howard and Laura Moretti, *Sound and Space in Renaissance Venice: Architecture, Music, Acoustics*, 8.

36. See Marshall McLuhan, *Understanding Media*; E. A. Havelock, *The Muse Learns to Write;* and Ong, *Orality and Literacy.*

37. Steven Connor develops this theme in "Edison's teeth."

38. R. M. Schafer, *The Tuning of the World*, 90.

39. David Sonnenschein, *Sound Design*; Adam Krims (ed.), *Music/Ideology*. In a seminal work written in the 1850s dedicated to decoupling music and the emotions, Eduard Hanslick asserts: "there is no *causus nexus* between a musical composition and the feelings it may excite, as the latter vary with our experience and impressibility." Eduard Hanslick, *The Beautiful in Music: A Contribution to the Revisal of Musical Aesthetics*, 25.

40. See, for example, Bernard Tschumi, *Architecture and Disjunction* (Cambridge, MA: MIT Press, 1994); Bernard Tschumi, *The Manhattan Transcripts*; Bernard Tschumi, "One, two, three: jump"; Rem Koolhaas, "Junk space."

41. Heesang Lee, "Mobile networks, urban places and emotional spaces," 56.

42. Schafer, *The Tuning of the World*, 7.

43. Thaler and Sunstein, *Nudge*, 78.

44. Marc Augé, *Non-places*. Also see Richard Coyne and Martin Parker, "Voices out of place"; and Richard Coyne, "Space without ground."

45. See Andy Clark, *Being There*; Andy Clark, "Reasons, robots and the extended mind"; Andy Clark, *Natural-Born Cyborgs*: and Rolf Pfeifer and Josh C. Bongard, *How the Body Shapes the Way We Think*. Also see Richard Coyne, "Thinking through virtual reality."

46. Clark, *Being There*, 135.

47. See Steven H. Strogatz, "Exploring complex networks": M. E. J. Newman, "The structure and function of complex networks." See also Richard Coyne, "The net effect"; and Richard Coyne, "Wicked problems revisited."

48. For an optimistic account of group behavior in the context of the Internet, see Charles Leadbeater, *We-Think*.

49. Howard Rheingold, *Smart Mobs*.

50. T Berners-Lee, Jay Hendler, and O. Lassila, "The semantic web."

51. For a systematic account of grassroots appropriations of digital technologies in an urban context, see Mark Gaved and Paul Mulholland, "Pioneers, subcultures and cooperatives."

52. Bruno Latour, *Reassembling the Social*, 46. See also Bruno Latour, "On recalling ANT."

53. Donald A. Norman, *Emotional Design.*

54. This orientation toward pleasure is exemplified in the account of the "affective" aspects of interaction design given by Yvonne Rogers, Jenny Preece, and Helen Sharp, *Interaction Design,* 180–215. See also Norman, *Emotional Design.*

55. See Manuel Castells et al., *Mobile Communication and Society,* 51.

56. Sigmund Freud, "Beyond the pleasure principle."

57. The uncanny is emerging as a strong theme in the analysis of digital media. See for example Geert Lovink, *Uncanny Networks;* and Richard Coyne, "The digital uncanny."

58. See, for example, Umberto Eco, *Travels in Hyperreality;* Robert Venturi, Denise Scott Brown, and Steven Izenour, *Learning from Las Vegas;* Jean Baudrillard, "Simulacra and Simulations."

59. Peter Cook and Warren Chalk, "Amazing Archigram."

60. Sigfried Giedion, *Space, Time and Architecture,* xxxii.

61. For a philosophical discussion of the character of irony, see Richard Rorty, *Contingency, Irony, and Solidarity.*

62. I explore these themes at length in Richard Coyne, *Cornucopia Limited.*

Chapter 2

1. *Breakdown* is a term adopted by Martin Heidegger to account for a major aspect of our experience. See Heidegger, *Being and Time* ; Hubert L. Dreyfus, *Being-in-the-world;* and Terry Winograd and Fernando Flores, *Understanding Computers and Cognition.*

2. Brad Johanson, Amando Fox, and Terry Winograd, "The Interactive Workspaces Project," 69.

3. Calibration is relevant to much art production. Artist Tony Longson provides an account of his fine-line 3D geometrical etchings that involve close attention to adjustment: "Making this work was tedious. It involved putting a small mark on the Plexiglas sheet then walking back to the fixed viewpoint to see if the mark coincided with the lines on the grid. Inevitably the mark was in the wrong place, and had to be readjusted. It took many days to complete the image, so these were 'one-off' 3D drawings." Longson, "Reconstruction," 154.

4. I discuss this process in terms of the gift in Richard Coyne, *Cornucopia Limited,* 119.

5. See T Berners-Lee, J. Hendler, and O. Lassila, "The semantic web."

6. See, for example, Dave Raggett, *Report: W3C Workshop.*

7. See the discussion by Ken Ping Hew, Norman Fisher, and B. Hazim, "Towards an integrated set of design tools." The International Alliance for Interoperability advances this cause (see http://www.iai-na.org/).

8. For an early examination of the issues see Aart Bijl, *Computer Discipline and Design Practice.*

9. A term coined by the social theorist Max Weber. See Weber, *The Protestant Ethic and the Spirit of Capitalism.*

10. Here I draw on theories of practice promoted in diverse fields: Stanley Fish, *Doing What Comes Naturally*; Donald A. Schön, *Reflective Practitioner*; John McCarthy and Peter Wright, *Technology as Experience*; Richard Coyne, *Designing Information Technology in the Postmodern Age*; Robin Williams and David Edge, "The social shaping of technology."

11. See Heidegger, *Being and Time*, 172.

12. Note the fragile nature of the standard. Apparently the official kilogram is now 50 micrograms lighter than its copies (see http://www.sciencedaily.com/releases/2007/09/070921110735.htm).

13. Robert John Ackerman, *Data, Instruments, and Theory.*

14. See W. E. Knowles Middleton, *A History of the Thermometer*, 289; Arnold Court, "Concerning an important invention"; Nancy C. Flores and Elizabeth A. E. Boyle, *Thermometer Calibration Guide.*

15. Middleton, *A History of the Thermometer.*

16. For helpful discussions of scientific realism and the importance of instrumentation, see Bruce Gregory, *Inventing Reality*; and Don Ihde, *Instrumental Realism.*

17. Mary Hesse, "The explanatory function of metaphor"; Hesse, *Models and Analogies in Science.* For a similar account of the role of metaphor in biology, see Evelyn Fox Keller, *Refiguring Life.*

18. As elaborated by Thomas Kuhn, *The Structure of Scientific Revolutions.*

19. For a standard description of the definition of temperature, see Francis Weston Sears and Mark W. Zemansky, *College Physics*, 289. There is economy in the process of calibration and recalibration. In the case of the thermometer, only two measurements are made to establish the extremes of the scale. The 50-degree point could be mapped by mixing boiling water with the same quantity of ice water, but this would be difficult to control, and is not necessary anyway. The 50-degree mark and every other step between 0 and 100 is calculated or interpolated using the convention of marking off the distance between 0 and 100 in even units. In fact, this is the definition of temperature. The convention defines temperature as a linear scale

relative to the expansion of a fluid. Calibration often involves taking a few strategic measurements. If the instrument required that every graduation on the scale had to be decided by a direct procedural mapping, then the procedure would be more difficult to reproduce, and the accuracy of the instrument would not be easy to verify.

20. S. Drake, *Discoveries and Opinions of Galileo,* 115–116; Jignesh Khakhar, "Data graphics and interactive information environments," 13. Edward R. Tufte draws attention to the influential role of Galileo's drawings in the context of graphic imagery, particularly as it pertains to the "small increments": see Tufte, *Envisioning Information.*

21. Note that precision design and manufacture have effectively rendered invisible to the user the need to calibrate in some cases.

22. Andy Clark, *Natural-Born Cyborgs,* 18–19. Also see Rolf Pfeifer and Josh C. Bongard, *How the Body Shapes the Way We Think.*

23. Private conversation with Kevin Warwick, May, 22, 2002.

24. Clark, *Natural-Born Cyborgs,* 122.

25. Manfred E. Clynes, "Cyborg II; Manfred E. Clynes and Nathan S. Kline, "Cyborgs and space."

26. M. Brown and D. G. Lowe, "Recognising panoramas."

27. The functions and issues surrounding digital social networks are described in Ofcom, *Report: Social Networking.*

28. Available at http://labs.live.com/.

29. Carlo Ratti and Paul Richens demonstrate just how much can be revealed by automated calculations from aerial views, taken pixel by pixel: building shapes, heights, and environmental performance. See Ratti and Richens, "Raster analysis of urban form."

30. I. Amidror, *The Theory of the Moiré Phenomenon.*

31. Available at http://www.mathematik.com/Moire/.

32. J. Murray Barbour, *Tuning and Temperament.*

33. The tuning of an orchestra is such a process. Performers come out on stage and adjust their instruments to a standard. In a classical Western orchestra this is usually the A note on an oboe, 440 Hz (cycles per second). Of course it is not only the third string of each violin that has to be so tuned, but also all of the other strings on each violin relative to it. Performers will also quietly adjust their instruments during periods when they are not playing.

34. Philip Bonello et al., "Designs for an adaptive tuned vibration absorber."

35. Available at http://aardvark.co.nz/pjet/.

36. Robert M. Pirsig, *Zen and the Art of Motorcycle Maintenance*, 98–99. This book is in turn a reference to Eugen Herrigel, *Zen in the Art of Archery*. The latter obsesses over the matter of the archer relaxing into the feel of the bow's tension, and the sense of when to release the arrow: "Is it 'I' who draws the bow, or is it the bow that draws me into the state of highest tension? Do 'I' hit the goal, or does the goal hit me? . . . 'Now at last,' the Master broke in, 'the bow-string has cut right through you" (85–86).

37. Nicolas Collins, *Handmade Electronic Music: The Art of Hardware Hacking*, 11.

38. See Norbert Weiner, *The Human Use of Human Beings*.

39. Ranulph Glanville, "Try again," 1181.

40. Ferdinand de Saussure, *Course in General Linguistics*, 116.

41. Richard Coyne, *Technoromanticism*.

42. McCarthy and Wright, *Technology as Experience*. Also see Coyne, *Designing Information Technology in the Postmodern Age*.

43. P. Dourish, *Where the Action Is*, 189–190.

44. Malcolm McCullough, *Digital Ground*, 92.

45. Ibid., 118.

46. Curtis Roads, *Microsound*, 21.

47. Iannis Xenakis, *Formalized Music*, 9.

48. Russell Foster and Leon Kreitzman, *Rhythms of Life*, 35. Also see http://www.npl.co.uk/time/.

49. See Thomas Kuhn, *The Copernican Revolution*, 11.

50. Available at http://www.npl.co.uk/time/.

51. Were it not for the insertion of leap years, it would be easy to calculate that the yearly cycle would drift across the seasons such that New Year's Day would alternate between mid-winter and mid-summer about every seven hundred years!

52. Foster and Kreitzman, *Rhythms of Life*, 181.

53. According to studies into jet lag, we are also better at accommodating the changes to daily cycles when traveling in an easterly direction across time zones than when traveling west (ibid.).

54. This critique focuses on call centers and the idea of a 24-hour labor force. See Manuel Castells, *The Rise of the Network Society*, 476.

55. Vitruvius, *The Ten Books on Architecture*, 26-31; Indra McEwen, *Vitruvius*.

56. Plotinus, *The Essence of Plotinus*; Slavoj Žižek, *The Indivisible Remainder*, 42.

57. See Arnold Pacey, *Meaning in Technology*.

58. The enthusiasm for listening to the stars persists in the Acoustic Space Program: "It will enable listeners to tune into different celestial frequencies, hearing planets, stars, and the constant hiss of cosmic noise. It will reveal the sonic character of objects in our galaxy, and in the process perhaps make these phenomena more tangible and comprehensible" (http://www.radioqualia.net/rt32/announce.html).

59. Pacey, *Meaning in Technology*, 26.

60. Johannes Kepler, *Harmonies of the World* (1939), 1031. There is an interesting subtheme here about the priority of light and vision that preserve the harmonies, as there is no sound in the space of the heavens, as there is nothing to rub against.

61. Kepler, *Harmonies of the World*, 1061.

62. Hesse, *Models and Analogies in Science*, 26.

63. Kuhn, *The Structure of Scientific Revolutions*.

64. Leon Battista Alberti, *On the Art of Building in Ten Books*, 156. This echoes Aristotle for whom: "it is customary to say of well-executed works that nothing can be added to them or taken away, the implication being that excess and deficiency alike destroy perfection, while the mean preserves it." Aristotle, *The Ethics of Aristotle*, 101.

65. Vaughan Hart and Robert Tucker, "Imaginacy set free."

66. Adrian B. Snodgrass, *Architecture, Time and Eternity*, vol. 1, 171. The Aztec calendar gives similar accord to the five uncounted and unnamed days of the year. See Snodgrass, *Architecture, Time and Eternity*, vol. 2, 521.

67. Snodgrass, *Architecture, Time and Eternity*, vol. 1, 173. I return to the issue of sacrifice in the context of a discussion of noise in chapter 11.

68. Barbour, *Tuning and Temperament*. The composer La Monte Young has worked with a piano tuned to the Just intonation. The result is described by Piero Scaruffi: "The performer begins playing the given notes, but soon the piano, because of its [J]ust intonation, provokes certain modulations and, after the performer adjusts to these changes, he must adjust to the subsequent changes forced by the piano's tuning, and so on during the course of the performance. In this sense the piece is like an organism that grows little by little. Over time, the performance becomes frenetic and hypnotic." Scaruffi, *LaMonte Young*.

69. That the discrepancy for both the days of the year and the musical comma is approximately one quarter is clearly coincidental, and does not seem to have been

accorded any significance. Kepler described the discrepancies between the harmonic ratios of planetary movement in terms of units such as the comma, but not as cyclical discrepancies derived from mapping cycles of octaves to cycles of fifths as in musical scales.

70. Note that the word *temperament* in German is *Stimmung*, the same word to denote attunement in Heidegger's writing.

71. According to Gustav Engel, reported in Barbour, *Tuning and Temperament*, 198.

72. See for examples William A. Sethares, *Tuning, Timbre, Spectrum, Scale.*

73. Max Weber, *The Rational and Social Foundations of Music.* Theodor W. Adorno advances a related claim that of all the musical scales or modes, the Platonic tradition favors those that are the most militaristic. See Adorno, *The Culture Industry*, 31.

74. Kathryn Vaughn, "The influence of tambura drone."

75. Such anomalies are by now familiar features of logic and mathematics, as evident in Gödel's significant theorem about undecidability, which is said to "prove" by logic itself that there are statements that are palpably true but unprovable. See Kurt Gödel, *On Formally Unprovable Propositions*; and Douglas R. Hofstadter, *Gödel, Escher, Bach.*

Chapter 3

1. Much derives from Plato's account of the Demiurge, the divine creator, dividing up through geometrical constructions the matrix of formless matter. See Plato, *The Republic of Plato.*

2. According to Rudolph Arnheim there is a psychological aspect to this tendency. We have an inbuilt capability to see the straightness of things that are nearly straight, and the triangularity in things nearly triangular. See Arnheim, *Art and Visual Perception.* For David Pye, in assessing the workmanship of a joiner or sculptor the critic may designate as rough those objects that exhibit deviations from perfection. This deviation can be deliberate, the result of a constraint on time and resources, or because the craft worker is incapable of achieving perfection. Rough workmanship is an acquired art. See Pye, *The Nature and Art of Workmanship*, 32.

3. See Alexandre Koyré, *From the Closed World to the Infinite Universe.*

4. Thomas Kuhn, *The Copernican Revolution*, 221.

5. For elaboration on the theme of *phronesis* in design, see Adrian Snodgrass and Richard Coyne, *Interpretation in Architecture.*

6. Pye, *The Nature and Art of Workmanship*, 64.

7. For the application of some of these issues to communications in building construction, see Dermott McMeel, "The Artistry of Construction".

8. Colin Rowe, *The Mathematics of the Ideal Villa*, 14.

9. Ibid.

10. Vitruvius, *The Ten Books on Architecture*, 114.

11. Ibid., 13.

12. Ibid., 84.

13. Ibid., 86. See further elaboration by Vila Domini and A. David, "The diminution of the classical column."

14. Ibid., 308–309.

15. The Latin word for *wedge* is *cuneus*, from which we derive cuneiform, wedge-shaped.

16. Lewis Mumford, *Technics and Civilization*, 77.

17. Vitruvius, *The Ten Books on Architecture*, 190.

18. Ibid., 274.

19. Ibid., 298.

20. See Pye, *The Nature and Art of Workmanship*, 35.

21. Arnheim, *Art and Visual Perception*, 181.

22. Such devices are receiving prominence in high-profile museums. Of note are the codebreaking exhibits at Bletchley Park and the reconstruction of Babbage's Difference Engine at the London Science Museum, both in the United Kingdom. For a history of computing see Sadie Plant, *Zeros and Ones*.

23. Deborah Howard and Laura Moretti, *Sound and Space in Renaissance Venice: Architecture, Music, Acoustics*, 6.

24. Ibid., 110.

25. Leon Battista Alberti, *On Painting*, 43.

26. Arnheim, *Art and Visual Perception*, 289.

27. John Hospers, *An Introduction to Philosophical Analysis*, 81.

28. Such emergent shard-like forms are theorized to be the result of overlaid and transparent methods of organization, which might produce a "rich fabric of spaces in which the two directions are accommodated and conflated." Colin Rowe and Robert Slutzky, *Transparency*, 103.

29. Martin Parker, "A response to 'Athens by Sound,'" 32.

30. Steven Connor, *Dumbstruck*, 20.

31. In fact what I am describing here is a common property of complex networks, where there are lots of interconnected devices, or agents, that depend on each other for information. The elusive goal described here is simply the problem of how to get the devices to interoperate effectively. Tuning a stringed instrument such as a guitar is typically a multivariate problem. There are six strings, and increasing the tension in one bends the fret board slightly, which reduces the tension in the other five strings and puts them at a slightly lower pitch. So each string needs to be adjusted in turn, and repeatedly, until the six strings are suitably tuned (E, A, D, G, B, E). There is a co-dependence between the individual strings. In the technical literature *multivariate calibration* means using known variable values (e.g., barometric pressure, wind speed, rainfall) to infer a value for something that has not been measured for whatever reason (e.g., air temperature). For technical discussions of the calibration problem in various complex domains, see Harald Martens, *Multivariate Calibration*; Thomas Pyzdek and Paul A. Keller, *Quality Engineering Handbook*; and Marko Hofmann, "On the complexity of parameter calibration in simulation models," *The Journal of Defense Modeling and Simulation*.

32. Norbert Weiner, *The Human Use of Human Beings*.

33. Conversation is so described by Hans-Georg Gadamer as a process of play. See Gadamer, *Truth and Method*; and Snodgrass and Coyne, *Interpretation in Architecture*.

34. See Rolf Pfeifer and Josh C. Bongard, *How the Body Shapes the Way We Think*.

35. Alfred Schutz, "Making music together," 161–162. Also see Paul Filmer, "Songtime," 96.

36. From Duchamp's notes, reported in Craig Adcock, "Marcel Duchamp's gap music," 128.

37. Arnold Pacey, *Meaning in Technology*, 23.

38. Mumford, *Technics and Civilization*, 13–14.

39. Edwin Hutchins, *Cognition in the Wild*, 316.

40. See Marshall McLuhan, *The Gutenberg Galaxy*, Marshall McLuhan and R. Bruce Powers, *The Global Village;* and Marshall McLuhan, *Understanding Media*. I expand further on these themes in Richard Coyne, *Designing Information Technology in the Postmodern Age*.

41. Here I am repeating observations and summaries I developed in Coyne, *Designing Information Technology in the Postmodern Age*.

42. John Stuart Mill, *On Liberty*.

43. Mary Hesse, *Models and Analogies in Science*, 76.

44. See A. B. Snodgrass and R. D. Coyne, "Models, metaphors and the hermeneutics of designing."

45. Connor, *Dumbstruck*, 20.

46. Jonathan Donner, "What can be said with a missed call?"

47. Donald Schön discusses such shifts in thinking in Schön, *Displacement of Concepts*.

48. See Michel Foucault, *The Order of Things*; Michel Foucault, *Discipline and Punish*.

49. Michel de Certeau, *The Practice of Everyday Life*, xiv.

50. Ibid., xvii.

51. Ibid.

52. Ibid., xviii.

53. Ibid., xix–xx. For an account of *metis* as a guiding strategy in architectural and urban design, see Mark Dorrian and Adrian Hawker, *Metis*.

54. de Certeau, *The Practice of Everyday Life*, 32.

55. Jean-François Augoyard, *Step by Step*, 24.

56. Christopher Alexander, *Notes on the Synthesis of Form*.

57. John H. Miller and Scott E. Page, *Complex Adaptive Systems*.

58. Fitness concepts are concomitant with notions of ideal, smooth urbanism, and a romance with wholeness, redemptive narratives, and utopianism. They also align with dystopian laments, as if fractured urbanism needs to be repaired. Splintered urbanism carries pejorative notions of an urban existence that is fragmented and lacking coherence, drifting out of alignment.

59. Pfeifer and Bongard, *How the Body Shapes the Way We Think*, 266. Also see D. J. Bakkum et al., "Remove some 'A' from AI"; B. D. Reger et al., "Connecting brains to robots."

60. Lewis Mumford, *Technics and Civilization*, 13–14.

61. Sean Cubitt, *Digital Aesthetics*, 47.

62. For an extended discussion of design as metaphor play, see Richard Coyne, Adrian Snodgrass, and David Martin, "Metaphors in the Design Studio."

63. Manuel Castells et al., *Mobile Communication and Society*, 2.

Chapter 4

1. For an interesting account of the use of mobile phones in everyday life, see Larissa Hjorth, "Imaging communities."

2. D. K. Arvind and K. J. Wong, "Speckled computing."

3. Alex S. Taylor and Richard Harper, "Age-old practices in the 'New World.'" Taylor and Harper elaborate on such exchanges in terms of the gift society. On the reception by teenagers of digital media see Robson, Matthew. *Report: How teenagers consume media.*

4. Sigmund Freud, *The Psychopathology of Everyday Life.*

5. See Henri Lefebvre, *Critique of Everyday Life*; Hakim Bey, *T.A.Z.: The Temporary Autonomous Zone.*

6. Anne Galloway, "Intimations of everyday life."

7. Harold Garfinkel, *Studies in Ethnomethodology*, 1. See also Garfinkel, "Studies of the routine grounds of everyday activities." Jean-François Augoyard says of this approach that it "favours observation of the most unremarkable of feelings and actions." Augoyard, *Step by Step*, 20.

8. For discussions of the tension between the everyday and theatricality in the conception of the user of architectural space, see Stephen A. Gage, "Constructing the user"; and François Penz, "The architectural promenade as narrative device."

9. See Tarmo Virko, *Global cell phone use at 50 percent.*

10. An idea amplified and critiqued in Manfredo Tafuri, *Architecture and Utopia.*

11. I elaborate on related experiments in chapter 10.

12. Mizuko Ito, Daisuke Okabe, and Misa Matsuda (eds.), *Personal, Portable, Pedestrian.*

13. The discussion pertains to the censorship of Yoani Sánchez's Generation Y blog site about life in Cuba. (http://www.desdecuba.com/generationy/). "This aspect of a personal account is very powerful in a place like Cuba, she became a personality because she blogs about her daily life and that's what annoys the government. The daily routine of Cubans is exposed to the press of the world, their lack of choice and lack of things to buy, she became a celebrity by exposing this and showing how difficult life is in Cuba." Americo Martins, in Alka Marwaha, Blogging all over the World, 13:50 GMT, Monday, 22 June 2009 14:50 UK. http://news.bbc.co.uk/1/hi/technology/8102803.stm. Full interview: http://www.bbc.co.uk/worldservice/business/2009/06/090616_digitalplanet_160609.shtml Global Blogging and Censorship, broadcast 16 June 2009.

14. William James develops the theme of habit at length, as a means of keeping any individual within their social stratum: "An invisible law, as strong as gravitation, keeps him within his orbit, arrayed this year as he was the last" (James, *The Principles of Psychology*, 125–126, quoted by Richard Shusterman, *Body Consciousness*, 140–141). See also Leonidas Koutsoumpos, *Inhabiting Ethics.*

15. Michael Bull, "The intimate sounds of urban experience," 171.

16. The Oxford English Dictionary also relates "haven," the safe place for sheltering boats, to the verb "to have."

17. Mark Griffiths, "Sex on the Internet," 278.

18. Martin Heidegger makes much of dwelling as inhabiting, but favors the word *dwell* (*Gewohnen*): "Building as dwelling, that is, as being on the earth, however, remains for man's everyday experience that which is from the outset "habitual"—we inhabit it, as our language says so beautifully: it is the *Gewohnte*. For this reason it recedes behind the manifold ways in which dwelling is accomplished, the activities of cultivation and construction. These activities later claim the name of *bauen,* building, and with it the fact of building, exclusively for themselves. The real sense of *bauen,* namely dwelling, falls into oblivion." Heidegger, "Building, dwelling, thinking," 147–148.

19. Martin Heidegger elaborates on the term *in*. See Heidegger, *Being and Time,* 78–81.

20. Heidegger, "Building, dwelling, thinking," 147.

21. Samuel Butler, *Life and Habit*.

22. For a helpful discussion relating habit to habitat and debates surrounding Darwin's theories, see Jodie A Nicotra, *The Force of Habit*.

23. Available at http://www.biology-online.org/dictionary/Ecological_Niche.

24. Mary Douglas, "The idea of a home," 261.

25. See Sherry Turkle (ed.), *Evocative Objects*.

26. For a description of Le Corbusier's housing complex and the symbol, see Sarah Menin and Flora Samuel, *Nature and Space*, 66.

27. Among other factors for life. See Peter D. Ward and Donald Brownlee, *Rare Earth*.

28. Henri Lefebvre, *Rhythmanalysis*, 15.

29. Russell Foster and Leon Kreitzman, *Rhythms of Life*.

30. See for example Anne Trafton, "Wearable blood pressure sensor offers 24/7 continuous monitoring."

31. Note that there is a tradition of scholarship contesting the distinction between instinct and habit. See for example Knight Dunlap, "The Identity of Instinct and Habit."

32. Alain De Botton, *The Art of Travel*, 247.

33. Butler, *Life and Habit*.

34. For an account rehabilitating notions of prejudice, see Hans-Georg Gadamer, *Truth and Method*; and Adrian Snodgrass and Richard Coyne, *Interpretation in Architecture.*

35. Andy Clark, *Natural-Born Cyborgs*. Also see Edwin Hutchins, *Cognition in the Wild.*

36. See Richard Coyne, "Thinking through virtual reality."

37. Clark, *Natural-Born Cyborgs*, 30.

38. David Morley, *Home Territories*, 90.

39. For an explanation of the impact of illegal file sharing in the UK see Stephen Carter, *Digital Britain*. Michael Bull sees iPod culture in general as a way of fighting "against the imposed rhythms and timings of the everyday world." See Michael Bull, *Sound Moves*.

40. Kathryn Vaughn, "The influence of tambura drone."

41. Eugen Herrigel, *Zen in the Art of Archery*, 58.

42. E. A. Havelock, *The Muse Learns to Write*, 71; Walter J. Ong, *Orality and Literacy*, 34.

43. Ong, *Orality and Literacy*, 41.

44. For example, B. J. Fogg asserts: "Unlike human persuaders, computers don't get tired; they can implement their strategies over and over again." Fogg, *Persuasive Technology*, 216.

45. For Freud the game is a response to the child's apparent distress at losing sight of his mother as she periodically enters and leaves the room. For Freud, this is the condition of us all, coming to terms with the loss of comfort and the loss of security of the mother's presence. (If we want to take this further, according to Freud the game also invokes recollections of the threat of castration by the father.) In certain cases Freud would identify such repetitive behavior as pathologically obsessive. But most of the time such enactments or encounters with repetition are simply reminders of this primal conflict: loss of the mother, and all she symbolizes, with oneness, nurture, and so on.

46. S. Freud, "The 'uncanny.'" For an expansion of the application of the uncanny to architectural spaces, see A. Vidler, *The Architectural Uncanny*. Also, see Richard Coyne, "The digital uncanny."

47. Vidler, *The Architectural Uncanny*.

48. See Karl Marx, "Capital."

49. I discuss the phenomenon of repetition in the context of computer games and in the context of Marxist theory elsewhere. See Richard Coyne, *Cornucopia Limited.*

50. Friedrich Wilhelm Nietzsche, *Thus Spoke Zarathustra*. Johan Huizinga refers to the sophistry and word play of Nietzsche as possibly restoring philosophy to its play origins. See Huizinga, *Homo Ludens*, 152. See also Gilles Deleuze, *Difference and Repetition* for a detailed treatment of Nietzsche's concepts of repetition. Soren Kierkegaard also develops the theme. See Kierkegaard, "Repetition."

51. Jacques Derrida, *Of Grammatology*; and Jacques Derrida, "Freud and the scene of writing." See also Gilles Deleuze and Felix Guattari, *Anti-Oedipus*.

52. Think of the twentieth-century revival of concept of homeland, *Heimat*, in Germany, and as documented in Edgar Reitz's long-running serialized drama by the same name.

Chapter 5

1. Alexander Tzonis and Liane Lefaivre, *Classical Architecture*, 118.

2. Henri Lefebvre, *Rhythmanalysis*, 79.

3. Mark Johnson, *The Body in the Mind*.

4. Walter J. Ong, *Orality and Literacy*, 72

5. Sigmund Freud, "Beyond the pleasure principle."

6. See Oliveros's study into the sounds of cisterns and garden hoses (http://music.msn.com/artist/default.aspx?artist=115797) and Rebelo's work in Lisbon on water cisterns and spatial resonances (http://www.sarc.qub.ac.uk/~prebelo/folio/aquasliberas/).

7. Russell Foster and Leon Kreitzman, *Rhythms of Life*.

8. Frances A. Yates, *The Art of Memory*.

9. See for example P. Turner and E. Davenport, *Spatiality, Spaces and Technology*; Alessandro Aurigi and Fiorella de Cindio (eds.), *Augmented Urban Spaces*.

10. William Etkin, "Co-operation and competition in social behaviour."

11. Ibid., 22–23.

12. David McFarland, *Animal Behavior*, 416.

13. Jean-François Augoyard and Henry Torgue, *Sonic Experience*, 94.

14. Donald MacKenzie and Yuval Millo, "Constructing a Market, Performing Theory."

15. Alain Corbin, "The auditory markers of the village," 118.

16. Augoyard and Torgue, *Sonic Experience*, 62.

17. Walter Benjamin, "The work of art in the age of mechanical reproduction."

18. No doubt the account I have given here will appear quaint in five years' time, when we take such connectivity for granted. Any impediments to interoperability currently reside with the adoption of standard communication protocols, competition in the marketplace, who controls production and upkeep of networks, and how costs are disbursed.

19. Christy Desmet, "Reading the Web as fetish."

20. David Morley, *Home Territories*, 97.

21. Karl Marx, "Capital."

22. Edward R. Tufte, *Envisioning Information, 67.*

23. Martin Heidegger, "The age of the world picture," 129.

24. The notion of scanning probably derives from poetry: to scan a poem is to test its meter. According to the *OED* "to scan" derives from "to climb," as if to ascend a ladder, a procedure followed step by step.

25. Edwin Hutchins, *Cognition in the Wild.*

26. In audio engineering, the way a sound source moves across the acoustical field is regarded as panning.

27. Available at http://photosynth.net/.

28. It even generates three-dimensional models of these sites from subtle shifts in point of view and parallax.

29. http://www.geograph.org.uk/. For a sonic equivalent see http://www.soundaroundyou.com.

30. Robert Baker's 1796 patent for the panorama emphasizes the importance of keeping the surface on which the panorama is painted at a suitable distance from the viewing public, and that there should be a canopy above the viewer and platform extensions to occlude the apparent limits of the rendered surface. Sectional drawings through panorama buildings make apparent the visual contrivance of occlusion, recesses beneath the platform for storage and maintenance, and the delivery of illumination and optical special effects. Panoramas were not only large canvases, but large and elaborate buildings.

31. As exemplified in the popular computer game *Myst IV* and as deployed in QuickTime VR.

32. H. Maturana and F. G. Varela, *Autopoiesis and Cognition*; Humberto Maturana, "Reality." Also see N. Katherine Hayles, *How We Became Posthuman*, 131–135.

33. Surveillance cameras perpetuate the repetitive scan. Cameras reveal insecurity, suspicion, delinquency, and crime. Antisocial and illegal uses of image media

include exposure (on social networks), "happy slapping" (recording violence via mobile cameras), and "griefing" (spoiling other people's online social interaction), libel, and intrusion. Online and everyday spatial categories of transgression converge. Some everyday places are ordinarily immune to the tourist gaze: places of only local concern, not regularly photographed, deemed ugly, out of character, inaccessible, or shameful, or as attractions on the "dark tourism" itinerary.

Chapter 6

1. To tag something arguably absolves us from having to remark on it. I want to suggest that tagging is ordinary and everyday; tagging is not a remarkable activity and we do not tag only remarkable things.

2. Tags appear as insertions in the text, such as <b>this</b>. An HTML interpreter, such as a web browser, will identify the tag and print the words enclosed by the tags in bold. The tag itself, or at least the start and the end tags, <b></b>, will not be printed onto the computer screen and will be invisible.

3. For example, all the words related to computers in this chapter could be tagged with <digital></digital>. It would then be simple for an XML parser (such as most web browsers) with a set of instructions (a style sheet) to only print out those words, or to print them in bold, or to link them to other digital words.

4. Malcolm McCullough, *Digital Ground*, 80–83.

5. John Counsell and Marie-Cecile Puybaraud, "Visible display of automated observation of collaborative workspaces."

6. Mark S. Nixon, Tieniu Tan, and Rama Chellappa, *Human Identification Based on Gait.*

7. A landscape of tags may be a world preoccupied with security and control, but there is more to be said about tagging before foreclosing on the issue of its desirability. I suspect that the specter of bureaucratic control that haunts modern societies usually is based on the cumbersome processing of paper ledgers and lists rather than digital records per se. See Walter J. Ong, *Ramus.*

8. For some, the tag is "the designation of a difference." See Vlad Tanasescu, Dumitri Roman, and John Domingue, "Service selection via extreme geotagging."

9. There is no space to go into the intricacies of language theory relevant here. See John Austin, *How to Do Things with Words*; Michael Reddy, "The conduit metaphor"; Ludwig Wittgenstein, *Philosophical Investigations.*

10. One of the first accounts of this obsession with depositing signatures in public landmarks as graffiti was a 1971 *New York Times* article by Anon., "'Taki 183' spawns pen pals." More recent engagement with graffiti commonly invokes the name of

the artist who goes by the name of Banksy and relies on the World Wide Web to publicize and advertise his audacious productions.

11. Ferdinand de Saussure, *Course in General Linguistics*; Fredric Jameson, *The Prison-House of Language*.

12. See Tanasescu, Roman, and Domingue, "Service selection via extreme geotagging."

13. Charles Sanders Peirce, "On the algebra of logic," 181.

14. A reviewer of an earlier draft of this manuscript dissuaded me from overuse of the terms *we, us,* and *our,* which amount to using indexicals in a very unspecific way, prompting the perplexed reader to ask, "Who are we?"

15. The usual commerce involves pointers and memory addresses, each of which can be treated as variables.

16. Tim Guest, *Second Lives*.

17. The cognitive operation of landmarks is explored by Kevin Lynch, *The Image of the City*; and from the point of view of situation cognition, by Edwin Hutchins, *Cognition in the Wild*, 134–136.

18. See Arno Sharl, "Towards the geospatial web."

19. I pursue the theme of location-aware computing in more detail in chapter 8.

20. For a discussion of the significance of the threshold in ritual, see Victor Turner, *The Forest of Symbols*.

21. James Hays and Alexei A. Efros, "IM2GPS."

22. I describe our own experimentation with context-based locational tagging in chapter 10.

23. For real-time video streaming from smartphone cameras see www.qik.com

24. Hutchins, *Cognition in the Wild*, 105.

25. I describe GPS in greater detail in chapter 8.

26. Adam Mathes, *Folksonomies*.

27. Ella Chmielewska, "Logos or the resonance of branding."

28. See Douglas B. Holt, "Why do brands cause trouble?"; Tomi Ahonen and Alan Moore, *Communities Dominate Brands*; and Naomi Klein, *No Logo*.

29. Saussure, *Course in General Linguistics*.

30. Roland Barthes, *Mythologies*.

31. Joseph Conrad, *Heart of Darkness*, 105.

32. See Chmielewska, "Logos or the resonance of branding."

33. The latter is an attempt to encapsulate Foucault's account of social ordering.

34. For a discussion of some of the issues in the case of the Internet in China, see Guobin Yang, "The co-evolution of the Internet and civil society in China."

35. Henri Lefebvre, *The Production of Space*, 75.

36. Gaston Bachelard, *The Poetics of Space*, 26.

37. Ibid., 27.

38. The latter is an attempt to encapsulate the Marxist and neo-Marxist critique of modernity.

39. Jean-François Augoyard, *Step by Step*, 80

40. Bachelard, *The Poetics of Space*, 17.

41. Ibid.

42. As in the case of the fetish explored in chapter 5.

43. Christy Desmet, "Reading the Web as fetish."

44. See Ciro Cattuto, Vittorio Loreto, and Luciano Pietronero, "Semiotic dynamics and collaborative tagging"; Peter Morville, *Ambient Findability*, 134–143.

45. Saussure, *Course in General Linguistics*, 66.

46. William T. Keeton, *Biological Science*, 633.

47. If a new homeowner arranged furniture in this way, she might put all the chairs in one room, the tables in another, and so on.

48. To identify members of a student group, academics often resort to a more surreptitious form of tagging: a "lookup table" in the form of a matrix of students' photographs with their names printed beneath.

49. Frances A. Yates, *The Art of Memory*.

50. Ibid., 25.

51. Ibid.

Chapter 7

1. The Italian *toccare* (to touch) is the derivation of *toccata*, a musical piece written to exercise the performer's technique.

2. Research by Ishii attempts to demonstrate how touch can be communicated across distance by digital means. See Hiroshi Ishii and Brygg Ullmer, "Tangible bits."

3. Whose dress is presumed to resemble rags as in the Scottish-Irish traditional song, "The Raggle Taggle Gypsy".

4. In some of our own experiments we have encouraged users to post their most commonly used brand logos on a social network site. Apart from helping to form identities, such branding has a mnemonic function, providing people with reminders of their daily consumption practices and those aspects of their lives with which the brands are associated: sitting down for meals, working in the garden, taking out the garbage, going for a jog, watching television. Brands and tags invoke nostalgia for the past, recalling childhood bath time, one's first computer, playing with model trains, granddad's smoking habits.

5. For a helpful discussion of network security that draws on architectural metaphors, see Neal Kumar Katyal, "Digital architecture as crime control." Also see Richard Coyne, John Lee, and Martin Parker, "Permeable portals."

6. Katyal, "Digital architecture as crime control."

7. Note that the term in wide use now is *captcha,* in lower case.

8. Another automated spam strategy is to grab the captcha image and send it to another webpage set up as a puzzle site for a human user to translate unwittingly. The machine thus entices humans to do the image matching. See Janet Meiners, "Spammers getting around captchas."

9. For an examination of the value of such voice tags as mnemonic devices, see Bruce Smith, "Listening to the wild blue yonder," 24.

10. Steven Connor, *Dumbstruck.*

11. The term is an oblique reference to the cliché that people who live in landscapes dominated by snow have an inordinate number of words for snow: likewise, presumably, the British have many words for rain.

12. See http://snowclones.org/.

13. Jean-François Augoyard, *Step by Step,* 88.

14. This latter phrase from the Barack Obama presidential campaign was adopted as the name of an activist website in Vietnam. See Alka Marwaha, *Blogging all over the world.*

15. Michel Serres, *The Parasite.*

16. Ibid., 15–16.

17. Joseph Weissman and Taylor Adkins, "Science and parasites."

18. Pfeifer and Bongard, *How the Body Shapes the Way We Think,* 255.

19. "The Flea," by John Donne (1572–1631).

20. As explored in the novel by Tim Guest, *Second Lives.*

21. Naomi Klein, *No Logo,* 28.

22. Ibid.

23. The error of which is exemplified in the Midas myth. For a helpful summary of different standpoints on the value of money, see Chris Robinson and Elton G. McGoun, "The sociology of personal finance."

24. Themes explored by Steven Levitt and Stephen J. Dubner, *Freakonomics.*

25. Klein, *No Logo,* 281.

26. Ibid., 300. Italics are in the original.

27. See http://www.a-i-u.net/wishtree2.html. Tying a ribbon or tag on a tree or a knot in a handkerchief indicates that there is something important to be associated with the host, even though the tag may not indicate what it is. By virtue of being unusual, the tag acts as a reminder, hopefully recalling the context in which the attachment was made. Tags remind people of the tag's host, or make the host memorable. Web pages are now populated with special symbols that act as reminders, even if net surfers do not attend to their messages: star ratings, Digg rankings (one particular web service that automatically scores websites on the basis of popularity), compliance symbols, copyright and creative commons marks (e.g., the reversed "c" in a circle to indicate "copy left," permitting others to copy and adapt the material with certain caveats), and of course brand logos.

28. Hal Berghel, "Identity theft, social security numbers, and the web."

29. Plato, "Cratylus," 126.

30. The hunter attracts a wild duck with a wooden replica, a fake pond, or a synthetic duck call.

31. Roger Caillois, "Mimicry and legendary psychasthenia."

32. Charles Darwin, *The Descent of Man and Selection in Relation to Sex.*

33. Marc Naguib and R. Haven Wiley, "Estimating the distance to a source of sound."

Chapter 8

1. For an introduction of the theme of locative media and lessons from archeology, see Anne Galloway and Matt Ward, "Locative media as socialising and spatializing practice." For examples of the use of GPS and other technologies in wayfinding, see Philip Berridge, Volker Koch, and Andre G. P. Brown, "Information spaces for mobile city access"; and Wanji Mai, Gordon Dodds, and Chris Tweed, "A PDA-based system for recognizing buildings from user-supplied images."

2. J. E. D. Williams, *From Sails to Satellites.*

3. Paul Virilio, *Speed and Politics.*

4. According to William Mitchell: "We experience networks at their interfaces, and only worry about the plumbing behind the interfaces when something goes wrong." Mitchell, *City of Bits*, 15.

5. Tacitus, *The Histories Volume 1*, 123.

6. According to Tacitus, "On their arrival at Aquileia they had mobbed the couriers who brought the news of Otho's fall, and torn to pieces the standards bearing Vitellius' name, finally looting the camp-chest and dividing the money among themselves. These were hostile acts." Ibid., 191.

7. For a different elaboration of the postal metaphor applied to mobile phone communications, see Larissa Hjorth, "Locating Mobility."

8. Manuel Castells, *The Internet Galaxy.*

9. Williams, *From Sails to Satellites.*

10. Ibid., 24.

11. See ibid., 85–106; Dava Sobel, *Longitude.* Already in this discussion you will notice the ease with which one slips into a series of assumptions about the actuality and reality of a position. After all, one must be somewhere. It is only the accuracy of the fix that is in question. Later we will see how the focus on small increments draws us to consider the discrepancies between frames of reference rather than anomalies between maps and actualities. This recalls the argument in chapter 2 that calibration is a matter of comparing models, representations, frames of reference, or, we may add here, maps.

12. Williams, *From Sails to Satellites*, 37.

13. Ibid., 21.

14. See http://asa.usno.navy.mil/.

15. Williams, *From Sails to Satellites*, 98–99.

16. I explore these themes elsewhere. See Richard Coyne, *Technoromanticism.*

17. For an early and seminal collection of debates about usability and metaphor in interaction design, see Brenda Laurel (ed.), *The Art of Human-Computer Interface Design.*

18. Art often deploys languages derived from esoteric navigational practices. John Donne wrote his sonnets at the time of the great explorers, and expanded the language of navigation to intimacy between lovers: "maps to other, worlds on

worlds have shown; Let us possess one world; each hath one, and is one." "The Good-Morrow," by John Donne.

19. See http://www.lalalab.org/redvisible/index_en.htm.

20. Roy Rosenzweig, "Can History Be Open Source?"

21. M. Hazas, J. Scott, and J. Krum, "Location-aware computing comes of age."

22. Arnold Scharl, "Towards the geospatial web."

23. John D. Bossler (ed.), *Manual of Geospatial Science and Technology.*

24. Scharl, "Towards the geospatial web," 4.

25. Martin Heidegger, "The age of the world picture," 129. For a discussion of the problem with the ocularcentric world picture and its implications for understanding digital media, see Don Ihde, *Bodies in Technology*, 72.

26. Heidegger, "The age of the world picture," 132. See chapter 5.

27. Scharl, "Towards the geospatial web," 4.

28. Don Jewell, "GPS Insights."

29. Bossler, *Manual of Geospatial Science and Technology*, 78–84.

30. The Interplanetary Internet uses Internet-type package switching, rerouting protocols, and hosts distributed across probes already sent from Earth into the solar system to support communication. See www.ipnsig.org/home.htm.

31. Vitruvius, *The Ten Books on Architecture*, 26.

32. More precisely, the GPS receiver picks up ephemeris data from satellites that are within range, i.e. the precise position of the satellites relative to the Earth at the time of the reading. The almanac contains approximate positions. See Joel McNamara, *GPS for Dummies*, 53–54.

33. Sometimes simply called *triangulation*. *Multilateration* is the term used for an indefinite number of reference points.

34. The GPS device calculates its distance through quadrilateration. If the distances were the same, the GPS receiver would be roughly at the position of the center of the Earth, an impossible position not least because the mass of the Earth would block the signals. The variation in distances at the surface of the Earth will be between about 25,800 km to a satellite near the horizon and about 22,200 km to a satellite directly overhead. We may wonder that any such fix is possible, considering the distances and the small differences involved. Even knowing which satellite transmissions you are receiving, i.e., that are in the line of sight in the sky at any moment, without distance readings, will tell you where you are within ten to a few hundred kilometers

on the surface of the earth—at least you can determine which hemisphere you are in. Richard B. Thompson describes the process of fixing a location thus: "To summarize our results so far, the receiver is expected to (i) receive time and position information from the satellites, (ii) maintain a steady (but not necessarily accurate clock), (iii) select four satellites with a good range of positions, (iv) find an approximate numerical solution for a system of four equations, and (v) make a transformation of coordinates. Given the current state of electronics, these are easy tasks for a small hand-held instrument." Thompson, "Global positioning system."

35. The distances to stellar objects are too great to vary appreciably across the face of the Earth, and so would be useless in triangulation even if it could be calculated on the fly.

36. A delay of 0.086 seconds would indicate a distance of about 25,800 km. A delay of 0.067 seconds would yield a distance of 22,200 km.

37. In fact two hyperboloids are created, each with a base station as its focal point, but one of these can be eliminated if it is known which of the two towers receives the signal first.

38. Differential GPS involves a network of fixed reference stations that broadcast corrections to compensate for local inaccuracies. See en.wikipedia.org/wiki/Differential_GPS.

39. Rob Sharp, "The curse of satnav."

40. Peter Morville, *Ambient Findability*, 71.

41. Mitchell, *City of Bits*, 59.

42. Doreen Massey, *For Space*, 94.

43. Jean-François Augoyard, *Step by Step.*

44. For Vitruvius, humankind is different from the animals in that we are able to walk upright and look up at the "splendor of the starry firmament." Vitruvius, *The Ten Books on Architecture*, 38.

45. Augoyard, *Step by Step*, 19. That walking might be "forgetful" is an example of the conflation of thinking and walking.

46. Ibid. These themes are also developed by Michel de Certeau, whose chapter "Walking in the City" is particularly relevant to this discussion. See de Certeau, *The Practice of Everyday Life*, 91–110. New media theorist Lev Manovich makes the connection between de Certeau's concepts of walking and navigation through computer spaces. See Manovich, *The Language of New Media*, 268.

47. Edwin Hutchins, *Cognition in the Wild.*

48. Augoyard, *Step by Step*, 129. According to Augoyard: "The production and organization of the built and developed world have privileged a kind of manipulation

of space that is based on a logic of repetition as well as the following fundamental principal: produce first the urban habitat so as to hand it over then for use." This is a "relation of container to contained" (p. 8).

49. See Gilles Deleuze and Felix Guattari, *A Thousand Plateaus;* and Edward S. Casey, *The Fate of Place*. On the theme of drifting and urbanism, see Stephen Cairns, *Drifting*.

50. Manovich, *The Language of New Media*, 269.

51. Clifford Geertz, *The Interpretation of Cultures*.

52. For an interesting discussion of skateboarders as a cultural subgroup, who deploy the Internet (e.g., YouTube) in articulating urban space, see Mark Gaved and Paul Mulholland, "Pioneers, subcultures and cooperatives," 176–177.

53. Michael Bull, *Sounding Out the City*; Michael Bull, "The intimate sounds of urban experience." Bull also explores the use of the iPod as a digital "Sherpa," a cognitive guide that also carries information. See Michael Bull, *Sound Moves: iPod Culture and Urban Experience*, 132.

54. See Alka Marwaha, "Blogging all over the world."

55. Roy Want et al., "The active badge location system." The observation about evading and confusing detection comes from my conversations with researchers at Olivetti's research laboratory (Olivetti Research Ltd) in Cambridge, UK, in 1992. Modern devices for tracking the movement of adolescents come with wristbands and safety locks. See Morville, *Ambient Findability*.

56. Augoyard, *Step by Step*, 40.

57. Ibid., 73.

58. For reference to concepts of non-place in the context of new media, see Manovich, *The Language of New Media*, 280.

59. Marc Augé, *Non-places*.

60. Augoyard, *Step by Step*, 24.

61. Bernard Arthur Owen Williams, *Shame and Necessity*, 89.

62. Non-place also implicates the human voice. According to Williams: "The most primitive experiences of shame are connected with sight and being seen, but . . . guilt is rooted in hearing, the sound in oneself of the voice of judgment; it is the moral sentiment of the word." Ibid. This sentiment derives from Herbert Morris, *On Guilt and Innocence*. Non-places are populated by textual signs that impinge on the visual field, but these echo the rule of law, the voice of reproach. Here it is appropriate to think of how psychoanalytic theory relates the rule of law to the voice of the father. See for example Jacques Lacan, *The Four Fundamental Concepts of Psychoanalysis*; and Slavoj Žižek, *Looking Awry*.

63. John Bunyan, *Grace Abounding to the Chief of Sinners.*

64. The British Broadcasting Commission's children's website, http://www.bbc.co.uk/cbbc/.

65. "Not proven" has been an option in Scots law for many years. In Scotland a judge may pronounce you innocent of the charge, but if the evidence is insufficient for the charge to stick may resort to the third category of "not proven." Though the effect may be the same as innocence, technically the case can be reopened by other means. G. C. Gebbie, S. E. Jebens, and A. Mura, "'Not proven' as a juridical fact."

66. Furthermore, under UK Freedom of Information legislation this information may have to be disclosed on receipt of a formal request.

67. Augé, *Non-places.*

68. John Urry, *The Tourist Gaze.*

69. For an example of contextual labeling of museum exhibits based on natural language generation, see J. Oberlander et al., "Conversation in the museum."

70. Augé, *Non-places*, 97.

71. In chapter 10, I describe an experiment that attempts to extend such graffiti using mobile phones.

72. Augoyard, *Step by Step*, 85.

73. Ibid., 86.

74. Iain Borden, *Skateboarding, Space and the City. Parkour* is the sport of running through an urban environment and climbing over obstacles as if effortlessly.

75. As for leftover spaces, digital devices are used for purposes outside of their design, regardless of their customary functions. Such accidental and erratic uses include pretending to type notes at a meeting while answering emails, feigning receipt of an important phone call to get out of a meeting, and wearing earphones just to signal that you don't want to be disturbed.

76. Augé, *Non-places*, 71.

Chapter 9

1. P. Dourish, *Where the Action Is*, 189–190.

2. For a fulsome examination of the human need for mobility see John Urry, *Mobilities.*

3. Howard Rheingold, *Smart Mobs.*

4. Available at http://www.geocaching.com. See also Joel McNamara, *GPS for Dummies*, 117–141.

5. Much of the less flattering information, like graffiti on important public buildings, seems to get removed.

6. With this kind of license the originator of the resource specifies that people may use it for nonprofit purposes, but they in turn must make resources derived from it available to others under the same conditions. See http://creativecommons.org.

7. Mark Monmonier, *How to Lie with Maps*, 1–2.

8. Ibid., 2.

9. A company specializing in communications-tower camouflage in the UK advertises: "We removed the original timber louvers on the church towers and replaced them with our radio transparent replicas accurately crafted from our Transclad material range allowing the operator to install the equipment behind, without it being visible from the external of the building." And: "Using our moulding skills and innovative Transclad radio transparent materials, we recreated a chimneystack and pots in the style of the surrounding architecture and painted it to match the colors and ageing of the surrounding stonework." See http://www.dynamicconcepts.co.uk/Product.aspx?id=187.

10. Urban dwellers might be anxious on several counts. A kind of paranoia sets in as concerned citizens seek to identify these hidden objects, and wonder at the ready complicity of churches, mosques, temples, and government institutions to rent out their landmarks and symbols, and to succumb to architectural and ornamental subterfuge. People may wonder at the relationship between radio emissions and the symbolism of the tower, dome, and spire. I may also wonder why my particular cell phone service provider is not better represented in the electromagnetic landscape.

11. See http://www.navizon.com.

12. See Adrian Snodgrass, "Random thoughts on the way."

13. Adrian Snodgrass and Richard Coyne, *Interpretation in Architecture*, 246.

14. Ibid., 247.

15. Ibid.

16. Ibid.

17. Jane M. Jacobs, "Too many houses for a home," 168.

18. Snodgrass and Coyne, *Interpretation in Architecture*, 244.

19. Victor Turner, *The Forest of Symbols*.

20. John Urry, *The Tourist Gaze*, 11. See also Urry, *Mobilities*.

21. Urry, *The Tourist Gaze*, 13.

22. Ibid., 155. From the point of view of way-ism this pleasure is subservient to the processes of transformation, which the traveler may permit in greater or less measure. Walking is about *being* before it is about pleasure.

23. Michael Bull, "Thinking about sound, proximity and distance," 189. Also see Michael Bull, Sound Moves: iPod Culture and Urban Experience.

24. See http://www.lftk.org/tiki/tiki-index.php.

25. Urry, *The Tourist Gaze*, 150.

26. Jean-François Augoyard, *Step by Step*, 96. Cooking odors are also so described.

27. Urry, *The Tourist Gaze*, 155.

28. Ibid., 152.

29. See Guy Debord, *The Society of the Spectacle.*

30. For an account of the Situationist movement and examples of contemporary works, see Francesco Careri, *Walkscapes*.

31. R. Murray Schafer, *The Soundscape*, 33.

32. "In the design of the edified space, where arrangements have been made either to favor one's 'view' or to mask, through architectural forms, the private sphere, the auditory sense comes to undo the territorial limits that had been set between private and public." Augoyard, *Step by Step*, 132.

33. Alain De Botton, *The Art of Travel*, 252. Notably, he enlists this observation in an argument for traveling alone.

34. Urry, *The Tourist Gaze*, 152.

35. Ibid., 153.

36. Ibid., 154.

37. Ann Light, "Transports of delight?"; see also Ann Light, "Negotiations in space."

38. Colin Rowe and Robert Slutzky, *Transparency*.

39. Alasdair Turner et al., "From isovists to visibility graphs"; Bill Hillier, "A theory of the city as object"; Alasdair Turner and Alan Penn, "Encoding natural movement as an agent-based system."

40. Turner et al., "From isovists to visibility graphs," 118.

41. Such calculations assume you are looking at eye level and need to be expanded to consider elevation.

42. Viewshed maps coded into digital city guides have been used as a means of alerting visitors to "features of interest" in the city landscape. See Phil J. Bartie

and William A. Mackaness, "Development of a speech-based augmented reality system."

43. Jean-Paul Thibaud, "The sonic composition of the city," 332.

44. Jean-François Augoyard and Henry Torgue, *Sonic Experience*, 29.

45. The overlay provides a common urban metaphor that has also been related to digital augmentation: "The changes in the tension between spaces of movement and social spaces of quality usage, given by the increased fluidity and overlapping of—virtual—mobility and socially-conducive spatial settings" (Alessandro Aurigi, "Epilogue," 349).

46. Architect Rem Koolhaas draws attention to the congestion and convergence of the city. See Rem Koolhaas, *Delirious New York*

47. Snodgrass and Coyne, *Interpretation in Architecture*, 197.

48. Barack Obama, *The Audacity of Hope*, 223.

49. Hans-Georg Gadamer, *Truth and Method*, 301.

50. Ibid., 305.

51. Thomas Kuhn, *The Structure of Scientific Revolutions.*

52. Jay Appleton, *The Experience of Landscape.*

53. Richard Coyne, *Cornucopia Limited.*

54. Lewis Hyde, *Trickster Makes This World*, 7.

55. Ibid., 6.

56. Quentin Skinner, *Machiavelli*, 48.

57. Andy Clark, *Natural-Born Cyborgs*, 198.

58. At the time of writing the investigation of such technologies became common. See for example the Urban Atmospheres projects at http://www.urban-atmospheres.net/projects.htm. Ronald Lenz provides a helpful series of links to current projects on the theme of locative media at http://spesearch.waag.org/images/LocativeMedia.pdf.

Chapter 10

1. Developed by a team at the University of Edinburgh that included James Stewart, Mark Wright, Henrik Ekeus, and Penny Travlou.

2. See Lowell Feld and Nate Wilcox, *Netroots Rising*. The U.S. presidential election campaigns of 2008 also demonstrated the emerging role of social media.

3. Lisa Gye, "Picture This."

4. Available at http://cabspotting.org; see Reena Jana, "Web Design Case Study."

5. See Richard Coyne et al., "Virtual flagships and sociable media."

6. See, for example, Kristóf Nyíri (ed.), *A Sense of Place*.

7. The system uses a server and database of images and content, and sophisticated image-recognition algorithms to match captured images to data records. A cell phone user photographs an image of a designated object (poster, label, sign) using her camera phone and sends the image to the server. The content associated with that image is returned as text, graphics, web content, or a voice message. The software deploys a highly reliable smart image-matching algorithm that accounts for different angles of view, light conditions, and noisy data. The user can also store content associated with that site, available for someone else to collect when they too visit the site and take a picture of the object. The commercial application of Spellbinder is for brands, logos, or any graphical image, either extant or planted in the environment by advertisers, to be deployed to trigger communication flows between consumers and providers.

8. See Richard H. Thaler and Cass R. Sunstein, *Nudge*.

9. C. Frayling, *Research in Art and Design*; Richard Coyne and Jenny Triggs, "Training for practice-based research"; Chris Argyris and Donald Schön, "Participatory action research and action science compared."

10. Naomi Klein, *No Logo*.

11. As highlighted by Klein, in an odd twist, some brand managers have reappropriated the culture-jamming concept as a means of marketing. See ibid.

12. Constance Penley, "Brownian motion."

13. R. V. Kozinets, "E-Tribalized Marketing?"

14. See M. Robson, *Report: How teenagers consume media*.

15. Stephen Graham and Simon Marvin, *Splintering Urbanism*, 186.

16. Ekeus and Wright have developed further techniques for mapping images of live human forms onto moving objects in Second Life. As you move about the actual room, someone in Second Life could see you as a ghostly apparition that was walking around. The technique uses motion tracking as well as image projection.

17. The creation of a voice service able to run across different mobile platforms was an illusive challenge. AudioBoo, by Vimeo LLC, is an audio blogging service for the iPhone. See http://audioboo.fm/.

18. On the theme of user-centered security measures, see Richard Coyne, John Lee, and Martin Parker, "Permeable portals."

Chapter 11

1. Claude E. Shannon and William Weaver, *The Mathematical Theory of Communication*, 51. See also the translation of this theory into a provocative account of noise and music: Jacques Attali, *Noise*, 27. For a critique of Shannon and Weaver's model see Michael Reddy, "The conduit metaphor."

2. This much is evident in the early diagram in Ferdinand de Saussure's earlier work on communication (published in 1916). See Saussure, *Course in General Linguistics*.

3. The theories build on the earlier work of R. V. L. Hartley, "Transmission of information."

4. The likelihood of errors in digital transmissions is reduced considerably by the parity check protocol. Characters and numbers are transmitted as strings of bits (1s and 0s). Included in that string is a bit that indicates whether the string is equivalent to an odd or even number. A stray bit is soon detected by the receiver, as there will be a mismatch between the parity bit and the odd-even parity of the string, invoking a resend. This capability is built into microchips, and the 7-bit ASCII data format assumes parity checking.

5. JPEG compression reduces the color range in areas where there is a lot of contrast, such as around the edges of objects, and preserves subtle color discrimination across large areas. It performs these calculations across a grid that may become visible at high rates of compression.

6. See Scot Hacker, *MP3*.

7. "Theorem 1: If a function *f(t)* contains no frequencies higher than *W* cps, it is completely determined by giving its ordinates at a series of points spaced 1/2 *W* seconds apart." Claude E. Shannon, "Communication in the presence of noise," 448.

8. Emily Thompson, *The Soundscape of Modernity*, 120.

9. Claude E. Shannon, "A mathematical theory of communication," 397.

10. Ibid., 20. Gregory Bateson talks similarly of redundancy: "The regularity called signal/noise ratio is really only a special case of redundancy . . . the concept 'redundancy' is at least a partial synonym of 'meaning.'" Bateson, *Steps to an Ecology of Mind*, 420.

11. Douglas Kahn, *Noise, Water, Meat*, 22.

12. And here I invoke Ludwig Wittgenstein's famous characterization of meaning: "Meaning is the *use* we make of the word." See Wittgenstein, *Philosophical Investigations*, 53.

13. See http://adam-buxton.co.uk.

14. R. Murray Schafer adds: "The important thing to realize is this: to have Sacred Noise is not merely to make the biggest noise; rather it is a matter of having the authority to make it without censure." Schafer, *The Soundscape*, 76.

15. Kahn, *Noise, Water, Meat*, 214.

16. In keeping with Aristotle's understanding of sound as arising from the striking of two objects, referred to in the introduction to this book. Many of the attributes we ascribe to sound are more appropriately labeled as properties of noise. For Brandon LaBelle: "Sound thus *performs* with and through space: it navigates geographically, reverberates acoustically, and structures socially, for sound amplifies and silences, contorts, distorts and punches against architecture; it escapes rooms, vibrates walls, disrupts conversation; it expands and contracts space by accumulating reverberation, relocating place beyond itself, carrying it in its wave, and inhabiting always more than one place; it misplaces and displaces; like a car speaker blasting too much music, sound overflows borders. It is boundless on the one hand, and site specific on the other" Brandon LaBelle, *Background Noise*, xi.

17. Michael Kirby and Victoria Nes Kirby, *Futurist Performance*. For an account of the violent reception such works often received, see Thompson, *The Soundscape of Modernity*, 130–144. On violence see Steve Goodman, *Sound Warfare*.

18. Attali, *Noise*, 3. He also states: "Listening to music is listening to all noise, realizing that its appropriation and control is a reflection of power, that it is essentially political. . . . More than colors and forms, it is sounds and their arrangements that fashion societies. With noise is born disorder and its opposite: the world. With music is born power and its opposite: subversion" (6).

19. Ibid.

20. "Make people Forget, make them Believe, Silence them. In all three cases, music is a tool of power: of ritual power when it is a question of making people forget the fear of violence; of representative power when it is a question of making them believe in order and harmony; and of bureaucratic power when it is a question of silencing those who oppose it." Ibid., 19.

21. This is a further argument against the predominance of the visual sense in the considerations of design: "What is heard, whether collective rumour or disturbing noise, covers over and deconstructs the visual realm, which ordinarily is predominant." Jean-François Augoyard, *Step by Step*, 107.

22. Michel Chion, *Audio-Vision*, 57. For vivid examples of the role and implementation of silences in film, see Walter Murch, "Touch of Silence."

23. John Cage, *Silence*, 51. He then invites us to consider the sounds of our nervous system and circulation of blood while standing in an anechoic chamber. See also Douglas Kahn, "John Cage."

24. Michel Chion, *The Voice in Cinema*, 8.

25. An expanded variation of Saussure's characterization of the residency of meaning within phonetic *difference*.

26. Deborah Howard and Laura Moretti, *Sound and Space in Renaissance Venice: Architecture, Music, Acoustics*, 2. See also Deborah Howard, "The innocent ear."

27. Juhani Pallasmaa, *The Eyes of the Skin*, 52.

28. Martin Heidegger relates this condition of being unable to speak to what he terms anxiety, which is a primal, unavoidable, and not altogether undesirable way of dealing with the nothing that confronts us: such "anxiety robs us of speech." The word for entunement in German is *Stimmung*, which derives from the German word for *voice*. Heidegger, "What is metaphysics?," 101.

29. Immanuel Kant and Paul Guyer, *Critique of the Power of Judgment*, 141.

30. Ibid.

31. Adrian Snodgrass and Richard Coyne, *Interpretation in Architecture*, 224.

32. Steven Connor, "The help of your good hands," 73.

33. See Michel Foucault, *Discipline and Punish*. Issues of quietness, noise, spontaneity, control, and politics coalesce in debates about certain meditative practices. For example, Thomas Ots discusses the political role of *qigong*, the Chinese exercise and meditative practice of controlled, relaxed body movement. Conflict arises in the discussion of this practice and the extent to which it allows wild, uncontrolled movement. The received wisdom is, "Big movement is not as good as small movement, small movement is not as good as no movement, no movement is not as good as quietness." Ots, "The silenced body."

34. Thomas More, *Utopia*, 84.

35. Snodgrass and Coyne, *Interpretation in Architecture*, 224.

36. For analyses of this work, see LaBelle, *Background Noise*; and Kahn, "John Cage."

37. http://mrogalsky.web.wesleyan.edu\.

38. Architectural theorist Helen Mallinson captures this sentiment in affirming that the voice is associated with air in any case: "Air as spirit represented both the word and the light. Air was the medium of speech, the literal voice, and its reception as sound. It was thus linked to thought, inspired or demonic." Mallinson, "Metaphors of experience," 165.

39. Howard and Moretti, *Sound and Space in Renaissance Venice*, 146.

40. Vitruvius, *The Ten Books on Architecture*, 143–153.

41. Howard and Moretti, *Sound and Space in Renaissance Venice, 146.*

42. Ibid., 107.

43. Ibid., 149.

44. Barry Blesser and Linda-Ruth Salter, *Spaces Speak, Are You Listening?*, 71–72.

45. For an extensive analysis of this piece, see LaBelle, *Background Noise*, 123–146.

46. Available at http://www.davidbyrne.com.

47. John Urry, *Mobilities*, 175.

48. Michael Bull, "The intimate sounds of urban experience," 177–178.

49. Michel de Certeau, *The Practice of Everyday Life*, 154.

50. Alfred Schutz, "Making music together."

51. Jean Baudrillard, *Simulacra and Simulation*, 6.

52. Jacques Attali links the performance of sound to rituals of sacrifice. His activist philosophy reinforces the equation of noise to violence and even murder. Noise interrupts a transmission, it disturbs and kills: "It is a simulacrum of murder." Attali, *Noise*, 26. For Attali, history suggests that civil society transforms murder into rituals of animal sacrifice. Ritual sacrifice is the transformation of violence. It involves extinguishing life, but generally not human life, and in controlled circumstances, according to a code. If noise is related to violence, then what is music? In the same way that sacrifice is the respectable and tamed simulation of violence, music is the respectable and tamed simulation of noise. By analogy, for Attali, music is "ritual sacrifice, the scapegoat" (Ibid., 20). The scapegoat was the poor animal on whom was attached, symbolically, the guilt of the supplicant prior to its slaughter or release into the wilderness. I explore the theme of sacrifice in relation to digital commerce elsewhere, drawing on Jacques Derrida's writing on the subject. See Derrida, *Given Time: 1*; and Richard Coyne, *Cornucopia Limited*. Attali's strategy here is to enliven the theory of music by placing it in a strange category. Whether or not we are convinced by his argument, his move serves our purposes in legitimating the alignment of noise with ritual sacrifice, the absent other, and the tuning of place.

53. David Gill, "Trapezomata," 137. Gill adds, "Later, . . . The god is more in the background, more a spectator at than a partaker in the sacral banquet."

54. See Georg Simmel, "Sociology of the meal." I referred to companionship in the context of walking. The *OED* shows the origin of "companion" in two Latin words: together (*com*) and bread (*panis*).

55. There are obvious associations between the everyday meal and Passover, Mass, Holy Communion, and sacrifice in general. Any meal might act as a reminder of a prototypical meal, of a sacrificial event in which the blood of the slaughtered animal is offered to God. Conversely, the sacrifice of an animal on an altar can be thought of as an enactment of an everyday meal. Concepts of animal sacrifice may seem far

removed from contemporary uses of ubiquitous devices, but sacrifice highlights the role of absence, noise, and ambiguity, and as we shall see reveals their calibration as ambiguous and tricky.

56. Lewis Hyde, *Trickster Makes This World,* 33. The god Hermes is commonly invoked in the context of sacrifice, often considered to be its originator. After stealing cattle from his brother, Hermes butchers and prepares two of them. Though he is hungry, he does not eat but stores the carcasses away in a barn. Later, he says to his mother, "Why should we be the only gods who never eat the fruits of sacrifice and prayer?" To eat meat is to be a mortal. In his aspiration to assert his position among the gods, Hermes denies his appetites and sticks to fruit and the smoke of sacrifice.

57. Ibid., 36.

58. Recall the discussion in chapter 2 of the symbolic role of the remainder in certain calendars and mandala forms.

59. Hyde, *Trickster Makes This World,* 37. I elaborate further on the relevance of the trickster to understandings of electronic commerce in Coyne, *Cornucopia Limited.* Also see Richard Coyne et al., "Co-operation and complicity."

60. Gill, "Trapezomata," 118.

61. Michel Serres, *The Parasite,* 16.

62. Ibid., 53–54.

63. Ibid., 52.

64. Mikhail Bakhtin, *The Dialogic Imagination,* 259.

65. Ibid., 293.

66. Ibid.

67. Ibid., 294.

68. Hubert J. M. Hermans and Harry J. G. Kempen, *The Dialogical Self,* 25.

69. Hubert J. M. Hermans and Els Hermans-Jansen, "The dialogical construction of coalitions."

70. Ibid., 125.

71. Sigmund Freud, "The ego and the id"; Jacques Lacan, *The Four Fundamental Concepts of Psychoanalysis;* Gilles Deleuze and Felix Guattari, *A Thousand Plateaus.*

72. Foucault, *Discipline and Punish.*

73. Public spaces are characteristically noisy. There is the well-known phenomenon—the "cocktail party phenomenon"—whereby we are able to discriminate the

voice of a friend from a background of babble. We tune in to the familiar voice. The voice off invites calibration with what is in the frame, with what we see.

74. For seminal work in this area, see Sherry Turkle, *Life on the Screen,* and her earlier work on Lacan and Freud, *Psychoanalytic Politics.*

75. Compare this with a more postmodern treatment, where you might confront the character head on: "The Thing itself as the incarnated, materialized emptiness" (Slavoj Žižek, *Looking Awry,* 145).

76. See Chion, *The Voice in Cinema.* I have already rehearsed the issue of voice and space elsewhere. Here I amplify the theme in the context of the tuning of place. See Richard Coyne et al., "The augmented marketplace"; Richard Coyne and Martin Parker, "Voices out of place"; and Richard Coyne and Martin Parker, "Voice and space."

77. Chion, *The Voice in Cinema,* 21.

78. Ibid., 24.

79. The ending of Manoj Night's 1999 film *The Sixth Sense,* ostensibly a mystery about ghosts, requires a similar recalibration. Enthusiastic amateur weblog reviews attest to the need to see the film again to recalibrate the events with the new information that is revealed only at the end of the film.

80. The building so described is the Church of Santa Maria dei Derelitti at the Ospedaletto. Howard and Moretti, *Sound and Space in Renaissance Venice: Architecture, Music, Acoustics,* 181–182. Telephones are a means of keeping people invisible but also confining the voice. Head-height screens in offices preserve a degree of visual privacy but are not intended to enhance the effects of the acousmêtre.

81. Chion, *The Voice in Cinema,* 85.

82. Steven Connor, *Dumbstruck.*

83. Ibid., 215.

84. Impersonation is a further means by which the voice of another is applied, as if grafted, to one's own body. Impersonation, or mimicry, is a common social device, even away from the stage. Mimicry is a route to learning. Copying others facilitates Foucault's disciplinary body, and social cohesion. Exaggerated impersonation of the voice and mannerisms of others can provide vehicles for communicating endearment, contempt, or ridicule, much of which passes as habit.

85. See Stephen Feeke, "John Logie Baird and Stooky Bill."

86. Ventriloquism is but one specialized instance of the everyday performance of mimicry. In public spaces people have been observed to assume the vocal manners

of those near to them, as if unconsciously. Social practices are explicable in terms of the functions of mimesis as well as of agency. On occasion, people will mime the voice of a singer in piped music. On a train, certain individuals will impersonate idiosyncratic public announcements. The grafted voice draws on concepts of role playing. DeNora discusses the way people make use of public spaces such as shops and arcades in acting out a role (Tia deNora, *Music and Everyday Life*), one of glamour, coolness, piety, intelligence, or loutishness, abetted by sounds and decor. Music and the voice are factors in this narrative invention. People use spaces and music to construct themselves for the moment. Spatial designers are involved not so much in engineering people's behaviors and the way they use the voice, as in setting a stage, providing an environment for the mimetic fantasy, the calibration of personas, voices, and places.

87. As pointed out by my colleague Martin Parker, there are two methods for synthesizing the voice. The most familiar uses combinations of synthetic sound sources, filters, and a collection of preformed, synthesized phonetics to produce low-fidelity voice-bytes. The second method deploys a database of audio samples gathered from a human voice to produce high-fidelity utterances. Small phonetic grains are reconstituted to form any word and phrase and inflect it with natural intonation. The conditioning of the acousmêtre permits us to graft agency onto a machine, to imagine that a machine can speak, even with expressionless low-fidelity speech synthesis. The acousmêtre of the hi-fi (high fidelity) synthetic voice is closer to our own, but betrays its synthetic origins through imperfections that emerge irregularly when the voice makes a question of a statement or tells a joke without chuckling. The hi-fi acousmêtre is inevitably imperfect. Paradoxically, the seasoned ear finds it difficult to trust and believe the agency and autonomy of the hi-fi synthesized voice.

This lack of confidence in the synthetic voice seems to deter companies from replacing human telephone operators with convincing digital voices. However, human-operated call centers are already synthetic grafts. The flat, scripted voice that results from reciting preplanned clauses constitutes the company speaking through the mouths of human operatives. The acousmêtre of this dynamic is doubly vexed. Callers using the service are obliged to accord courtesy to the voice, and call center operatives risk complications if they deviate from their scripts.

The depersonalized synthetic voice is also vulnerable. In the film *2001,* Stanley Kubrick represents the breakdown of the Hal 9000 computer as an acousmatic event. Throughout the film, Hal is an all-seeing voice, insistent, controlling, and synthetically cold. But his dismantling is unnervingly accompanied by his reversion to a primal condition, revealing his digital substrate as he is reduced to an infantile recitation. Once the voice has died, Hal's physical menace ceases: "A strange death, leaving no trace, no body," (Chion, *The Voice in Cinema,* 46) and no echo.

Chapter 12

1. On the phenomenon of the blog for which no one posts a comment, see Geert Lovink, *Zero Comments*. For Slavoj Žižek the anxiety built into such recordings and broadcasts (which border on surveillance) is that, after all, no one will be interested enough to watch. See Žižek, "Big brother."

2. Adrian Snodgrass and Richard Coyne, *Interpretation in Architecture*, 234.

3. Ibid., 233.

4. Ibid.

5. See Richard Coyne and Martin Parker, "Voice and space."

6. Roland Barthes, *The Responsibility of Forms*.

7. Steven Connor, "Edison's teeth."

8. John Dewey, *Art as Experience*.

9. John Ruskin and J. G. Links (eds.), *The Stones of Venice*.

10. Richard Coyne, *Cornucopia Limited*.

11. Greg Lynn, *Animate Form*.

12. Psychoanalytic theory has made much of the importance of the looped visual structure: a defining moment comes for the infant when she sees her reflection in a mirror, a moment that indicates separateness and alterity from the rest of the world, a moment often related back to the myth of Narcissus, the god who fell in love fatally with his own reflection in a pool. Vision entails a sense of seeing, being seen, and seeing oneself, a kind of looped perceptual field. See Jacques Lacan, "The mirror stage as formative."

13. Mladen Dolar, "The object voice," 14.

14. Robert Graves, *The Greek Myths*, 287.

15. Connor, "Edison's teeth."

16. Ibid.

17. Gilles Deleuze, *The Fold*, 14.

18. Mary Douglas, *Purity and Danger*, 44–45.

19. Ibid., 46.

20. On the theme of children's access to online material, see Kathryn C. Montgomery, *Generation Digital*.

21. Douglas, *Purity and Danger*, 46–47.

22. Ibid., 49.

23. In a later passage Douglas asserts: "Pollution is like an inverted form of humour. It is not a joke for it does not amuse. But the structure of its symbolism uses comparison and double meaning like the structure of a joke." Ibid., 151.

24. Ibid., 47.

25. This is the annealing process induced by the blacksmith pounding hot metal with a hammer.

26. Iannis Xenakis, *Formalized Music*, 9.

27. Ludwig Wittgenstein, *Philosophical Investigations*, 20.

28. Iain Borden, *Skateboarding, Space and the City*, 1. "Through an everyday practice—neither consciously theorized nor programmed—skateboarding suggests that pleasure rather than work, use values rather than exchange values, activity rather than passivity, performing rather than recording, are potential components of the future, as yet unknown city" (173).

29. These are some of the "apps" released for the iPhone at the time of writing.

30. Supporting this common view of the role of music, see David Sonnenschein, *Sound Design*. For a nuanced study and discussion of how people "use" music to enhance or dispel certain moods, see Tia deNora, *Music and Everyday Life*.

31. Craig Adcock, "Marcel Duchamp's gap music," 126.

32. Ibid., 128.

33. See for example Cristian Suau, "Potential Public Spaces in the Modern Suburbia."

34. Available at http://www.comob.org.uk.

35. See Eric von Hippel, *Democratizing Innovation*.

36. See John Counsell and Marie-Cecile Puybaraud, "Visible display of automated observation of collaborative workspaces," 195.

37. Cristian Suau, "Potential Public Spaces in the Modern Suburbia," 36.

38. There are analogies here with the small irritant that produces the oyster's pearl. The inconspicuous particle calls into play complex processes that converge on something of value.

39. Sadie Plant, *Zeros and Ones*.

40. They also engage in the alternative, activist motivations and practices of participative architecture, urbanism, and social organization. See for example PEVRAV, *Urban Act*.

41. Vincente Rafael, "The Cell Phone and the Crowd: Messianic Politics in the Contemporary Philippines, " 305–306.

42. Plato, *The Republic of Plato*.

43. Gregory Bateson, *Steps to an Ecology of Mind*, 416. Italics in the original.

References

Ackerman, Robert John. 1985. *Data, Instruments, and Theory: A Dialectical Approach to Understanding Science*. Princeton, NJ: Princeton University Press.

Adcock, Craig. 1992. "Marcel Duchamp's gap music: Operations in the space between art and noise." In *Wireless Imagination: Sound, Radio, and the Avant-Garde*, ed. Douglas Kahn and Gregory Whitehead, 105–138. Cambridge, MA: MIT Press.

Adilkno. 1998. *The New Media Archive*. Brooklyn, NY: Autonomedia.

Adorno, Theordor W. 1991. *The Culture Industry: Selected Essays on Mass Culture*. London: Routledge.

Ahonen, Tomi, and Alan Moore. 2005. *Communities Dominate Brands: Business and Marketing Challenges for the 21st Century*. London: Futuretext.

Alberti, Leon Battista. 1996. *On the Art of Building in Ten Books*. Trans. Joseph Rykwert, Neil Leach, and Robert Tavernor. Cambridge, MA: MIT Press. First published in Latin ca. 1450.

Alberti, Leon Battista. 2004. *On Painting*. Trans. Cecil Grayson and Martin Kemp. London: Penguin. First published in 1435.

Alexander, Christopher. 1964. *Notes on the Synthesis of Form*. Cambridge, MA: Harvard University Press.

Alexander, Christopher. 1988. "A city is not a tree." In *Design After Modernism*, ed. John Thackara, 67–84. London: Thames and Hudson.

Amidror, I. 2000. *The Theory of the Moiré Phenomenon*, vol. 1: Periodic Layers. Dordrecht: Kluwer.

Anon. 1971. "'Taki 183' spawns pen pals." *New York Times*, 21 June, 37. http://www.ni9e.com/blog_images/taki_183.pdf.

Appleton, Jay. 1975. *The Experience of Landscape*. London: John Wiley.

Argyris, Chris, and Donald Schön. 1989. "Participatory action research and action science compared: A commentary." *American Behavioral Scientist* 32 (5):612–623.

Aristotle. 1976. *The Ethics of Aristotle: The Nicomachean Ethics*. Trans. J. A. K. Thomson. London: Penguin. Written ca. 334–323 BCE.

Aristotle. 1986. *De Anima (On the Soul)*. Trans. Hugh Lawson-Tancred. London: Penguin. Written about 350 BCE.

Arnheim, Rudolph. 1956. *Art and Visual Perception: A Psychology of the Creative Eye*. London: Faber and Faber.

Arvind, D. K., and K. J. Wong. 2004."Speckled computing: Disruptive technology for networked information appliances." *Proceedings of the IEEE International Symposium on Consumer Electronics*: 219–223.

Attali, Jacques. 1985. *Noise: The Political Economy of Music*. Minneapolis: University of Minnesota Press.

Augé, Marc. 1995. *Non-places: Introduction to an Anthropology of Supermodernity*. Trans. John Howe. London: Verso.

Augoyard, Jean-François. 2007. *Step by Step: Everyday Walks in a French Urban Housing Project*. Trans. David Ames Curtis. Minneapolis: University of Minnesota Press. First published in French in 1979.

Augoyard, Jean-François, and Henry Torgue. 2005. *Sonic Experience: A Guide to Everyday Sounds*. Trans. Andra McCartney and David Paquette. Montreal: McGill-Queen's University Press.

Aurigi, Alessandro. 2008. "Epilogue: Towards designing augmented places." In *Augmented Urban Spaces: Articulating the Physical and Electronic City*, ed. Alessandro Aurigi and Fiorella de Cindio, 331–350. Aldershot, Hampshire, UK: Ashgate.

Aurigi, Alessandro, and Fiorella de Cindio, eds. 2008. *Augmented Urban Spaces: Articulating the Physical and Electronic City*. Aldershot, Hampshire, UK: Ashgate.

Austin, John. 1966. *How to Do Things with Words*. Cambridge, MA: Harvard University Press.

Bachelard, Gaston. 1964. *The Poetics of Space*. New York: Orion Press.

Badaracco, Joseph L. 2002. *Leading Quietly: An Unorthodox Guide to Doing the Right Thing*. Boston: Harvard Business School Press.

Bakhtin, Mikhail. 1981. *The Dialogic Imagination: Four Essays*. Austin: University of Texas Press.

Bakkum, D. J., A. C. Shkolnik, G. Ben-Ary, P. Gamblen, T. B. DeMarse, and S. M. Potter. 2004. "Remove some 'A' from AI: Embodied cultural networks." In *Embodied Artifical Intelligence*, ed. F. Iida, R. Pfeifer, L. Steels, and Y. Kuniyoshi, 130–145. Berlin: Springer.

Banham, Reyner. 1969. *The Architecture of the Well-tempered Environment.* London: University of Chicago Press.

Barthes, Roland. 1973. *Mythologies*. Trans. Annette Lavers. London: Paladin.

Barthes, Roland. 1991. *The Responsibility of Forms: Critical Essays on Music, Art, and Representation.* Trans. Richard Howard. Berkeley and Los Angeles: University of California Press.

Bartie, Phil J., and William A. Mackaness. 2006. "Development of a speech-based augmented reality system to support exploration of cityscape." *Transactions in GIS* 10 (1):63–86.

Bateson, Gregory. 2000. *Steps to an Ecology of Mind.* Chicago: University of Chicago Press.

Baudrillard, Jean. 1994. *Simulacra and Simulation.* Trans. Sheila Faria Glaser. Ann Arbor: University of Michigan Press.

Baudrillard, Jean. 2001. "Simulacra and Simulations." In *Selected Writings*, ed. Mark Poster, 169–187. Cambridge: Polity.

Benjamin, Walter. 1992. "The work of art in the age of mechanical reproduction." In *Illuminations*, ed. Hannah Arendt, 1–58. London: Fontana First published in German in 1936.

Berghel, Hal. 2000. "Identity theft, social security numbers, and the web." *Communications of the ACM* 43 (2):17–21.

Bergson, Henri. 1919. *Time and Free Will.* Trans. F. L. Pogson. London: George Allen and Unwin. First published in French in 1889.

Berners-Lee, T., J. Hendler, and O. Lassila. 2001. "The semantic web." *Scientific American* 284 (5):34–43.

Berridge, Philip, Volker Koch, and Andre G. P. Brown. 2003. "Information spaces for mobile city access." *International Journal of Architectural Computing* 1 (1):34–45.

Bey, Hakim. 2003. *T.A.Z. The Temporary Autonomous Zone, Ontological Anarchy, Poetic Terrorism.* Brooklyn, NY: Autonomedia.

Bijl, Aart. 1989. *Computer Discipline and Design Practice: Shaping Our Future.* Edinburgh: Edinburgh University Press.

Blesser, Barry, and Linda-Ruth Salter. 2006. *Spaces Speak, Are You Listening? Experiencing Aural Architecture.* Cambridge, MA: MIT Press.

Bolter, J. David, and Diane Gromola. 2003. *Windows and Mirrors: Interaction Design, Digital Art, and the Myth of Transparency.* Cambridge, MA: MIT Press.

Bolter, J. David, and Richard A. Grusin. 1999. *Remediation: Understanding New Media.* Cambridge, MA: MIT Press.

Bonello, Philip, and J. Michael Brennan, Stephen J. Elliott, Julian F. V. Vincent, and George Jeronimidis. 2005. "Designs for an adaptive tuned vibration absorber with variable shape stiffness element." *Proceedings of the Royal Society* 461:3955–3976.

Borden, Iain. 2001. *Skateboarding, Space and the City: Architecture and the Body.* Oxford: Berg.

Bossler, John D., ed. 2002. *Manual of Geospatial Science and Technology.* London: Taylor and Francis.

Brown, M., and D. G. Lowe. 2003. "Recognising panoramas." *Proceedings of Ninth IEEE International Conference on Computer Vision* 2:1218–1225.

Bull, Michael. 2000. *Sounding Out the City: Personal Stereos and the Management of Everyday Life.* Oxford: Berg.

Bull, Michael. 2004. "Thinking about sound, proximity and distance in Western experience: The case of Odyssius's walkman." In *Hearing Cultures: Essays on Sound, Listening and Modernity*, ed. Veit Erlmann, 173–190. Oxford: Berg.

Bull, Michael. 2005. "The intimate sounds of urban experience: An auditory epistemology of everyday mobility." In *A Sense of Place: The Global and the Local in Mobile Communication*, ed. Kristóf Nyíri, 169–178. Vienna: Passagen Verlag.

Bull, Michael. 2007. *Sound Moves: iPod Culture and Urban Experience.* Abingdon: Routledge.

Bunyan, John. 1987. *Grace Abounding to the Chief of Sinners.* London: Penguin. First published in 1666.

Butler, Samuel. 1910. *Life and Habit.* London: Jonathan Cape.

Cage, John. 1968. *Silence: Lectures and Writings.* London: Marion Boyars.

Caillois, Roger. 1961. *Man, Play, and Games.* New York, NY: The Free Press of Glencoe.

Caillois, Roger. 1984. "Mimicry and legendary psychasthenia." October 31 (Winter): 17–32. First published in *Minotaure* in 1935.

Cairns, Stephen. 2003. *Drifting: Architecture and Migrancy.* London: Routledge.

Careri, Francesco. 2001. *Walkscapes: Walking as an Aesthetic Practice.* Barcelona: Gustavo Gili.

Cariani, Peter. 1993. "To evolve an ear: Epistemological implications of Gordon Pask's electrochemical devices." *Systems Research* 10 (3):19–33.

Carter, Stephen. 2009. *Digital Britain Final Report.* London: Department for Culture, Media and Sport, and Department for Business, Innovation and Skills.

Casey, Edward S. 1997. *The Fate of Place: A Philosophical History*. Berkeley: University of California Press.

Castells, Manuel. 2001. *The Internet Galaxy: Reflections on the Internet, Business, and Society*. Oxford: Oxford University Press.

Castells, Manuel. 1997. "An introduction to the information age." *City: Information, Identity and the City* 7:6–16.

Castells, Manuel. 1996. *The Rise of the Network Society*. Malden, MA: Blackwell Publishers.

Castells, Manuel, Mireia Fernandez-Ardevol, Jack Linchuan Qiu, and Araba Sey. 2007. *Mobile Communication and Society: A Global Perspective*. Cambridge, MA: MIT Press.

Cattuto, Ciro, Vittorio Loreto, and Luciano Pietronero. 2007. "Semiotic dynamics and collaborative tagging." *Proceedings of the National Academy of Sciences of the United States of America* 4 (5):1461–1464.

Chalmers, Matthew. 2003. "Seamful design and ubicomp infrastructure." In *Proceedings of Ubicomp 2003 Workshop at the Crossroads: The Interaction of HCI and Systems Issues in UbiComp*. Seattle, WA. http://www.dcs.gla.ac.uk/~matthew/papers/ubicomp2003HCISystems.pdf.

Chion, Michel. 1999. *The Voice in Cinema*. Trans. Claudia Gorbman. New York: Columbia University Press. First published in French in 1982.

Chion, Michel. 1994. *Audio-Vision: Sound on Screen*. Trans. Claudia Gorbman. New York: Columbia University Press.

Chmielewska, Ella. 2005. "Logos or the resonance of branding: A close reading of the iconosphere of Warsaw." *Space and Culture* 8 (4):349–380.

Clark, Andy. 1997. *Being There: Putting Brain, Body and World Together Again*. Cambridge, MA: MIT Press.

Clark, Andy. 2001. "Reasons, robots and the extended mind." *Mind & Language* 16 (2):121–145.

Classen, Constance. 1993. *Worlds of Sense: Exploring the Senses in History and across Cultures*. London: Routledge.

Clynes, Manfred E. 1995."Cyborg II: Sentic space travel." In *The Cyborg Handbook*, ed. Chris H. Gray, 35–42. New York: Routledge. First published in 1970.

Clynes, Manfred E., and Nathan S. Kline. 1995. "Cyborgs and space." *The Cyborg Handbook*, ed. Chris H. Gray, 29–33. New York: Routledge. From an article published in 1960.

Collins, Nicolas. 2006. *Handmade Electronic Music: The Art of Hardware Hacking*. New York: Routledge.

Connor, Steven. 2004. "Edison's teeth: Touching hearing." In *Hearing Cultures: Essays on Sound, Listening and Modernity*, ed. Veit Erlmann. 153–172. Oxford: Berg.

Connor, Steven. 2003. "The help of your good hands: Reports on clapping." In *The Auditory Culture Reader*, ed. Michael Bull and Les Back, 67–76. Oxford: Berg.

Connor, Steven. 2000. *Dumbstruck: A Cultural History of Ventriloquism*. Oxford: Oxford University Press.

Conrad, Joseph. 1993. *Heart of Darkness*. New York: New American Library.

Cook, Peter, and Warren Chalk. 1967. "Amazing archigram: A supplement." *Perspecta* 11:131–154.

Corbin, Alain. 2003. "The auditory markers of the village." In *The Auditory Culture Reader*, ed. Michael Bull and Les Back, 117–125. Oxford: Berg.

Counsell, John, and Marie-Cecile Puybaraud. 2006. "Visible display of automated observation of collaborative workspaces." In *Visible Display of Automated Observation of Collaborative Workspaces*, ed. Y. Luo, 192–199. Heidelberg: Springer Berlin.

Court, Arnold. 1967. "Concerning an important invention (review article)." *Science* 156:812–813.

Coyne, Richard. 1995. *Designing Information Technology in the Postmodern Age: From Method to Metaphor*. Cambridge, MA: MIT Press.

Coyne, Richard. 1999. *Technoromanticism: Digital Narrative, Holism, and the Romance of the Real*. Cambridge, MA: MIT Press.

Coyne, Richard. 2005. *Cornucopia Limited: Design and Dissent on the Internet*. Cambridge, MA: MIT Press.

Coyne, Richard. 2005. "The digital uncanny." In *Spaces, Spatiality and Technology*, ed. P. Turner and E. Davenport, 5–18. Dordrecht: Springer.

Coyne, Richard. 2005. "Wicked problems revisited." *Design Studies* 26 (1):5–17.

Coyne, Richard. 2006. "Space without ground." In *Architecture in Scotland*, ed. Morag Bain, 94–99. Glasgow: The Lighthouse Trust.

Coyne, Richard. 2007. "Thinking through virtual reality: Place, non-place, and situated cognition in technological society." *Techné: Research in Philosophy and Technology, Special Issue: Real and Virtual Places* (http://scholar.lib.vt.edu/ejournals/SPT/v10n3/pdf/) 10 (3):26–38.

Coyne, Richard. 2008. "The net effect: Design, the rhizome, and complex philosophy." *Futures* 40:552–561.

Coyne, Richard, and Martin Parker. 2009. "Voice and space: The agency of the acousmêtre in spatial design." In *Exploration of Space, Technology and Spatiality: Interdisciplinary Perspectives*, ed. P. Turner, S. Turner, and E. Davenport, 102–112. Hershey, PA: Information Science Reference.

Coyne, Richard, and Martin Parker. 2006. "Voices out of place: Voice, non-place and ubiquitous digital communications." In *Mobile Understanding: The Epistemology of Ubiquitous Communication*, ed. Kristóf Nyíri, 171–182. Vienna: Passagen Verlag.

Coyne, Richard, and Jenny Triggs. 2007. "Training for practice-based research: Adaptation, integration and diversity." In *Creativity or Conformity: Building Cultures of Creativity in Higher Education, 8–10 January*, ed. Tony Bianchi. Cardiff: Metropolitan University. Full paper at http://www.creativityconference07.org/abstracts.php.

Coyne, Richard, John Lee, and Martin Parker. 2005. "Permeable portals: Designing congenial web sites for the e-society." *Tangentium* 2 (1): http://personalpages.manchester.ac.uk/staff/andrew.whitworth/tangentium/jan05/feature1.html

Coyne, Richard, Hoon Park, and Dorian Wiszniewski. 2002. "Design devices: Digital drawing and the pursuit of difference." *Design Studies* 23 (3):263–286.

Coyne, Richard, Hoon Park, and Dorian Wiszniewski. 2000. "Design devices: What they reveal and conceal." *Kritische Berichte: Zeitschrift für Kunst- und Kulturwissenschaften* 3:55–69.

Coyne, Richard, Pedro Rebelo, and Martin Parker. 2004. "Resisting the seamless interface." *International Journal of Architectural Computing* 4 (2):430–442.

Coyne, Richard, Adrian Snodgrass, and David Martin. 1994. "Metaphors in the design studio." *JAE* 48 (2):113–125.

Coyne, Richard, Mark Wright, James Stewart, and Henrik Ekeus. 2009. "Virtual flagships and sociable media." In *Flagship Marketing: Concepts and Places*, ed. Anthony Kent and Reva Brown, 46–62. London: Routledge.

Coyne, Richard, Raymond Lucas, Jia Li, Martin Parker, and John Lee. 2007. "Co-operation and complicity: Voices, robots, and tricksters in the digital marketplace." *International Journal of Architectural Computing* 5 (1):161–175.

Coyne, Richard, Raymond Lucas, Jia Li, Martin Parker, and John Lee. 2006. "The augmented marketplace: Voices, robots and tricksters." In *Keynote Speakers: Proc. Communicating Space(s)*, ed. Vassilis Bourdaksi and Dimitris Charitos, ii–ix. Volos: University of Thessaly, Greece.

Crabtree, Andy, and Tom Rodden. 2008. "Hybrid ecologies: Understanding cooperative interaction in emerging physical-digital environments." *Personal and Ubiquitous Computing* 12 (7):481–493.

Cubitt, Sean. 1998. *Digital Aesthetics*. London: Sage.

Darwin, Charles. 2004. *The Descent of Man and Selection in Relation to Sex*. London: Penguin Classics. First published in 1871.

Darwin, Charles. 2007. *The Formation of Vegetable Mould Through the Action of Worms with Observations on Their Habits*. Charleston, SC: BiblioBazaar. First published in 1881.

De Botton, Alain. 2002. *The Art of Travel*. London: Penguin.

de Certeau, Michel. 1984. *The Practice of Everyday Life*. Trans. Steven Rendall. Berkeley: University of California Press.

de Souza e Silva, Adriana. 2006. "From cyber to hybrid: Mobile technologies as interfaces of hybrid spaces." *Space and Culture* 9 (3):261–278.

de Zegher, Catherine, and Mark Wigley, eds. 2001. *The Activist Drawing: Retracing Situationist Architecture from Constant's New Babylon to Beyond*. Cambridge, MA: MIT Press.

Debord, Guy. 1983. *The Society of the Spectacle*. Detroit, MI: Black and Red.

Deleuze, Gilles. 1993. *The Fold: Leibniz and the Baroque*. Trans. Tom Conley. Minneapolis: University of Minnesota Press.

Deleuze, Gilles. 1994. *Difference and Repetition*. Trans. Paul Patton. London: Athlone Press.

Deleuze, Gilles, and Felix Guattari. 1977. *Anti-Oedipus: Capitalism and Schizophrenia*. New York: Viking Press.

Deleuze, Gilles, and Felix Guattari. 1988. *A Thousand Plateaus: Capitalism and Schizophrenia*. Trans. Brian Massumi. London: Athlone Press.

deNora, Tia. 2000. *Music and Everyday Life*. Cambridge, UK: Cambridge University Press.

Derrida, Jacques. 1976. *Of Grammatology*. Trans. Gayatri Chakravorty Spivak. Baltimore, MD: Johns Hopkins University Press.

Derrida, Jacques. 1978. "Freud and the scene of writing." In *Writing and Difference*, Trans. and ed. Alan Bass, 196–231. Chicago: Chicago University Press.

Derrida, Jacques. 1992. *Given Time: 1. Counterfeit Money*. Trans. Peggy Kamuf. Chicago: University of Chicago Press.

Desmet, Christy. 2001. "Reading the Web as fetish." *Computers and Composition* 18:55–72.

Dewey, John. 1980. *Art as Experience*. New York: Wideview Perigee.

Dolar, Mladen. 1996. "The object voice." In *Gaze and Voice as Love Objects*, ed. Renata Saleci and Slavoj Žižek, 7–31. Durham, NC: Duke University Press.

Donner, Jonathan. 2005. "What can be said with a missed call? Beeping via mobile phones in sub-Saharan Africa." In *Proceedings of Seeing, Understanding, Learning in the Mobile Age*, ed. Kristóf Nyíri, 267–276. Budapest: Institute for Philosophical Research of the Hungarian Academy of Sciences and T-Mobile Hungary Co Ltd.

Dorrian, Mark, and Adrian Hawker. 2002. *Metis: Urban Cartographies*. London: Black Dog.

Douglas, Mary. 1966. *Purity and Danger: An Analysis of Concepts of Pollution and Taboo*. London: Routledge and Kegan Paul.

Douglas, Mary. 1991. "The idea of a home: A kind of space." In *Home: A Place in the World*, ed. Arien Mack, 261–281. New York: New York University Press.

Dourish, P. 2001. *Where the Action Is: The Foundations of Embodied Interaction*. Cambridge, MA: MIT Press.

Drake, S. 1957. *Discoveries and Opinions of Galileo*. New York: Doubleday.

Dreyfus, Hubert L. 1990. *Being-in-the-World: A Commentary on Heidegger's Being and Time Division I*. Cambridge, MA: MIT Press.

Dunlap, Knight. 1922. "The identity of instinct and habit." *Journal of Philosophy* 19 (4):85–94.

Eckermann, Johan Peter. 1998. *Conversations of Goethe with Johann Peter Eckermann*. Trans. John Oxenford. New York: Da Capo Press. First published in German in 1836–1848.

Eco, Umberto. 1986. *Travels in Hyperreality*. Trans. William Weaver. San Diego, CA: Harcourt Brace Jovanovich.

Etkin, William. 1964. "Co-operation and competition in social behaviour." In *Social Behaviour and Organization Among Vertebrates*, ed. William Etkin, 1–34. Chicago: University of Chicago Press.

Evans, Robin. 1997. *Translations from Drawing to Building and Other Essays*. London: Architectural Association.

Feeke, Stephen. 2004. "John Logie Baird and Stooky Bill: Ventriloquism in early television." In *With Hidden Noise: Sculpture, Video and Ventriloquism*, ed. Stephen Feeke and Jon Wood, 9–13. Leeds, UK: Henry Moore Institute.

Feld, Lowell, and Nate Wilcox. 2008. *Netroots Rising: How a Citizen Army of Bloggers and Online Activists is Changing American Politics*. Santa Barbara, CA: Greenwood.

Filmer, Paul. 2003. "Songtime: sound culture, rhythm and sociality." In *The Auditory Culture Reader*, ed. Michael Bull and Les Back, 91–112. Oxford: Berg.

Fish, Stanley. 1989. *Doing What Comes Naturally: Change, Rhetoric, and the Practice of Theory in Literary and Legal Studies*. Durham, SC: Duke University Press.

Flores, Nancy C., and Elizabeth A. E. Boyle. 2000. *Thermometer Calibration Guide.* Manhattan, KS: Kansas State University Agricultural Experiment Station and Cooperative Extension Service.

Fogg, B. J. 2003. *Persuasive Technology: Using Computers to Change What We Think and Do.* Amsterdam: Morgan Kaufmann.

Foster, Russell, and Leon Kreitzman. 2004. *Rhythms of Life.* London: Profile Books.

Foucault, Michel. 1970. *The Order of Things: An Archaeology of the Human Sciences.* New York: Random House.

Foucault, Michel. 1977. *Discipline and Punish: The Birth of the Prison.* London: Penguin.

Foucault, Michel, and P. Rabinow, eds. 1984. *The Foucault Reader: An Introduction to Foucault's Thought.* London: Penguin.

Frayling, C. 1993. *Research in Art and Design.* Royal College of Art Research Papers series, vol. 1 no. 1. London: Royal College of Art.

Freedman, Richard D., and Stephen A. Stumpf. 1980. "Learning style theory: Less than meets the eye." *Academy of Management Review* 5 (3):445–447.

Freud, Sigmund. 1990. "Beyond the pleasure principle." In *The Penguin Freud Library, Volume 11: On Metapsychology,* ed. Angela Richards, 269–338. Harmondsworth, Middlesex, UK: Penguin. First published in German in 1920.

Freud, Sigmund. 1990. "The ego and the id." In *The Penguin Freud Library, Volume 11: On Metapsychology,* ed. Angela Richards, 339–407. Harmondsworth, Middlesex, UK: Penguin. First published in German in 1920.

Freud, Sigmund. 2003. *The Psychopathology of Everyday Life.* Trans. Anthea Bell. New York: Penguin. First published in German in 1901.

Fullam, Scott. 2004. *Hardware Hacking: Projects for Geeks.* Sebastopol, CA: O'Reilly.

Gadamer, Hans-Georg. 2004. *Truth and Method.* Trans. Joel Weinsheimer and Donald G. Marshall. New York: Continuum. Originally published in German in 1960.

Gage, Stephen A. 2007. "Constructing the user." *Systems Research and Behavioral Science* 24:313–322.

Galloway, Anne. 2004. "Intimations of everyday life: Ubiquitous computing and the city." *Cultural Studies* 18 (2–3):384–408.

Galloway, Anne. 2007. "Seams and scars, or how to locate accountability in collaborative work." In *Uncommon Ground,* ed. Cathy Brickwood, Bronac Ferran, David Garcia, and Tim Putnam. Amsterdam: BIS Publishers, 152–158.

Galloway, Anne, and Matt Ward. 2006. "Locative media as socialising and spatializing practice: Learning from archaeology." *Leonardo Electronic Almanac* 14 (3) http://leoalmanac.org/journal/vol_14/lea_v14_n03-04/gallowayward.asp.

Garfinkel, Harold. 1964. "Studies of the routine grounds of everyday activities." *Social Problems* 11 (3):225–250.

Garfinkel, Harold. 1967. *Studies in Ethnomethodology*. Cambridge, UK: Polity Press.

Garrod, Simon, and Martin J. Pickering. 2003. "Why is conversation so easy?" *Trends in Cognitive Sciences* 8 (1):8–11.

Gates, Bill, and Collins Hemingway. 1999. *Business @ the Speed of Thought: Using a Digital Nervous System*. London: Penguin.

Gaved, Mark, and Paul Mulholland. 2008. "Pioneers, subcultures and cooperatives: the grassroots augmentation of urban places." In *Augmented Urban Spaces: Articulating the Physical and Electronic City*, ed. Alessandro Aurigi and Fiorella de Cindio, 171–199. Aldershot, Hampshire, UK: Ashgate.

Gebbie, G. C., S. E. Jebens, and A. Mura. 1999. "'Not proven' as a juridical fact in Scotland, Norway and Italy." *European Journal of Crime Criminal Law and Criminal Justice* 7 (3):262–276.

Geertz, Clifford. 1971. *The Interpretation of Cultures*. New York: Basic Books.

Giaccardi, Elisa. 2008. "Cross-media interaction for the virtual museum: Reconnecting to natural heritage in Boulder, Colorado." In *New Heritage: New Media and Cultural Heritage*, ed. Yehuda E. Kalay, Thomas Kvan, and Janice Affleck, 112–131. London: Routledge,

Giedion, Sigfried. 1962. *Space, Time and Architecture: The Growth of a New Tradition*. Cambridge, MA: MIT Press.

Gill, David. 1974. "Trapezomata: A neglected aspect of Greek sacrifice." *Harvard Theological Review* 67 (2):117–137.

Gladwell, Malcolm. 2000. *The Tipping Point: How Little Things Can Make a Big Difference*. London: Abacus.

Gladwell, Malcolm. 2006. *Blink: The Power of Thinking Without Thinking*. London: Abacus.

Glanville, Ranulph. 2007. "Try again. Fail again. Fail better: The cybernetics in design and the design in cybernetics." *Kybernetes* 36 (9/10):1173–1206.

Gödel, Kurt. 1962. *On Formally Unprovable Propositions*. New York: Basic Books.

Goffman, Erving. 1969. *The Presentation of Self in Everyday Life*. London: Penguin.

Goodman, Steve. 2009. *Sonic Warfare: Sound, Affect, and the Ecology of Fear*. Cambridge, MA: MIT Press.

Graham, Stephen, and Simon Marvin. 2001. *Splintering Urbanism: Networked Infrastructures, Technological Mobilites and the Urban Condition*. London: Routledge.

Graves, Robert. 1960. *The Greek Myths*, vol. 1. London: Penguin.

Gregory, Bruce. 1988. *Inventing Reality: Physics as Language*. New York: Wiley.

Griffiths, Mark. 2003."Sex on the Internet: Issues, concerns, and implications." In *The Wired Homestead: An MIT Press Sourcebook on the Internet and the Family*, ed. Joseph Turow and Andrea L. Kavanaugh, 261–281. Cambridge, MA: MIT Press.

Guest, Tim. 2007. *Second Lives: A Journey Through Virtual Worlds*. London: Hutchinson.

Gye, Lisa. 2007. "Picture this: The impact of mobile camera phones on personal photographic practices." *Continuum* 21 (2):279–288.

Hacker, Scot. 2000. *MP3: The Definitive Guide*. Cambridge, MA: O'Reilly.

Hanslick, Eduard.1974. *The Beautiful in Music: A Contribution to the Revisal of Musical Aesthetics*. New York: Da Capo Press. First published in German in 1854.

Haraway, Donna J. 1991. *Simians, Cyborgs, and Women: The Reinvention of Nature*. London: FAb.

Hart, Vaughan, and Robert Tucker. 2001. "Imaginacy set free: Aristotelian ethics and Inigo Jones's banqueting house at Whitehall." *Research Journal of Anthropology and Aesthetics* 39:151–167.

Hartley, R. V. L. 1928. "Transmission of information." *Bell System Technical Journal* (July):535–563.

Havelock, E. A. 1986. *The Muse Learns to Write: Reflections on Orality and Literacy from Antiquity to the Present*. New Haven, CT: Yale University Press.

Hayes, Brian. 2008. "Cloud computing." *Communications of the ACM* 51 (7):9–11.

Hayles, N. Katherine. 1999. *How We Became Posthuman: Virtual Bodies in Cybernetics, Literature, and Informatics*. Chicago: University of Chicago Press.

Hays, James, and Alexei A. Efros. 2004. "IM2GPS: Estimating geographic information from a single image." *Proceedings of the IEEE Conference on Computer Vision and Pattern Recognition (CVPR)* http://graphics.cs.cmu.edu/projects/im2gps/im2gps.pdf.

Hazas, M., J. Scott, and J. Krumm. 2004. "Location-aware computing comes of age." *Computer Supported Cooperative Work* 37 (2):95–97.

Heidegger, Martin. 1971."Building, dwelling, thinking." In *Poetry, Language, Thought*, 143–161. New York: Harper and Row.

Heidegger, Martin. 1962. *Being and Time*. Trans. J. Macquarrie and E. Robinson. London: SCM Press.

Heidegger, Martin. 1977. "The age of the world picture." In *The Question Concerning Technology and Other Essays*. Trans. W. Lovitt, 115–154. New York: Harper and Row.

Heidegger, Martin. 1978. "What is metaphysics?" In *Martin Heidegger: Basic Writings*, ed. David Farrell Krell. 93–110. London: Routledge.

Hermans, Hubert J. M., and Els Hermans-Jansen. 1993. "The dialogical construction of coalitions in a personal position repertoire." In *The Dialogical Self: Meaning as Movement*, ed. Hubert J.M. Hermans and Harry J.G. Kempen, 124–137. San Diego, CA: Academic Press.

Hermans, Hubert J. M., and Harry J. G. Kempen. 1993. *The Dialogical Self: Meaning as Movement*. San Diego, CA: Academic Press.

Herrigel, Eugen. 1953. *Zen in the Art of Archery*. London: Penguin.

Hesse, Mary. 1970. *Models and Analogies in Science*. Notre Dame, IN: University of Notre Dame Press.

Hesse, Mary. 1980. "The explanatory function of metaphor." In *Revolutions and Reconstructions in the Philosophy of Science*, ed. Mary Hesse, 111–124. Brighton, Sussex, UK: Harvester Press.

Hew, Ken Ping, Norman Fisher, and Hazim B. Awbi. 2001. "Towards an integrated set of design tools based on a common data format for building and services design." *Automation in Construction* 10:459–476.

Hill, Jonathan, ed. 2001. *Architecture: The Subject is Matter*. London: Routledge.

Hillier, Bill. 2002. "A theory of the city as object: Or, how spatial laws mediate the social construction of urban space." *Urban Design International* 7:153–179.

Hippel, Eric von. 2005. *Democratizing Innovation*. Cambridge, MA: MIT Press.

Hjorth, Larissa. 2004."Imaging communities: Gendered mobile media in the Asia-Pacific." *The Asia-Pacific Journal: Japan Focus*: http://www.japanfocus.org/-Larissa-Hjorth/3064.

Hjorth, Larissa. 2005."Locating Mobility: Practices of co-presence and the persistence of the postal metaphor in SMS/MMS mobile phone customization in Melbourne." *Fibreculture* 6: http://journal.fibreculture.org/issue6/issue6_hjorth.html.

Hofmann, Marko. 2005. "On the complexity of parameter calibration in simulation models" *Journal of Defense Modeling and Simulation* 2: 217–226.

Hofstadter, Douglas R. 1979. *Gödel, Escher, Bach: An Eternal Golden Braid*. New York: Basic Books.

Holt, Douglas B. 2002. "Why do brands cause trouble? A dialectical theory of consumer culture and branding." *Journal of Consumer Research* 29:70–90.

Hospers, John. 1997. *An Introduction to Philosophical Analysis*. London: Routledge.

Howard, Deborah. 2006. "The innocent ear: Subjectivity in the pereption of acoustics." In *Architettura e Musica Nella Venezia del Rinascimento*, ed. Deborah Howard and E. Alura Moretti, 239–257. Milan: Bruno Mondadori.

Howard, Deborah, and Laura Moretti. 2009. *Sound and Space in Renaissance Venice: Architecture, Music, Acoustics*. New Haven and London: Yale University Press.

Howes, David, ed. 2005. *Empire of the Senses: The Sensual Culture Reader*. Oxford: Berg.

Howes, David. 2005. "Hyperesthesia, or, the sensual logic of late capitalism." In *Empire of the Senses: The Sensual Culture Reader*, ed. David Howes. Oxford: Berg, 281–303.

Huizinga, Johan. 1955. *Homo Ludens: A Study of the Play Element in Culture*. Boston: Beacon Press.

Hutchins, Edwin. 1996. *Cognition in the Wild*. Cambridge, MA: MIT Press.

Hyde, Lewis. 1998. *Trickster Makes This World: Mischief, Myth and Art*. New York: North Point Press.

Ihde, Don. 1991. *Instrumental Realism: The Interface between Philosophy of Science and Philosophy of Technology*. Bloomington: Indiana University Press.

Ihde, Don. 2002. *Bodies in Technology*. Minneapolis: University of Minnesota Press.

Innis, Harold A. 1951. *The Bias of Communication*. Toronto, Canada: University of Toronto Press.

Inns, Tom, ed. 2007. *Designing for the 21st Century: Interdisciplinary Questions and Insights*. Farnham, Surrey, UK: Gower Ashgate.

Ishii, Hiroshi, and Brygg Ullmer. 1997. "Tangible bits: Towards seamless interfaces between people, bits and atoms." *Proceedings of CHI '97, March 22–27, Atlanta, Georgia*, 234–241.

Ito, Mizuko, Daisuke Okabe, and Misa Matsuda, eds. 2006. *Personal, Portable, Pedestrian: Mobile Phones in Japanese Life*. Cambridge, MA: MIT Press.

Jacobs, Jane M. 2003. "Too many houses for a home: Narrating the house in the Chinese diaspora." In *Drifting: Architecture and Migrancy*, ed. Stephen Cairns, 164–183. London: Routledge.

James, William. 1950. *The Principles of Psychology*. New York: Dover. First published in 1890.

Jameson, Fredric. 1972. *The Prison-House of Language: A Critical Account of Structuralism and Russian Formalism*. Princeton, NJ: Princeton University Press.

Jana, Reena. 2008. "Web Design Case Study: Data Visualization." *BusinessWeek Online* (June 24): http://www.businessweek.com.

Jaskot, Paul B. 1996. "Anti-semitic policy in Albert Speer's plans for the rebuilding of Berlin." *Art Bulletin* 78 (4):622–632.

Jewell, Don. "GPS Insights." 2007.*GPS World* (May): http://mg.gpsworld.com/gpsmg/article/articleDetail.jsp?id=425488.

Johansen, T. K. 2007. *Aristotle on the Sense-Organs*. Cambridge, UK: Cambridge University Press.

Johanson, Brad, Amando Fox, and Terry Winograd. 2002. "The Interactive Workspaces Project: Experiences with Ubiquitous Computer Rooms." *Pervasive Computing*, April-June, 67–74.

Johnson, Mark. 1987. *The Body in the Mind: The Bodily Basis of Meaning, Imagination, and Reason*. Chicago: University of Chicago Press.

Jones, Caroline A. 2006. *Sensorium: Embodied Experience, Technology, and Contemporary Art*. Cambridge, MA: MIT Press.

Jones, J. C. 1970. *Design Methods: Seeds of Human Futures*. London: Wiley.

Jordan, David P. 2004. "Haussmann and Haussmannisation: The legacy for Paris." *French Historical Studies* 27 (1):87–113.

Kahn, Douglas. 1997. "John Cage: Silence and silencing." *Musical Quarterly* 81 (4):556–598.

Kahn, Douglas. 2001. *Noise, Water, Meat: A History of Sound in the Arts*. Cambridge, MA: MIT Press.

Kant, Immanuel, and Paul Guyer. 2000. *Critique of the Power of Judgment*. Cambridge, UK: Cambridge University Press.

Katyal, Neal Kumar. 2003. "Digital architecture as crime control." *Yale Law Journal* 112 (8):2261–2289.

Katz, James E., and Mark Aakhus. 2002. *Perpetual Contact: Mobile Communication, Private Talk, Public Performance*. Cambridge, UK: Cambridge University Press.

Kay, Alan. 1990. "User interface: A personal view." In *The Art of Human-Computer Interface Design*, ed. Brenda Laurel, 191–207. Reading, MA: Addison Wesley.

Keeton, William T. 1972. *Biological Science*. New York: Norton.

Keller, Evelyn Fox. 1995. *Refiguring Life: Metaphors of Twentieth Century Biology*. New York: Columbia University Press.

Kepler, Johannes. 1939. *Harmonies of the World*. Trans. Charles Glenn Wallis. Chicago: Great Books of the Western World. First published in 1619.

Khakhar, Jignesh. 2007. "Data graphics and interactive information environments." PhD dissertation. Cardiff: Welsh School of Architecture.

Kierkegaard, Soren. 2001. "Repetition: An essay in experimental psychology by Constantin Constantius." In *The Kierkegard Reader*, ed. Jane Chamberlain and Jonathan Rée, 115–150. London: Blackwell. First published in 1843.

Kirby, Michael, and Victoria Nes Kirby. 1971. *Futurist Performance*. New York: PAJ Publications.

Klein, Naomi. 2005. *No Logo*. London: Harper Perennial.

Kline, Stephen, Nick Dyer-Witheford, and Greig de Peuter. 2003. *Digital Play: The Interaction of Technology, Culture and Marketing*. Montréal: McGill-Queen's University Press.

Kolb, David. 1984. *Experiential Learning as the Source of Learning and Development*. Englewood Cliffs, NJ: Prentice-Hall.

Koolhaas, Rem. 1994. *Delerious New York*. New York: Monacelli Press.

Koolhaas, Rem. 2004. "Junk space." In *Content*, ed. Rem Koolhaas, AMO and OMA, 162–171. Cologne: Taschen.

Koutsoumpos, Leonidas. 2008. "Inhabiting Ethics: Educational Praxis in the Design Studio, the Music Class and the Dojo", PhD Thesis. Edinburgh: The University of Edinburgh.

Koyré, Alexandre. 1958. *From the Closed World to the Infinite Universe*. New York: Harper and Row.

Kozinets, R. V. 1999. "E-tribalized marketing?: The strategic implications of virtual communities of consumption." *European Management Journal* 17 (3):252–264.

Krims, Adam, ed. 1998. *Music/Ideology: Resisting the Aesthetic*. Amsterdam, The Netherlands: G+B Arts International.

Kuhn, Thomas. 1957. *The Copernican Revolution: Planetary Astronomy in the Development of Western Thought*. Cambridge, MA: Harvard University Press.

Kuhn, Thomas. 1970. *The Structure of Scientific Revolutions*. Chicago: University of Chicago Press.

LaBelle, Brandon. 2006. *Background Noise: Perspectives on Sound Art*. New York: Continuum.

Lacan, Jacques. 1977. "The mirror stage as formative of the function of the I as revealed in psychoanalytic experience." In *Écrits: A Selection*. Trans. Alan Sheridan, 1–7. London: Tavistock.

Lacan, Jacques. 1979. *The Four Fundamental Concepts of Psychoanalysis*. Trans. Alan Sheridan. London: Penguin.

Lakoff, George. 2003. *Women, Fire, and Dangerous Things: What Categories Reveal about the Mind*. Chicago: University of Chicago Press.

Lakoff, George, and Mark Johnson. 1980. *Metaphors We Live By*. Chicago: University of Chicago Press.

Langheinrich, Marc, Vlad Coroama, Jürgen Bohn, and Michael Rohs. 2002. "As we may live—Real-world implications of ubiquitous computing." http://www.vs.inf.ethz.ch/publ/papers/langhein_aswemaylive_2002.pdf

Latour, Bruno. 1999. "On recalling ANT." In *Actor Network Theory and After*, ed. J. Law and J. Hassard, 15–25. Oxford: Blackwell.

Latour, Bruno. 2005. *Reassembling the Social: An Introduction to Actor-network-theory*. Oxford: Oxford University Press.

Latour, Bruno. 2008. "A Cautious Prometheus? A Few Steps Toward a Philosophy of Design (with Special Attention to Peter Sloterdijk)". Keynote lecture, Networks of Design meeting of the Design History Society in Falmouth, Cornwall, September 3, 2008: http://www.bruno-latour.fr/articles/article/112-DESIGN-CORNWALL.pdf.

Laurel, Brenda, ed. 1990. *The Art of Human-Computer Interface Design*. Reading, MA: Addison Wesley.

Leadbeater, Charles. 2008. *We-Think: Mass Innovation, Not Mass Production*. London: Profile.

Lee, Heesang. 2008. "Mobile networks, urban places and emotional spaces." In *Augmented Urban Spaces: Articulating the Physical and Electronic City*, ed. Alessandro Aurigi and Fiorella de Cindio, 41–59. Aldershot, Hampshire, UK: Ashgate.

Lefebvre, Henri. 1991. *The Production of Space*. Trans. D. Nicholson-Smith. Oxford: Blackwell. First published in French in 1974.

Lefebvre, Henri. 2004. *Rhythmanalysis: Space, Time and Everyday Life*. Trans. Stuart Elden and Gerald Moore. London: Continuum.

Lefebvre, Henri. 2009. *Critique of Everyday Life*. Trans. John Moore. London: Verso.

Leibniz, Gottfried Wilhelm. 1964. "The relational theory of space and time." In *Problems of Space and Time*, ed. J. J. C. Smart, 89–98. New York: Macmillan.

Levitt, Steven, and Stephen J. Dubner. 2005. *Freakonomics: A Rogue Economist Explores the Hidden Side of Everything*. London: Penguin.

Light, Ann. 2008. "Negotiations in space: The impact of receiving phone calls on the move." In *The Reconstruction of Space and Time: Mobile Communication Practices*, ed. Rich Ling and Scott Campbell, 191–214. Piscataway, NJ: Transaction.

Light, Ann. 2008. "Transports of delight? What the experience of receiving (mobile) phone calls can tell us about design." *Personal and Ubiquitous Computing* 12 (5):391–400.

Ling, R. 2004. *The Mobile Connection: The Cell Phone's Impact on Society*. San Francisco: Morgan Kaufmann.

Longson, Tony. 2008. "Reconstruction." In *White Heat Cold Logic: British Computer Art, 1960–1980*, ed. Paul Brown, Charlie Gere, Nicholas Lambert, and Catherine Mason, 151–162. Cambridge, MA: MIT Press.

Lovano-Kerr, Jessie. 1983. "Cognitive style revisited: Implications for research in art production and art criticism." *Studies in Art Education* 24 (3):195–205.

Lovink, Geert. 2003. *Uncanny Networks: Dialogues with the Virtual Intelligentsia*. Cambridge, MA: MIT Press.

Lovink, Geert. 2003. *Zero Comments: Blogging and Critical Internet Culture*. London: Routledge.

Lynch, Kevin. 1960. *The Image of the City*. Cambridge, MA: Technology Press.

Lynn, Greg. 1999. *Animate Form*. New York: Princeton Architectural Press.

Mackenzie, Adrian. 2006. *Cutting Code: Software and Sociality*. New York: Peter Lang.

Mackenzie, Adrian. 2002. *Transductions: Bodies and Machines at Speed*. London: Continuum.

MacKenzie, Donald, and Yuval Millo. 2003. "Constructing a Market, Performing Theory: The Historical Sociology of a Financial Derivatives Exchange." *American Journal of Sociology* 109 (1):107–145.

Mai, Wanji, Gordon Dodds, and Chris Tweed. 2003. "A PDA-based system for recognizing buildings from user-supplied images." In *Mobile and Ubiquitous Information Access*, ed. F. Crestani , 143–157. Berlin: Springer-Verlag.

Mallinson, Helen. 2004. "Metaphors of experience: The voice of air." *Philosophical Forum* 35 (2):161–177.

Malnar, Joy Monice, and Frank Vodvarka. 2004. *Sensory Design*. Minneapolis: University of Minnesota Press.

Mann, Steve. 1997. "Smart clothing: The wearable computer and WearCam." *Personal Technologies* 1:21–27.

Manovich, Lev. 2002. *The Language of New Media*. Cambridge, MA: MIT Press.

Markopoulos, P., and G. W. M. Rauterberg. 2001. *LivingLab: A white paper, IPO Annual Progress Report 35*. Eindhoven: TU/e.

Martens, Harald, and Tormod Naes. 1989. *Multivariate Calibration*. Hoboken, NJ: Wiley.

Marwaha, Alka. 2009. "Blogging All Over the World." Digital Planet: BBC News Channel http://news.bbc.co.uk/1/hi/technology/8102803.stm.

Marx, Karl. 1977. "Capital." In *Karl Marx: Selected Writings*, ed. David McLellan, 415–507. Oxford: Oxford University Press. First published in 1887.

Massey, Doreen. 2005. *For Space*. London: Sage.

Mathes, Adam. 2004. *Folksonomies—Cooperative Classification and Communication Through Shared Metadata*. http://www.adammathes.com/academic/computer-mediated-communication/folksonomies.html.

Maturana, H., and F. G. Varela. 1980. *Autopoiesis and Cognition*. Dordrecht: Reidel.

Maturana, Humberto. 1988. "Reality: The search for objectivity or the quest for a compelling argument." *Irish Journal of Psychology* 9 (1):25–82.

McCarthy, John, and Peter Wright. 2004. *Technology as Experience*. Cambridge, MA: MIT Press.

McCullough, Malcolm. 2004. *Digital Ground: Architecture, Pervasive Computing, and Environmental Knowing*. Cambridge, MA: MIT Press.

McEwen, Indra. 2003. *Vitruvius: Writing the Body of Architecture*. Cambridge, MA: MIT Press.

McFarland, David. 1999. *Animal Behaviour*. London: Prentice Hall.

McLuhan, Marshall. 1962. *The Gutenberg Galaxy: The Making of Typographic Man*. Toronto: University of Toronto Press.

McLuhan, Marshall. 1994. *Understanding Media, The Extensions of Man*. Cambridge, MA: MIT Press.

McLuhan, Marshall, and R. Bruce Powers. 1989. *The Global Village: Transformations in World Life and Media in the 21st Century*. New York: Oxford University Press.

McMeel, Dermott. 2008. "The artistry of construction: An investigation into construction as a creative process and the influence of mobile phones within domestic scale construction projects," PhD Thesis. Edinburgh: The University of Edinburgh.

McNamara, Joel. 2004. *GPS for Dummies*. Hoboken, NJ: Wiley.

Meiners, Janet. 2007. "Spammers getting around captchas." *WebProNews* 31 (October): http://www.webpronews.com/blogtalk/2007/2010/2031/spammers-getting-around-captchas.

Menin, Sarah, and Flora Samuel. 2003. *Nature and Space: Aalto and Le Corbusier*. London: Routledge.

Meyrowitz, Joshua. 1985. *No Sense of Place: The Impact of Electronic Media on Social Behavior*. New York: Oxford University Press.

Middleton, W. E. Knowles. 1966. *A History of the Thermometer and Its Uses in Meteorology*. Baltimore, MD: John Hopkins.

Mill, John Stuart. 1991. *On Liberty*. London: Routledge.

Miller, John H., and Scott E. Page. 2007. *Complex Adaptive Systems: An Introduction to Computational Models of Social Life*. Princeton, NJ: Princeton University Press.

Mitchell, William J. 1995. *J. City of Bits: Space, Place, and the Infobahn*. Cambridge, MA: MIT Press.

Mitchell, William J. 2005. *Placing Words: Symbols, Space, and the City*. Cambridge, MA: MIT Press.

Monmonier, Mark. 1991. *How to Lie with Maps*. Chicago: University of Chicago Press.

Montgomery, Kathryn C. 2009. *Generation Digital: Politics, Commerce, and Childhood in the Age of the Internet*. Cambridge, MA: MIT Press.

Moran, Thomas P., and Paul Dourish. 2001. "Introduction to this special issue on context-aware computing." *Human-Computer Interaction* 16:87–95.

More, Thomas. 1965. *Utopia*. Trans. Paul Turner. Harmondsworth, Middlesex, UK: Penguin. First published in 1516.

Morley, David. 2000. *Home Territories: Media, Mobility and Identity*. London: Routledge.

Morris, Herbert. 1976. *On Guilt and Innocence: Essays in Legal Philosophy and Moral Psychology*. Berkeley: University of California Press.

Morville, Peter. 2005. *Ambient Findability: What We Find Changes Who We Become*. Beijing: O'Reilly.

Mugerauer, Robert. 1994. *Interpretations on Behalf of Place: Environmental Displacements and Alternative Responses*. Albany, NY: SUNY Press.

Mumford, Lewis. 1934. *Technics and Civilization*. London: Routledge.

Murch, Walter. 2003. "Touch of Silence." In *Soundscape: The School of Sound Lectures 1998–2001*, ed. Larry Sider, Diane Freeman, and Jerry Sider, 83–102. London: Wallflower Press.

Murray Barbour, James. 2004. *Tuning and Temperament: A Historical Survey*. Mineola, NY: Dover.

Naguib, Marc, and R. Haven Wiley. 2001. "Estimating the distance to a source of sound: Mechanisms and adaptations for long-range communication." *Animal Behaviour* 62 (5):825–837.

Negroponte, Nicholas. 1973. *The Architecture Machine*. Cambridge, MA: MIT Press.

Negroponte, Nicholas. 1995. *Being Digital*. London: Hodder and Stoughton.

Newman, M. E. J. 2003. "The structure and function of complex networks." *SIAM Review* 45:167–256.

Nicotra, Jodie A. 2005. "The Force of Habit: Rhetoric, Repetition, and Identity from Darwin to Drugs." PhD dissertation. University Park, PA: Pennsylvania State University.

Nietzsche, Friedrich Wilhelm. 1961. *Thus Spoke Zarathustra: A Book for Everyone and No One*. Trans. R. J. Hollingdale. London: Penguin Books. First published in German in 1892.

Nixon, Mark S., Tieniu Tan, and Rama Chellappa. 2006. *Human Identification Based on Gait*. New York: Springer.

Norman, Donald A. 2004. *Emotional Design: Why We Love (Or Hate) Everyday Things*. New York: Basic Books.

Nyíri, Kristóf, ed. 2005. *A Sense of Place: The Global and the Local in Mobile Communication*. Vienna: Passagen Verlag.

Obama, Barack. 2007. *The Audacity of Hope: Thoughts on Reclaiming the American Dream*. Edinburgh: Canongate Books.

Oberlander, J., M. O'Donnell, A. Knott, and C. Mellish. 1998. "Conversation in the museum: Experiments in dynamic hypermedia with the intelligent labelling explorer." *New Review of Hypermedia and Multimedia* 4:11–32.

Ofcom. 2008. *Social Networking: A quantitative and qualitative research report into attitudes, behaviours and use*. London: Ofcom (Office of Communications).

Oliver, Julian Holland. 2002. "The similar eye: Proxy life and public space in the MMORPG." In *Proceedings of Computer Games and Digital Cultures Conference,* ed. Frans Mäyrä, 171–184. Tampere, Finland: Tampere University Press.

Ong, Walter J. 2002. *Orality and Literacy: The Technologizing of the Word*. London: Routledge.

Ong, Walter J. 1972. *Ramus: Method, and the Decay of Dialogue from the Art of Discourse to the Art of Reason*. New York: Octagon.

Ots, Thomas. 1994. "The silenced body—the expressive Leib: On the dialectic of mind and life in Chinese cathartic healing." In *Embodiment and Experience: The Existential Ground of Body and Self,* ed. Thomas J. Csordas, 116–136. Cambridge, UK: Cambridge University Press.

Pacey, Arnold. 1999. *Meaning in Technology*. Cambridge, MA: MIT Press.

Pallasmaa, Juhani. 2005. *The Eyes of the Skin: Architecture and the Senses*. Chichester, UK: Wiley.

Parker, Martin. 2008. "A response to 'Athens by Sound." In *Athens by Sound*, ed. Anastasia Karandinou, Christina Achtypi, and Stylianos Giamarelos, 32–34. Athens: Hellenic Ministry of Culture.

Peirce, Charles Sanders. 1885. "On the algebra of logic: A contribution to the philosophy of notation." *American Journal of Mathematics* 7 (2):180–196.

Penley, Constance. 1991. "Brownian motion: Women, tactics, and technology." In *Technoculture*, ed. Constance Penley and Andrew Ross, 135–161. Minneapolis: University of Minnesota Press.

Penz, François. 2004. "The architectural promenade as narrative device: practice-based research in architecture and the moving image." *Digital Creativity* 15 (1):39–51.

PEVRAV. 2008. *Urban Act: A Handbook of Alternative Practice*. Paris: European Platform for Alternative Practice and Research on the City, Atalier d'Architecture Autogérée.

Pfeifer, Rolf, and Josh C. Bongard. 2006. *How the Body Shapes the Way We Think: A New View of Intelligence*. Cambridge, MA: MIT Press.

Pirsig, Robert M. 1999. *Zen and the Art of Motorcycle Maintenance: An Inquiry into Values*. London: Vintage. First published in 1974.

Plant, Sadie. 1998. *Zeros and Ones: Digital Women and the New Technoculture*. London: Fourth Estate.

Plato. 1997. "Cratylus." In *Complete Works*, ed. John M. Cooper, 101–156. Indianapolis, IL.: Hackett. Written about 360 BCE.

Plato. 1941. *The Republic of Plato*. Trans. Francis MacDonald Cornford. London: Oxford University Press. Written about 380 BCE.

Plotinus. 1948. *The Essence of Plotinus: Extracts from the Six Enneads and Porphyry's Life of Plotinus*. Trans. Stephen Mackenna. New York: Oxford University Press. Compiled and edited about 270 AD.

Pye, David. 2007. *The Nature and Art of Workmanship*. Cambridge, UK: Cambridge University Press.

Pyzdek, Thomas, and Paul A. Keller.2003. *Quality Engineering Handbook*. West Palm Beach, Florida: CRC Press.

Rafael, Vincente. 2006. "The Cell Phone and the Crowd: Messianic Politics in the Contemporary Philippines." In *New Media Old Media*, ed. Wendy Hui Kyong Chun and Thomas Keenan, 297–314. London: Routledge.

Raggett, Dave. 2006. *Report: W3C Workshop on the Ubiquitous Web (*http://www.w3.org/2006/03/ubiweb-workshop-summary*)*. Keio University, Japan: W3C.

Rank, Stephen, Carl O'Coill, Cornelia Boldyreff, and Mark Doughty. 2004. "Software, architecture, and participatory design." In *Proc. WISER'04*. Newport Beach, CA: ACM. http://eprints.lincoln.ac.uk/28/1/f18-rank.pdf.

Ratti, Carlo, and Paul Richens. 2004. "Raster analysis of urban form." *Environment and Planning B: Planning & Design* 31:297–309.

Reddy, Michael. 1979. "The conduit metaphor: A case of frame conflict in our language about language." In *Metaphor and Thought*, ed. Andrew Ortony, 284–324. Cambridge, UK: Cambridge University Press.

Reger, B. D., K. M. Flemming, V. Sanguineti, S. Alford, and F. A. Mussa-Ivaldi. 2001. "Connecting brains to robots: An artificial body for studying the computational properties of neural tissues." *Artificial Life* 6:307–324.

Relph, Edward. 1976. *Place and Placelessness*. London: Pion.

Relph, Edward. 2007. "Spirit of Place and Sense of Place in Virtual Realities." *Techné: Research in Philosophy and Technology, Special Issue: Real and Virtual Places* (http://scholar.lib.vt.edu/ejournals/SPT/v10n3/pdf/) 10 (3):17–25.

Rheingold, Howard. 2002. *Smart Mobs: The Next Social Revolution*. Cambridge, MA: Basic Books.

Rhodes, Bradley J., Nelson Minar, and Josh Weaver. 1999. "Wearable computing meets ubiquitous computing: reaping the best of both worlds." In *Proceedings of The Third International Symposium on Wearable Computers*, 141–149. San Francisco: ISWC.

Roads, Curtis. 2001. *Microsound*. Cambridge, MA: MIT Press.

Robins, Kevin, and Les Levidow. 1995. "Soldier, Cyborg, Citizen." In *Resisting the Virtual Life: The Culture and Politics of Information*, ed. James Brook and Iain A. Boal, 131–143. San Francisco: City Lights.

Robinson, Chris, and Elton G. McGoun. 1998. "The sociology of personal finance." *Financial Services Review* 7:161–173.

Robson, Matthew. 2009. *Report: How teenagers consume media*. New York: Morgan Stanley.

Rogers, Yvonne, Jenny Preece, and Helen Sharp. 2007. *Interaction Design: Beyond Human-Computer Interaction*. Chichester, West Sussex, UK: Wiley.

Rorty, Richard. 1980. *Philosophy and the Mirror of Nature*. Oxford: Basil Blackwell.

Rorty, Richard. 1989. *Contingency, Irony, and Solidarity*. Cambridge, UK: Cambridge University Press.

Rosenzweig, Roy. 2006. "Can History Be Open Source? Wikipedia and the Future of the Past." *Journal of American History* 93 (1):117–146.

Rothensee, Matthias. 2008."User acceptance of the intelligent fridge: empirical results from a simulation." In *The Internet of Things*. Christian Floerkemeier, Marc Langheinrich, Elgar Fleisch, Friedemann Mattern, and Sanjay E. Sarma,eds., 123–139. Berlin: Springer.

Rowe, Colin. 1976. *The Mathematics of the Ideal Villa and Other Esssays*. Cambridge, MA: MIT Press.

Rowe, Colin, and Robert Slutzky. 1997. *Transparency*. Basel, Switzerland: Birkhäuser Verlag.

Ruskin, John. 1960. *The Stones of Venice*. New York: Da Capo Press. First published 1853.

Rymaszewski, Michael, Wagner James Au, Mark Wallace, Catherine Winters, Cory Ondrejka, and Benjamin Batstone-Cunningham. 2007. *Second Life: The Official Guide*. Indianapolis, IN: Wiley.

Saussure, Ferdinand de. 1983. *Course in General Linguistics*. Trans. Roy Harris. London: Duckworth. Originally published as *Cours de Linguistique Générale* (Paris: Payot, 1916).

Scaruffi, Piero. 1999. *LaMonte Young*. http://www.scaruffi.com/oldavant/young.html.

Schafer, R. Murray. 1977. *The Tuning of the World*. Toronto: McClelland & Stewart.

Schafer, R. Murray. 1993. *The Soundscape: Our Sonic Environment and the Tuning of the World*. Rochester, VT: Destiny. First published in 1977.

Scharl, Arnold. 2007. "Towards the geospatial web: Media platforms for managing geotagged knowledge repositories." In *The Geospatial Web: How Geo-Browsers, Social Software and the Web 2.0 are Shaping the Network Society*, ed. Arno Scharl and Klaus Tochtermann, 3–14. London: Springer.

Schelling, F. W. J. 1989. *The Philosophy of Art*. Trans. D. W. Stott. Minneapolis, Minnesota: University of Minnesota Press.

Schön, Donald. 1963. *Displacement of Concepts*. London: Tavistock.

Schön, Donald. 1979. "Generative metaphor: A perspective on problem-setting in social policy." In *Metaphor and Thought*, ed. Andrew Ortony, 254–283.Cambridge, UK: Cambridge University Press.

Schön, Donald. 1983. *Reflective Practitioner: How Professionals Think in Action*. London: Temple Smith.

Schutz, Alfred. 1964. "Making music together." In *Alfred Schutz, Collected Papers II: Studies in Social Theory*, ed. Arvid Brodersen, 159–178. The Hague: Martinus Nijhoff.

Sears, Francis Weston, and Mark W. Zemansky. 1960. *College Physics*. Reading, MA: Addison Wesley.

Sellars, John. 1999. "The point of view of the cosmos: Deleuze, romanticism, stoicism." *Pli* 8:1–24.

Serres, Michel. 2007. *The Parasite*. Trans. Lawrence R. Schehr. Minneapolis: University of Minnesota Press.

Sethares, William A. 1998. *Tuning, Timbre, Spectrum, Scale*. London: Springer.

Shannon, Claude E. 1948. "A mathematical theory of communication." *Bell System Technical Journal* 27:379–423, 623–656.

Shannon, Claude E. 1949. "Communication in the presence of noise." *Proc. Institute of Radio Engineers* 37 (1):447–457.

Shannon, Claude E., and William Weaver. 1963. *The Mathematical Theory of Communication*. Urbana: The University of Illinois Press.

Sharl, Arno. 2007. "Towards the geospatial web: Media platforms for managing geotagged knowledge repositories." In *The Geospatial Web: How Geo-Browsers, Social Software and the Web 2.0 are Shaping the Network Society*, ed. Arno Scharl and K. Tochtermann, 3–14. London: Springer.

Sharp, Rob. 2008. "The curse of satnav: On a road to nowhere. . . ." *The Independent* (April 9): http://www.independent.co.uk/life-style/gadgets-and-tech/features/the-curse-of-satnav-on-a-road-to-nowhere-806268.html.

Shepard, Roger N., and Jacqueline Metzler. 1971. "Mental Rotation of Three-Dimensional Objects." *Science, New Series* 171, no. 3972:701–703.

Shipman, Stephanie, and Virginia C. Shipman. 1985. "Cognitive styles: Some conceptual, methodological, and applied issues." *Review of Research in Education* 12:229–291.

Shusterman, Richard. 2008. *Body Consciousness: A Philosophy of Mindfulness and Somaesthetics*. Cambridge, UK: Cambridge University Press.

Silberman, Neil. 2008. "Chasing the unicorn? the quest for 'essence' in digital heritage." In *New Heritage: New Media and Cultural Heritage*, ed. Yehuda E. Kalay, Thomas Kvan, and Janice Affleck, 81–111. London: Routledge.

Simmel, Georg. 1997. "Sociology of the meal." In *Simmel on Culture: Selected Writing*, ed. Georg Simmel, David Frisby, and Mike Featherstone, 130–135. London: Sage.

Simmel, Georg. 2004. "The metropolis and mental life." In *Urban Culture: Critical Concepts in Literary and Cultural Studies*, ed. Chris Jenks, 349–360. London: Taylor & Francis.

Skinner, Quentin. 2000. *Machiavelli: A Very Short Introduction*. Oxford: Oxford University Press.

Smith, Bruce. 2004. "Listening to the wild blue yonder: The challenges of acoustic ecology." In *Hearing Cultures: Essays on Sound, Listening and Modernity*, ed. Veit Erlmann, 21–41.Oxford: Berg.

Snodgrass, Adrian B. 1990. *Architecture, Time and Eternity: Studies in the Stellar and Temporal Symbolism of Traditional Buildings*, vol. 1. New Delhi, India: Aditya Prakashan.

Snodgrass, Adrian B. 1990. *Architecture, Time and Eternity: Studies in the Stellar and Temporal Symbolism of Traditional Buildings*, vol. 2. New Delhi, India: Aditya Prakashan.

Snodgrass, Adrian B. 2006. "Random thoughts on the way." In *Interpretation in Architecture: Design as a Way of Thinking*, ed. Adrian B. Snodgrass and Richard Coyne, 243–254. London: Routledge.

Snodgrass, Adrian B., and Richard Coyne. 1992. "Models, metaphors and the hermeneutics of designing." *Design Issues* 9 (1):56–74.

Snodgrass, Adrian B., and Richard Coyne. 2006. *Interpretation in Architecture: Design as a Way of Thinking*. London: Routledge.

Sobel, Dava. 1995. *Longitude*. London: Fourth Estate.

Sonnenschein, David. 2001. *Sound Design: The Expressive Power of Music, Voice, and Sound Effects in Cinema*. Studio City, CA: Michael Wiese Productions.

Sterne, Jonathan. 2005. *The Audible Past: Cultural Origins of Sound Reproduction*. Durham, NC: Duke University Press.

Strogatz, Steven H. 2001. "Exploring complex networks." *Nature* 410:268–276.

Suau, Cristian. 2005. "Potential Public Spaces in the Modern Suburbia: Urban Reflections for the Regeneration of Free Spaces." *Nordisk Arkitekturforskning* 4:31–41.

Tacitus. 1912. *The Histories Volume 1*. Trans. W. Hamilton Fyfe. Oxford: Clarendon. Produced first century AD. Available online: http://www.gutenberg.org/files/16927/16927-h/i.html.

Tafuri, Manfredo. 1996. *Architecture and Utopia: Design and Capitalist Development*. Trans. Barbara Luigia La Penta. Cambridge, MA: MIT Press. First published in Italian in 1973.

Tanasescu, Vlad, Dumitru Roman, and John Domingue. 2009. "Service selection via extreme geotagging." In *Proceedings of the International Conference on Advanced Geographic Information Systems & Web Services (GEOWS 2009)* 189–194. Cancun, Mexico.

Taylor, Alex S., and Richard Harper. 2002. "Age-old practices in the 'New World': A study of gift-giving between teenage mobile phone users." In Proc. CHI 2002, Minneapolis, MN. 439–446. http://research.microsoft.com/en-us/um/people/ast/files/chi_2002.pdf.

Thaler, Richard H., and Cass R. Sunstein. 2008. *Nudge: Improving Decisions about Health, Wealth and Happiness*. London: Penguin.

Thibaud, Jean-Paul. 2003. "The sonic composition of the city." In *The Auditory Culture Reader*, ed. Michael Bull and Les Back, 329–341. Oxford: Berg.

Thompson, Emily. 2004. *The Soundscape of Modernity: Architectural Acoustics and the Culture of Listening in America, 1900–1933*. Cambridge, MA: MIT Press.

Thompson, Richard B. 1998. "Global positioning system: The mathematics of GPS receivers." *Mathematics Magazine* 71 (4):260–269.

Trafton, Anne. 2009. "Wearable blood pressure sensor offers 24/7 continuous monitoring." *MIT Tech Talk* (April 8):4.

Tschumi, Bernard. 1994. *Architecture and Disjunction*. Cambridge, MA: MIT Press.

Tschumi, Bernard. 1994. *The Manhattan Transcripts*. London: Academy Editions.

Tschumi, Bernard. 1995. "One, two, three: jump." In *Educating Architects*, ed. Martin Pearce and Maggie Toy, 24–25.London: Academy Editions.

Tufte, Edward R. 1990. *Envisioning Information*. Cheshire, CT: Graphics Press.

Turkle, Sherry. 1992. *Psychoanalytic Politics: Jacques Lacan and Freud's French Revolution*. New York: Guilford.

Turkle, Sherry. 1995. *Life on the Screen: Identity in the Age of the Internet*. London: Weidenfeld and Nicolson.

Turkle, Sherry, ed. 2007. *Evocative Objects: Things We Think With*. Cambridge, MA: MIT Press.

Turner, Alasdair, and Alan Penn. 2002. "Encoding natural movement as an agent-based system: An investigation into human pedestrian behaviour in the built environment." *Environment and Planning. B, Planning & Design* 29:473–490.

Turner, Alasdair, Maria Doxa, David O'Sullivan, and Alan Penn. 2001. "From isovists to visibility graphs: A methodology for the analysis of architectural space." *Environment and Planning. B, Planning & Design* 28:103–121.

Turner, P., and E. Davenport. 2005. *Spatiality, Spaces and Technology*. Dordrecht: Kluwer.

Turner, Victor. 1967. *The Forest of Symbols: Aspects of Ndembu Ritual*. Ithaca, NY: Cornell University Press.

Tzonis, Alexander, and Liane Lefaivre. 1986. *Classical Architecture: The Poetics of Order*. Cambridge, MA: MIT Press.

Urry, John. 1990. *The Tourist Gaze: Leisure and Travel in Contemporary Societies*. London: Sage.

Urry, John. 2007. *Mobilities*. Cambridge, UK: Polity.

Vaughn, Kathryn. 1993. "The influence of tambura drone on the perception of proximity among scale types in North Indian classical music." *Contemporary Music Review* 9:21–33.

Veblen, Thorstein. 1998. *The Theory of the Leisure Class*. Amherst, NY: Prometheus, First published in 1899.

Venturi, Robert, Denise Scott Brown, and Steven Izenour. 1993. *Learning from Las Vegas: The Forgotten Symbolism of Architectural Form*. Cambridge, MA: MIT Press.

Vidler, Anthony. 2002. *Warped Space: Art, Architecture, and Anxiety in Modern Culture*. Cambridge, MA: MIT Press.

Vila Domini, David A. 2003. "The diminution of the classical column: Visual sensibility in antiquity and the renaissance." *Nexus Network Journal* 5 (1):99–124.

Virko, Tarmo. 2007. *Global cell phone use at 50 percent*. http://www.reuters.com/article/technologyNews/idUSL2917209520071129.

Virilio, Paul. 1986. *Speed and Politics: An Essay on Dromology*. Trans. Mark Polizzotti. New York: Semiotext(e).

Vitruvius, Pollio. 1960. *The Ten Books on Architecture*. Trans. Morris Hicky Morgan. New York: Dover Publications. Written ca. 50 AD.

Want, Roy, Andy Hopper, Veronica Falcão, and Jonathan Gibbons. 1992. "The active badge location system." *ACM Transactions on Information Systems* 10 (1):91–102.

Ward, Peter D., and Donald Brownlee. 2000. *Rare Earth: Why Complex Life is Uncommon in the Universe*. New York: Springer-Verlag.

Weber, Max. 1958. *The Rational and Social Foundations of Music*. Carbondale: Southern Illinois University Press.

Weber, Max. 1992. *The Protestant Ethic and the Spirit of Capitalism*. Trans. Talcott Parsons. London: Routledge. First published in German 1904–1905.

Weiner, Norbert. 1950. *The Human Use of Human Beings*. Cambridge, MA: Da Capo Press.

Weiser, Mark. 1991 "The computer for the 21st century." *Scientific American* 265:66–75.

Weiser, Mark, and John Seely Brown. 1996."The coming age of calm technology." *Xerox Parc Report,* http://www.ubiq.com/hypertext/weiser/acmfuture2endnote.htm.

Weissman, Joseph, and Taylor Adkins. 2007. "Science and parasites: Michel Serres and the unification of human and natural sciences." *Fractal Ontology* at fractalontology.wordpress.com.

Wigley, Mark. 1998. "The architecture of atmosphere." *Daidalos* 68:18–27.

Williams, Bernard Arthur Owen. 1993. *Shame and Necessity*. Berkeley: University of California Press.

Williams, J. E. D. 1992. *From Sails to Satellites: The Origin and Development of Navigational Science*. Oxford: Oxford University Press.

Williams, Robin, and David Edge. 1996. "The social shaping of technology." In *Information and Communication Technologies,* ed. William H. Dutton, 53–67. Oxford: Oxford University Press.

Winograd, Terry, and Fernando Flores. 1986. *Understanding Computers and Cognition: A New Foundation for Design*. Reading, MA: Addison Wesley.

Wittgenstein, Ludwig. 1953. *Philosophical Investigations*. Trans. G. E. M. Anscombe. Oxford: Blackwell.

Wittkower, Rudolf. 1998. *Architectural Principles in the Age of Humanism*. Chichester: Academy Editions.

Xenakis, Iannis. 1992. *Formalized Music: Thought and Mathematics in Music*. Stuyvesant, NY: Pendragon Press.

Yang, Guobin. 2003. "The co-evolution of the Internet and civil society in China." *Asian Survey* 43 (3):405–422.

Yates, Frances A. 1966. *The Art of Memory*. London: Routledge and Kegan Paul.

Žižek, Slavoj. 1991. *Looking Awry: An Introduction to Jacques Lacan through Popular Culture*. Cambridge, MA: MIT Press.

Žižek, Slavoj. 1996. *The Indivisible Remainder: An Essay on Schelling and Related Matters*. London: Verso Books.

Žižek, Slavoj. 2002. "Big brother, or, the triumph of the gaze over the eye." In *CTRL [SPACE]: Rhetorics of Surveillance from Bentham to Big Brother,* ed. Thomas Y. Levin, Ursula Frohne and Peter Weibel, 224–227. Cambridge, MA: MIT Press.

Index